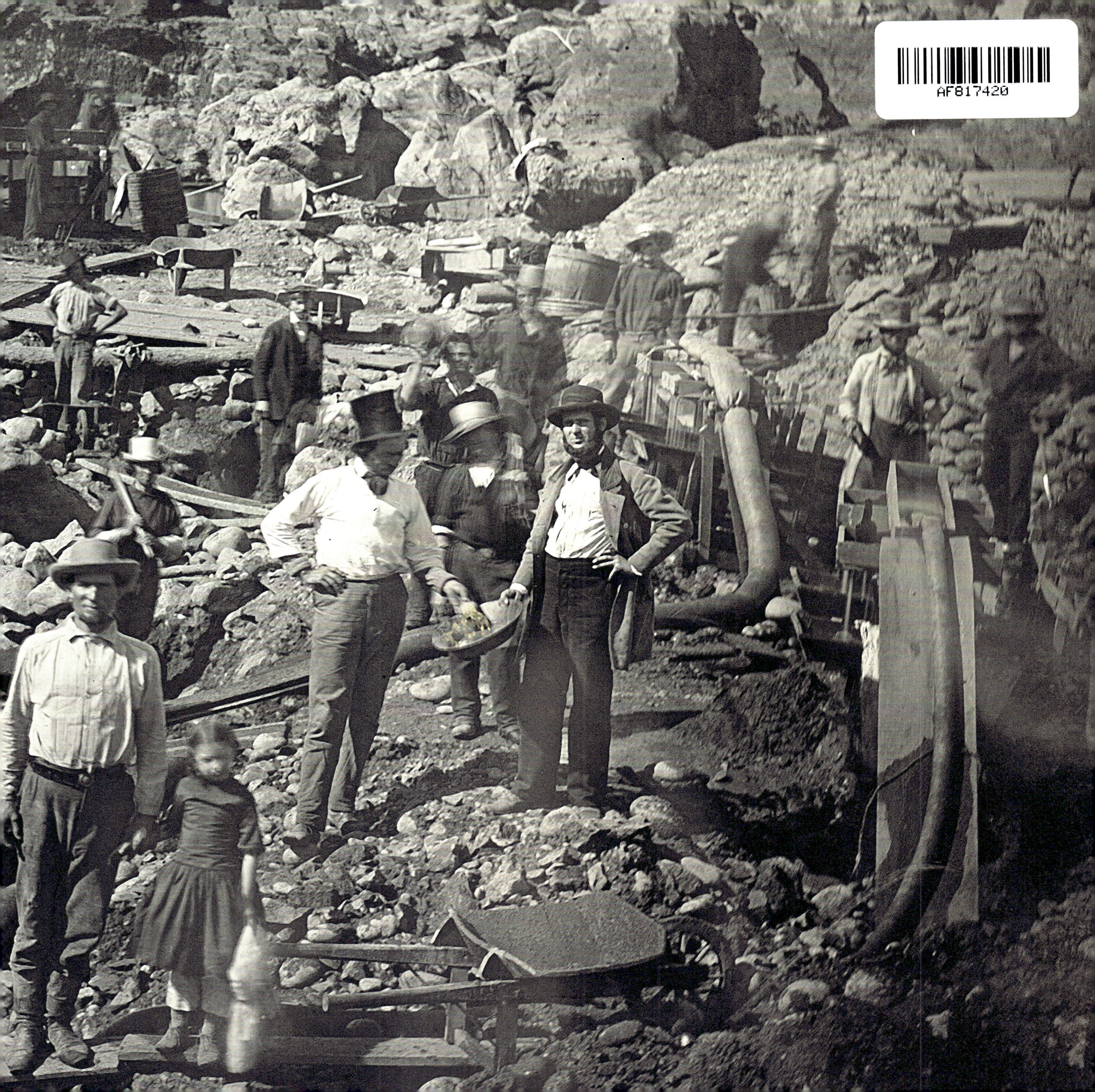

GOLDEN PROSPECTS

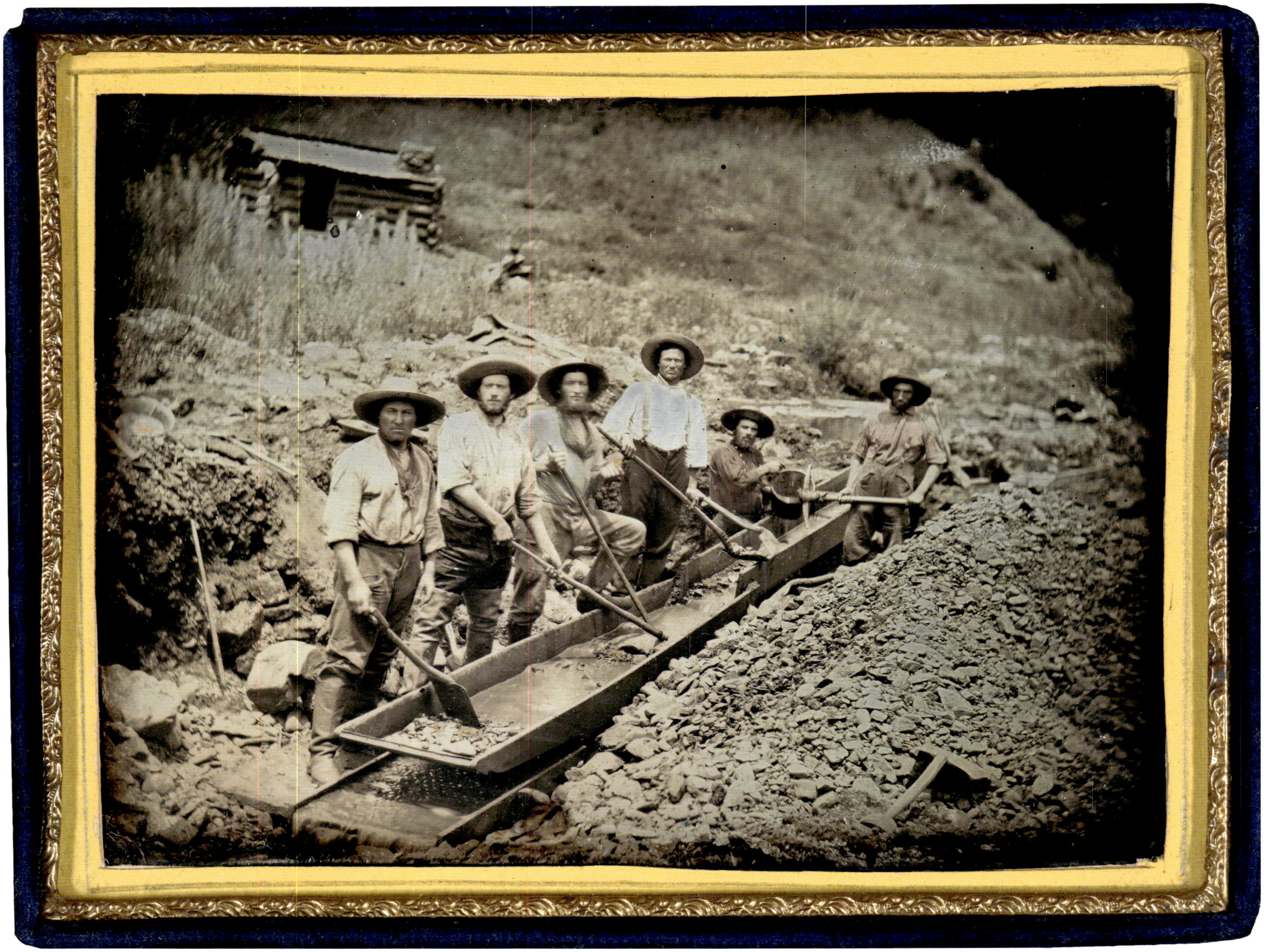

FRONTIS **Unknown maker**, American. *California gold miners with long tom,* ca. 1850. Quarter-plate daguerreotype.

GOLDEN PROSPECTS

Daguerreotypes of the California Gold Rush

JANE L. ASPINWALL

with contributions by

KEITH F. DAVIS

Director's Foreword by

JULIÁN ZUGAZAGOITIA

Hall Family Foundation
in association with
The Nelson-Atkins Museum of Art
Kansas City, Missouri

Distributed by Yale University Press
New Haven and London

This volume is one in a series based on the Hallmark Photographic Collection at The Nelson-Atkins Museum of Art. Previous titles, all distributed by Yale University Press, include *The Origins of American Photography, 1839–1885: From Daguerreotype to Dry-Plate* (2007); *The Photographs of Homer Page: The Guggenheim Year, New York, 1949–50* (2009); *Timothy H. O'Sullivan: The King Survey Photographs* (2011); *The Photographs of Ray K. Metzker* (2012); *Heartland: The Photographs of Terry Evans* (2012); *Impressionist France: Visions of Nation from Le Gray to Monet* (2013); *Alexander Gardner: The Western Photographs, 1867–1868* (2014); *Multitude, Solitude: The Photographs of Dave Heath* (2015); *Eugene Richards: The Run-On of Time* (2017); and *The Photographs of Ralston Crawford* (2018). In addition, a short history of the program, *The Big Picture: The Hallmark Photographic Collection at The Nelson-Atkins Museum of Art*, was issued in 2018.

Financial support for this publication has been provided by the Hall Family Foundation, and by the Mellon-Frick-Rothschild Publication Fund, The Nelson-Atkins Museum of Art.

The text of this volume is based on Jane L. Aspinwall, *From Pan to Plate: Cased Images of the California Gold Rush*, PhD dissertation, University of Missouri-Kansas City, 2019.

GOLDEN PROSPECTS

Daguerreotypes of the California Gold Rush

Published to accompany the exhibition *Golden Prospects: California Gold Rush Daguerreotypes* at The Nelson-Atkins Museum of Art, September 6, 2019–January 26, 2020; Peabody Essex Museum, April 4–July 12, 2020; and Yale University Art Gallery, August 28–November 29, 2020.

Unless otherwise noted, all photographs reproduced in this volume are in the collection of The Nelson-Atkins Museum of Art, Kansas City, Missouri. Images FRONTIS, 3, 4, 6, 20, 22, 28, 30, 56, 58, 59, 61, 72, 75, 82, 84, 85, 99, 103, 112, 115, 127, 132, 144, Gift of Hallmark Cards, Inc., 2005; Images 2, 5, 7–9, 11–14, 19, 21, 24, 29, 31, 32, 42, 44, 45, 54, 55, 60, 62–64, 67, 70, 74, 76, 80, 92, 94, 97, 104, 107, 117–122, 124, 130, 133, 137, 147, Gifts of the Hall Family Foundation, 2006–2019.

COVER: **Unknown maker**, American. *Portrait of a California miner with pan of gold*, ca. 1852. Sixth-plate daguerreotype.

FRONT ENDSHEET: **George H. Johnson**, American (1823–ca. 1880s). *Large mining operation at North Fork of American River*, ca. 1852. Whole-plate daguerreotype, detail of [**41**]. National Gallery of Canada, Ottawa.

BACK ENDSHEET: **Unknown maker**, American. *Street in mining town with American flag*, ca. 1852. Half-plate daguerreotype, detail of [**102**]. National Gallery of Canada, Ottawa.

ISBN 978-0-300-24621-6

Library of Congress Control Number: 2019908919

HALL FAMILY FOUNDATION

P.O. Box 419580, MD 323
Kansas City, Missouri 64141-6580
www.hallfamilyfoundation.org

The Nelson-Atkins Museum of Art

4525 Oak Street
Kansas City, Missouri 64111
www.nelson-atkins.org

Distributed by
Yale University Press, New Haven and London
302 Temple Street
P.O. Box 209040
New Haven, Connecticut 06520-9040
www.yalebooks.com/art

Contents

DIRECTOR'S FOREWORD

Julián Zugazagoitia
Menefee D. and Mary Louise Blackwell Director/CEO
The Nelson-Atkins Museum of Art

The California gold rush remains one of the most important episodes in American history. The wild scramble for wealth that began in 1848 transformed the nation and gave rise to the modern American West. The gold rush was that era's Great Adventure—an almost mythic quest involving long travel, hard work, and the lure of unimaginable riches. The gold rush reflected something essential about the nation itself—the character of its people and the potential of the land.

The importance of this story lies in its complexity. Seemingly overnight, the massive influx of new arrivals created a network of transient settlements, two major cities, and the nation's thirty-first state. This frenzied process of growth resulted in an unprecedented mixing of peoples and cultures, racial and ethnic tensions, the decimation of indigenous American Indian populations, and significant environmental damage. In this process, many prospectors and businessmen did become rich, thanks to their ingenuity, labor, and luck. But of course, just as many returned home exhausted and disappointed. What they all shared was the *experience* of California. Looking back now, after 170 years, we see the gold rush as an overlapping set of narratives, a rich and complex blend of reality and myth.

Jane L. Aspinwall has long recognized the importance of this subject. With her special expertise in early American photography and the daguerreotype, she has been studying gold rush–era photographs for years. Her vision is all-inclusive: she begins by celebrating these works *as pictures*, as an integral part of both our artistic and cultural heritage. She then looks carefully at their content, highlighting the visual choices made by the original photographers as well as the significance of what they recorded. This dual perspective—looking at these pictures as both art and information—does real justice to the richness of these rare works. It allows us to appreciate the context from which these photographs arose as well as their place in modern visual culture. The result is a new understanding of a pivotal historical era and a reminder that important pictures are as fresh and meaningful as the quality of attention we bring to them.

This volume, with its accompanying exhibition, builds on a series of earlier books and exhibitions dealing with the daguerreotype or the history of photography in the American West. These include *The Origins of American Photography, From Daguerreotype to Dry-Plate, 1839–1885* (2007); *Timothy H. O'Sullivan: The King Survey Photographs* (2011); and *Alexander Gardner: The Western Photographs, 1867–1868* (2014). This gold rush project underscores once again the depth and significance of the photography program at The Nelson-Atkins Museum of Art. As part of our comprehensive survey of nineteenth-century American photographs, NAMA has one of the nation's largest holdings of California daguerreotypes and ambrotypes. As a result, more than half the works in the accompanying exhibition are drawn from our permanent collection.

This museum began exhibiting photographs in 1936 and made its first major purchase in 1957.[1] In late 2005, it was transformed with the acquisition of the famed 6,500-piece Hallmark Photographic Collection. Since then, the museum has boasted dedicated exhibition space for the medium and an extraordinarily talented and active curatorial department. With continued growth, our photography collection now includes about 15,000 works, ranging in date from 1826 to the present. We take great pride in our public's interest in these activities, and in the national and international significance of this program.

This volume and the accompanying exhibition are the result of a truly collaborative effort. Jane L. Aspinwall has devoted several years of intensive work to this project, conducting original research in major archives nationwide and further deepening her understanding of works in our permanent collection. Keith F. Davis, our senior curator, assisted with the shaping of this book, and Kaitlyn Bunch, exhibitions and publications coordinator, provided support and guidance on both book and exhibition. This project has been aided in innumerable ways by the other members of the photography department: April M. Watson, curator; Natalie Boten, senior department coordinator; Tara Brungardt, collections manager; and Saori Lewis, associate conservator. We also celebrate the

1 This history has been documented in Keith F. Davis, *The Big Picture: The Hallmark Photographic Collection at The Nelson-Atkins Museum of Art* (Kansas City: Hall Family Foundation/The Nelson-Atkins Museum of Art, 2018).

essential contributions of the museum's various divisions, including Conservation and Collections Management, Curatorial, Education, Presentation, and our own Spencer Art Reference Library.

Beyond our museum, I am tremendously thankful to those directors, curatorial colleagues, and museum professionals who have supported this effort. We are excited that this exhibition will be so widely seen. After it debuts here at The Nelson-Atkins Museum of Art, it will travel to the Peabody Essex Museum, Salem, Massachusetts; and the Yale University Art Gallery, New Haven, Connecticut. For their enthusiasm for this project, we sincerely thank the directors and staffs of both of our exhibition partners. For their essential loans to this exhibition, we also extend sincere thanks to the National Gallery of Canada, Ottawa; the Bancroft Library, University of California, Berkeley; and the Art Institute of Chicago.

As always, we are grateful to our distribution partner, Yale University Press, and our copublisher, the Hall Family Foundation, for their enthusiasm for this project. The Hall Family Foundation continues to stand as a model of generous and enlightened patronage. After more than seventy-five years of charitable activity, the Foundation's contributions to this community continue to be transformative. For their vision and commitment, we again thank the Foundation, its board of directors, and, in particular, Donald J. Hall and William A. Hall.

INTRODUCTION

Jane L. Aspinwall
Curator, Photography
The Nelson-Atkins Museum of Art

As word of the California gold rush spread around the world, it was difficult to know what to believe. In October 1850, the *Illustrated London News* reported: "The existence of California has, at length, become a 'great fact.' . . . The most incredulous sceptics [*sic*] are at last convinced; several of the localities have been Daguerreotyped. . . . To refuse the evidence of the Daguerreotype is to deny the existence of the 'prime cheerer' of light, and the Sun and his works."[1] The daguerreotype, it would seem, had the ability to stand in for reality, to make the incredible credible. It was assumed that the photograph simply could not lie. As curator and print historian William Ivins observed, "The nineteenth century began by believing that what was reasonable was true and it would end up by believing that what it saw a photograph of was true. The photograph has been accepted as showing that impossible desideratum of the historian—how it actually was."[2] But what truths do daguerreotypes of the California gold rush actually reflect?

After gold was discovered at Sutter's Mill in 1848, gold fever swept the nation. Prior to 1848, there were around 14,000 inhabitants living in the territorial area that would later become the state of California.[3] Word spread slowly at first, starting in California towns and among the resident American Indian population. Soon, immigrants from Chile and Mexico and settlers who had previously traveled west to Oregon began to arrive. The response on the East Coast of the United States was delayed until President Polk announced the discovery in his annual address to Congress, in December 1848. He stated, "The accounts of the abundance of gold . . . are of such an extraordinary character as would scarcely command belief were they not corroborated by the authentic reports of officers . . . who have visited the mineral district and derived the facts . . . from personal observation."[4] After the spring snowmelt, the rush began in earnest.

The rush for gold was driven by a quest for wealth, but nationalistic notions about nature, the West, and man's right to dominion shaped the larger narrative.[5] Manifest Destiny, as it was termed in 1845, reflected the view that Americans were on a divinely ordained mission: "[It] is by the right of our manifest destiny to overspread and to possess the whole of the continent."[6] In "going West," white men were engaged in what they saw as an ostensibly heroic effort to conquer Nature and remove its resident enemies to establish rightful ownership to the land. Whether the West was transformed by "the individualist agrarian ideal of continuous divinely ordained progress [to] transform wild nature into a civilized garden" or by "man's materialist, capitalist development and the technology it possessed (its machines, its engineering)," Americans had an unwavering belief in this "myth of the West."[7] The idea of American exceptionalism was reinforced in Frederick Jackson Turner's famous 1893 thesis defining the American frontier as "the meeting point between savagery and civilization."[8] Unfortunately, of course, this "myth of the West" ignored historical reality by omitting the region's existing populations, the diffusion of races and immigrant cultures, and environmental destruction.

Thousands made the journey to California, often with money borrowed from friends and family. The trip was made by land or by sea and typically took four to six months. Most journeys began in an eastern US port; ships sailed around Cape Horn with a brief stop in Valparaiso, Chile. Continuing on, the gold seekers arrived in California at the port of San Francisco; from April 1849 to April 1850, 62,000 people arrived there by ship. For the overland trek, many traveled westward by wagon from St. Joseph, Missouri; an additional 32,000 made the journey this way, pushing west despite harsh weather, food deprivation, and the threat of conflict. In California, San Francisco was the initial gathering point for many and the area's financial hub; Sacramento was the largest city close to the gold fields.

Along with the tens of thousands of would-be miners, merchants flocked to the region to seek their own fortunes selling supplies. Lured by the ready market of potential customers, daguerreotypists also made their way to the area. Most daguerreotypists set up portrait studios in the larger cities of San Francisco or Sacramento, though some ventured into the smaller towns and directly into the gold fields in photographically outfitted wagons.

Early California photography falls into two basic categories: indoor studio portraiture and outdoor views. Studio portraiture, the bread-and-butter work of most daguerreians, included both standard images of residents and occupational portraits of miners. Outdoor views make up a significant portion of California daguerreotypes. In the rapidly expanding cities of San Francisco and Sacramento, daguerreotypists made multi-plate panoramas, as well as street views. They also traveled through the gold region, seeking business where miners worked in the field and in the small towns that sprang up around successful strikes. Some special skill was required to make consistent outdoor daguerreotypes, but it is clear that many practitioners mastered this aspect of the business.

In the prologue to his book *Reading American Photographs*, Alan Trachtenberg described Charles Wilson Peale's painting *The Artist and His Museum* (1822). This work depicts the artist standing front and center, as he lifts a dark curtain to reveal his room-sized cabinet of curiosities. A vast row of compartments is filled with specimens of nature, all neatly organized and labeled; a nearly endless variety of species is rendered comprehensible through categorization and organization. Here, Peale assumes the artist's role as the intermediary between the "raw material and the finished art, between things unsorted and unclassified and things rearranged, reassembled, [and] placed in compartmental spaces."[9]

During the California gold rush, daguerreotypists were similarly faced with "raw material" that required logical organization. The California landscape was like nothing they had seen before. The human environment was also unprecedented: the region's population comprised a complex mix of racial and ethnic cultures, some native to the area (Mexican, American Indian, Californian), many more from distant lands (Chilean, Chinese, European, Hawaiian, etc.). Challenging the American notion of who could participate in the gold rush were African Americans (both enslaved and free) and women. Gold towns appeared and disappeared, as gold claims were discovered and depleted. Mining technologies evolved from individuals with a pickaxe, shovel, and pan; to groups of men with rockers, long toms, and sluices; to large companies engaged in river diversion and hydraulic mining. Nothing remained the same for long in gold rush California.

To make sense of what they were seeing, daguerreotypists created a distinctive pictorial vocabulary. In this way, each daguerreotypist became "the mediator of the world's truth" in the hopes of revealing "the true order hidden within things, an invisible order he brings to view."[10] Inevitably, of course, daguerreotypists brought their own views and values to the task. Historian William H. Goetzmann noted that western explorers and artists, "as they go out into the unknown, are 'programmed' by the knowledge, values and objectives" of the society that shaped them.[11] According to historian Peter Hales, to study the visual products of daguerreotypists "is to educate ourselves in the deepest concerns of American culture. At the same time, their cultural 'programming' had a profound effect on the "photographs they made."[12] California daguerreotypists "transformed that new and unsettling world into acceptable and comprehensible patterns."[13] Tapping into the "artistic conventions dominant in the civilized culture of the day," they detected the sublime in the untamed expanse of the California landscape, the picturesque in views of encampments and small villages beside mountain streams, and the power of human ingenuity in the riches pulled from this terrain.[14]

The daguerreotype was a vital facet of the gold rush experience. The world's first practical method of photography, the daguerreotype was introduced in 1839. The process began with a sheet of copper being plated with a thin layer of silver. After being buffed to a mirrorlike finish, the plate was sensitized by the fumes of iodine and bromine, to create a light-sensitive silver-halide emulsion. The sensitized plate was then inserted into a plate holder and placed in a camera, which had been previously positioned and focused. Exposure times typically varied—depending on lens, light, and plate size—from about one to thirty seconds.[15] In the darkroom, the plate was removed from the plate holder and developed over a heated pot of (poisonous) mercury. After the image appeared on the plate, it was fixed by immersion in a solution of salt or sodium thiosulfate. The plate was then toned with gold chloride in order to increase image contrast and permanence, and washed in water. For an additional cost, plates could be hand-colored—touches of pigment added to a subject's cheeks or clothing. The finished plate was then fitted with a brass mat, covered with glass, and sealed with a brass preserver. This package was then secured in a leather or thermoplastic case, lined in velvet or silk. The daguerreotype is a one-of-a-kind, direct-positive process. Technically, each plate functions as both a "positive" and a "negative," depending on the angle at which the plate is viewed.

Despite the enormous amount of literature dedicated to the California gold rush, the scholarship on gold rush daguerreotypes remains limited.[16] This project seeks to revitalize the conversation about this important work by taking a fresh approach, beginning with a focus on their status as beautiful visual objects. Through a systematic analysis of known gold rush images, previously unrecognized patterns in this overall production have been revealed.

This new perspective is based on the author's personal research database of over 500 cased images (daguerreotypes and ambrotypes) made in California during the gold rush era, 1849 to 1865. This compilation was created from thirty-three institutional and private collections, as well as from auction records, exhibition catalogues, and related research materials.[17] Of the thirty-three institutions, five were deemed to have the largest holdings relevant to this project. Together, the holdings of these five institutions comprise two-thirds of the total database: the Bancroft Library, University of

California, Berkeley; the California State Library, Sacramento; The Nelson-Atkins Museum of Art, Kansas City, Missouri; the Matthew Isenburg collection at the National Gallery of Canada, Ottawa, Ontario; and the Oakland Museum, Oakland, California. Other significant past or existing holdings include: the Stephen Anaya collection, auctioned by Sotheby's Inc., New York, April 6, 2000; the W. Bruce and Delaney H. Lundberg Collection at The Art Institute of Chicago; the Society of California Pioneers, the Presidio, San Francisco; the California Historical Society, San Francisco; the J. Paul Getty Museum, Los Angeles; and the private collections of Michael Peterson and Doug Scougale. Other significant works are held by the Amon Carter Museum of Art, Fort Worth, Texas; the Metropolitan Museum of Art, New York City; the Seaver Center at the Los Angeles County Museum of Natural History; the George Eastman Museum, Rochester, New York; the San Francisco Maritime National Historic Park Museum; the Beinecke Library at Yale University, New Haven, Connecticut; the Huntington Library, San Marino, California; the Library of Congress, Washington, DC; the New-York Historical Society, New York City; the Wells Fargo History Museum, San Francisco; the Minnesota Historical Society, St. Paul; the Siskiyou County Historical Society Museum, Yreka, California; the University of New Mexico Art Museum, Albuquerque; the Henry Ford Museum, Dearborn, Michigan; the Searls Historical Library of the Nevada County Historical Society, Nevada City, California; the private collections of Greg French and Len Walle; private collections included in the exhibition catalogue *Silver & Gold: Cased Images of the California Gold Rush* (1998); and the privately held research materials of Robert A. Weinstein.[18]

This is not to be considered a definitive database. Because of the one-of-a-kind nature of the daguerreotype and the absence of a worldwide daguerreotype inventory system, it would be impossible to account for all extant gold rush cased images. The goal was to compile a critical mass of images for the purpose of identifying visual and thematic patterns. It is hoped, however, that this study will provide a productive starting point for future research.

The same information was collected for each image: maker (when known); presence of maker mark (either on brass mat or on the velvet liner); geographic location; title; medium (daguerreotype or ambrotype); size (whole, half, quarter, sixth, or ninth plate); known or probable date; and subject category. Identification of source institution/private collection with associated accession number, notes, and jpeg image were also included. Written inscriptions, use of hand-coloring, and (if the object was personally viewed) overall condition were also noted. For search purposes, various keywords were also assigned.

The resulting database is divided into six basic categories: Gold Fields, Gold Towns, Portraiture, San Francisco, Sacramento, and Stockton.[19] The Gold Fields category includes views of large and small groups of miners working in the field with various types of mining and excavation technologies, water fluming operations, and miner accommodations. The Gold Towns category focuses on towns outside the urban centers of San Francisco, Sacramento, and Stockton, and includes street views, merchant housing, cemeteries, and distant views. The Portraiture category is limited to studio portraits of miners. This includes men in recognizable mining attire often holding a pickaxe, shovel, knife, or gold nugget/ore specimen.

For unknown locations, geographic indicators like vegetation, topography, and distinct topographical formations were noted. Miners were carefully studied for unusual poses and the specifics of dress. The composition of the mining population was always of interest—information about race, gender, the presence of children, and nationality was noted.

Although the identities of most of the photographers are unknown, trends in photographers' choices were recorded. Variations in vantage point from differing camera positions—either eye-level, slightly elevated, or distant from the subject—were noted. Other object-specific decisions included the vertical or horizontal orientation of the plate, and the choice of mats.[20]

Informed by this wealth of data, the chapters of this volume offer an in-depth analysis of California gold rush daguerreotypes: an overview of the earliest daguerreian projects completed in California by Robert Vance and J. Wesley Jones, a summary of notable California daguerreotypists working outside the studio, views of gold towns, the evolution of mining technologies, and the contributions of people of various cultures and races.

California gold rush daguerreotypes offer more than a simple documentation of a major cultural and historical event. These images provide an extraordinary glimpse into the transformation of the American West: a mass migration led to a complex mix of peoples and cultures, cities arose almost overnight, and mining technology altered the landscape. While daguerreotypists found many ways to explore the reality of the gold rush, existing images do not—and perhaps could not—fully convey the experience in all the ways we now might wish. This volume focuses on what is visually represented in California gold rush daguerreotypes, while addressing what tended to be ignored.

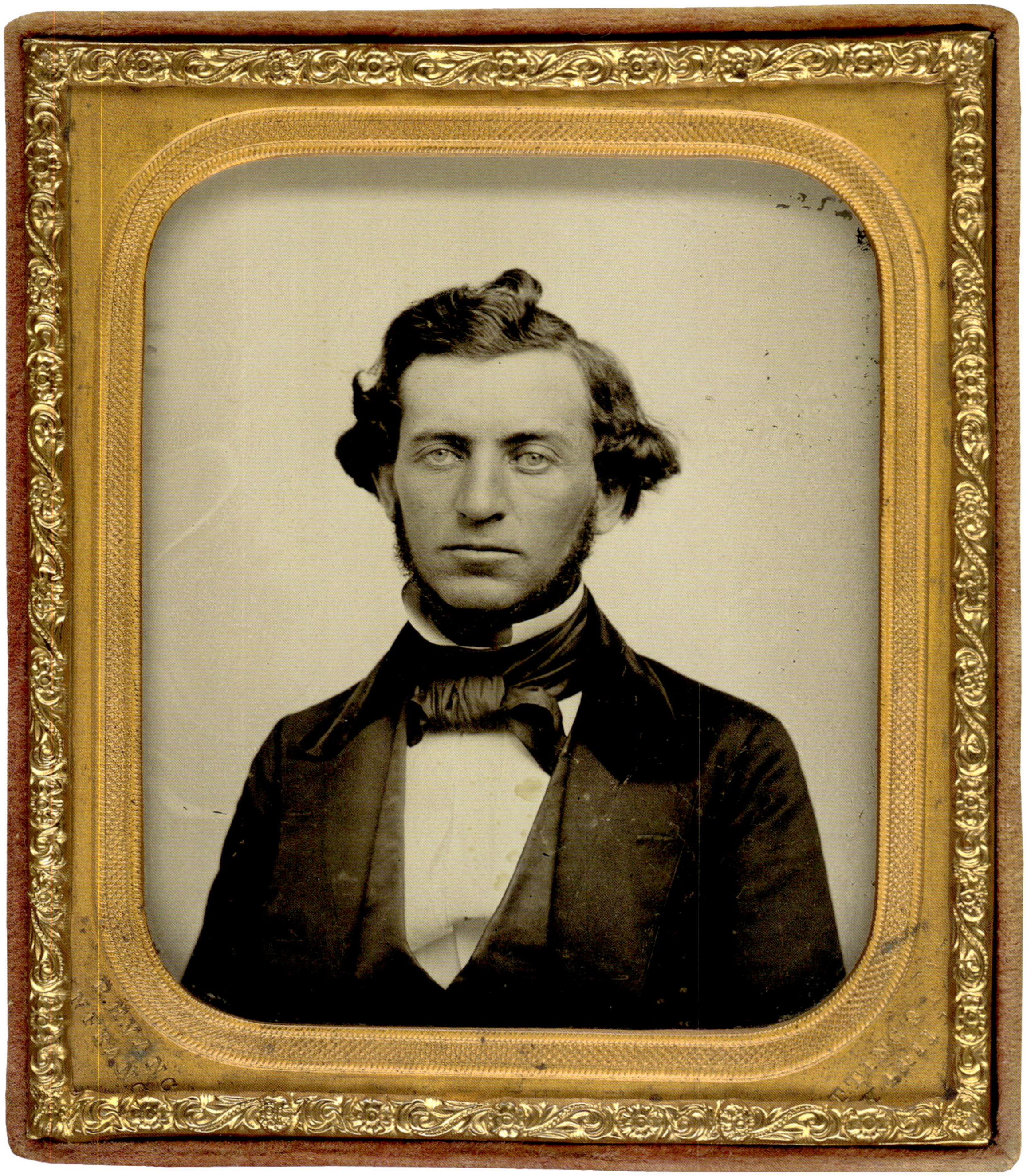

1 **Robert H. Vance**, American (1825–1876). *Self-portrait*, ca. 1854. Sixth-plate ambrotype. National Gallery of Canada, Ottawa.

CHAPTER 1 *Early Daguerreian Projects in California: Vance and Jones*

Two of the earliest daguerreotypists in California were Robert H. Vance and J. Wesley Jones. Traveling through the gold region at roughly the same time, in 1851, Vance and Jones recorded many of the same areas. Both understood what they saw in the broadest terms: as a cultural event—and adventure—of unprecedented historical importance. With remarkable entrepreneurial imagination, each conceived of a grand public showing of views, but with one important difference: Vance's daguerreotypes were made exclusively for exhibition while Jones's were created as references for painters. While their motivations varied, both Vance and Jones understood the power of the daguerreotype image to accurately represent this rich, newly acquired territory.

Robert Vance was already a skilled photographer when he arrived in California by ship from South America in 1850. Eager to daguerreotype the region—its cities, towns, mining sites, and indigenous inhabitants—Vance envisioned a massive exhibition of 300 whole-plate daguerreotypes that would tour cities in the eastern United States. J. Wesley Jones, on the other hand, was lured to California as part of a gold mining company. As he made the arduous trip overland, Jones determined to daguerreotype this entire experience: his tour of the California gold fields and his return across the continent to Missouri. The resulting plates would be used by painters in Boston to create a large-scale painted panorama. Jones was a daguerreian artist of convenience, and his interest in the medium ceased once this project was complete. Vance, on the other hand, enjoyed a long career as a photographic artist in California.

Unfortunately, all the daguerreotypes produced for these ventures are gone: Jones's daguerreotypes and the resulting painting are assumed lost, and Vance's daguerreotypes are almost certainly destroyed.[1] While no longer extant, these two projects are of special importance to the subject of the California gold rush. Both Vance's and Jones's journeys, resulting in large monographic collections, constituted a seminal use of the medium; notably, the camera was employed in a multifaceted enterprise involving documentation, art, education, entertainment, and entrepreneurship. These projects illuminate the central themes of the gold rush narrative—its most important sites and visual motifs—and its enormous public appeal.

J. WESLEY JONES

Working as a lawyer in Illinois when gold was discovered in California, John Wesley Jones originally had no plans to travel out west. However, he did invest in a company heading to the gold fields, and after one of the leaders of the company was detained, Jones was appointed in his place. He traveled overland to California in the spring of 1850 and arrived at Placerville in the spring of 1851. He worked variously as an attorney, census taker, and shopkeeper, and later hired miners to work for him at his claim near the Cold and Diamond Springs area.

Inspired by his journey to California, Jones conceived of an ambitious project to sketch and daguerreotype the entire California Trail, from the Missouri River to the gold fields.[2] Back east, painters would use the resulting images to create a large-scale moving panorama called a pantoscope.[3] Jones hoped that the pantoscope, accompanied by his lecture, would tour large cities throughout the eastern United States. While he had filled notebooks with pencil sketches on his trip westward, Jones was unsatisfied with his skill as a draftsman. Thus, despite lacking any previous experience with photography, he resolved in San Francisco that the daguerreotype would be the most trustworthy medium to record such views, despite the "great cost of means and toil."[4]

Jones became acquainted with Seth Shaw, a daguerreotypist from Nashville who had made the overland trip to California at about the same time and was running a successful daguerreotype studio in San Francisco.[5]

The two formed Shaw, Jones and Company, and in April 1851, the firm began work in San Francisco and the surrounding area. The *Alta California* newspaper noted,

> We learn that a company of enterprising young artists are now engaged in taking daguerreotype views of San Francisco, San Jose, Stockton, and along the San Joaquin and Sacramento Rivers. About the 1st of June they start across the plains . . . through to Independence, Missouri. The Panorama will be painted from the daguerreotype views in Lowell, Mass., and will be the largest ever exhibited in the United States.[6]

Shortly before the planned departure for the East, Shaw dropped out of the project, choosing to remain in business in San Francisco.[7] Fortunately, Jones quickly found a replacement for him in Jacob Shew.[8] Shew had immigrated to California in 1849 and may have been the earliest daguerreotypist to open a studio in the area. He was later joined by his brother, William, in March 1851. Jones wasted no time in hiring the two brothers for his pantoscope project. By late May, it was reported that

> Wesley Jones and William Shew, daguerreotype artists, are in our city taking views for the grand panorama. . . . Two excellent views have been taken of the United States Hotel and the office of the "Marysville Herald" by these admirable artists.[9]

Throughout the spring of 1851, Jones and his team made views of San Francisco, Sacramento, and Stockton, and throughout the gold mining region. By early July, both William and Jacob Shew had ended their tenures with the project, leaving Jones as the primary daguerreotypist for the remainder of the journey.[10] While it is unknown from whom he learned the craft, Jones most likely gained this expertise in his association with Shaw and the Shews.

From Placerville, Jones and his company left the western gold mining region behind and set off on the eastward leg of their overland journey, making both daguerreotypes and pencil sketches along the way. In St. Louis in November, Jones visited the newspaper offices of the *St. Louis Republican*. There, he treated the editorial staff to

> a glimpse of his choice Daguerreotypes of scenery, curiosities, and stupendous rocks; embracing a vast collection of all that is rich and rare, among the deep gorges, and "Ranges" of the Rocky and Sierra Nevada mountains. The Desert, and Plains . . . Mr. Jones has also Daguerreotypes of the various animals, and the different tribes of Indians, and a complete collection representing California scenery, the Gold Regions, and the towns and cities of the "Eureka State," the Quicksilver Mines, &c., &c.[11]

With the journey completed and 1,500 daguerreotype views secured, Jones relocated to Melrose, Massachusetts, to prepare for the production of the pantoscope. Three of the artists who had accompanied Jones on the overland trip—Alonzo Chappell, William N. Bartholomew, and W. Pearson—were joined by Thomas Burnham to complete the artistic team. Combining their various talents for landscape, architecture, and figural studies, the team embarked on the work, using the daguerreotypes and field sketches as a guide. The resulting pantoscope, ten feet tall and hundreds of yards long, was first presented in December 1852 at Boston's Armory Hall. A popular success, it played in Boston for six months before touring to the nearby cities of Lowell and Bedford. It then was taken to New York City in the fall of 1853, where it played for eleven months. That seemed to mark the end of its popular appeal. By 1855, Jones had returned to Illinois, and the pantoscope faded from the public memory, presumably discarded or destroyed.

Since the original daguerreotypes no longer exist, our knowledge of this work is dependent on period sources. A copy of Jones's illustrated lecture has survived, now in the collection of the California Historical Society, and Jones's work was documented and celebrated by George Spencer Phillips.[12] Under the pseudonym John Ross Dix, Phillips published a thirty-four-page booklet titled *Amusing and Thrilling Adventures of a California Artist while Daguerreotyping a Continent* (1854) to accompany the pantoscope. His aim was to provide "a hand book or guide to this great masterpiece of art, which has for so long a time graced our city [Boston], and delighted and instructed thousands."[13] Dix's sensationalized narrative was full of humorous and harrowing anecdotes about unusual happenings, deadly encounters with American Indians, and the treacherous nature of overland travel. But it was Jones's extraordinary character that truly captured Dix's esteem. Jones had fought "his way stubbornly through Indian territory, daguerreotyping every point of the way, gun in hand, though deserted by his artists." Stamped "as a man of genius," Jones persevered after "hardship, disease and death had robbed him of the counsel and aid of his faithful companions."[14] Part Two of Dix's narrative is titled *A Poetical Companion of Jones' Pantoscope of California, Nebraska, Utah, and the Mormons.* Broken into geographical sections from east to west, this narrative was meant to be held in hand and read while actively engaged with the pantoscope. Most of the passages are short and titled to orient the reading material with the visual experience.

When Jones made his documentary journey, he began in California and traveled eastward toward the plains. The pantoscope was painted in the reverse direction, from the plains westward to California.[15] Working on the assumption that many if not most geographical areas in the pantoscope were painted directly from daguerreotype views, we can glean important information from Dix's narrative, Jones's lecture notes, and contemporary newspaper articles and reviews.[16] A careful combined reading of the California section of Jones's lecture and of Dix's *Poetical Companion* gives a more complete picture of people, the California landscape, and the gold mining region, as well as tantalizing glimpses into the process of making those views.

In the *Poetical Companion* section of Dix's narrative, the descriptions of the first impressions of California are dramatic. The initial view, made from the snowy summit of the Sierra Nevada, was "inexpressively sublime and almost boundless, looking down upon mountains and forests, as they stretch out in every direction, sparkling with snow and glaciers."[17] This perspective, focused on the majesty of the scenery, had nationalistic implications about Manifest Destiny and the "divine right" to take possession of the land; it represents an implicit move away from European-centric art traditions. Jones made this clear in the excerpt following the description of the view:

> As we climbed on the highest crags our German artist threw down his book in excessive delight and admiration of the gorgeous scenery before him. Never have I seen such magnificence before he exclaimed as a student and artist I treaded the mazes and mountain paths of the Alps . . . but never have I beheld such vastness and sublimity. Every thing in America is grand your mountains—your rivers—your lakes—your glorious institutions—An Empire—a world in itself—and from 'yon tall boulder He gave "Three long cheers" for "America as she came from the hands of her God and her Washington."[18]

The entry point for overland travelers to the gold fields was through Hangtown (later named Placerville). Jones remarked that after "toiling four months over arid plains, Deserts, and snows," Hangtown signaled the merciful "end of his journey."[19] Here, Jones daguerreotyped from a distant and elevated position, perhaps as one would have first seen the town on arrival. After Hangtown, the illustrations in the lecture are based on sketches by Jones's artists or daguerreotypes by the Shews.[20] The narrative next focused on Weberville and the eastern portion of the gold mining region, an ethnically diverse area made up of Chileans, Chinese, Mexicans, and American Indians.

After the village of Cold Spring and the beautiful rolling hills of the valley of the Sacramento River, Jones arrived in bustling Sacramento. This city of 12,000 residents was of great interest to Jones, and he had the Shews make a nine-plate panorama of the place. In his text, Jones used nearby Sutter's Fort as an opportunity to discuss again the perceived divine right of Anglo men to appropriate territory for themselves.

In 1839, Swiss immigrant John A. Sutter had established an agricultural and trading post and a fortified settlement near the confluence of the Sacramento and American Rivers. In 1841, he received a land grant from Mexico for a large swath of property north from Sutter's Fort along the Feather River to Marysville. He then relocated his residence about forty-five miles north to Hock Farm, near Yuba City on the Feather River.[21] Most travelers journeying through the region made stops at either Sutter's Fort or Hock Farm, where the weary "found a refuge in his heart and in his hospitality."[22]

Upon arrival, Sutter's faulty impression was that the indigenous Mexican and American Indian population were undeserving and ill-equipped to recognize the full potential of the land. From Jones's perspective, Sutter exerted "an influence over savage tribes"[23] by "persevering, by kindness, and the exercise of skill, and well timed authority."[24] Clearly exploitative, Sutter relied completely on American Indians to build his fort, and his attempts to acculturate them included supplying "clothing, hats and every thing necessary to humanize, and civilize them."[25] Dix noted that "Indian villages abound" along the banks of the Sacramento and Feather River.[26] One of these was located at

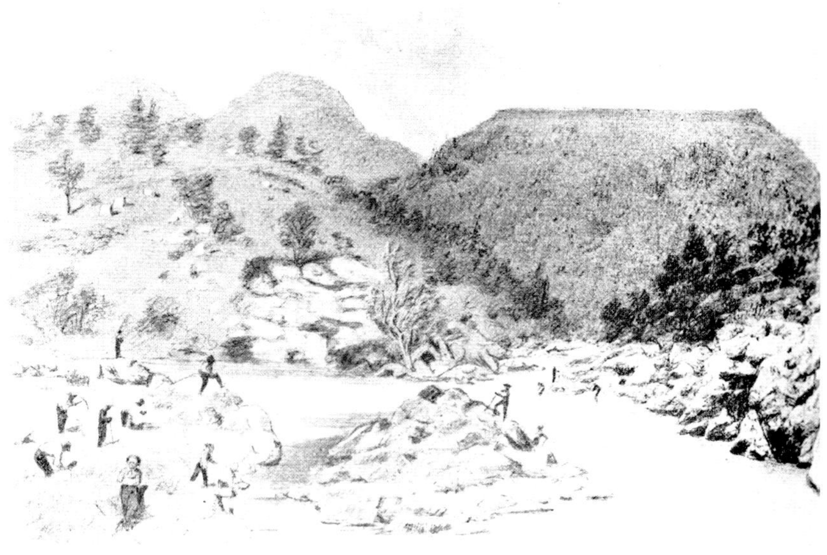

FIG. 1 **Alonzo Chappell**. *Table Mountain on the Feather River*, from "Jones' Pantoscope of California (Concluded)," *California Historical Society Quarterly* 6, no. 3 (September 1927).

Hock Farm. Jones described the village and its American Indian inhabitants in derogatory terms (for example, calling the women in the view weaving willow baskets "loathsome creatures, the worst of slaves").[27] Not far from the village, Jones daguerreotyped Sutter's residence—a large two-story structure with out-buildings and cultivated gardens surrounded by a picket fence.[28]

Immediately across the Feather River from Yuba City, the town of Marysville marked the beginning of the northern mining region. This portion of Jones's narrative revealed the ethnic diversity of the area and the ability of various groups to live and work together. Indeed, throughout his text, Jones references the activities of people of various nationalities and races: the equestrian skills of Mexican men, the industriousness of Chinese workers, and the tireless work of American Indian women.[29]

The scene that Jones encountered upon reaching the Feather River mining area was considered so central to his entire undertaking that it warranted special authentication: "The rocky character of the streams, where gold is obtained here is faithfully represented from Daguerreotypes."[30] It was crucial to Jones that the viewer recognize the truthfulness of the view. He described the riverbed scene, with miners from the White Rock mining company "picking among the crevices in the rocks with their pick-axes and iron spoons," and the head of the firm leaning on his shovel in the center of the scene.[31] This company had built a dam in the Feather River and diverted the flow into a secondary channel. This method of mining was common but could be accomplished only by collective effort rather than a solitary individual. In the sketch by Chappell titled *Table Mountain on the Feather River* [FIG. 1], miners working in the streambed can be seen indistinctly in

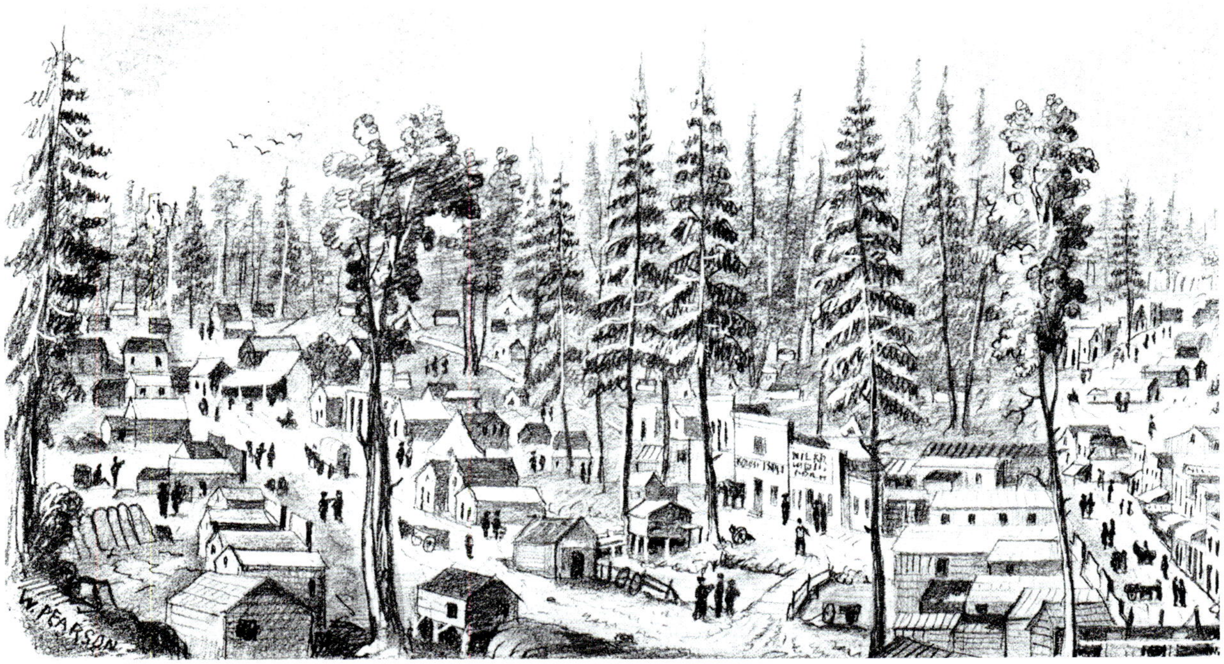

FIG. 2 **W. Pearson**. *Nevada City, California*, from "Jones' Pantoscope of California (Concluded)," *California Historical Society Quarterly* 6, no. 3 (September 1927).

the distance. Behind the river at Bidwell's Bar, a hillside is dotted with canvas tents; miner housing was often temporary as companies pulled up stakes and moved each time a claim was exhausted.

Continuing through the gold mining region, Jones was just as attentive to the landscape as he was to mining activity. He described the Yuba River and its winding route through the mountains. At Ousley's Bar, where miners worked, he was fascinated by the buckeye trees "growing with remarkable [symmetry] and beauty."[32]

Jones recognized the central importance of water to all forms of mining. "There being a scarcity of water through the greater portion of the year," he noted, companies were formed to dam rivers high up in the mountains. "Through Canals, and flumes, the water is brought, often over tree tops . . . and branched off in a thousand directions to supply the miners . . . [who] get it by paying from $16 to $30 per day."[33]

After the smaller gold mining towns, Nevada City must have felt like a metropolis. To properly convey its size and brisk commercial activity, Jones made his view from a relatively distant, elevated position. It is difficult to discern any signs in Pearson's sketch *Nevada City, California* [**FIG. 2**], but they would have been legible in the original daguerreotype view and in the pantoscope. Jones described several establishments, including Bower's Express, where miners received their mail; Milk Punch Depot; and the church and graveyard on the top of Zion's Hill. After passing through Greenwood Valley, "one of the most interesting areas in the dry diggings," Jones came to Sutter's Mill, where gold was first "accidentally discovered, and the destiny of California, and Millions of people changed."[34]

The area's third most important town after San Francisco and Sacramento, Stockton was located adjacent to the southern mining region. Steamboat service ran regularly between Sacramento and Stockton as a quick and efficient way for miners to reach the gold fields. The city straddled the San Joaquin River, and Jones described the most prominent buildings on both sides. On one, the El Placer gambling hall had a theater in its upper story; on the other was the Stockton House, a large hotel.

The rest of Jones's narrative covers areas outside the gold region. Views of the quicksilver mines near San Jose and of Mission Santa Clara have accompanying illustrations, but views of a large Mexican ranch, Mission Dolores, and San Francisco have been lost.[35] The quicksilver mines were essential to the gold mining (as well as the daguerreotype) process—from them, red cinnabar was quarried and heated to produce mercury, commonly known as quicksilver. Even then, however, mercury's toxic effects were apparent. As Jones noted, it was hard to find men to work in the mercury refining operation:

> The foreman had only been engaged about four months when we saw him, and he was so saturated with Mercury that he shook like an aspen Leaf, and could scarcely carry on a conversation . . . and where the vapor from the Chimneys settles upon the hillsides for any time Vegetation is destroyed.[36]

Reviews of Jones's Daguerreotypes and Pantoscope

Jones's pantoscope was enthusiastically received by critics and the public alike. Many of these reviews were cited at the end of Part One of Dix's narrative, in a "Miscellany" chapter. One section of this chapter, titled "Notices of the Artists, by The California Press. Daguerreotypes of California," commented specifically on the daguerreotypes created in California by Jones and his team for use in the pantoscope. Reviews from newspapers like the *Placer Times and Transcript, Sacramento Union, St. Louis Republican, Great Salt Lake Desert News*, and *Boston Journal* were included.[37] Another section of this chapter, titled "Encomiums of the Press," included testimonials by editors, excerpted articles, and reviews from newspapers including the *Boston Journal, Boston Bee, Boston Traveller, Boston Herald, Congregationalist and Christian Times, Portland Advertiser, New York Tribune, New York Herald, Providence Journal*, and *New York Mirror*.[38] These endorsements focused on the pantoscope painting, with occasional references to the original daguerreotypes.[39]

To these reviewers, Jones's success began with his use of the camera, "for the daguerreotype cannot fail to produce things as they really are."[40] As Robert Vance's daguerreotypes would later be described as the "impression of the real thing itself," so, too, were Jones's "a perfect view of California *as it is*."[41] With "the object to *illustrate California perfectly*," as reviewers acknowledged, Jones's daguerreotypes were valued for their "consummate accuracy."[42] From their position at the heart of the gold rush experience, the editors of the *Placer Times* stated that "*His view of California* is *complete, and truthful,—we can testify*."[43]

A darling of the press, Jones was lauded to the extreme. Perhaps the first to be viewed as an adventurer-photographer, Jones embodied the example set by Prussian-born Alexander von Humboldt, the greatest naturalist of his day. Humboldt's widely celebrated exploration of the Americas between 1799 and 1804 resulted in daring adventures and innumerable scientific discoveries.[44] Like Humboldt, Jones was seen as a man of "astonishing perseverance and triumph."[45] Jones's achievement was only magnified by the inevitable comparison to Colonel John C. Fremont, who failed in his 1842 attempt to make daguerreotypes across the West.

The concluding reviews in Dix's narrative focused on the pantoscope experience itself. The virtues of accuracy and faithfulness associated with the daguerreotypes were transferred to the painting derived from them. The truthfulness of the daguerreotype was seen to surpass that of the artist's hand: "In *accuracy* it probably *exceeds* any, as the daguerreotype has been used to give exactness to its delineations."[46] Thus, because the painting was based on the daguerreotype, "one feels confident assurance that [the images] accord with the realities."[47]

> All the varieties of mining life pass before us, and all the processes of mining. Nay, we see the very identical miners who were at work when the views were taken, in the very attitudes of real work; for they kept their positions for a time, by request, that the daguerreotypes might fix them *forever*. We see too the various stages of civilization, from the newest and most recent town, up to the metropolitan grandeur of San Francisco.[48]

This was recognized as a new kind of accuracy, transcending traditional modes of representation and reportage. Due to its derivation from photographs, the pantoscope had the power to virtually transport its viewers to California. This imaginary journey was at once exhilarating, all encompassing, and safe:

> Arrived in the Golden State, we are introduced to the miner in his home and at his labors; initiated to all the mysteries of mining life; visit all the principal miners, and after, walking the streets of Sacramento, Nevada, Marysville, Stockton and San Francisco, prying into all that's useful, and admiring all that's wonderful and sublime, in this land of novelties,—we return home perfectly delighted and almost persuaded that we have actually been to California and really "seen the elephant."[49]

ROBERT H. VANCE

As J. Wesley Jones was making his inaugural trip overland from Illinois in the spring and summer of 1850, Robert H. Vance [1] was also making plans to travel to California.[50] It is not known precisely where or when he first learned the daguerreotype art, but Vance's first advertised studio was located in Boston in 1846, with partner John Lerow. "For clearness, distinctness, and boldness of execution," Vance & Lerow's daguerreotypes were "unsurpassed."[51] The partnership was short lived, ending by 1847. At the beginning of 1847, Vance left Boston for South America. He opened studios in Valparaiso and Santiago, Chile, while making periodic trips to other parts of the region. In July 1848, he advertised in the *El Copiapino* newspaper in advance of his visit to the city of Copiapo, the center of the Chilean mining region.[52] While portraiture was certainly the most significant portion of his business, Vance refined his expertise in working outdoors. In Valparaiso, for example, he made at least three outdoor views: two plates of the city and one of an admiral's residence.[53]

By July 1850, gold fever had reached Chile.[54] Vance left shortly for San Francisco by ship, stopping briefly in Panama, where he made at least three views: a multi-plate panorama of the countryside, a view of a cathedral, and one of outlying islands.[55] On another stop in Acapulco, Mexico, he made two panoramic views of the city and its harbor.[56]

Vance arrived in San Francisco in late fall 1850 and established a studio there by December.[57] From the beginning, he was motivated by a most ambitious idea: an intensive, systematic photographic documentation of the region. Because the winter of 1850–51 "was a remarkable dry and pleasant one," Vance's opportunity to travel and photograph throughout the city and into the mining region was most likely immediate.[58] Moving eastward from San Francisco, he visited the northern, central, and southern mining regions. As historian Peter Palmquist has noted, Vance's chosen sites were often a day's travel apart and typically located along the route of the inland steamer.[59]

Seeking advance recognition for his work, Vance organized an entry in early 1851 to the Great Exhibition, or Crystal Palace Exhibition, scheduled to open in London on May 1. He initially intended to exhibit his full 300-plate exhibition, but "from an interruption to the Artist's work, from one of the San Francisco conflagrations, they could not be got together on time."[60] His final submission included a series of eight daguerreotype plates of San Francisco, "representing the whole of this city."[61] By the summer of that year, Vance's great project was complete. In September 1851, the *Photographic and Fine Art Journal* reported that he had amassed "three hundred California views, for exhibition."[62]

Vance's *Views in California*

Like Jones's collection, all 300 of Vance's daguerreotypes have been lost. The only remaining evidence of this remarkable project can be found in reviews of its showing in New York City and in the *Catalogue of Daguerreotype Panoramic Views in California*, published to accompany the exhibition. In the preface to this catalogue, Vance emphasized the importance of visual over textual information in his description of the California experience:

> Much valuable information has been given in regard to the country, by several excellent works, but inasmuch as the sight of a place affords so much more pleasure, and gives so much better knowledge than the bare description possibly can, the Artist flatters himself that the accompanying Views will afford the information so much sought after.[63]

He asserted that the daguerreotype was the only medium capable of accurately reflecting nature, assuring readers that the views they would see "are no exaggerated and high-colored sketches . . . but are as every daguerreotype must be, the stereotyped impression of the real thing itself." As a result, his collection of whole-plate daguerreotypes would provide the viewer "a complete picture of California."[64]

Unlike Jones's 1,500-plate collection, Vance's 300 California views were largely without narrative. The text of the catalogue was limited to the two-paragraph preface and a titled list of views, a total of 131 entries.[65] Sixty-one of these titles focus on the gold mining region, with nine explicitly referencing mining activity.[66] Vance's exact route through the mining region is not known. The titles in the catalogue do not appear to be in any specific order and are not listed chronologically. Based in San Francisco, he almost certainly made trips in and out of the gold region over a period of weeks or months rather than capturing all his views in one extended trip.[67] Vance's production covers roughly the same territory as Jones's, although Jones ventured farther north into Butte County (Bidwell's Bar) and Vance went farther south into Tuolumne and Stanislaus Counties.

In the northern mining region, Vance visited Nevada, Yuba, and El Dorado Counties. In Nevada County, the area around Nevada City was a hotbed of activity following major strikes in the ravines of Deer Creek and the "new and very rich diggings" of Gold Run.[68] In Nevada City, he made a view of the main street and a multi-plate panorama of the town. The latter emphasized the surrounding landscape, showing the great size of trees in this area, "some of them three hundred feet in height, and twenty-seven feet in circumference."[69] Underscoring the potential for lumbering in the region, Vance daguerreotyped the front and rear of a mule-powered sawmill. Interested in the latest mining technologies, he also daguerreotyped miners at work with a long tom near Nevada City and sluice washing on nearby Deer Creek. Gold Run, the subject of a multi-plate panorama, was of particular interest to him, "it being one of the first places" of gold discovery.[70] Fascinated by the intensity of activity here, Vance took the great majority of his mining views in Nevada County.

Moving on to the town of Marysville on the Yuba River, Vance daguerreotyped the levee and river steamers. He also took multiple views of the center of town, recording the main street, the California theater, the United States Hotel, and views of the town square from the west, south, and north. He photographed the scenery along the Yuba River and took an elevated multi-plate panorama of the town and its surroundings "from the top of the United States Hotel."[71]

Like Jones, once Vance arrived in Yuba and Sutter Counties, he visited the vast land holdings of John A. Sutter. Paying attention to the American Indians living on Sutter's land, he recorded their villages and huts, and made individual portraits of four chiefs and the "wife and sister of the celebrated chief Kasuse."[72] The most famous of all Sutter's properties was in El Dorado County just outside the town of Coloma. Sutter's Mill was a necessary pilgrimage site for any visitor, and Vance made multiple views of the sawmill where the first gold was found in January 1848.[73] He also made several views of the town of Coloma from various vantage points: from a northern hill on the west side of the river, an elevated view of Main Street from the courthouse, and a multi-plate panorama from the east side of the river. Highlighting the overall topography of the area, many of these views included the surrounding countryside.

South of Coloma, the town of Placerville was renowned as a place where "the surface of the earth yielded gold to the slightest touch; when fortunes oftentimes were made in a day."[74] Miners in the area dug into ancient streambeds to find gold hidden in cracks and crevices of the underlying rock in a process known as dry digging. Dirt unearthed at Placerville was hauled to a small feeder creek for washing. Here, Vance daguerreotyped miners at work, in the field and within the town limits. He also made a multi-plate panorama "from a Hill East of City; this being the first place of arrival for those crossing the Plains."[75] Curiously, two of Vance's views of the town were titled *Hangtown*, while the remaining three reflected the settlement's final name, *Placerville*, which may suggest that he made two or more trips to this town.[76]

Unlike Jones, Vance ventured into the southern mining region. In Calaveras County, Vance stopped in the town of Mokelumne Hill and at Carson's Creek, near the town of Melones, "at the foot of Gold Mountain, in which is the richest quartz vein in the world, one company alone taking out $25,000 per week!"[77] Farther south, in Tuolumne County, the town of Sonora was experiencing a similar gold boom.[78] Vance daguerreotyped Holden's Garden at Sonora, "from which the largest lump of Gold ever found, was taken, weighing twenty-eight pounds."[79] A group known as the Wheaton Company discovered this gold nugget in May 1851 (indicating that Vance's visit was after that date). In addition to daguerreotyping miners at work, Vance made a multi-plate panorama of the town, a view of Main Street, and an elevated view of Central Street "from a height south of the city."[80]

Following the Stanislaus River south into Stanislaus County, Vance was headed away from the gold mining region toward an area with a known American Indian population. In the region between and along the Stanislaus and Tuolumne Rivers, an early resident recounted, "In all directions, beneath the venerable oaks, were Indian Mounds, ancient and grass-grown, or modern and still swarming with swarthy life; and no evidence lacking to prove that this had long been a favorite rallying point for Indian tribes."[81] A white woman traveling from Stockton to Sonora at roughly the same time as Vance chronicled her impressions of the tribes living along the Stanislaus River:

> There were over a thousand, I was told, all neatly clad. To see their tents, wigwams and huts, lining this bold little stream—to see them in groups, of pastime or labor—to gaze . . . at Indians, river, shrubs, flowers, rocks, hills, all rugged and green, was a sight romantic, grand and imposing in the extreme.[82]

Similarly impressed, Vance took multiple views here: a village on the bank of the river, as well as some people cooking and others dressed for a "War Dance." Nearby, at the river town of Knight's Ferry, Vance daguerreotyped the valley of the Stanislaus River and made at least two additional views of the town itself, including an evening view.

With his grand project completed, Vance had some 300 whole-plate daguerreotypes, "elegantly framed in rosewood and gilding."[83] The group was first exhibited in New York City in October 1851.[84] Although the "grand exhibition attracted considerable attention through the month," it was poorly publicized and closed after only two months.[85] The editor of the *Photographic Art-Journal* noted that "although they are among the best daguerreotype views ever taken, they failed to attract that attention necessary to the support of an exhibition of any character."[86]

After the New York showing, Vance sought other exhibition venues. However, only one further presentation took place: a relatively short installation in a daguerreotypist's studio in New York City.[87] By early 1853, with little hope for future exhibitions, Vance was "desirous of selling" his collection, specifying that he would accept $1,500 for everything, or "half the collection for $900; one quarter for $500; or one eighth for $300."[88] In August 1853, the whole group was purchased at public auction by St. Louis daguerreotypist John Fitzgibbon.[89] It is not known what price was realized.[90]

Reviews of *Views in California*

Despite its commercial failure, Vance's exhibition was a critical success. In October and November 1851, his daguerreotypes were positively reviewed in four New York City–based publications, both those intended for general audiences (*United States Magazine and Democratic Review* and *Literary World*) and specialized journals for the photographic profession (*Photographic Art-Journal* and *Daguerreian Journal*).[91] These reviews provide a unique opportunity to explore the perceived characteristics of successful California daguerreotypes.

Critical reviews of early photography are problematic. The initial public reaction was often one of confusion about the nature of the medium and its relation to the more established fine arts. Painters were understood to render the world as they saw it—that is, as filtered and shaped by the interpretive mind of the artist. There was little question that the daguerreotype was uniquely accurate or faithful to the visible facts of the world. However, the medium's putatively mechanical nature led some art critics to pronounce it inherently inartistic, and useful only as a factual aid to painters. Daguerreotype views were difficult to discuss in pictorial terms because the standard of perfection for a work of art referenced painting. Straddling the line between factuality and artistry, daguerreotypists were expected to create both technically proficient and attractive images.

In their exquisite union of fact and aesthetics, Vance's daguerreotypes suggested a new kind of art—one that reflected a fresh respect for objective description. Praised for their "fidelity" to nature, his views were "accurate" and "thorough," with "every line faithfully portrayed."[92] This notion of "truth to nature" was promoted by the British art critic John Ruskin in his five-volume publication *Modern Painters* (1843–60). Ruskin believed that the principal role of the artist was to maintain the utmost truth to nature and that this fidelity to appearance would point to higher truths, both moral and spiritual. As historian Michael Harvey clarifies, in Ruskin's view, "It was important for the painter to remain faithful to the eye's vision. . . . Clarity of sight was paramount: through the eye it was possible to develop an understanding of the God-given intricacy of Nature."[93]

Ruskin was immediately drawn to photography's potential and first used the daguerreotype camera on an 1846 tour through France, Italy, and Switzerland. Made by his valet, John Hobbs, these daguerreotypes were used as source material for Ruskin's own drawings and watercolors and as the basis for illustrations in his publications. Finding the daguerreotype an indispensable tool, Ruskin was puzzled by its lack of use among artists: "I much regret that artists in general do not think it worth their while to perpetuate some of the beautiful effects which the daguerreotype alone can seize."[94]

Vance's California scenes were appreciated in a similar vein, as remarkable "evidence of the value of this art to the traveler."[95] The fine detail could not be grasped in a cursory view of the plates. Instead, critics suggested that "three or four hours can be very profitably and amusingly spent" in studying them.[96] Vance's daguerreotypes were clearly appreciated as both science and art, as "a valuable and interesting collection" and as "specimens worthy among the foremost in the [photographic] art."[97]

Lacking photographic terminology with which to describe landscape daguerreotypes, many reviewers defaulted to painting aesthetics. One insightful comment from the *Photographic Art-Journal* noted that Vance's 300 views of California evinced "an exquisite taste for the sublime and beautiful."[98] The "sublime" and "beautiful" were art historical terms highlighted by British philosopher Edmund Burke in 1757.[99] Long associated with landscape painting, Burke's terms provided a classification system for judgments about experience and a way to articulate feelings about nature. For Burke, a sublime landscape elicited feelings of horror, awe, and astonishment triggered by a sense of vastness, extreme height, peril, and ruggedness. The beautiful, on the other hand, described qualities conducive to relaxation and delight: balance, control, and harmony.

Studying the descriptive titles of Vance's daguerreotypes, one can easily imagine views of the sublime—gigantic trees towering 300 feet in height or expansive panoramic views taken from the tops of buildings or hills. Beautiful views, scenes on a comfortingly human scale, might include Hock Farm nestled into the landscape, an evening view of a river, or the rhythmic work of miners using a long tom. For many nineteenth-century art critics, beauty in the landscape was synonymous with the productive human presence. Reverend H. W. Bellows, a member of the National Academy of Design, asserted that "Nature never works so well in vegetation as when she unites with the industry of man."[100] He stated:

> All needful transformations of substance are but little lower than angelic. And, although it be a change to less external beauty, yet the higher human purpose served lends a higher beauty; so that an unsightly telegraph pole may be more noble than the tree from which it was formed, and a city may be grander than a forest.[101]

Nature's real beauty, it would seem, lay in its ability to provide raw materials for man's use; industrialization in all forms was indirectly the work of God. Bellows cited the discovery of ore deposits deep in the earth and "the recent and sublime science of physical geography, as well as geology, brilliantly proves that the earth was made for man, not man for the earth."[102]

The reliance on the painting aesthetic was particularly apparent in a report in the *Photographic Art-Journal* that "testimony to the excellence of Mr. Vance's Daguerreotypes" was provided by "one of our best landscape painters."[103] The unnamed painter was familiar with "all the painted panoramas that have been before the public for the last six years" and had expressed "delight at the many artistic beauties which they possessed." Despite the use of color in painted panoramas, the painter conceded that "Mr. Vance's views of California created . . . a greater degree of admiration than did Banvard's or Evers' great productions of the Mississippi and noble Hudson."[104] While admitting that "form, in color, is perhaps the greatest charm upon which the eye can dwell," the painter praised a new kind of aesthetic achievement—the idea that "detail, with general effect, should be the principal aim of all artists." And it was this quality that Vance had "achieved to the highest state of perfection." Clearly engaging with the daguerreotypes as works of art, the painter celebrated Vance's rendition of the gold mining landscape in explicitly aesthetic terms:

> Not a blade of grass, nor the most minute pebble—hardly perceptible to the naked eye—nor the fibres of the bark of the tree—nor the myriads of tinny [*sic*] leaves that compose the clustering foliage—nor the silver stretches in the zig-zag ripple of the water as it glides gently on, or meanders among the rocks, washing up in its passage the little spangles of gold which have made California the great attraction of the whole world—but are wonderfully portrayed . . . most incomparable.[105]

After carefully viewing Vance's entire collection, the painter focused on one plate that he had "no hesitation in saying is the finest daguerreotype view ever taken."[106] This view of untamed, raw beauty—including "a fallen tree over three hundred feet in length [and] sharp, angular rocks, &c."—could be described as "picturesque," a blending of the sublime and beautiful.[107] Similarly, the painter discovered "wild and romantic scenery" in many of the daguerreotype images, where "the general effect of the lights and shadows—the water especially, so life like in its reflections" resulted in superior views worthy of artistic study.[108]

For the editors of the *Daguerreian Journal*, only the daguerreotype could convey the "perfection of nature," with "every line faithfully portrayed and possessing a degree of minuteness in detail not to be equaled by the hand of man."[109] Inventor and artist Samuel Morse considered the "hand of man" fallible where nature was "subjected to [the artist's] imperfect, sketchy translations into crayon or Indian ink drawings, and occupying days, and even weeks, in their execution."[110] Seen as eliminating this imperfect human intervention, a daguerreotype plate was considered "painted by Nature's self with a minuteness of detail, which the pencil of light in her hands alone can trace" resulting in a "superabundance of *materials* and not *copies*; — *they cannot be called copies of nature, but portions of nature herself.*"[111] Writer Edgar Allan Poe also felt that daguerreotype views allowed for a more authentic experience with nature:

> In truth the daguerreotype plate is infinitely more accurate than any painting by human hands. If we examine a work of ordinary art, by means of a powerful microscope, all traces of resemblance to nature will disappear — but the closest scrutiny of the photographic drawing discloses only a more absolute truth, more perfect identity of aspect with the thing represented.[112]

It is telling that the catalogue accompanying Vance's exhibition was titled "Views *in* California" instead of "Views *of* California." This choice of words suggested an exhibition experience capable of mentally transporting the viewer directly to the gold region. The reviewer for the *Photographic Art-Journal* stated, "On looking upon these pictures, one can almost imagine himself among the hills and mines of California, grasping at the glittering gold that lies before him; wandering over the plains, along the beautiful rivers that flow into the California gulf . . . "[113] This was an idealized view, quite removed from the frequent realities of hard work, malnutrition, and failure. But for families back home, Vance's exhibition provided a virtual immersion in the experience, thus serving as both an education and a comfort — the best "presentation to people at a distance of California life."[114]

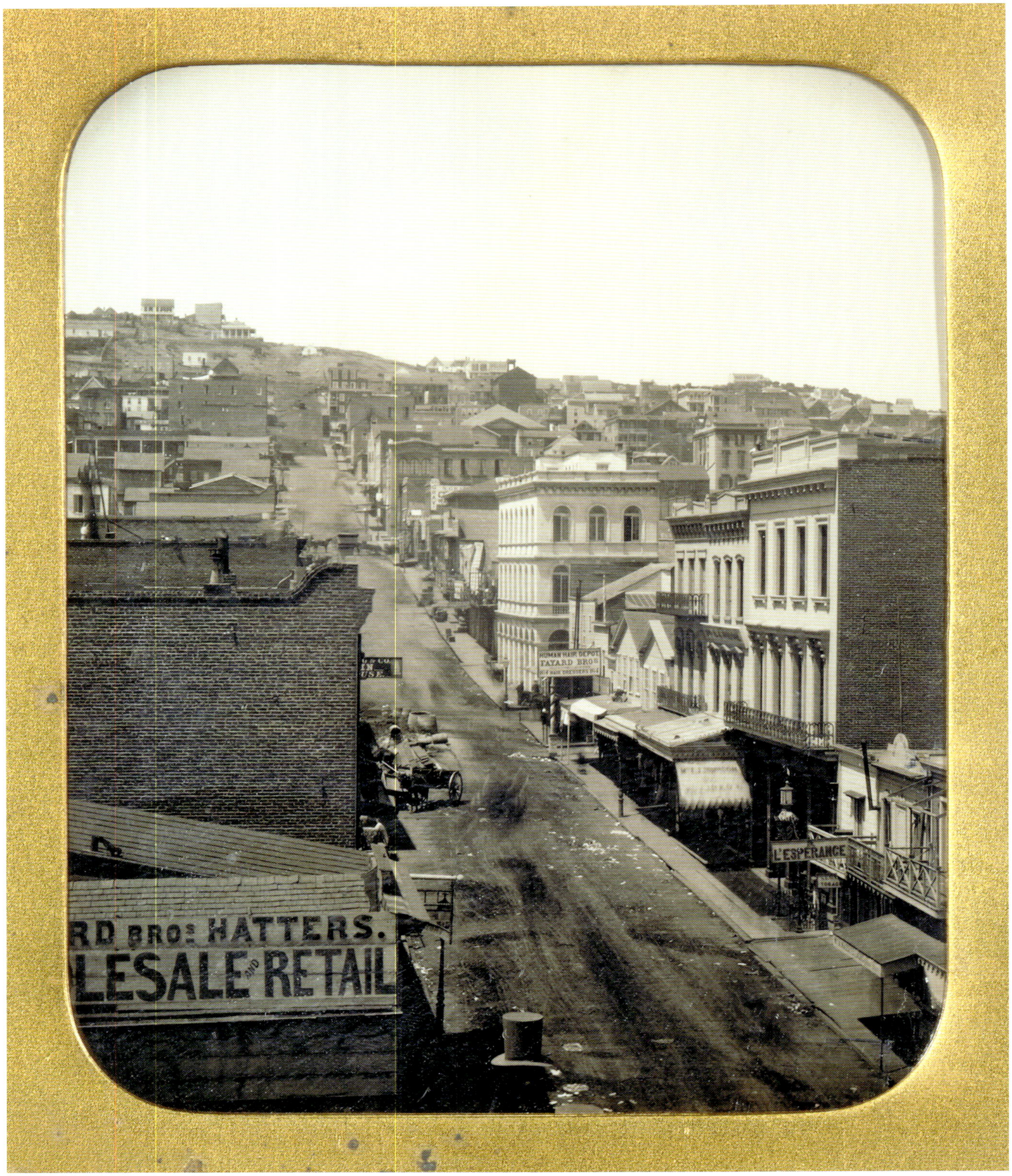

FIG. 3 **Robert H. Vance**, American (1825–1876). *View of Sacramento Street, San Francisco*, ca. 1854–56.
Stereo daguerreotype, detail of [22].

CHAPTER 2 *The Urban Gold Rush: The Daguerreotype in San Francisco and Sacramento*

Keith F. Davis

The most tangible legacy of the California gold rush is seen in the two largest cities it built: San Francisco and Sacramento.[1] Between 1848 and about 1860, this region witnessed a massive influx of immigrants and a veritable torrent of new wealth. Few of these new arrivals had any intention of staying in California—they aimed to strike it rich and return home. Likewise, much of the treasure pulled from the ground ended up in bank vaults on the other side of the American continent. Nonetheless, in this fundamentally transient and exploitative endeavor, it was inevitable that something would stick. The money and people that did stay in the region gave rise to San Francisco, one of the nation's most iconic cities, and Sacramento, the state capital.[2]

The European settlement of what is now San Francisco began as part of the Spanish Empire. In 1776, Spain established a religious mission and a small military garrison, or presidio, at Yerba Buena Cove on the west side of San Francisco Bay. When Mexico gained independence from Spain in 1821, Alta California, including all of the present-day state, came under Mexican control. The entire region was claimed by the United States in July 1846, at the start of the Mexican-American War, and California was admitted to the union as the thirty-first state in 1850.

For decades, Yerba Buena had been a small and relatively quiet trading post. The settlement was renamed San Francisco in January 1847 and, with a significantly increased American presence, it began growing—from about 200 residents in 1846 to something over 800 in early 1848. Gold was discovered in January 1848, but the news spread slowly at first. Following a major announcement in San Francisco, on May 12, 1848, much of the city was temporarily emptied out. As word spread over the following months, prospectors began arriving from elsewhere in California and from Oregon, the Hawaiian Islands, Mexico, Peru, and Chile. Following President Polk's confirmation of the find in his December 5, 1848, State of the Union address, the rush went global. With the arrival of the forty-niners, the population of San Francisco exploded: it reached 5,000 in July 1849 and an astounding 25,000 by the end of the year. The city had more than 36,000 residents in 1852 and nearly 57,000 in 1860.[3]

Modern historians have described San Francisco as an "instant city," the product of a wildly accelerated process of growth.[4] The city's population included white Americans, both free and enslaved African Americans, and others from Mexico, Chile, China, Australia, Hawaii, and various countries in Europe. While this diversity resulted in some racial and ethnic animosities, it produced a remarkable form of nineteenth-century cosmopolitanism. At least one historian has suggested that San Francisco's basic identity—as a place of cultural difference and tolerance—stems from the radical plurality of its formation.[5]

In the first years of the gold rush, San Francisco was seen as a port of transit and a commercial hub far more than a permanent place of residence. The majority of prospectors, and even many of the city's merchants, aimed to make their fortune and return home. Few devoted much thought or effort to the planning and administration of the city. As a result, officials tried to establish a normal urban infrastructure—for example, the police department was founded in 1849—but their efforts lagged well behind the community's actual needs. In the early years of the gold rush, San Francisco was a messy and chaotic place, characterized by muddy streets, cheap and temporary buildings, poor sanitation, political corruption, and crime.[6]

In this period of relentless change, San Francisco was transformed physically and economically.[7] To compensate for the shallow water near the shore, wharves were built out into the bay to allow large ships to unload cargo. At the same time, the city's steep hills were gradually shoveled away and dumped into the bay. By this process, wharves were transformed into streets, and "water lots" became solid ground. In 1847, the bay came up to Montgomery Street; by 1852, it had been pushed back more than three full city blocks. With the construction of the seawall (now the Embarcadero) in the 1860s, the city gained several more blocks of dry land.

Fire speeded the city's transformation. In a year and a half, San Francisco suffered six devastating fires: on December 24, 1849; May 4, June 14, and September 17, 1850; and May 3–4 and June 22, 1851. The latter two fires were the worst, together destroying more than thirty square blocks.[8] These blazes forced the adoption of new building practices—the replacement of temporary canvas-and-wood structures with fire-resistant buildings of brick and stone. As part of this overall improvement, a significant effort was made to grade, pave, plank, and sewer the city streets. Thus, in the span of only a few years, San Francisco went from a ragtag village to a much cleaner and more permanent city.

The city's economy was both supercharged and distorted by the wealth flooding in from the gold fields. The value of mining production peaked at a total of about $81 million in 1852, and then leveled off to about $50 million in the following few years. Next to gold, the region's most important export was mercury, or quicksilver, from the New Almaden mines near San Jose. Only in 1855–56, when it was obvious that gold field production had stagnated, did other export commodities such as flour, wheat, and barley take on significant economic value.[9]

A number of factors contributed to a chronic boom-and-bust economy in early San Francisco. The seasonal production in the gold fields led to a cycle of strong sales for the city's merchants in spring and fall, with reduced demand in summer and winter. Most merchants lived in an unpredictable world of scarcity and glut, always betting that the goods they ordered from far away would be in demand once they arrived. This led to both inflated and highly variable prices. Historian Roger W. Lotchin has observed,

> Nowhere was the instability of the market more in evidence than in the city's price index. In the years 1848–50, the fluctuation was enormous; but even in the relatively more stable years that followed, prices were very volatile. Flour, the leading staple for most of the period, reached a high of nineteen dollars per barrel in 1850, forty-seven in 1851, forty-two in 1852, thirty-one in 1853, thirteen in 1854, and fourteen and a half in 1855. However, these were only the highs. The lows for the year were frequently under ten dollars. These "California prices"—often very high, always unstable, and universally deplored—included nearly all goods at one time or another.[10]

When San Francisco emptied out in May and June 1848, it suffered a brief economic downturn. The first wave of affluence followed soon after, lasting from mid-1848 into early 1850. For most of 1850 and 1851, the city was economically depressed as a result of an overstock of commercial goods and a relative decline in immigration. The economy revived in early 1852 and remained strong for about a year and a half. Another slump beginning in late 1853 was prolonged by a banking crisis in early 1855 and the national financial panic of 1857; it did not lift until 1858 or 1859.

There was money to be made throughout this period, but nothing was guaranteed. Success depended on some vital combination of ambition and aggression, talent and guile, self-confidence and luck.

City Daguerreotypists

It is uncertain when the first photographer reached California. Given the significance of Yerba Buena / San Francisco as a trading post, it is possible that a daguerreotypist stopped there in the years between 1840 and 1848 on the way to another destination. At present, however, no relevant names or images from these years are known.

With his notice of January 25, 1849, in the *Alta California* newspaper, Richard H. Carr became the first in the city to advertise as a daguerreotypist. This enterprise lasted only about five weeks: by March 1, Carr had left San Francisco for the mines.[11] The city's second known daguerreotypist, E. Sutton, lasted somewhat longer, but he, too, has left little trace.[12] At least two of the earliest practitioners worked on something like a part-time basis. The city's first female daguerreotypist, Julia Shannon, offered her services as both a photographer and a midwife. She began advertising on January 29, 1850, using all capital letters to emphasize the novelty of her operation: "DAGUERREOTYPES TAKEN BY A LADY . . ."[13] Sterling C. McIntyre, who arrived in San Francisco in November 1850, had been working as both a dentist and a daguerreotypist for about six years. While he appears to have advertised only his services as a dentist in San Francisco, he made the first daguerreotype panorama of the city in January 1851. However, he left only three months later to make portraits and views in the gold fields.[14]

As these early practitioners demonstrate, the daguerreian business was like most other occupations in this raw, frenetic city—more a matter of opportunity and expediency than of great experience or technical sophistication. In truth, the profession was always in a dynamic process of adaptation: nothing remained constant for very long. Daguerreotypists routinely moved from one address to another, opened and closed branch operations, and engaged and disengaged in a sequence of partnerships and business relationships. The network of professional affiliations in the daguerreian world of San Francisco and Sacramento was remarkably dense and tangled.

Beginning in about 1850, the second wave of practitioners—including George H. Johnson, Henry W. Bradley, Frederick C. Coombs, James M. Ford, William Shew, Jacob Shew, and Robert H. Vance—viewed themselves as integral members of a national community of professionals. They ordered chemicals and supplies from wholesalers in New York, and they modeled their businesses on the leading galleries in that city.

The best studios in San Francisco and Sacramento had posing rooms on the upper level of a building, with a large skylight to allow for the best illumination and shortest possible exposures. By 1854, the peak year for daguerreian activity in San Francisco, the biggest of these studios were showplaces in their own right. The main waiting rooms often functioned as public picture galleries, with daguerreotype displays of notable scenes and personalities. The largest of these studios conveyed an atmosphere of aspiration and

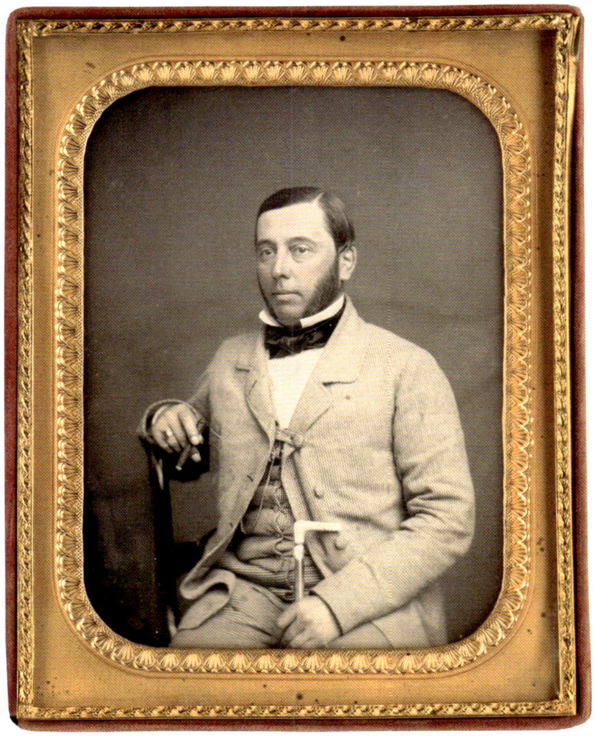

2 **George H. Johnson**, American (1823–ca. 1880s). *Portrait of a man*, ca. 1849. Half-plate daguerreotype.

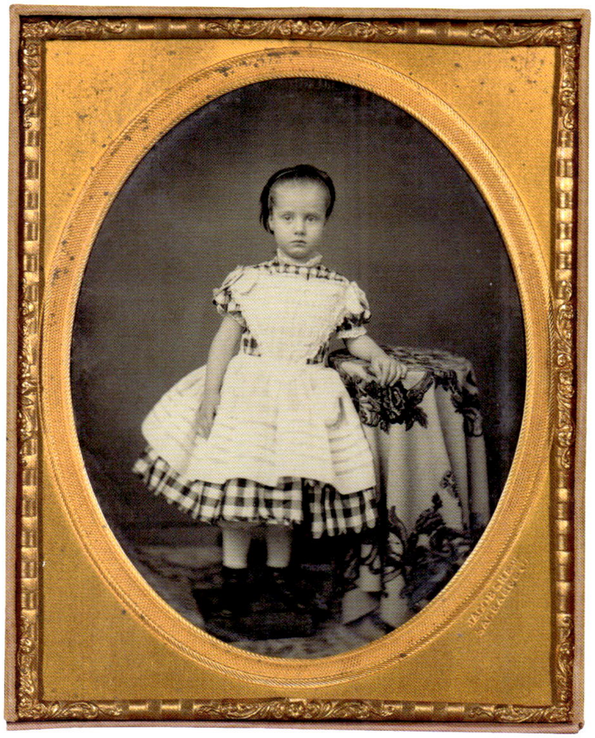

3 **Jacob Shew**, American (1826–1879). *Portrait of a girl*, ca. 1856–58. Half-plate daguerreotype.

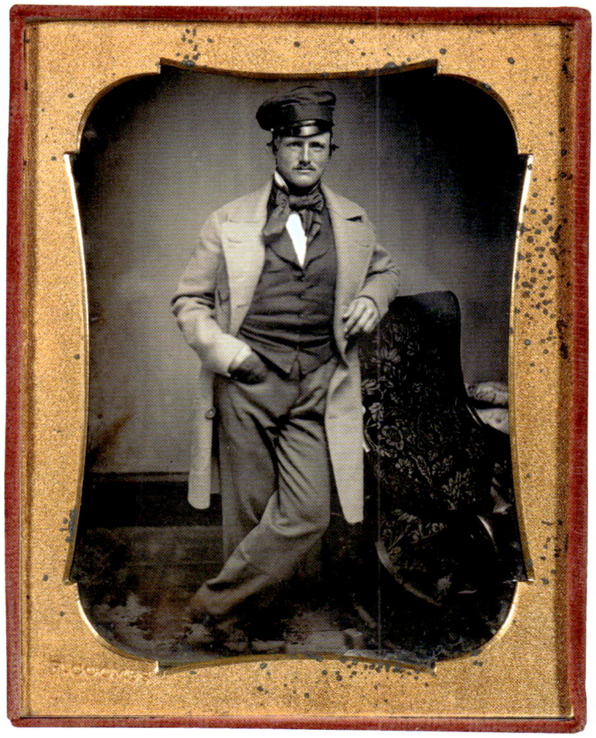

4 **Frederick Coombs**, American (1803–1874). *Portrait of John B. Newton*, ca. 1850–51. Quarter-plate daguerreotype.

refinement. In 1854, for example, Robert H. Vance opened a lavish new space on the corner of Montgomery and Sacramento Streets. One visitor observed,

> There are no less than eight elegantly finished reception rooms, and 12 operating rooms, used in the business. . . . On the lower story is the principal show room . . . its arrangement is the most complete we ever saw, and the display of pictures truly beautiful. There are ladies sitting and toilet rooms, where family parties may go, with a perfect assurance of privacy, and the premises are so arranged that there are at least three distinct galleries, each separate from the other. Magnificent chandeliers, lace curtains, oriental carpets, and the richest style of furniture seem to remind spectators that they are rather beholding the interior of a palace than a photographic gallery in San Francisco.[15]

Despite this outward image of permanence and prosperity, this was a period of rapid change for the photographic profession. The stereoscopic daguerreotype, introduced to the city by Vance in late 1853, was one of the first of these technical innovations. An upscale novelty in photographic portraiture, these images proved too expensive to really catch on. The introduction of the wet-collodion glass-negative process was vastly more consequential. This technique led to two new photographic forms, the paper photograph and the ambrotype, which made their first appearance in San Francisco in 1852 and 1854, respectively.[16] While more susceptible to fading than the daguerreotype, paper photographs could be printed in quantity from a single glass negative. East Coast practitioners began working with this technique in 1852–53, and it was in relatively widespread use by 1854.[17] The ambrotype is a thinly exposed glass negative that reads as a low-contrast positive when backed with black paper or lacquer. A less expensive alternative to the daguerreotype, the ambrotype is also a one-of-a-kind image, presented in a case. While immediately popular, the ambrotype lasted only about a decade. The paper print grew more slowly in popularity, but came to near-complete dominance in the field by about 1860. For a few years, in the last half of the 1850s, all three processes were used simultaneously.

Studio Portraiture

The making of a formal portrait was always something of a special occasion. Studio portraits aimed to create an elevating likeness, at once accurate and refined, which conveyed a "best" sense of the self.[18] By 1850, after a full decade of professional practice, the art of daguerreian portraiture was both sophisticated and relatively standardized. Daguerreotypists had established procedures for working with natural light, aiming for a soft and flattering quality of illumination. This left great latitude in posing one or more figures and the orchestration of body language and props. With very few exceptions, the best portraits were made in the leading city galleries, not by itinerants in the field.

A selection of portraits suggests both the quality and variety of the output of San Francisco and Sacramento studios in this era [2–9]. As a group, these works reveal something of the diversity of everyday practice, including

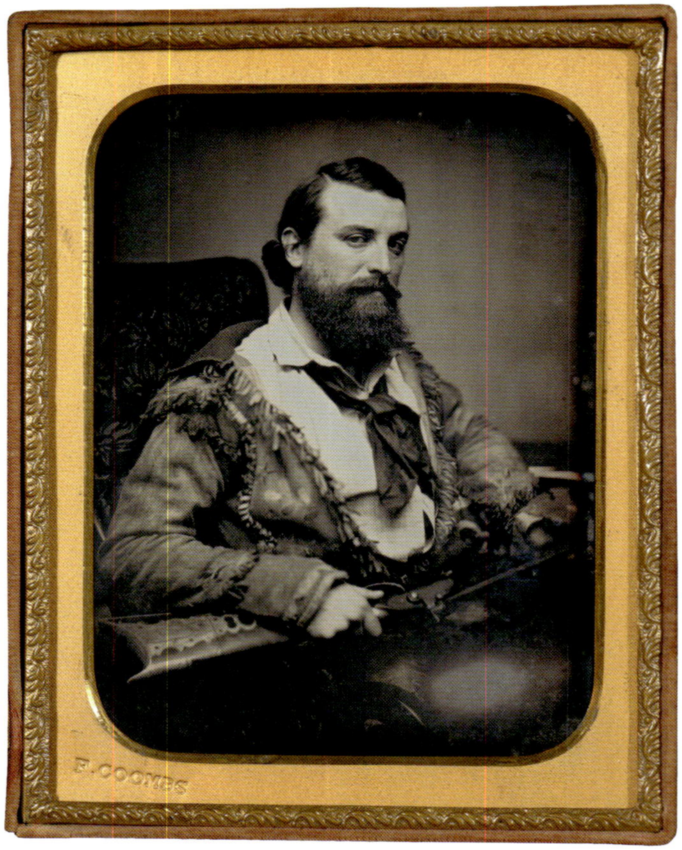

5 **Frederick Coombs**, American (1803–1874). *Portrait of a mountain man or trapper*, 1850–51. Quarter-plate daguerreotype.

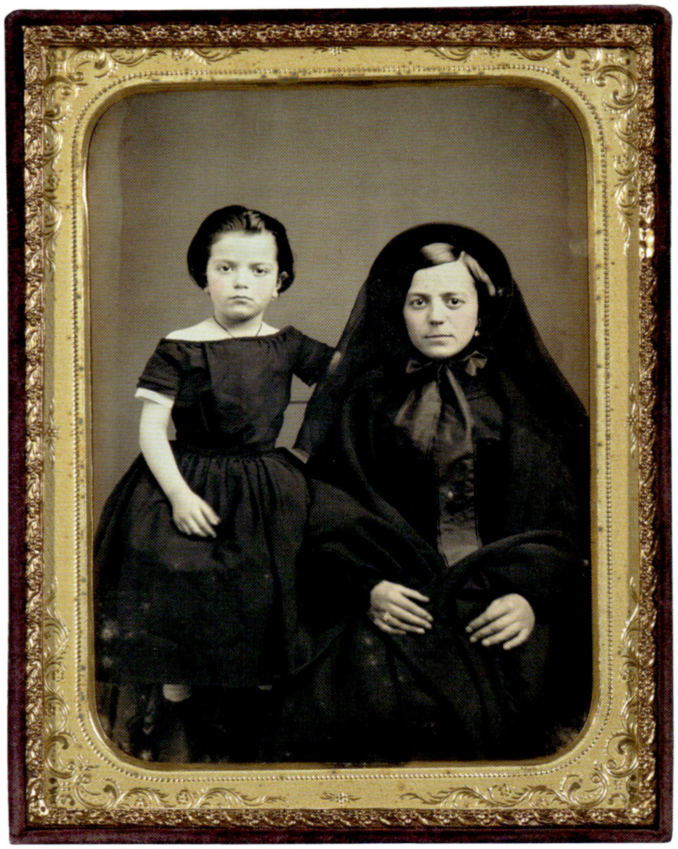

6 **Robert H. Vance**, American (1825–1876). *Woman in mourning with child*, ca. 1855. Quarter-plate daguerreotype.

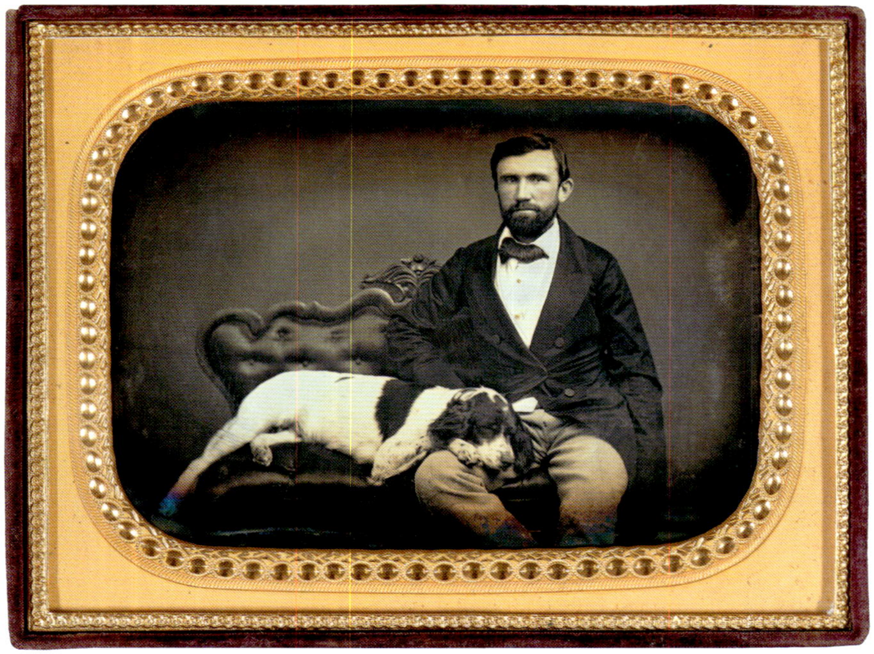

7 **Robert H. Vance**, American (1825–1876). *Man seated on loveseat with dog*, ca. 1855. Quarter-plate daguerreotype.

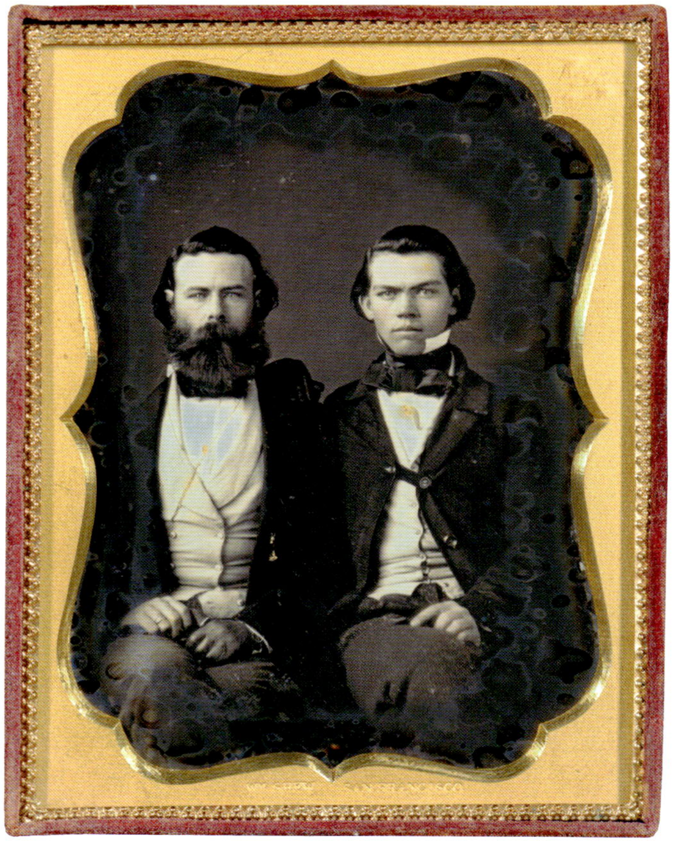

8 **William Shew**, American (1820–1903). *Portrait of two men*, ca. 1851–55. Quarter-plate daguerreotype.

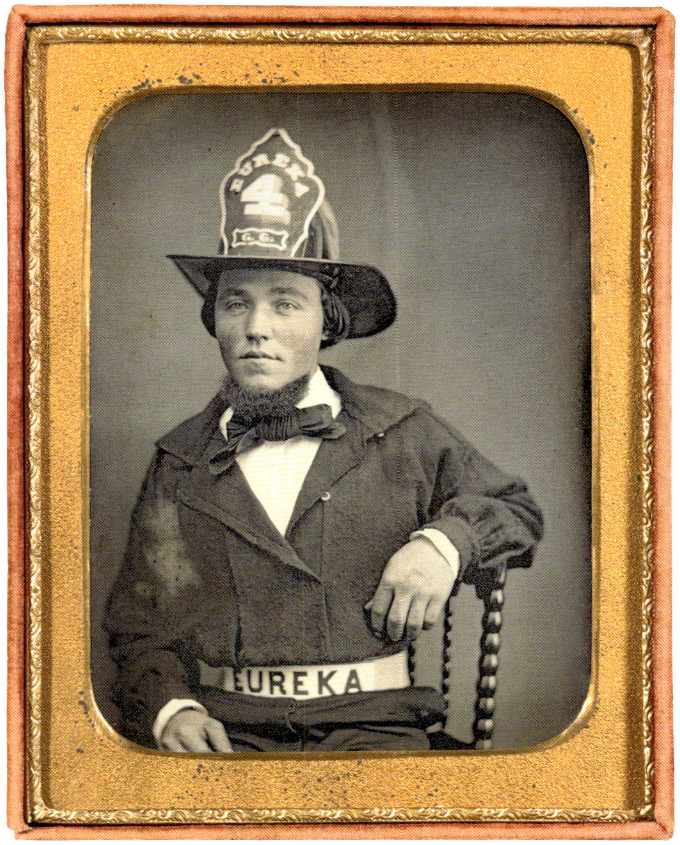

9 **Unknown maker**, American. *Portrait of a fireman, Eureka Company No. 4, Sacramento, California*, ca. 1850. Quarter-plate daguerreotype.

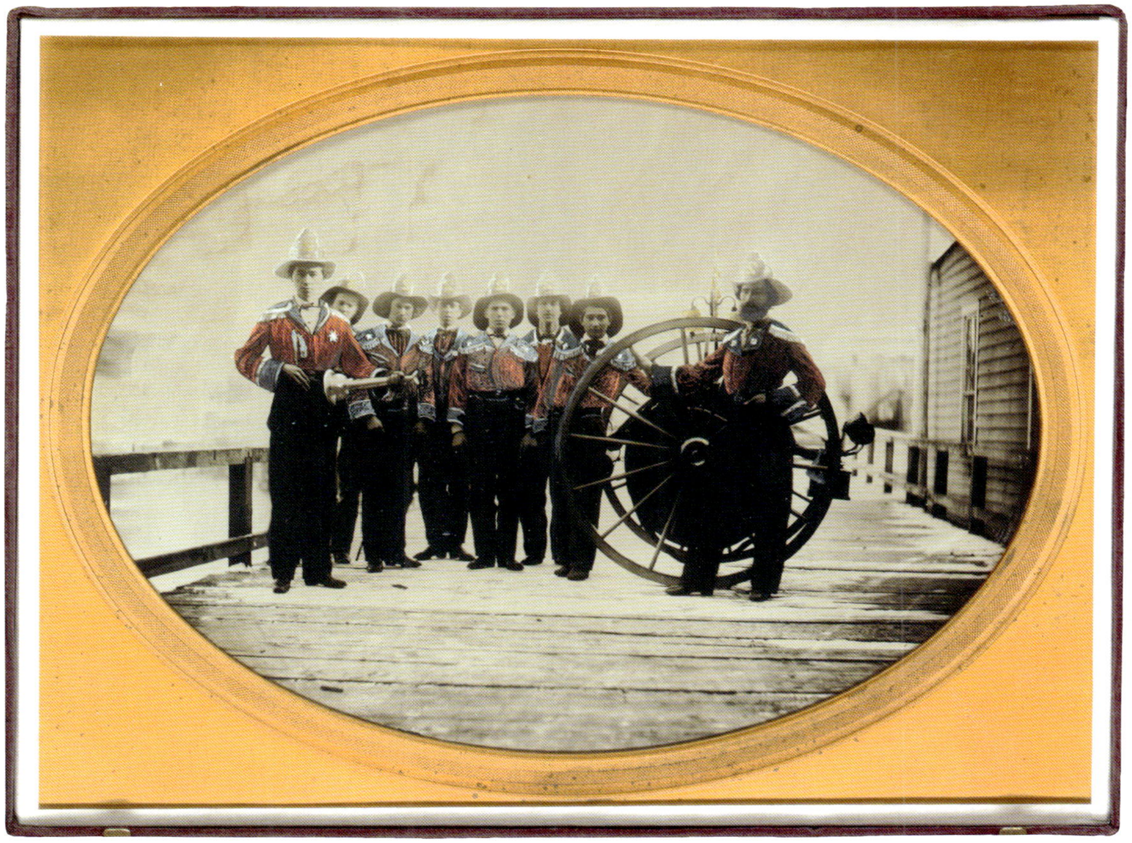

10 **Unknown maker**, American. *San Francisco Fire Brigade on Meiggs Wharf*, ca. 1855–58. Whole-plate ambrotype. Bancroft Library, University of California, Berkeley.

portraits of adults, a child, a woman and daughter in mourning, and a man with his beloved pet. Most of these subjects appear to be from the region's economic elite; as pictured by Frederick Coombs, for example, a self-confident John B. Newton looks every bit the prosperous businessman that he was. The other subjects in this selection of plates—including Coombs's intriguing portrait of a mountain man or trapper—remain unidentified.

The genre of the occupational portrait is exemplified in two works dealing with a timely and essential subject: fire protection. One plate depicts a member of the Eureka Company No. 4 fire station, probably in Sacramento [9]; the other is a group portrait of a San Francisco fire brigade on one of the wharfs in San Francisco Bay [10]. Both of these images engage issues of identity—personal and collective—while signaling a dedication to the welfare of the community.

Numerous portraits of noteworthy individuals in San Francisco and Sacramento have also survived. These include David T. Bagley [11], a leader of the First California Guard, formed in 1849, and a member of the Society of California Pioneers; and Armstead Calvin Brown [12], who grew rich in mining endeavors while living in the towns of Shasta and Jackson, California.

Noted ship captain Edgar Wakeman was recorded in an exquisite full-plate portrait [13], almost certainly by one of the leading studios in San Francisco or Sacramento. In addition to bringing prospectors to the region on trips around Cape Horn from the East Coast, Captain Wakeman spent about a year sailing the inland route between San Francisco and Sacramento. As a resident of San Francisco, he was active in a variety of civic causes, including the anti-crime Committee of Vigilance of 1856.

A daguerreotype by an unidentified photographer [14], probably taken in or near Sacramento, depicts one of the most colorful figures of gold rush–era California. Among the trio of California Rangers, Captain Harry Love sits in the center. A former Texas Ranger, Love came to California in 1850 to seek his fortune. After failing in the mines, he was made a commander of the California Rangers in 1853, tasked with apprehending the "Five Joaquins," a Mexican gang accused of murders and robberies in the gold fields. Love and his men claimed to have found the group and to have killed its leader, Joaquin Murrieta. The latter's severed head was brought to the governor, in Sacramento, and Love collected his reward. However, the truth of the story has long remained in doubt.[19]

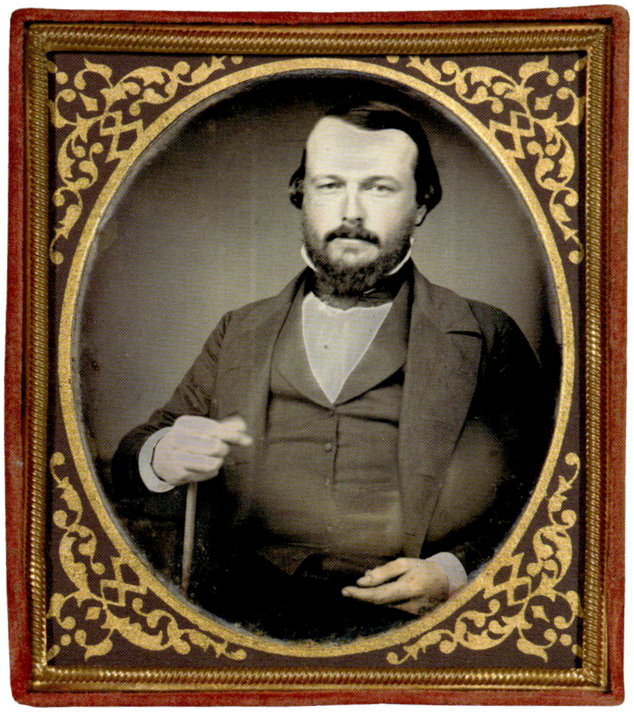

11 **Unknown maker**, American. *Portrait of David T. Bagley*, ca. 1850. Sixth-plate daguerreotype.

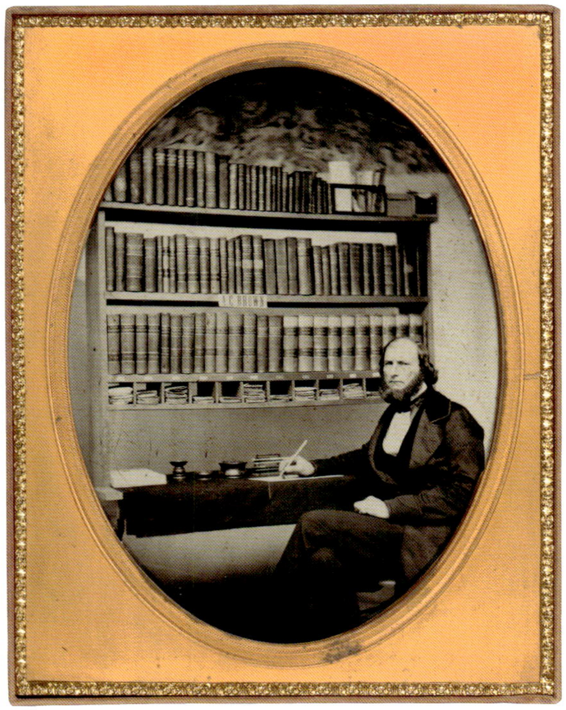

12 **Unknown maker**, American. *Armstead Calvin Brown, Assemblyman and Judge, in his office, Amador County, California*, ca. 1865. Whole-plate ambrotype.

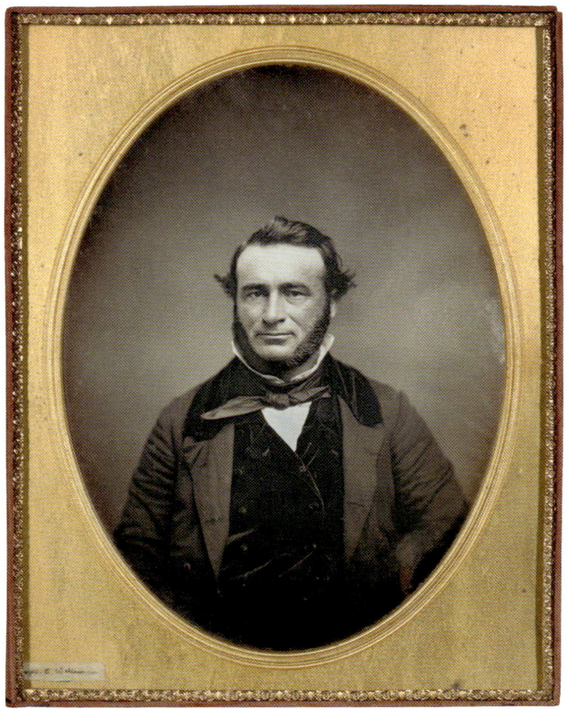

13 **Unknown maker**, American. *Portrait of Captain Edgar Wakeman*, ca. 1850. Whole-plate daguerreotype.

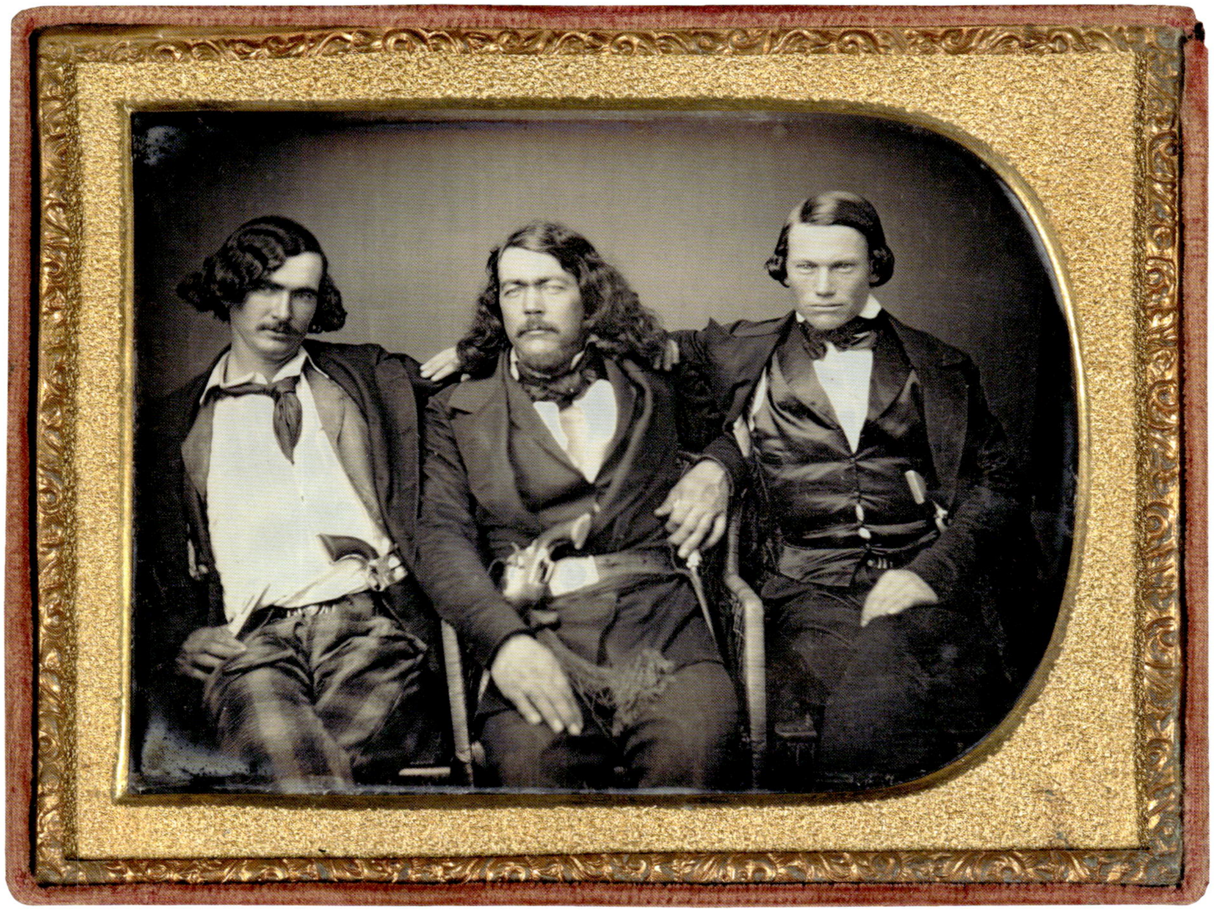

14 **Unknown maker**, American. *Captain Harry Love and California Rangers*, ca. 1853. Quarter-plate daguerreotype.

City Views

In addition to serving as the primary logistical and financial hub for the gold rush, San Francisco was itself a vitally important daguerreian subject. In fact, it may have been the most-recorded city in North America in this era. Sacramento, as the region's "second city," was also daguerreotyped repeatedly. Due to the photographic lure of the gold fields, both cities had a uniquely high proportion of daguerreotypists skilled in outdoor work. The process was not overly difficult, but it did require talents and equipment beyond those of the controlled environment of the studio.

Outdoor daguerreotypes were usually made with cameras and lenses designed for the purpose. Portrait lenses of this period emphasized light-gathering power over consistent sharpness; typically in the f/3.5 range, these lenses were sharper in the center, where a portrait subject would be recorded, than toward the edges of the plate. Landscape lenses — in the f/15 range — had less light-gathering power but were sharp across the visual field. In addition, to correct the inherent mirror-image reversal of the daguerreotype process, outdoor views were often made with a small mirror or prism placed in front of the lens. By this re-reversal technique, signage was recorded correctly. Given the abundance of right-reading outdoor views from this period, it is clear that many of the region's daguerreotypists were comfortable in this work.

The ability to create landscape and architectural daguerreotypes was amply rewarded in San Francisco and Sacramento. The demand for views of specific businesses would have been considerable. The ongoing state of construction, improvement, and expansion meant that most streets and structures were constantly changing; individual shop owners would have had continual incentive to commemorate their storefronts or business districts [15]. Beyond this, anyone involved in the overall promotion of these cities would have had reason to commission views testifying to their vitality and appeal. It could only help, of course, that San Francisco was famously scenic. The steep hills immediately west of the waterfront provided a perfect elevated perspective of the central business district, the ship-filled harbor, and the distant features of Alcatraz Island and the far side of San Francisco Bay. It is not surprising that more daguerreotype panoramas — at least nine — are known of San Francisco than of any other city in the world.[20]

Frederick Coombs was perhaps the first to make a series of daguerreotypes of San Francisco, between the spring of 1850 and early 1851. At least four of these plates are extant. A quarter-plate view of the ferry *Erastus Corning* in San Francisco Bay is in the collection of the San Francisco Maritime National Historical Park.[21] The George Eastman Museum holds three superb half plates by Coombs, focusing on the city's business district, centered on Montgomery Street, where Coombs had his gallery.[22] One of these [16], apparently made from a second-floor window or balcony, documents a structure containing a variety of businesses — including a bank, druggist,

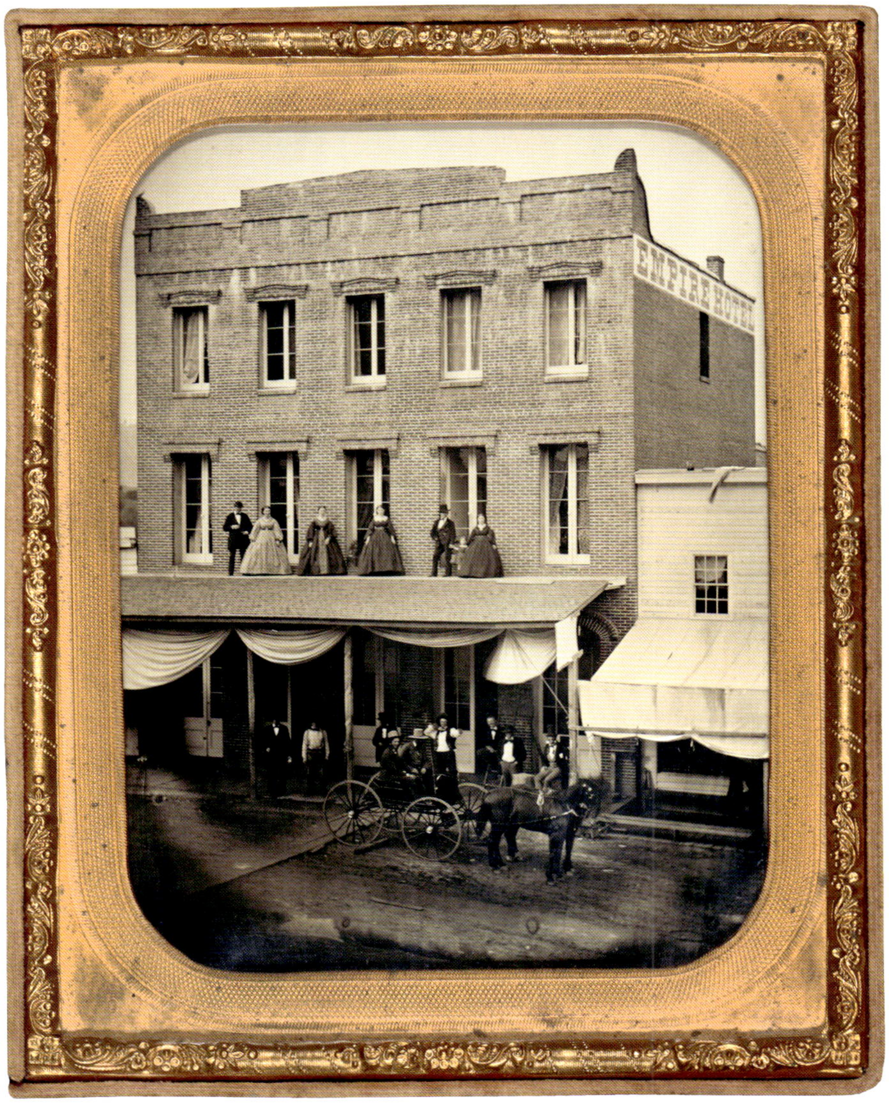

15 **Unknown maker**, American. *Empire Hotel, San Francisco*, ca. 1850–55. Half-plate daguerreotype. The Art Institute of Chicago, The W. Bruce and Delaney H. Lundberg Collection, restricted gift of The Phillip Leonian and Edith Rosenbaum Leonian Charitable Trust.

and land office — and a street busy with carts, horses, and human activity. The other two are more elevated views of Montgomery Street itself, looking north and south; one centers on the building in which Coombs worked, and the other may have been made from the roof of this structure.[23] Inasmuch as they emphasize carts and stacks of goods, all of these images testify to the city's economic vitality.

Sterling C. McIntyre made the first known panorama of San Francisco.[24] Shortly after arriving in the city, McIntyre dedicated himself to recording it — remarkably, there is no evidence that he engaged in studio portraiture at all in this period.[25] By mid-January 1851, McIntyre had succeeded in

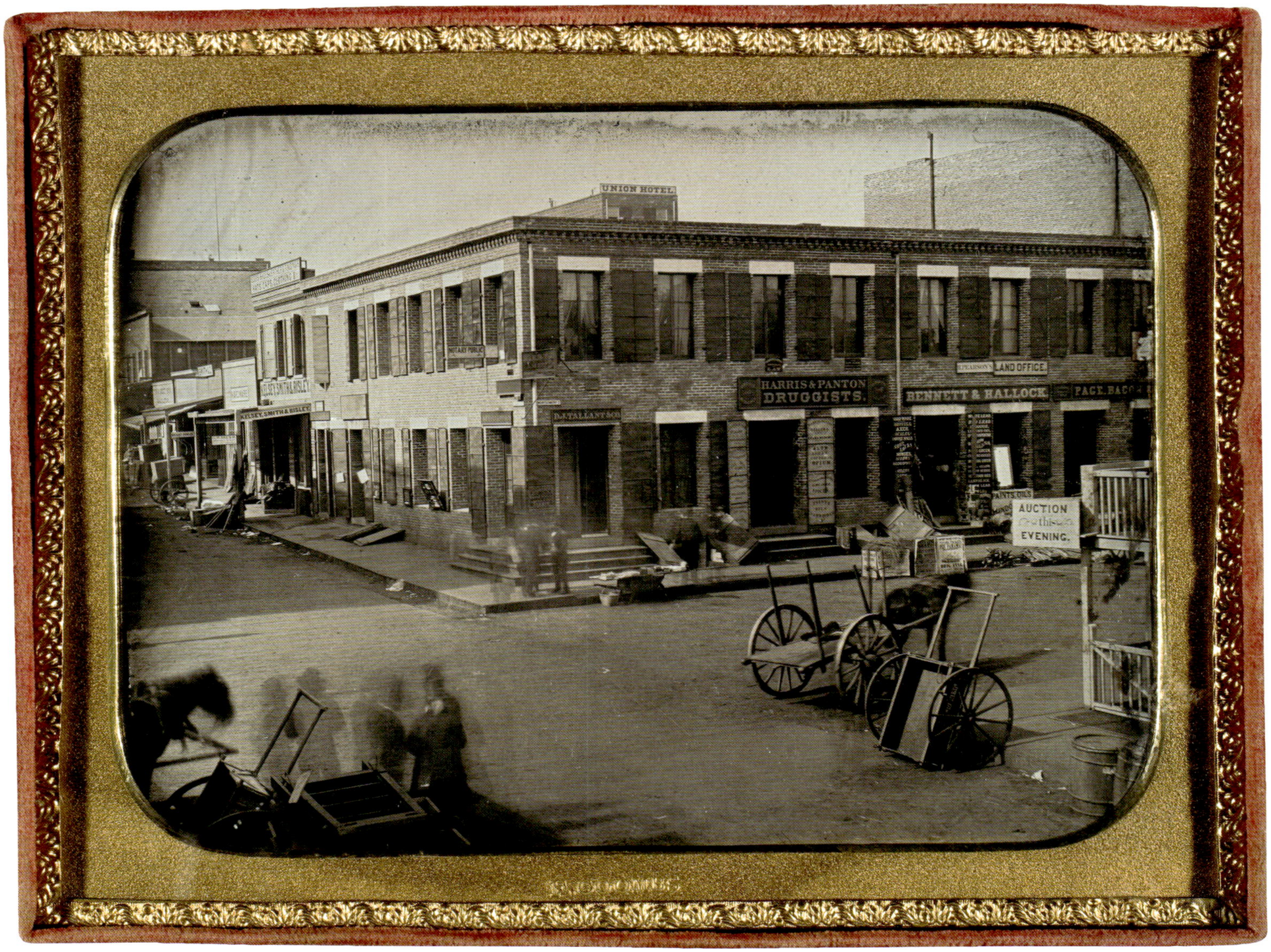

16 **Frederick Coombs**, American (1803–1874). *Corner of Clay and Montgomery Streets, San Francisco,* February 1851. Half-plate daguerreotype. George Eastman Museum.

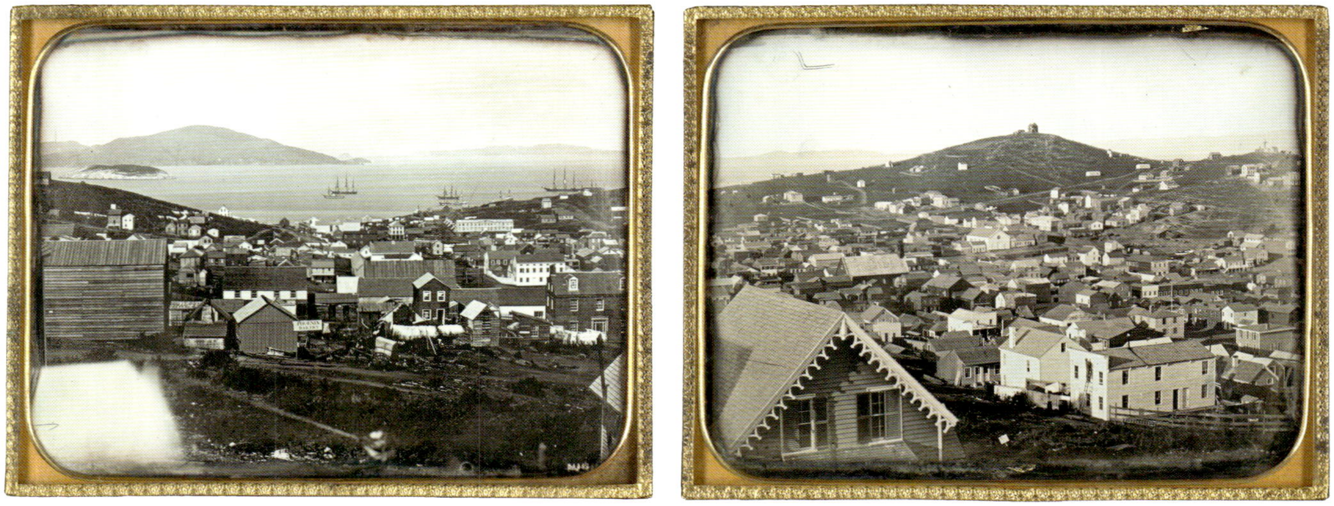

17 Attributed to **Sterling C. McIntyre**, American (active 1844–1852). *Panorama of San Francisco,* 1851. Half-plate daguerreotypes (with replacement middle plate by **Mike Robinson**, 2013). National Gallery of Canada, Ottawa.

making a superb panorama of five half plates, representing an elevated view from the north to the east, North Beach to Rincon Point. As part of his business strategy, McIntyre showed his panorama to the editor of the local newspaper, the *Alta California*. The paper published a glowing notice on January 19, 1851, calling this work "decidedly the finest thing in the fine arts produced in this city," and noting that McIntyre planned to send it to the Great Exhibition, scheduled to open in London on May 1, 1851. Finally, the paper reported McIntyre's intention "to finish and furnish duplicates of this excellent and artistical picture to the lovers of art, at one hundred dollars."[26] In the spirit of this period, McIntyre aimed for a combination of artistic originality, civic pride, international prestige, and profit-making. It is likely that he sold at least one more five-plate panorama of this scene [17]—another original view, not a copy of the first panorama.[27] Adding to his panoramic work, McIntyre made single half-plate views of notable San Francisco sites, including the harbor and Portsmouth Square.[28] McIntyre's plan to send his first panorama to London went unrealized, but he did ship it to the editor of the *Daguerreian Journal*, in New York City, garnering a laudatory mention.[29]

William Shew was also skilled in the production of city and topographic views. In his work for John Wesley Jones, in the first half of 1851, Shew created daguerreotypes of San Francisco, Sacramento, and Marysville. When Jones headed east, Shew returned to San Francisco, where, in addition to studio portraits, he made a specialty of architectural work. As the local newspaper reported on October 23, 1851, Shew "is now making a series of views of various prominent buildings in the city."[30] These included a study of the buildings at 120 and 122 Montgomery Street [18], which housed two newspapers—the *Evening Picayune* and the *San Francisco Herald*—as well as the office of influential citizen Samuel Brannan (who may be standing in the doorway on the right side of this view).[31] The Smithsonian National Museum of American History holds a superb example of Shew's multi-plate work: an 1852 panorama of San Francisco harbor composed of five whole-plate daguerreotypes.[32]

George Johnson also made fine architectural views in both Sacramento and San Francisco. By early April 1851, Johnson was advertising an improved gallery space—"decidedly the handsomest in the State," according to the local newspaper—on J Street, between Third and Fourth Streets, in Sacramento.[33] As part of a project to record key businesses in the city, Johnson photographed this address [20], in the recently opened brick block of Brown, Henry & Co. Centered on his own advertising banner, Johnson's photograph highlights both the newness of the structure and the vitality of local commerce. His other photographs in town include one of the *Daily Union* newspaper office resulting, predictably, in a positive mention in that paper.[34] While not maker marked, this view of the city's Boston Bakery [19] may also be his work. At his various addresses in San Francisco, Johnson continued to record architectural and city views—often in the whole-plate format [35]—including his own studio. This previously unpublished whole plate [21], depicting the corner of Clay and Montgomery Streets in San Francisco, is probably Johnson's work. The framing of the scene, from the skylight in the upper left to the bold signage on the right, confirm that this studio was the primary subject of this daguerreotype.[35]

Robert Vance, San Francisco's leading daguerreotypist in this era, was also the most prolific maker of urban views. In the spring of 1851, in the course of his great 300-plate project, Vance appears to have made nearly fifty whole-plate daguerreotypes of San Francisco, as well as views of Sacramento and Marysville. In San Francisco, he made more than thirty plates prior to

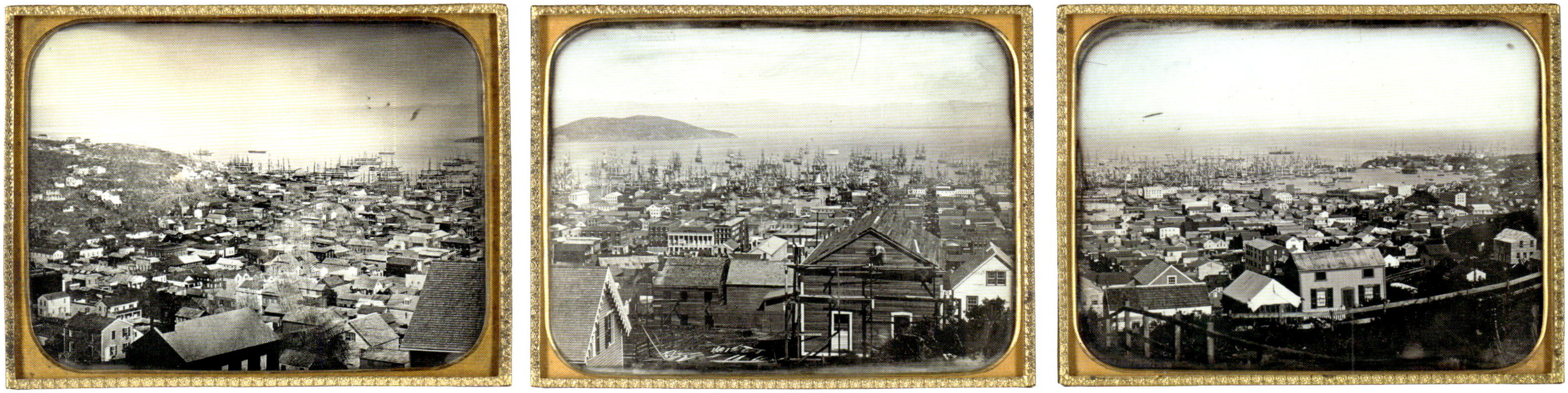

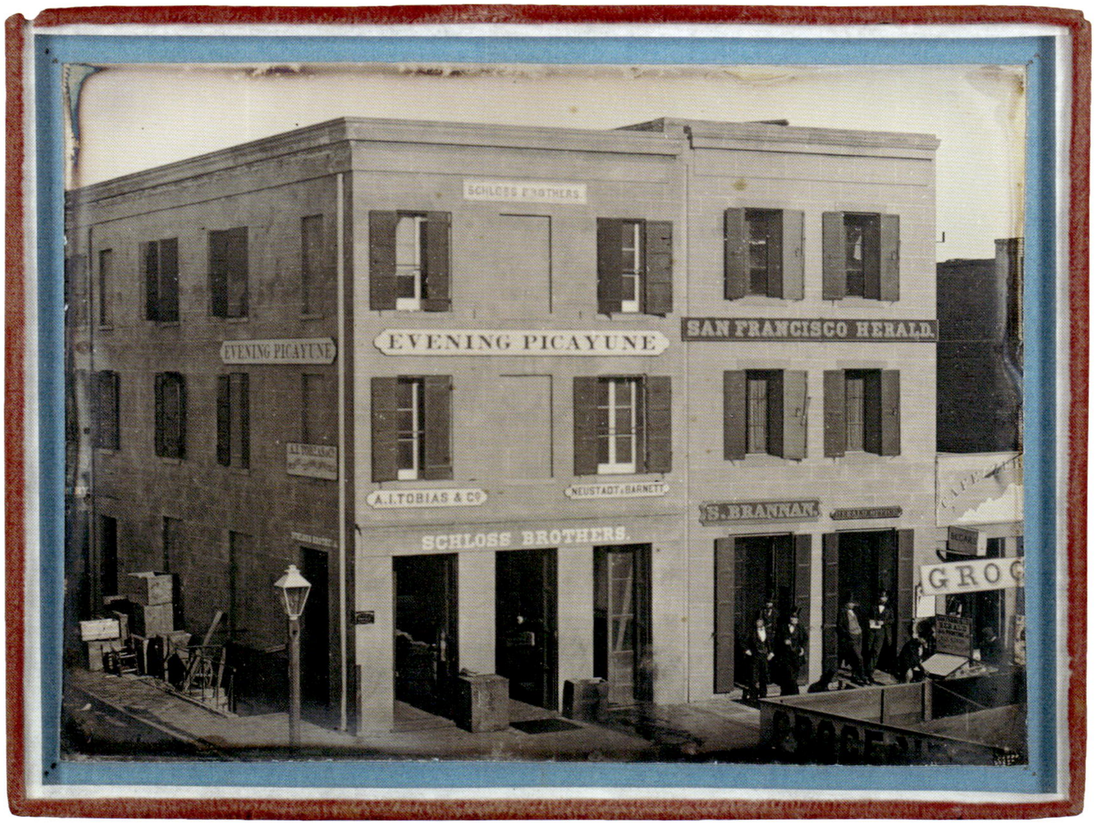

18 **William Shew**, American (1820–1903). *Newspaper offices on Montgomery and Sacramento Streets, San Francisco*, ca. 1850–52. Half-plate daguerreotype. Bancroft Library, University of California, Berkeley.

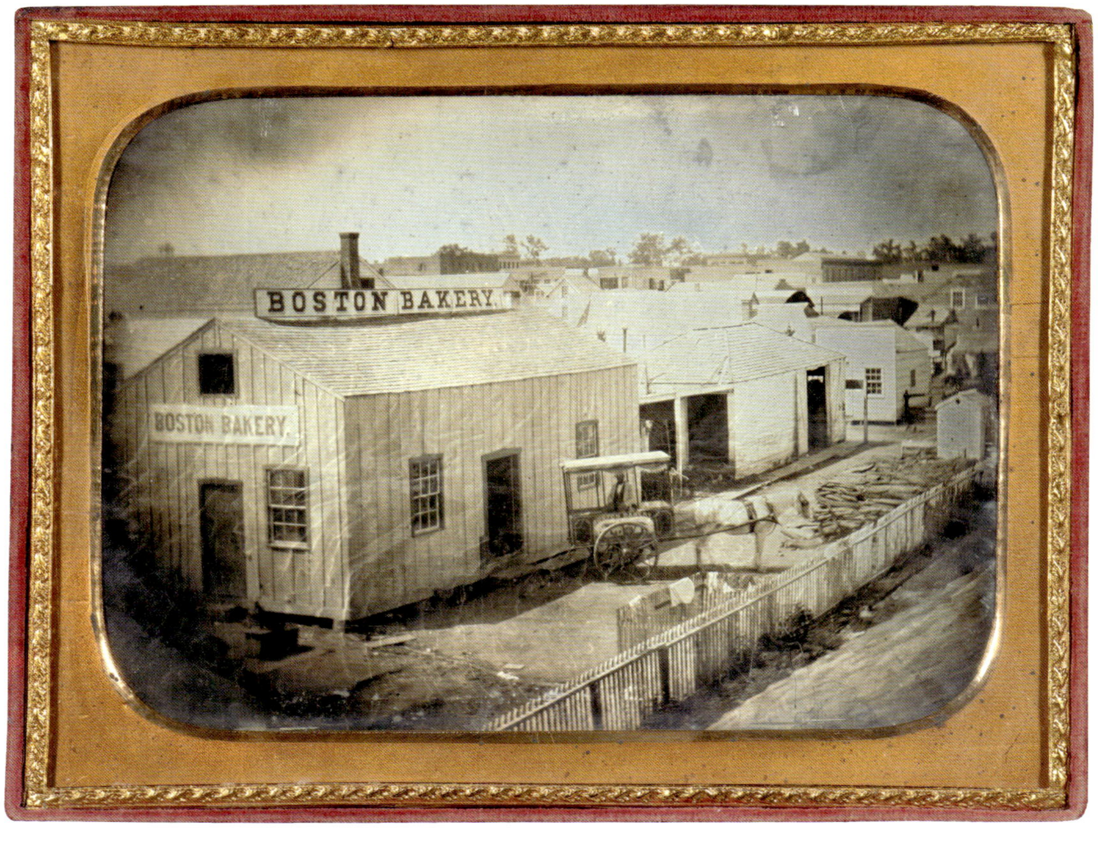

19 **Unknown maker**, American. *Boston Bakery, Sacramento, California*, ca. 1850–55. Half-plate daguerreotype.

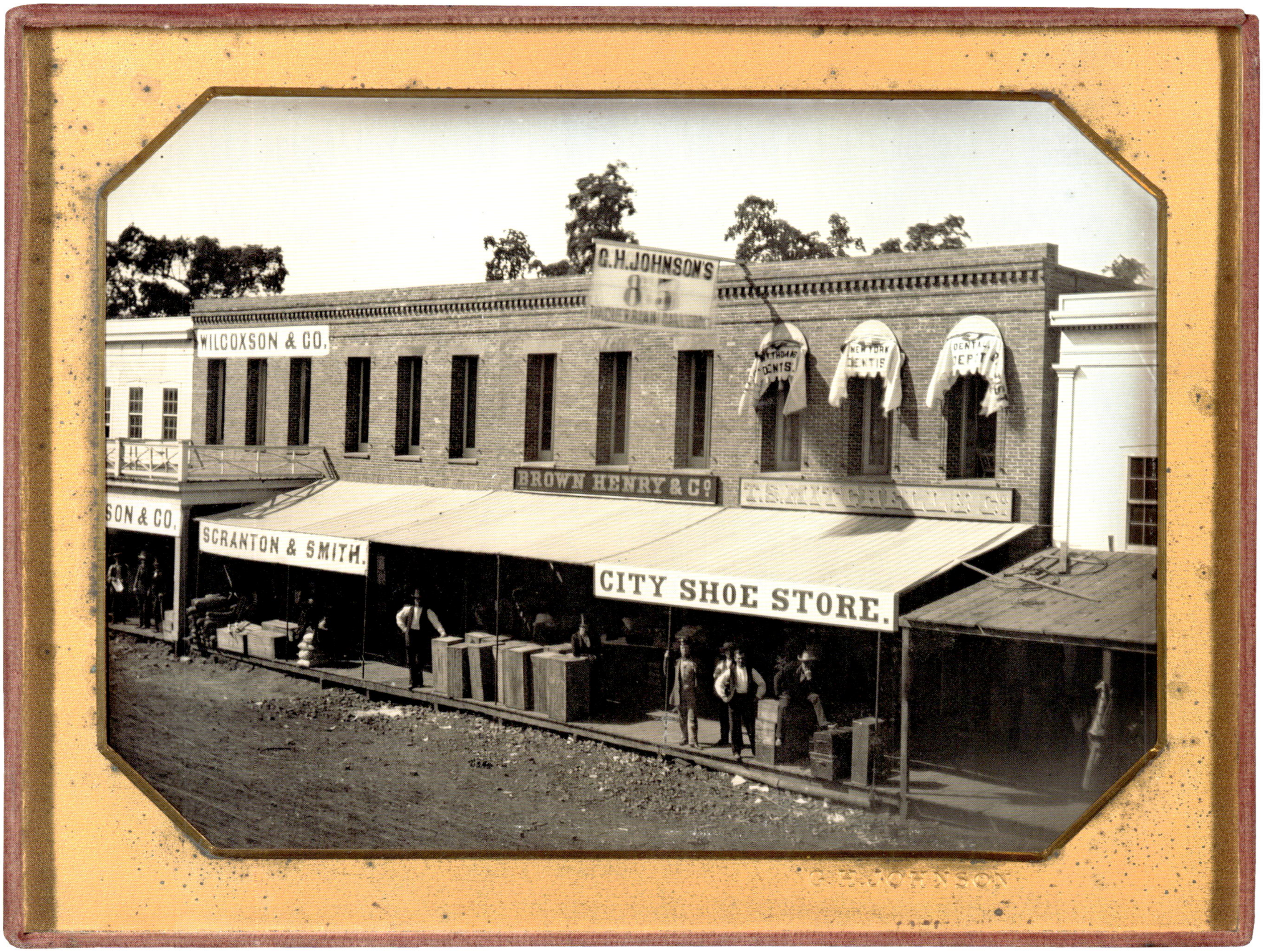

20 George H. Johnson, American (1823–ca. 1880s). *George Johnson's Daguerreian Gallery, Sacramento, California*, ca. 1850–55. Half-plate daguerreotype.

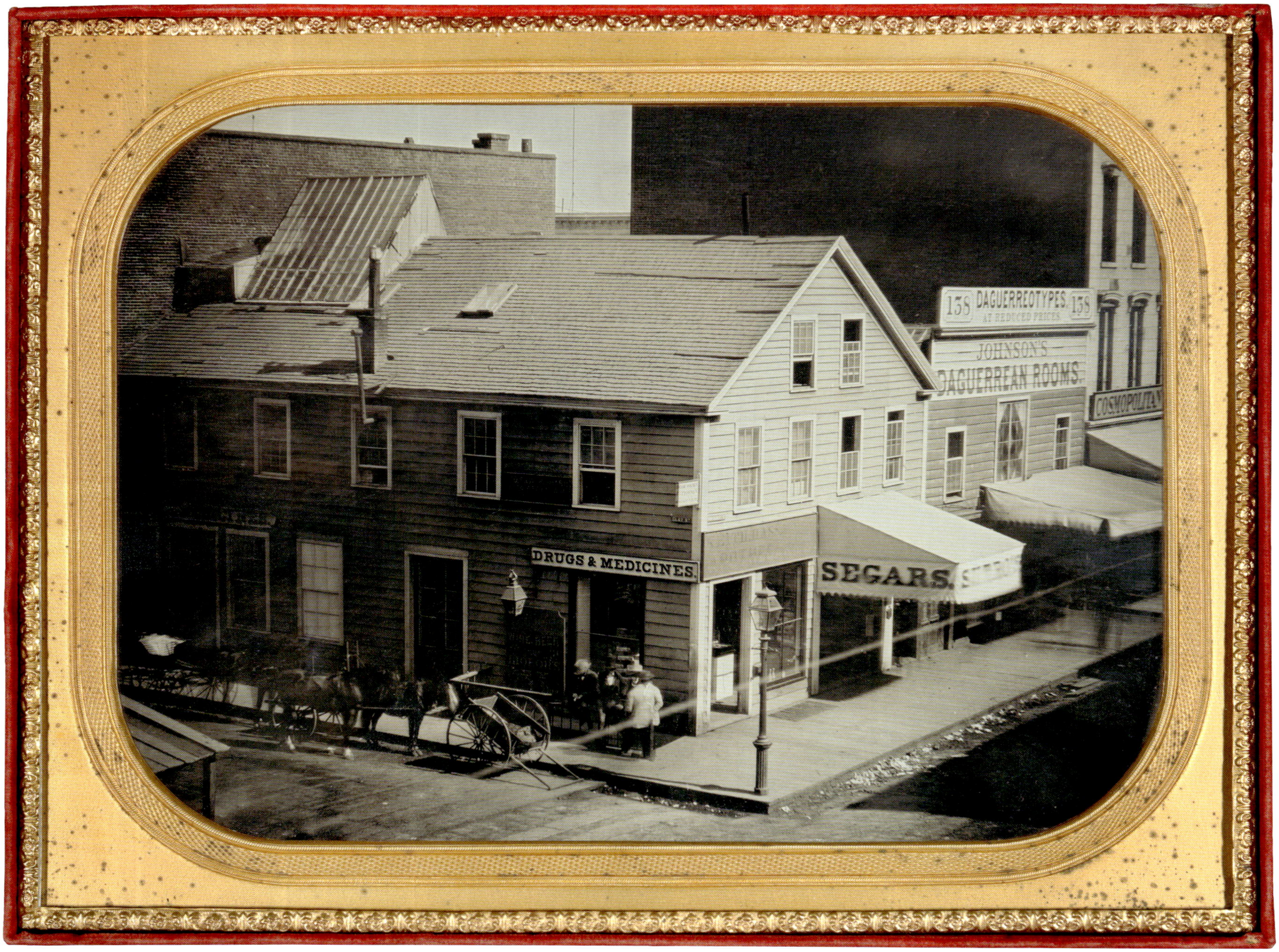

21 Attributed to **George H. Johnson**, American (1823–ca. 1880s). *Johnson's Daguerreian Rooms, San Francisco, California,* ca. 1854–55. Whole-plate daguerreotype.

the fire of May 3–4, including two multi-plate panoramas (one from the top of Telegraph Hill, the other from the Union Hotel, in Portsmouth Square), as well as individual overviews of the city and plates documenting notable streets, buildings, and wharves. Fully aware of the historical significance of the fire, Vance resumed work the very next day, focusing on what had been lost. By consciously duplicating vantage points he had used only weeks before, he created at least a dozen before-and-after pairs of plates for his celebrated *Views in California* installation in New York City. This phase of Vance's work in San Francisco extended into the last week of June, as indicated by two plates made after the city's subsequent fire on June 22.[36] As described elsewhere in this volume, all of this remarkable work has been lost.

Vance continued making architectural and urban views in the ensuing years. In Sacramento, he made a multi-plate panorama of the city after the fire of November 2, 1852, and an image of J Street following the flood of January 1, 1853. In San Francisco, he appears to have been the first to record the city in the stereo daguerreotype format, a technique he introduced there in late 1853. Several of these stereographs are known, including a magnificent view from the roof of his studio looking west on Sacramento Street [22, FIG. 3]. The generality of this perspective suggests that this image could have been made for Vance's own showroom, as a demonstration of both his skill and his place in town.[37] In 1853–54, Vance changed gallery spaces several times, but all of his addresses were on or near Sacramento Street.[38]

Vance was unexcelled at making commemorative architectural daguerreotypes—images that served as both a "portrait" of a building and as a record of a commercial or social milestone. For example, his iconic whole plate of the Excelsior Building [23] lends remarkable formal dignity to this modestly scaled structure. Vance made this photograph with a level camera from a second-floor window across the street. Emulating an ideal architectural elevation, he presents the building with rectilinear precision, describing the facade with meticulous clarity while suggesting its place in the city block. The scene is made complete by the well-dressed men posed in front, a gathering of those who designed, financed, or were now occupying the new building.

Vance recorded one of his most historically important commemorative architecture subjects in May 1856, following the death of a local newspaper editor with the unusual name of James King of William [24]. This whole-plate view depicts a bunting-draped building at Sacramento and Sansome Streets, one block from Vance's gallery, with a banner proclaiming "The Great Man Has Fallen. We Mourn His Loss." King of William, a muckraking journalist and editor of the *San Francisco Evening Bulletin*, had been a spirited foe of local political corruption. Enraged by one of his editorials, a rival editor and politician shot King of William on the street outside his office. He died six days later, on May 20, 1856. His supporters, spurred to form a civilian Committee of Vigilance, began demonstrating immediately after the shooting. Upon his death, this group removed the assassin from the

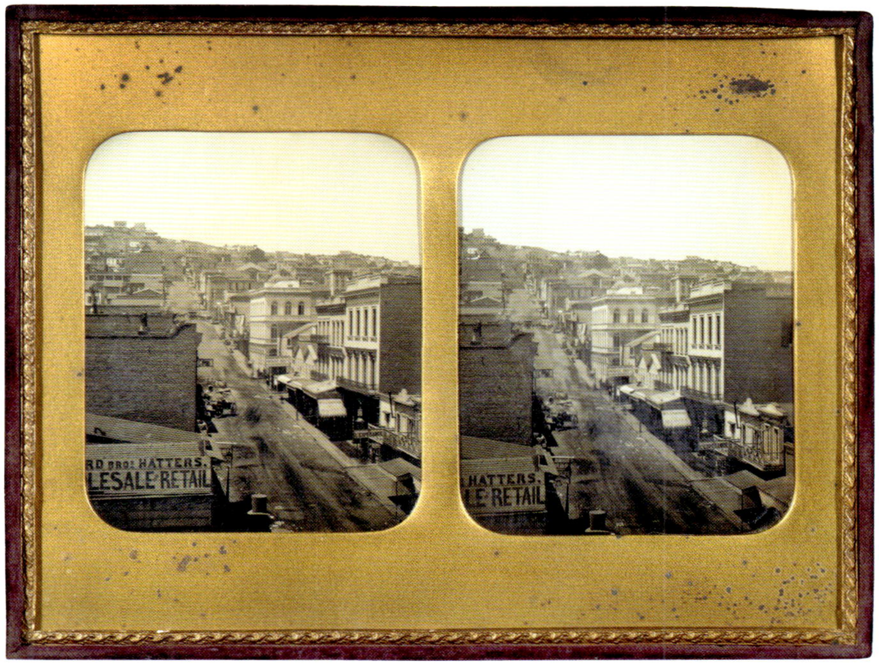

22 **Robert H. Vance**, American (1825–1876). *View of Sacramento Street, San Francisco, California*, ca. 1854–56. Stereo daguerreotype.

sheriff's office, gave him a pro forma hearing, found him guilty, and hanged him on May 22, the day of King of William's funeral. This extralegal civilian action occurred in a complex political climate—it reflected not only a concern for law and order, but also a struggle over economic dominance.[39] King of William had many supporters, including some of the community's most prosperous businessmen. As a result, it is likely that Vance would have found a ready market for daguerreotypes of this somber scene. Two nearly identical whole plates of it are known, and it is possible that Vance made even more from this camera position.[40]

Numerous other daguerreotypes of San Francisco are known today. The docks and San Francisco Bay were particularly popular subjects. An unidentified daguerreotypist made an elegantly composed view of a new warehouse on the waterfront [25], probably for the owner of the structure. In a similar vein, Silas Selleck's daguerreotype of merchant tailor E. A. Hulett [26] is at once an architectural study and an occupational portrait. A richly detailed view of the city and harbor, by an unidentified daguerreotypist, conveys the area's scenic grandeur [27]. Beautifully composed in its own right, this plate may have been made as part of a now-lost panorama.

Notably, San Francisco was the subject of a landmark work in early paper photography: George R. Fardon's *San Francisco Album* (1856), the first compilation of views of an American city. Fardon is an enigmatic figure in the medium's history; little is known about his arrival in San Francisco or his training in photography.[41] But by 1854, he was working actively with

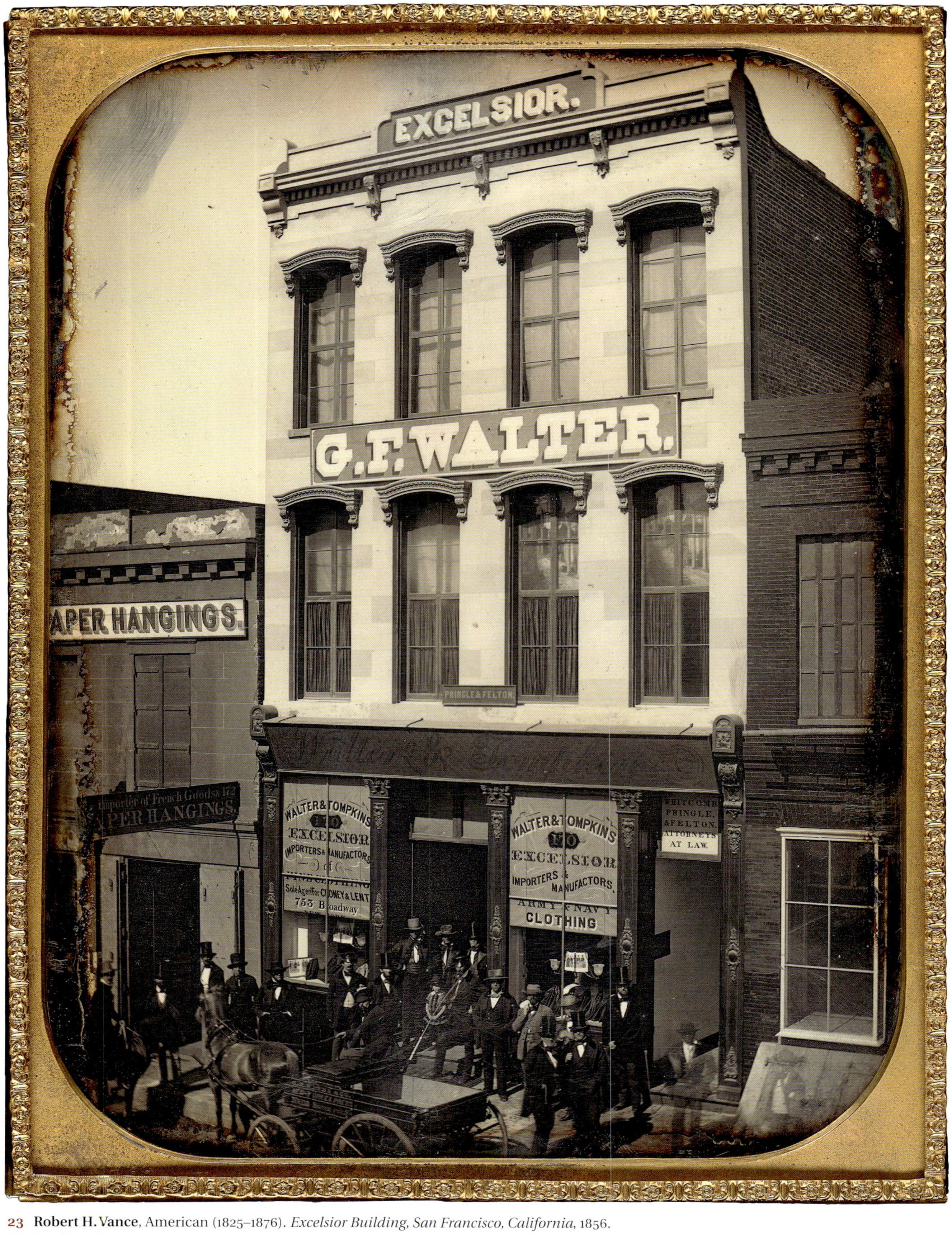

23 **Robert H. Vance**, American (1825–1876). *Excelsior Building, San Francisco, California*, 1856. Whole-plate daguerreotype. National Gallery of Canada, Ottawa.

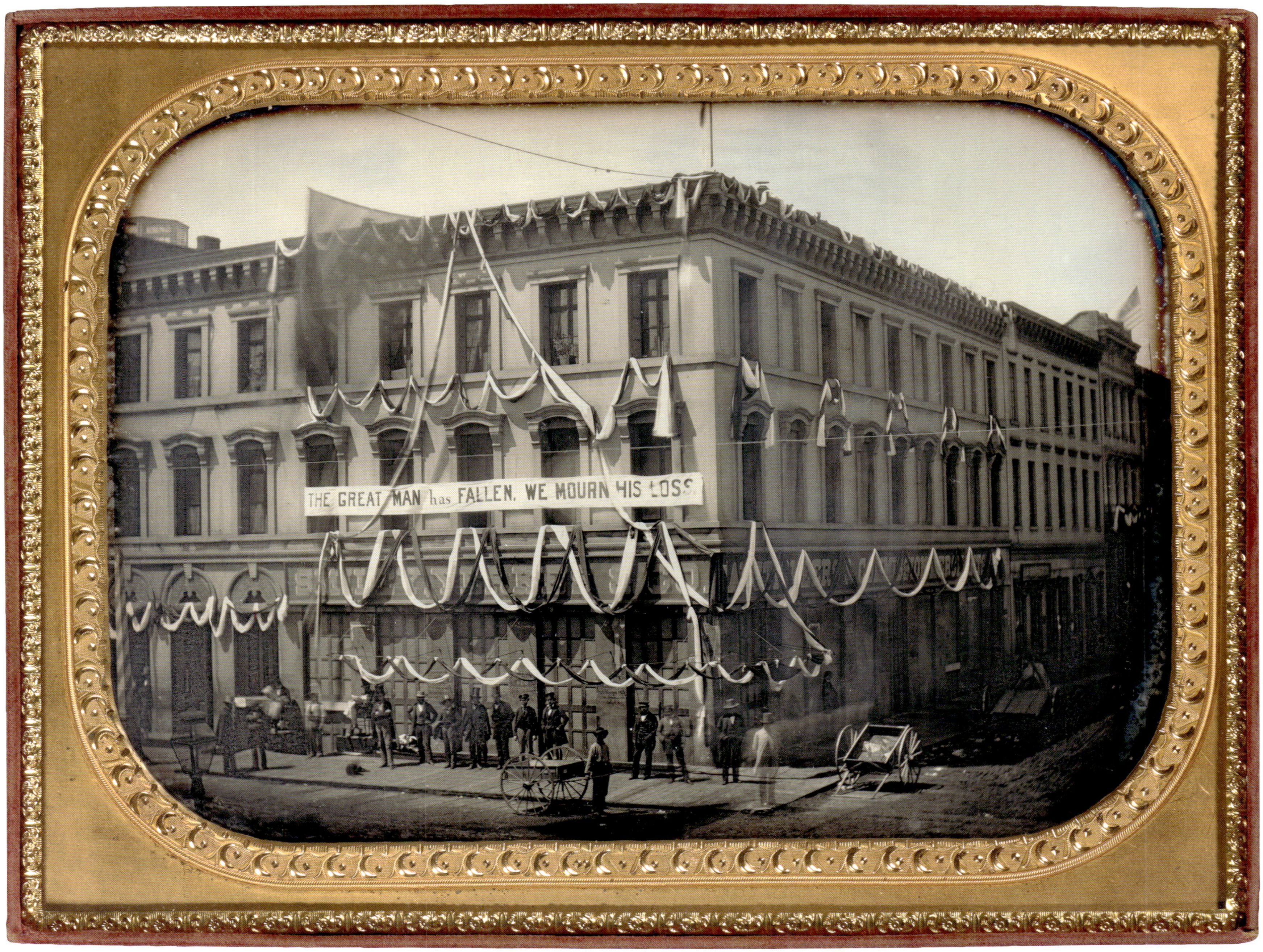

24 **Robert H. Vance**, American (1825–1876). *"The Great Man Has Fallen," San Francisco, California*, 1856. Whole-plate daguerreotype.

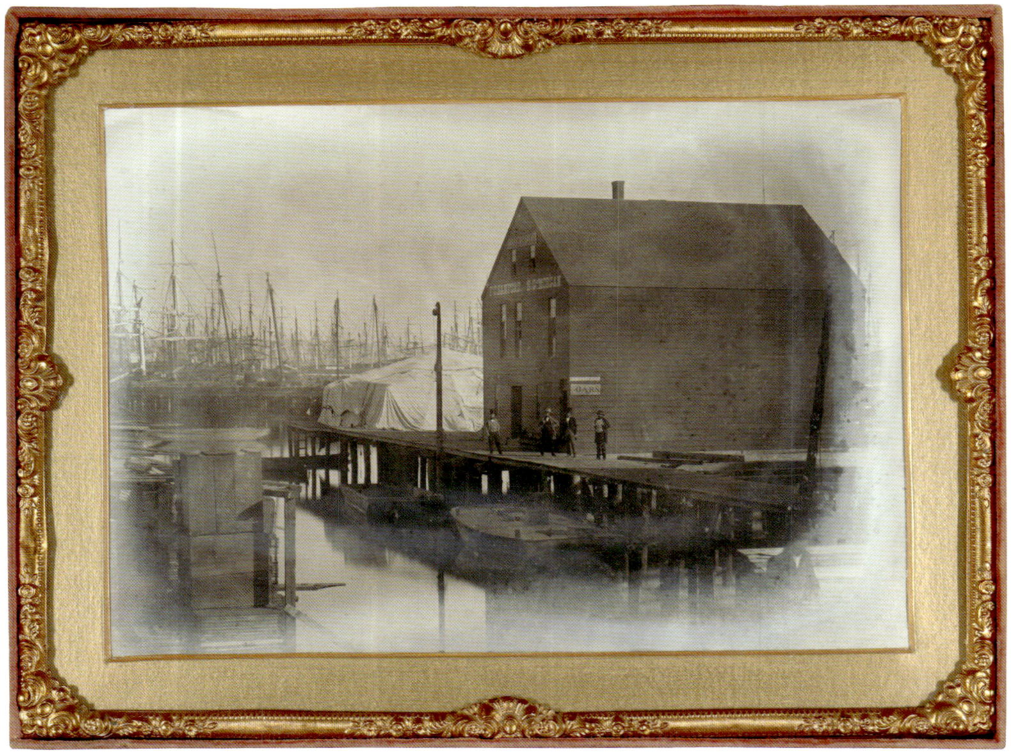

25 **Unknown maker**, American. *Warehouse on Wharf*, ca. 1850–55. Whole-plate daguerreotype. The Art Institute of Chicago, The W. Bruce and Delaney H. Lundberg Collection, restricted gift of The Phillip Leonian and Edith Rosenbaum Leonian Charitable Trust.

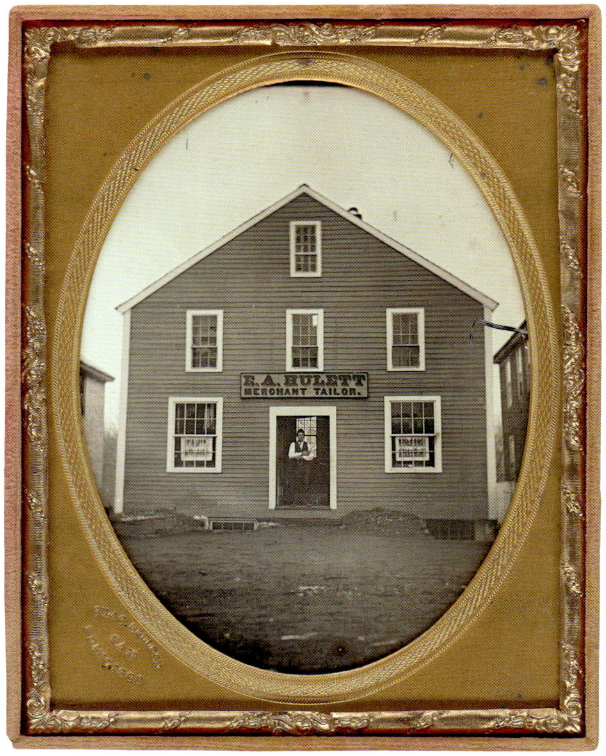

26 **Silas Selleck**, American (ca. 1828–1885). *E. A. Hulett in doorway of his merchant tailor shop, San Francisco*, ca. 1857. Quarter-plate daguerreotype. National Gallery of Canada, Ottawa.

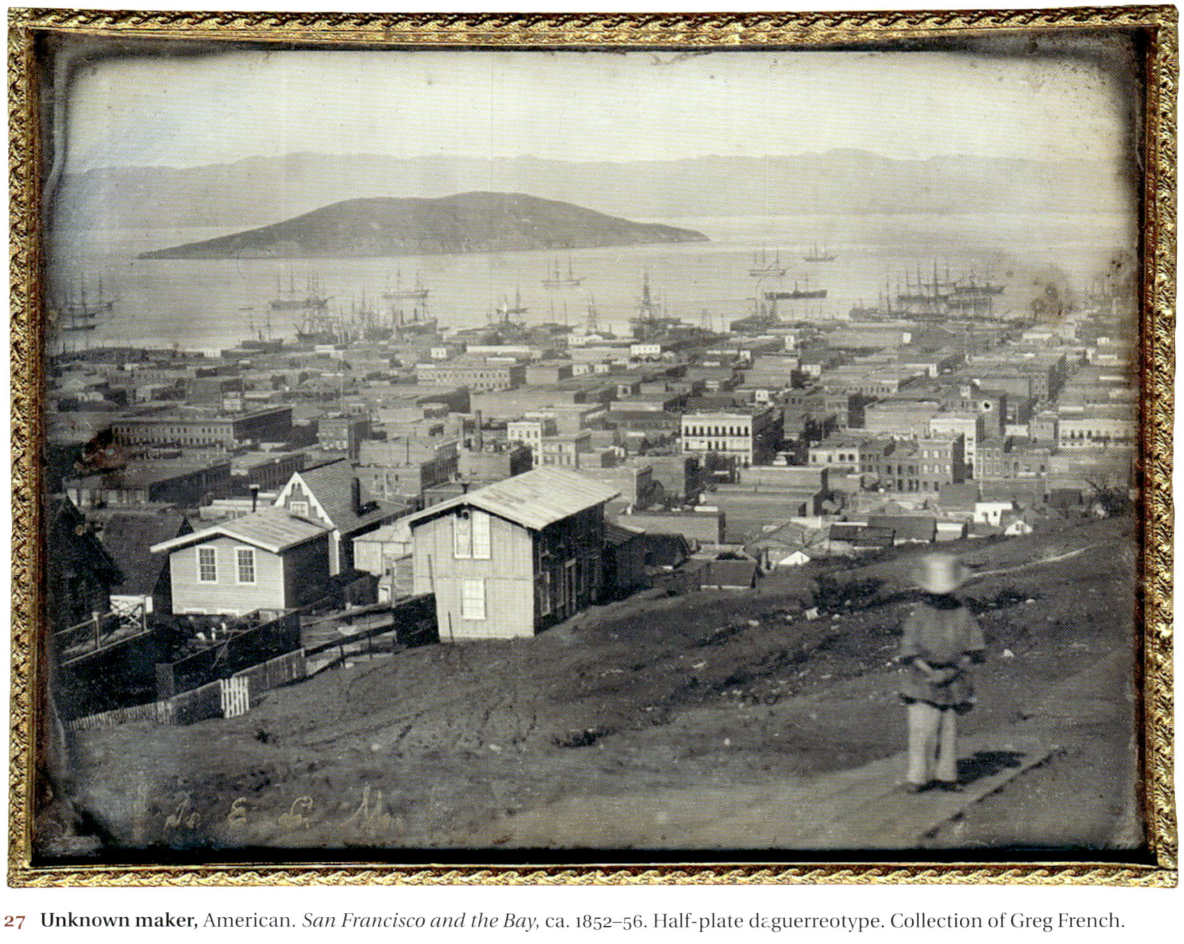

27 **Unknown maker,** American. *San Francisco and the Bay*, ca. 1852–56. Half-plate daguerreotype. Collection of Greg French.

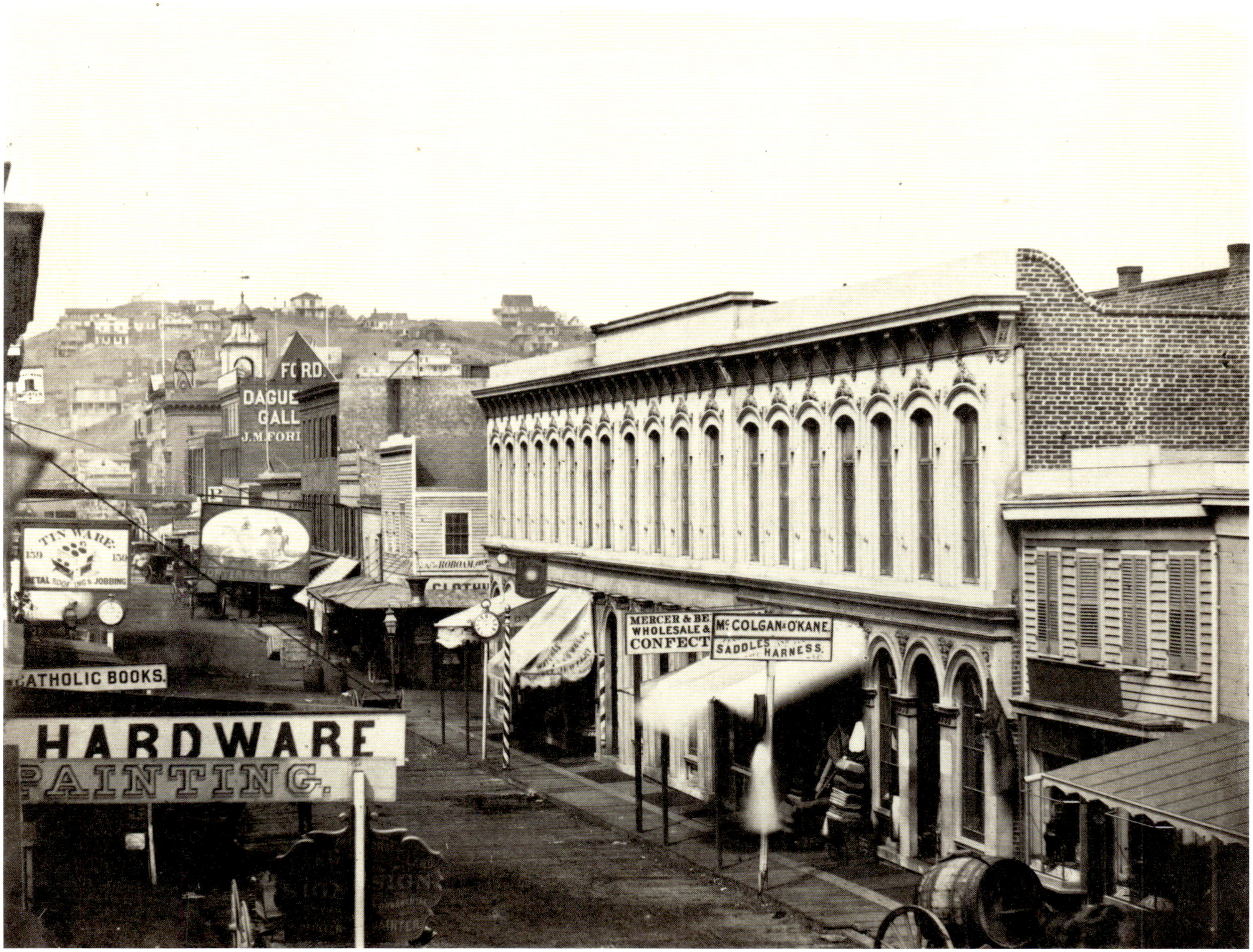

28 **George R. Fardon**, American, born England (1807–1886).
Kearny Street, San Francisco, ca. 1855–56. Salt print, 6¼ x 8 inches.

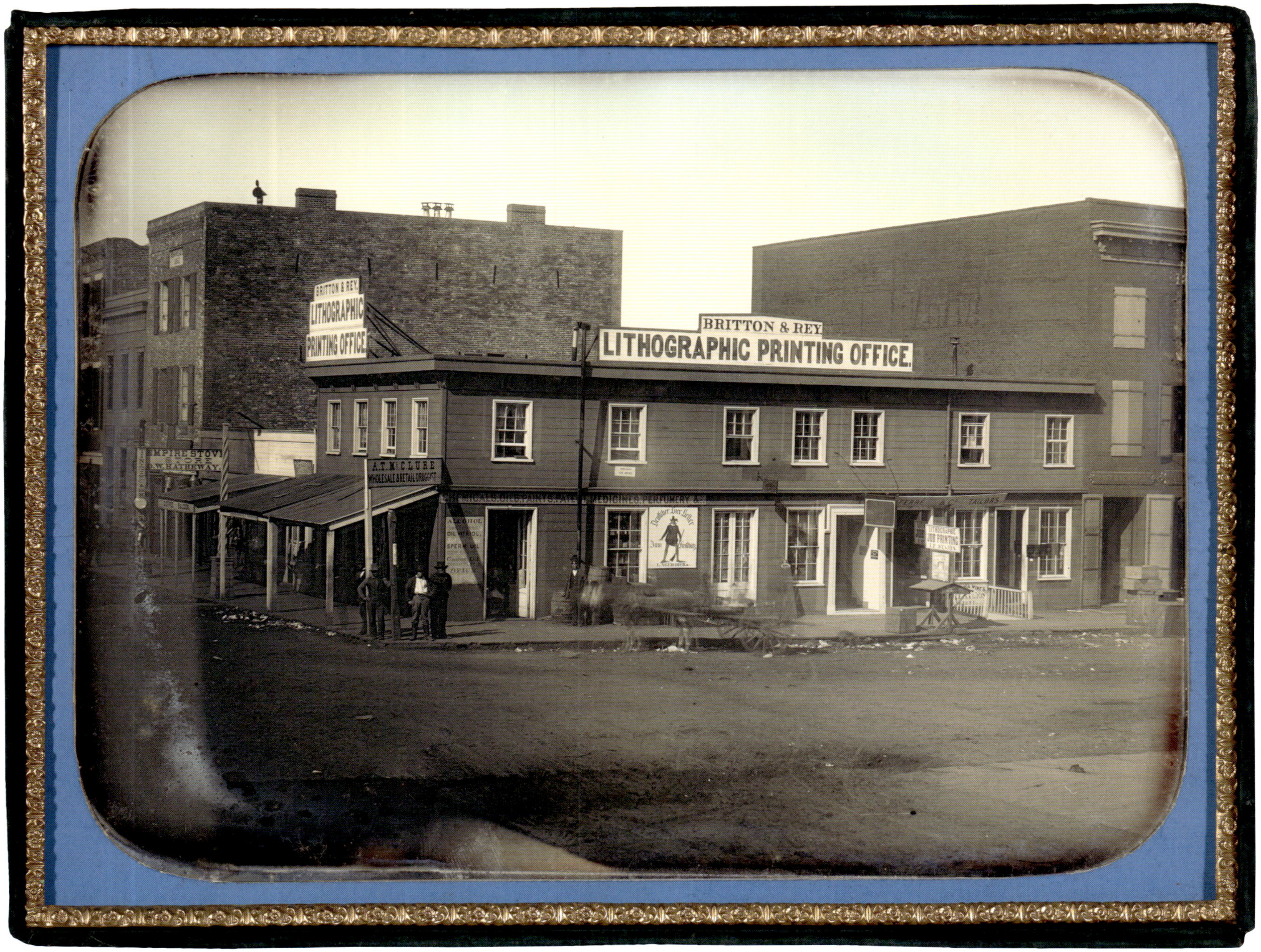

29 Unknown maker, American. *Britton & Rey Lithographic Printing Office, San Francisco, California*, ca. 1853. Whole-plate daguerreotype.

the wet-collodion glass-plate process, making city views in the whole-plate size. In 1856, these photographs were sold in a few hand-assembled albums comprising a title page, a printed list of subjects, and (typically) thirty-two original salted paper prints. The timing of this production appears to have been connected to the King of William affair and the activity of the Committee of Vigilance.[42] Fardon's views served the cause of civic boosterism, celebrating the city as prosperous, progressive, and safe: in addition to recording many key streets, commercial buildings, and churches, Fardon photographed no fewer than nine of the city's fire companies.[43] One of the most iconic of his views, looking north on Kearny Street [28], presents a rich visual inventory of buildings, storefronts, and signs. A large sign for the daguerreotype gallery of James M. Ford, at the corner of Clay Street, is seen clearly in the middle distance. While few, if any, human figures were captured in this long exposure, the economic vitality of the place is clear.

A Visual Economy

Photographers in San Francisco and Sacramento were integral to the larger business of making, publishing, and selling pictures in gold rush–era California. The visual economy included independent artists, painters, and photographers as well as publishers and retailers of art supplies.[44] While distinct in some respects, these varied enterprises had considerable social and economic overlap.

Inevitably, trade was centered in the largest cities, where these businesses were located. By the end of 1849, San Francisco was home to several dozen artists—sketch artists, painters, engravers, and lithographers. Like the photographers of this era, the most fortunate of these artists found a ready market in the steady flow of prospectors to and from the gold fields. A few of them became rich by catering to the city's business elite.[45] While portraits remained the primary focus, renderings of gold field subjects and California landscapes were also in high demand, as seen in the production of Charles Christian Nahl. The most notable of gold rush–era artists, Nahl was particularly interesting for the scope of his activities. In addition to his work at the easel, he operated a daguerreotype gallery, developed a method of photoengraving called the Nahlotype, and made prints for sale using the wood engraving and lithography processes.[46] Through the quantity and broad distribution of these images, Nahl contributed greatly to the popular image of the gold rush.

As these activities point up, a genuinely popular market for pictures depended on the ability to make images in multiple. Every daguerreotype studio had the ability to make a new copy of an existing daguerreotype, but it was an expensive, one-at-a-time process, and the resulting second-generation plates were usually lower in contrast and less sharp than the original. Daguerreotypists reached a larger audience when their works were used as the source for reproduction in newspapers and books. In 1856, for example, James Mason Hutchings began publishing his *California Magazine*, which included a number of illustrations based on photographs. However, these hand-engraved versions conveyed little of the photograph's factual specificity.

In this era, lithographers set the standard for the production of high-quality pictures in multiple. Many gold rush scenes, derived from sketches, watercolors, paintings, and sometimes daguerreotypes, were printed for popular sale.[47] Subjects ranged from panoramas of San Francisco to idealized vignettes of life in the gold mining camps. They were rendered in a variety of forms, including letter sheets, illustrated song and music sheets, maps, and larger lithographs, often in color, intended for wall display. As a result, lithographers were at the center of a professional network of sketch artists and painters, photographers, art dealers, and publishers.

The leading lithography firm in gold rush–era San Francisco was Britton & Rey [29]. Established in 1852 on Montgomery Street, the firm issued many prints of gold field and California subjects. In addition to creating their own designs, Joseph Britton and Jacques Joseph Rey also published lithographs by artists such as Charles Christian Nahl. Britton & Rey made something of a specialty of elevated views of cities and towns. At once descriptive and promotional in nature, these idealized renderings combined the virtues of both the panorama and the map.[48] Given the topographic exactitude of much of this work, it is not surprising that Britton & Rey—and similar firms—made some use of photographs as source material.

The paper photograph solved the basic problem of the daguerreotype's uniqueness, for the first time allowing photographic images to be created in editions of (relatively) identical originals. In the United States, this modern aspect of photographic practice increased steadily in importance in the last half of the 1850s. This transition changed photography's cultural reach and impact. At the same time, in bringing the era of the daguerreotype to an end, it profoundly altered the inherent nature of the medium. From this point forward, photographs would be cheaper and more widely disseminated, but they would never again have the extraordinary beauty and physical presence of the daguerreotype.

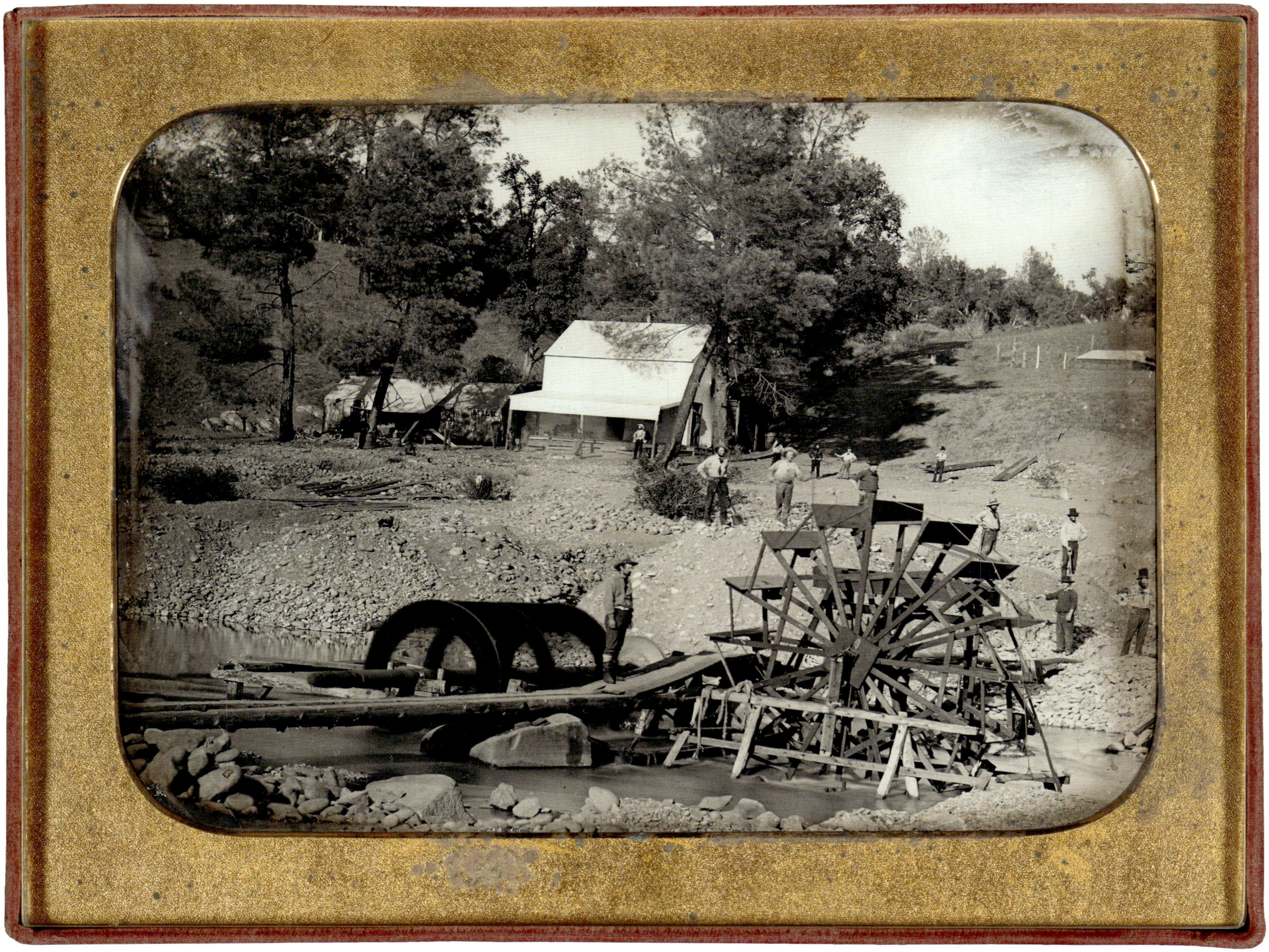

30 Attributed to **George H. Johnson**, American (1823–ca. 1880s). *River mining, North Fork, American River, California*, ca. 1850–55. Half-plate daguerreotype.

CHAPTER 3 *Daguerreotypists in the Gold Regions*

Photography very quickly had a firm foothold in the gold regions of California.[1] In addition to operating lavish studios in San Francisco and Sacramento, the better-known daguerreians like Robert Vance and George Johnson made frequent excursions into the gold fields to record miners and mining operations. Lacking fixed studios, some daguerreotypists, like Isaac Baker and Joseph Starkweather, photographed exclusively in gold country. Working outside the studio setup, daguerreotypists in the gold fields battled unpredictable weather conditions and challenging terrain to produce plates of astonishing quality and variety.

As Robert Vance methodically daguerreotyped for his grand showing of California views, Sterling McIntyre beat him to the punch. Originally from Pensacola, Florida, McIntyre was a trained dentist and practicing daguerreotypist capable of producing "perfect specimens of the beautiful art to which he has devoted himself."[2] Arriving in San Francisco in late 1850, McIntyre initially worked as a dentist. By January 1851, however, he was firmly established as a daguerreian phenom: "Decidedly the finest thing in the fine arts produced in this city . . . is a consecutive series of Daguerreian plates, five in number, arranged side by side so as to give a view of our entire city and harbor . . . the views were taken by Mr. McIntyre of this city."[3] Created for the Great Exhibition in London, the panoramic wonder was lauded by the editors of the *Alta California* newspaper:

> This picture, for such it may be termed, although the first attempt, is nearly perfect. It is admirable in execution as well as design. . . . We venture the assertion that nothing there will create greater interest than this specimen of Art among us, exhibiting a perfect idea of the city which of all the world carries with its name abroad more of romance and wonder than any other. It is a picture, too, which cannot be disputed—it carries with it evidence which God himself gives through the unerring light of the world's great luminary.[4]

By the next day, the panorama had generated palpable excitement. A "large number of gentlemen" visited the newspaper offices to proclaim it "the only picture of any description ever produced giving anything like a correct idea of the extent of our city."[5] Emboldened by his success, McIntyre produced additional plates in quick succession, including a view of Portsmouth Square.[6]

After viewing the San Francisco panorama, the editors of the *Sacramento Transcript* learned that McIntyre was considering a visit to Sacramento "for a like purpose." Moving into the gold fields, he also intended to take

> faithful pictures of the miner as he is engaged in his various styles of work. The whole country along the American River and its tributaries is of a bold character, and the artist need not travel far for either handsome or rugged prospects.[7]

The San Francisco panorama made its way to the office of the *Daguerreian Journal* in New York City. Quite enthused with the piece, the editors reprinted favorable reviews, including one claiming "a gush of rose tinted light [gave] an indescribable beauty to the sky of the picture just over the red-wood summit of Contra Costa."[8] Another daguerreotype by McIntyre was also of interest—a panorama of the gold diggings made up of six half plates, which pictured

> men, with spade and tin pan in hand, eagerly looking after the *dust*; some examining a lump just found, others up to their knees in water, and, among the rest is, in a bent position, a man, pan in hand, looking up with a grin, exhibiting "something" in his pan which he no doubt would try to make us believe was the metal.[9]

McIntyre may have hand-tinted the "something" in the pan with gold. The editors of the *Daguerreian Journal* explained the advantage of the daguerreotype for hand-tinting because "with [paper photography] there will be no use—can't pass off stones for gold!"[10] McIntyre's success was considerable but short-lived. In the spring of 1851, his studio was destroyed in one of the many San Francisco fires. By April of that year, he had opened another studio in Nevada City.[11]

Jacob and William Shew

Jacob Shew arrived in California in July 1849 from Baltimore, where he had managed John Plumbe's daguerreian studio.[12] Although some have reported his occupation as miner upon arrival in California, Shew claimed to have worked exclusively as a daguerreotypist.[13] Jacob was joined by his brother William in March 1851 and together they worked for J. Wesley Jones through the spring of that year.[14] By July, the brothers had left Jones to open their own separate daguerreian studios in San Francisco.[15]

On July 22, 1851, the *Alta California* reported on the commotion raised by a "big wagon which fills up a large portion of the Plaza, and which was yesterday being covered with a frame." This was identified as "a travelling daguerreotype establishment, with which the proprietor [William Shew] intends to travel around the city and country, taking views and portraits."[16] Impressed by his initiative, the editors noted that the "originality of the enterprise deserves success."[17] By this method, Shew made repeated trips into the gold fields, adding to his "collection of views taken in the mines and other parts of the state."[18]

Unfortunately, few of William Shew's daguerreotypes of the mining region still exist.[19] In Placer County, he made a whole-plate daguerreotype of the extensive hydraulic operation at Michigan Bluff [112]. The stripped and rocky landscape dominates the composition; only a sliver of sky is visible at the top where trestlework has been erected to supply water to the awaiting hoses. This detail dates the view to sometime after 1852, as it was not until "the winter of '53 . . . that the first hydraulic [operation was] erected here, having previous to that time worked with ground sluices."[20] Three figures, unable to keep still for the required exposure time, survey the scene.

Other known or attributed views by William Shew include two half plates, one made in Placer County near Lincoln and another in Calaveras Country, depicting miners at their diggings. Another half plate, made in an unidentified location, features a common but rarely depicted subject: a Chinese miner [31, FIG. 4].

William Rulofson

William Rulofson arrived in San Francisco, from Newfoundland, Canada, in June 1849.[21] He brought with him "his 'buff sticks' and 'coating boxes,' having no intention to exchange them for the miner's implements."[22] Like William Shew, Rulofson worked his way through the gold fields in a traveling daguerreian wagon, promoting his services as he went. Stopping for a brief time in Stockton, in summer 1850, Rulofson advertised his "perfect and lifelike Miniatures" and advised patrons to visit soon, "as his stay in town will be extremely limited."[23] Moving south to Sonora, he could not resist the urge to mine for gold but soon "relinquished the gold-washing cradle for the camera, and returned to his first love."[24] He formed a partnership with J. D. Cameron,

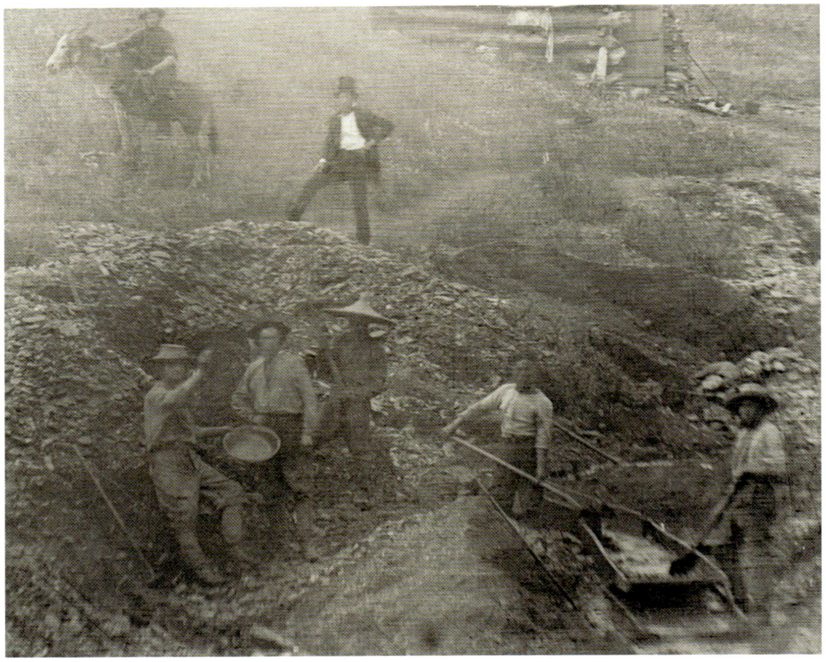

FIG. 4 **William Shew**, American (1820–1903). *California gold mining group including Chinese miner*, ca. 1853. Half-plate daguerreotype, detail of [31].

and "the artistic business of picture making which these men carried on quickly became celebrated throughout the mines."[25]

At some point between 1850 and 1852, Rulofson was introduced to Captain Charles M. Weber, an early California pioneer and the founder of Stockton. Weber commissioned Rulofson to daguerreotype his home and property, as well as various locations on the Stockton Channel.[26] In all, Rulofson made twelve half-plate views, including several close variants.

Denny and Edwin Hendee and Alfred Edwards

Denny Hendee was also operating in the mining fields by the spring of 1850, focusing on the southern region. Hendee and his brother Edwin arrived in San Francisco in January 1850 and were quickly employed by "the only art gallery in the city."[27] This studio may have belonged to Frederick Coombs, the only daguerreian in San Francisco mentioned in the *Daguerreian Journal* registry.[28] Denny and Edwin Hendee left San Francisco in May 1850, probably after a fire on May 4 destroyed the studio. They "went to the mines near Sonora, subsequently purchasing a daguerreotype outfit from an emigrant, then followed mining and taking pictures at each until January 1851 doing a prosperous business as well as meeting with great success in mining."[29] This daguerreotype [32], most likely taken by Edwin or Denny Hendee, features "Hendee's Daguerrean Rooms" as noted by the small sign next to the right-most front window of the upper story.

After the brothers parted ways, Denny Hendee "followed his artistic career at Stockton, Marysville, and through the mining camps, until the spring of 1853."[30] Indeed, by May 1851, he had "taken some admirable

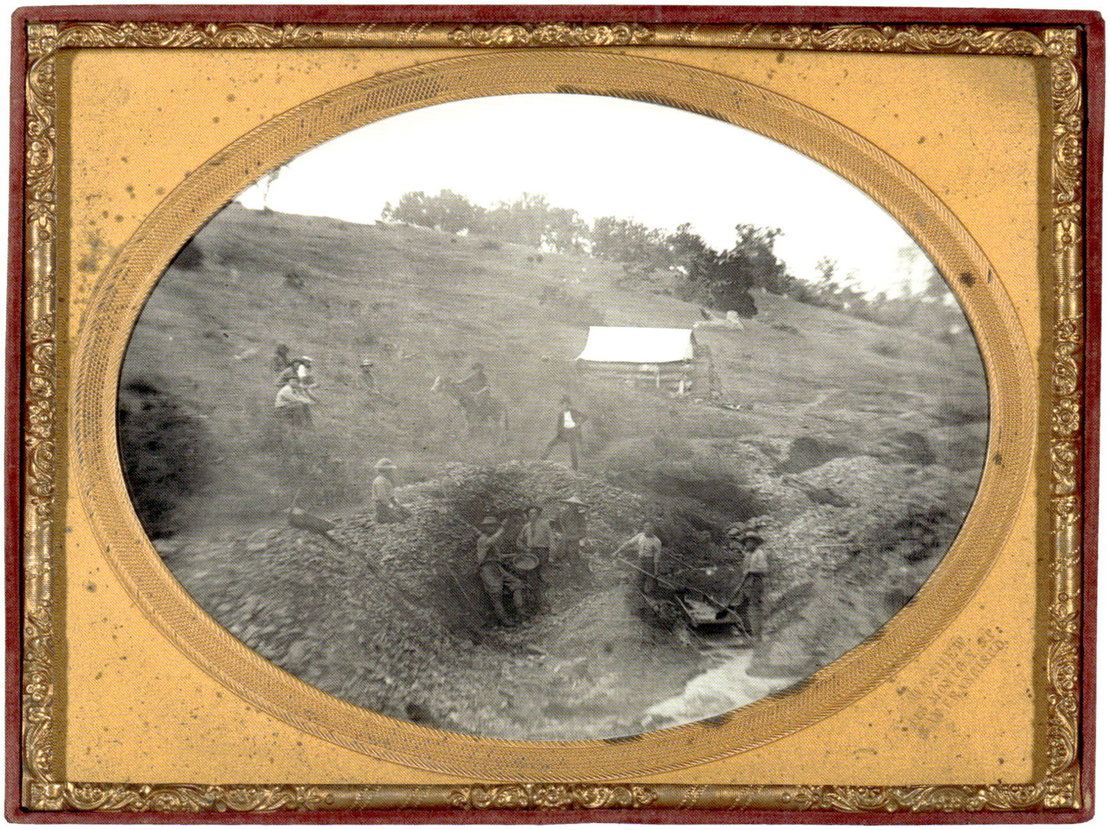

31 **William Shew**, American (1820–1903). *California gold mining group including Chinese miner*, ca. 1853. Half-plate daguerreotype.

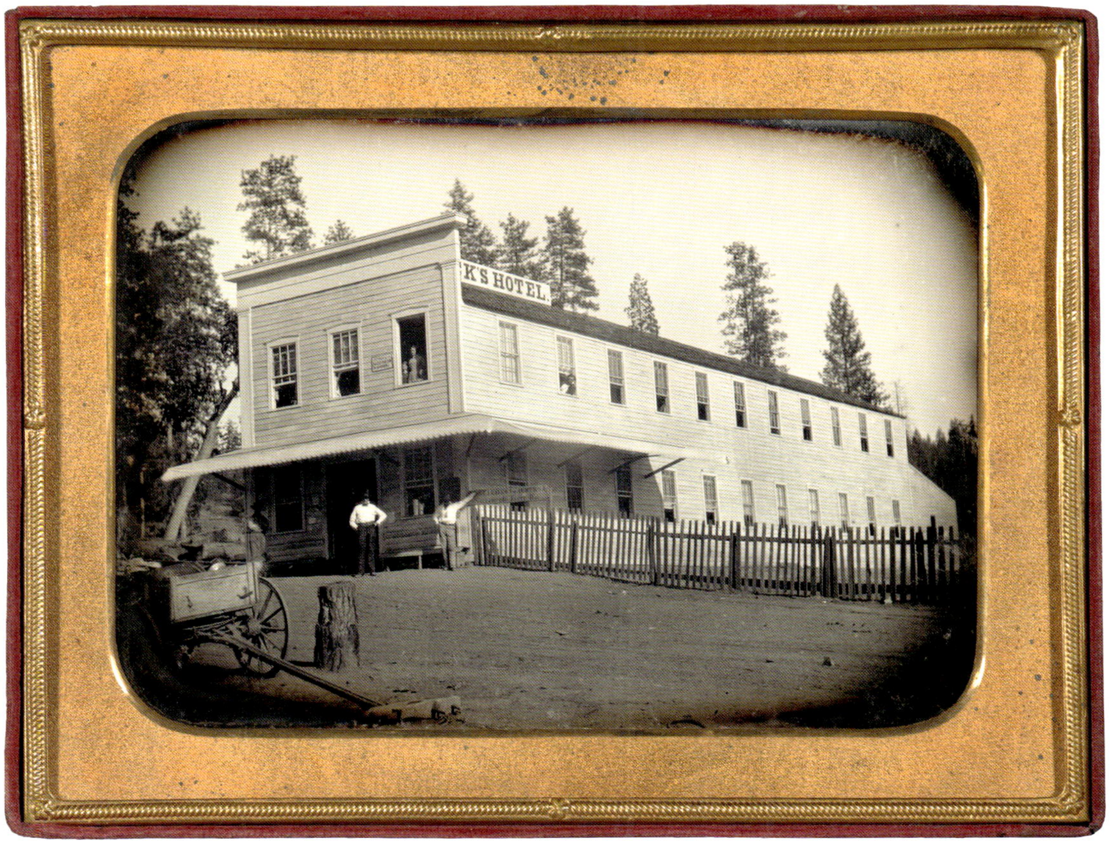

32 Attributed to **Denny Hendee**, American (1826–1907) and **Edwin Hendee**, American (1824–ca. 1900). *Hendee's Daguerreian Studio, California*, ca. 1850. Half-plate daguerreotype.

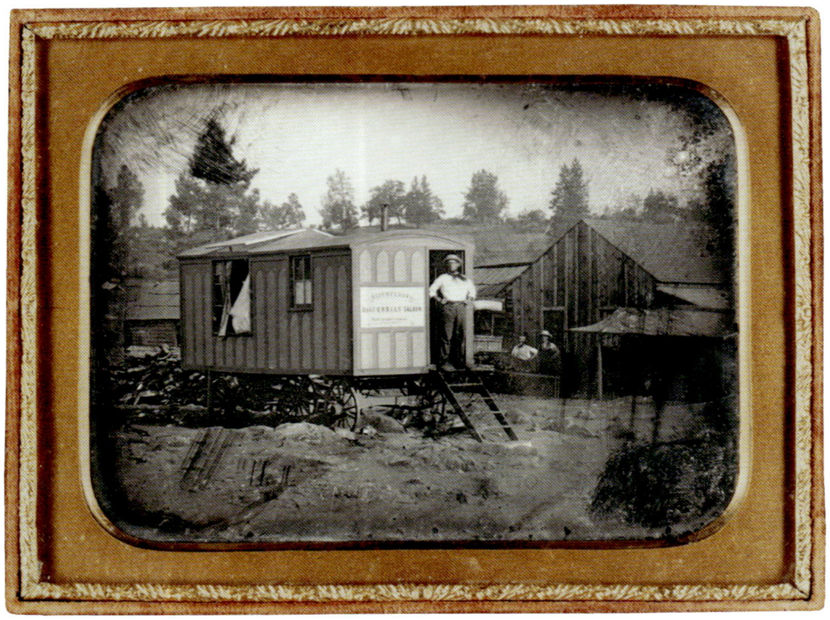

33 **Isaac W. Baker**, American (1810–?). *Isaac W. Baker in front of Batchelder's Daguerreian Saloon*, ca. 1853. Sixth-plate daguerreotype. Oakland Museum of California, Gift of an anonymous donor.

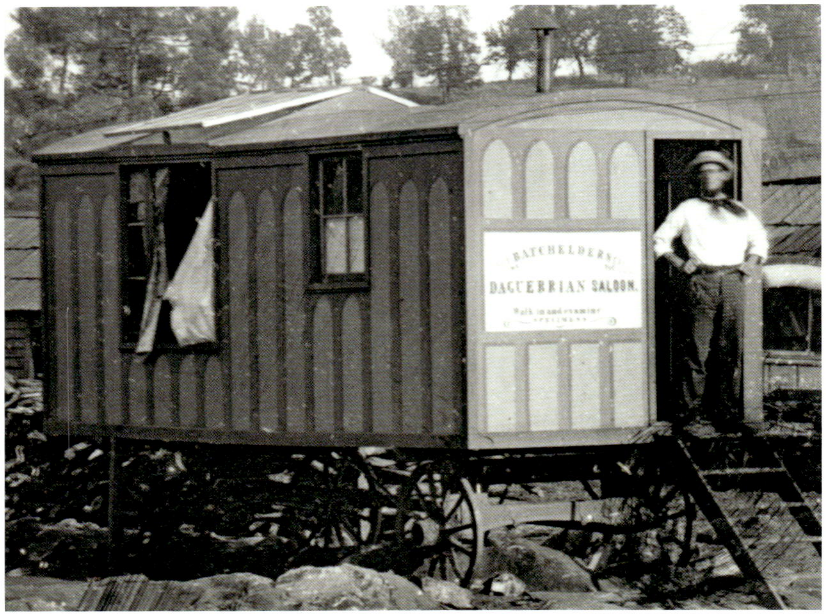

FIG. 5 **Isaac W. Baker**, American (1810–?). *Isaac W. Baker in front of Batchelder's Daguerreian Saloon*, ca. 1853. Sixth-plate daguerreotype, detail of [33].

likenesses" in Marysville and was about to relocate "to the rooms over Dr. Watts' city drug store."[31] In 1853, while in Marysville, he married and then moved to Portland, Oregon, where he continued his daguerreotype business. Hendee eventually returned to California, opening a studio in Oroville where he practiced paper photography until 1859.

The little-known daguerreotypist Alfred Edwards was also working in the mining region in 1850–51.[32] Originally from New York City, Edwards, it was noted in October 1851, had been "for the last year engaged in taking daguerreotype likenesses of diggers, as well as picturesque sketches of various mining localities."[33] In November 1852, Edwards partnered with one of the Hendee brothers and opened "Hendee and Edwards's Daguerrean Rooms" in Auburn, California. It is unknown whether he continued to make trips into the mining region to make views.

Perez and Benjamin Batchelder and Isaac Baker

Perez Batchelder and his brother Benjamin maintained a fleet of traveling daguerreian wagons primarily in the southern mining region. Headquartered in Sonora in 1851, they had relocated their wagon near the Stockton House in Stockton by fall 1852.[34] The brothers advertised skylights and camera equipment capable of producing superior portraits as well as "a splendid *View Camera*, for taking views without reversing."[35] By summer 1853, Perez and Benjamin were operating separate traveling wagons, working in various locations throughout the southern mining region.[36]

Enjoying brisk business, the Batchelder brothers employed additional operators, including Isaac Baker.[37] Arriving in California from Massachusetts

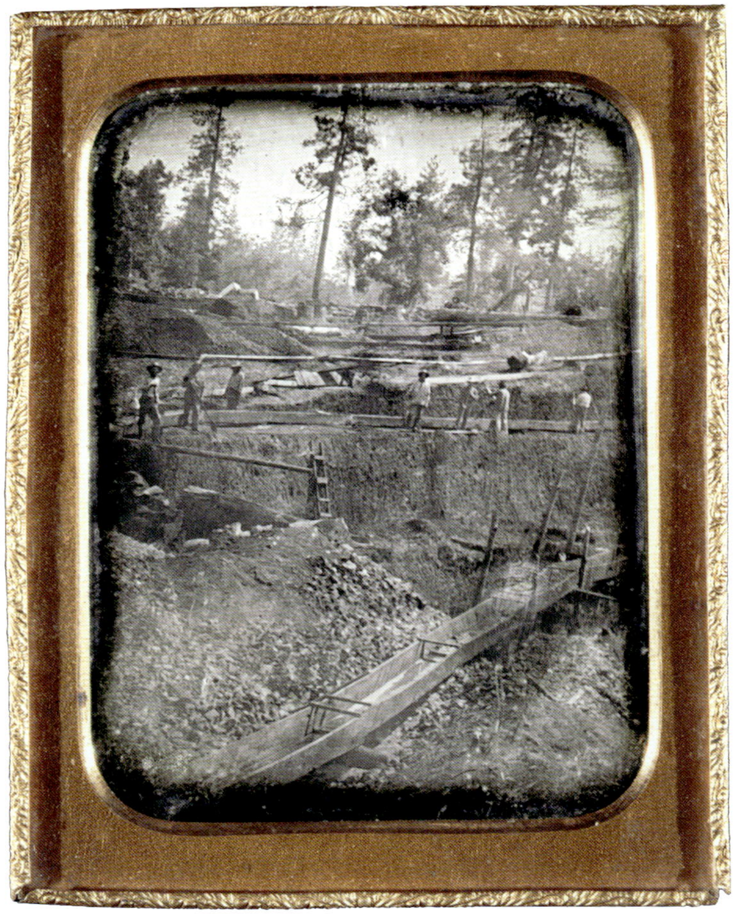

34 **Isaac W. Baker**, American (1810–?). *Gold miners and sluice boxes, Vallecito, California*, ca. 1853. Sixth-plate daguerreotype. Oakland Museum of California, Gift of an anonymous donor.

in January 1850, Baker first tried his hand at mining, only to return home in November.[38] Lured back to California in October 1852, he again stayed just one year before returning home. However, on this second trip, Baker learned the daguerreotype trade from Perez Batchelder. A willing and talented pupil, he quickly proved his skill and was sent out on his own in one of Batchelder's traveling studio wagons, as seen in [33, FIG. 5]. The figure posed proudly at the top of the stairs is believed to be Baker.

One of Baker's most sophisticated works was made in Vallecito.[39] An unusual vertical sixth-plate view, *Gold miners and sluice boxes, Vallecito, California*, depicts the deep trenches dug by the miners to reach underlying pay dirt [34]. Here, Baker creates a visually dynamic composition of this large operation: following the sluice in the foreground, our gaze zigzags along the horizontal lines of progressively distant trenches and sluices.

In July 1853, while working at Murphy's Camp, Baker wrote a poem for an advertising broadside, advising miners "to get a picture of your face . . . At MURPHY'S CAMP, and there's the place . . . walk in to 'BATCHELDER'S SALOON,' from morn, till late in afternoon." Resuming the rhyme, he promoted his skill with outdoor views, notifying miners, "if you want a 'view,' or 'claim,' Walk in and 'register your name.'"[40] While there, Baker recorded a view of the town's business-lined street, showing the place capable of sustaining a healthy economy. After his successful stint at Murphy's, Batchelder suggested a change in venue:

> I think you have done double the business at Murphy's that either David or Patch would have done. Indeed I think you have done *Muy Bien*, considering all things. I think if you can get down to Mokelumne Hill before the rains commence you will make a good winter's job of it. I thought at one time of taking the Saloon at Stockton there and I presume should have done so if I had not got a good location at Stockton. . . . Ben[jamin Batchelder] is in the Saloon at Jamestown. Have not heard from him don't know what he is doing.[41]

It is unclear whether Baker made it to Mokelumne Hill, but in October 1853, he departed California and returned to Massachusetts.

Robert H. Vance after 1851

Following the disappointing show of his *Views in California*, Robert Vance left New York City and was back in California by early 1852.[42] Laden with "$6,000 worth of Daguerreotype Stock and Instruments," he advertised that he was prepared to "commence taking Likenesses by an entirely new process," resulting in "a bolder, clearer and more durable picture than ever before made in California."[43]

Throughout the spring and summer of 1852, Vance received several shipments of goods from the East Coast, probably in anticipation of the opening of his new studio in Sacramento.[44] By June, Vance's Daguerrean Gallery was fully stocked and "just opened in the Post Office Building."[45] In addition to studio work, he likely continued his trips into the gold region. One of his views of Placerville was reproduced in the Sacramento newspaper as "an accurate and beautiful cut . . . from a daguerreotype view taken by Messrs. Salmon & Vance."[46] After a succession of fires and a flood destroyed his Sacramento studio, Vance relocated to San Francisco in 1853.[47] On January 1, 1853, the *Alta California* announced the opening of Vance's new, grandly appointed San Francisco studio. The newspaper encouraged the public to visit to see his impressive display of daguerreotypes, including "a collection of mining views."[48]

In Sacramento, there was no similar celebration on that day; the city was experiencing a catastrophic flood. Sensing a photographic opportunity, Vance rushed there to daguerreotype the event. One resulting plate served as the basis for a letter-sheet engraving. Although the plate is not extant, contemporary reviews document its success. In addition to its fine technical quality, the plate captured the stirring essence of the day, as revelers ringing in the New Year were simultaneously burdened with a natural disaster. "The artist has caught not only the form and outline of the varied persons and scenery forming the picture, but its spirit and *role* in the very height of merriment."[49] The letter sheet was intended to serve as a "perpetual memento" of this significant incident in Sacramento history, for locals to "transmit to their friends in the Atlantic States."[50] A copy of the letter sheet was sent to the *Photographic Art-Journal*. Predictably promoting the role of the camera in this endeavor, the journal's editor stated, "Nature furnished the original image, through the lenses of the daguerrean operator, from which a *fac simile* [*sic*] representation" was created.[51]

Vance continued to take outdoor and landscape scenes, advertising a recently acquired "entirely new and improved apparatus, expressly for taking views."[52] Processes were also improved and proprietary: Vance "chemicalizes and prepares his plates different from any other artist in California," giving a "beautiful, clear and perfect tone to the whole picture."[53] Traveling north from his San Francisco studio, Vance made daguerreotypes in Marysville and recorded mining scenes "at Parks's, Barton's, Reese's, and Landers' Bars, on the Yuba River."[54] He later opened an additional studio in Marysville in August 1853.[55]

Returning from Marysville in October 1853, Vance established temporary residence in Sacramento.[56] In December, he opened a daguerreotype studio in the city with partner Henry Sherman Beals. In addition to traditional portraiture work, Vance & Beals' Premium Daguerrean Gallery advertised the ability to copy "Daguerreotypes, Paintings, Drawings, &c." as well as their skill in making "Out-door Views . . . taken at the shortest notice."[57] The partners also advertised stereoscopic daguerreotypes, a new technique that Vance had introduced at his San Francisco location the previous month.[58] Editors of the *San Francisco Herald* found stereoscopic daguerreotypes to be an "improvement on the Daguerrean art, but few of which have heretofore been made in California, owing to the want of the proper instruments."[59] Vance's partnership with Beals ended in September 1854.[60]

Vance reopened his Sacramento studio with artist George Currier in November, but the competition from other studios was intense. Vance's advertisements were riddled with the language of a struggling business, with phrases such as "reduction of prices," "the best Daguerreotype for the least money," "one-half the former prices," and "Daguerreotypes for almost nothing." Adding insult to injury, Vance & Co. was listed on the front page of a supplemental issue of the *Sacramento Union* newspaper as one of several businesses delinquent in the payment of city tax.[61] Regardless of his financial circumstances, Vance maintained his reputation as an exceptional daguerreian artist. Visitors to his studio from outside the region continued to be strongly impressed with his skill, admiring, "several double whole [plates] four times the size of any in California."[62]

In late summer 1857, Vance made one of his last documented trips into the gold mining region (it is not known whether he had a camera with him).[63] Traveling to Solano County, he intended to confront settlers squatting on a tract of land he owned. One night, disguised intruders broke into his bedroom and after discharging a gun, kidnapped him. Vance managed to escape by running into the hills. Newspapers reported that "he had nothing but his shirt on when he was taken away, and this he had torn up and wrapped around his feet."[64] Naked, he was later administered aid at a local residence. The accounts in the press continued: "The cause of this murderous assault appears to have been that Mr. Vance bought a tract of land upon which the assaulting party were or are settlers, and failing to oust him by law, they perhaps thought that by killing him the title would be definitely settled in themselves. . . . Mr. Vance has had a very fortunate escape with his life."[65]

George H. Johnson

Born in New York State, George H. Johnson was one of the most prolific and important daguerreotypists to work in California. It is unclear where and when he learned the daguerreotype trade. An article in the *Illustrated California News* suggests the possibility of experience in Europe, noting that Johnson had "known this delicate art from its infancy, in the Old World as well as in the New."[66] He arrived in San Francisco in January 1849 from New York City, where he had been a daguerreotypist in at least 1847 and 1848.[67] In July 1849, the opening of his first studio in Sacramento warranted a mention in the local newspaper: "Mr. Johnson, Front St. next door to our Office, is taking some admirable pictures. Mr. J has recently arrived from New York and is an artist of skill and taste."[68] It is not surprising to find this early mention of Johnson in an article rather than an advertisement. Throughout his California career, Johnson maintained a cordial relationship with a number of newspapers. He understood how to promote his business through the press, regularly sending images to various publications in order to gain a positive mention or, better yet, an engraved reproduction of one of his views. In this way, Johnson made his name known to a wider audience than his actual plates could reach.

In Sacramento, Johnson probably exclusively produced portraits, including many of miners, into the spring of 1850.[69] His studio setup was primitive, "on the ground floor literally and had canvas sides and a roof."[70] By May 1850, he had moved to a more permanent location in the city, on J Street, and was ready to take likenesses "singly or in groups."[71] Notably, he was the only Sacramento-based daguerreotypist listed in the national registry of the first issue of the *Daguerreian Journal* in November 1850.[72] A later advertisement claimed that his "establishment was the first permanently located one of the kind on the Pacific."[73]

While Johnson is renowned for making views in the gold fields, it is not certain when this work began.[74] It seems unlikely that he daguerreotyped outside prior to spring 1850 due to heavy winter rains. However, Johnson's entry in the July 1850 city directory, as a "Daguerrean Artist, Facial and Landscape Gallery" indicates that he had undertaken outdoor views by this time.[75]

By July 1850, Johnson appears to have become a specialist in producing miner portraits, outfitting his studio with "a fine painting for a background, where miners desire to be represented at work."[76] The editors of the *Sacramento Transcript* encouraged readers to obtain a daguerreotype "to convey to their friends and relatives at home something of an idea of their appearance in *this* country, where razors have become obsolete, and digging gold works such a powerful change in every man." Johnson, it would seem, had a special ability for showing the essence of the miner, so that each man could see the true nature of "*themselves reflected*."[77] With a "living-like impress," these portraits were acceptable surrogates to be sent home in lieu of wayward miners. The editors continued, "We recommend such of our friends as promised to return to their early homes this season, and who have failed in their promise, to drop in at Johnson's to get a picture, and it will obviate the necessity for an early return."[78] Johnson's new studio on J Street included a skylight "and various important alterations made to insure the success of the operation."[79]

In August 1850, Johnson provided the editors of the *Illustrated California News* (in San Francisco) with several daguerreotype views of the location of a Sacramento riot, from which one could be chosen to make an engraving for the publication. The Sacramento squatters' riot of August 12–14, 1850, took place between the established landowners and newly arrived persons who had taken up residence on their land.[80] The groups converged violently on the city center, and several men were killed. Johnson recorded the scene of the action, utilizing a working method to which he would later return when photographing in the gold fields. He took multiple views of the location, "unweariedly, one after another, from different places of observation,

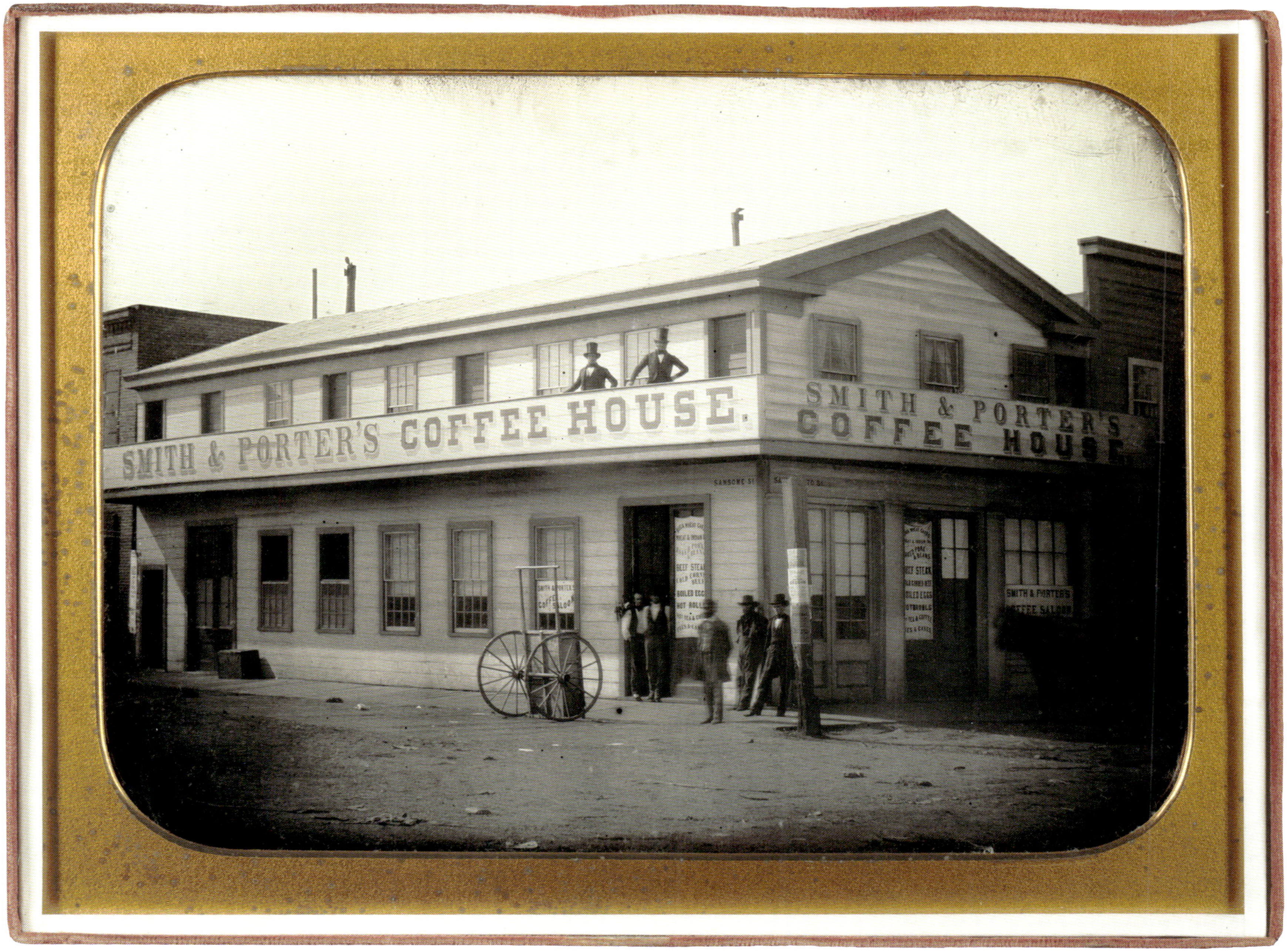

35 **George H. Johnson**, American (1823–ca. 1880s) and **Seth Lewis Shaw**, American (1816–1872). *Smith and Porter's coffee house and hotel on the corner of Sansome and Sacramento Streets, San Francisco*, ca. 1852. Whole-plate daguerreotype. Bancroft Library, University of California, Berkeley.

in order that the most advantageous points of view might be decided on by actual comparison."[81]

One of Johnson's first advertisements for "views of buildings" was in April 1851.[82] Understanding the power of the press, Johnson daguerreotyped the *Sacramento Union* newspaper building and gifted the view to the editors, prompting another positive mention in the paper.[83] By May, he had embarked on a project "taking views of the different blocks and stores of this city" [19] and was ready to provide "citizens a perfect counterpart of their dwellings, or places of business . . . the perfection to which . . . has excited the astonishment of all who have ever seen them."[84]

Johnson's business was clearly booming, and in January 1852, he opened his Eureka Daguerrean Rooms in San Francisco.[85] His partner, Seth Shaw, had arrived in that city in 1850 and run a successful daguerreian studio until he was recruited by J. Wesley Jones to act as daguerreotypist on Jones's overland journey.[86] Shaw left Jones's party in May 1851, returned to San Francisco, and later joined Johnson in the opening of his studio. Johnson and Shaw worked together from at least January to March 1852 taking city and gold mining views.

Existing plates by Johnson and Shaw include an impressive whole plate of Smith & Porter's Coffee House in San Francisco [35] and at least three gold field views in the quarter- and half-plate sizes.[87] In early March, Johnson advertised "Daguerreotype likenesses and Views taken at short notice, in any weather" and notified the public that there were "SOME BEAUTIFUL MINING VIEWS ON HAND."[88] Shaw may have continued to work with Johnson until August, at which time he and his brother Stephen purchased a homestead in Humboldt County and became farmers.[89]

By September 1852 at the Sacramento studio, Johnson had partnered with Silas Selleck, who had recently arrived from New York City.[90] Previously employed by Mathew Brady, Selleck was praised as "a first class artist."[91] An unsettled character in the early years, Selleck worked for nearly every major daguerreotypist in San Francisco and Sacramento at one point or another.[92] After Johnson's Sacramento studio burned in a citywide fire in November 1852, the pair moved their operation to San Francisco, opening Johnson and Selleck's Pacific Pioneer Daguerrean Gallery at 142 Montgomery Street. Although no daguerreotypes bearing a "Johnson and Selleck" stamp have to date been identified, the *Alta California* editors were familiar with their work, noting that they had been provided with "a fine daguerreotype landscape from Messrs. Johnson & Selleck, and have since seen other pictures from the same artists."[93] The pair also opened a small satellite studio at the Yerba Buena Cemetery in San Francisco "for the special purpose of taking daguerreotype views of the last resting place of those whose friends, either here or in the Atlantic States, may desire such a memento."[94] By October 1853, the partners were busy in the gold mining region, reportedly doing a "fine business in that part of the diggings."[95] Selleck continued to work with Johnson through the end of that year, but later opened his own studio in San Francisco [26].[96]

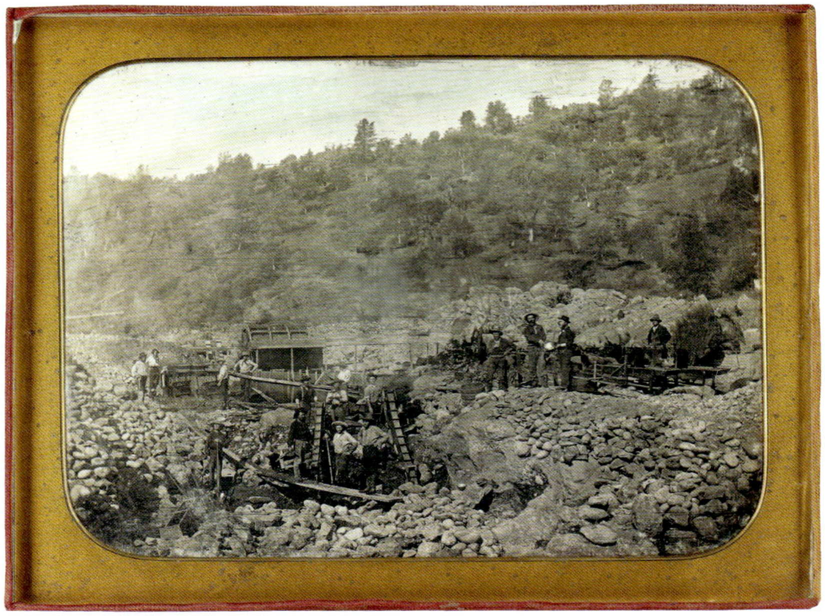

36 **George H. Johnson**, American (1823–ca. 1880s). *Gold mining operation*, ca. 1853. Whole-plate daguerreotype. National Gallery of Canada, Ottawa.

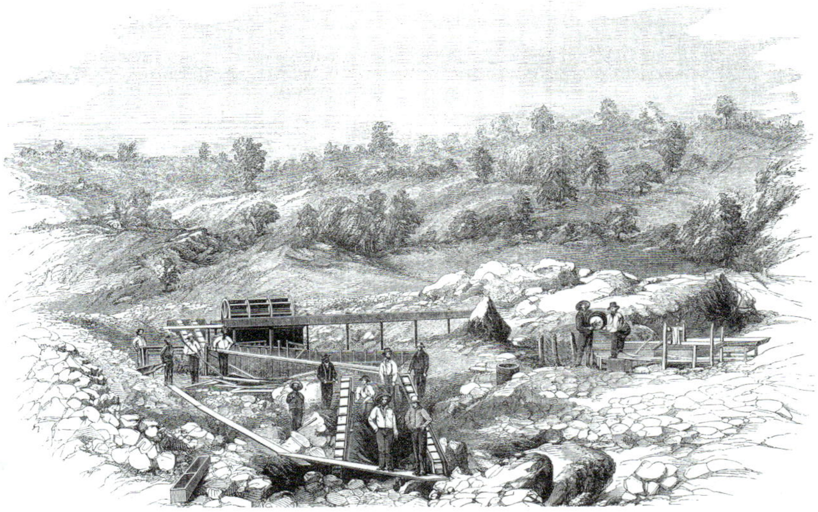

FIG. 6 *Notion Company's Works, California*, from *Gleason's Pictorial, Scenes in California*, 6, no. 12 (March 25, 1854). California History Room, California State Library, Sacramento.

As Johnson spent more time daguerreotyping in the gold fields, he realized the appeal of these views to a wider audience. Building on his earlier partnership with the press, he provided a daguerreotype view to the *Sacramento Union* for reproduction as an engraving. It was also used as the basis for a letter sheet (sold for twenty-five cents); the editors announced the availability "at the counter of this office, beautiful letter sheets with a spirited and correct view of 'Industry Bar,' on the Yuba river. This view is taken from a daguerreotype by Johnson, one of the most celebrated artists of this State, and will prove a valuable souvenir to friends at the East."[97] Intended as stationery, letter sheets were an inexpensive way for miners to share California experiences and views with family and friends back home.

Most engravings, once produced, were used repeatedly in various publications.[98] An engraving of Industry Bar—probably the same one used in the letter sheet—appeared as an illustration in the *Sacramento Union Steamer* newspaper. The October 28, 1852, issue was "embellished by a beautiful engraving of Industry Bar, on the Yuba river, from a daguerreotype by Mr. Geo. H. Johnson, of this city."[99] This engraving was again reproduced for an article in the *Illustrated London News* and for the book *Voyages en Californie et dans l'Orégon*.[100]

The March 1854 issue of *Gleason's Pictorial Drawing-Room Companion* featured a two-page spread with four large engravings of mining methods and scenes in California. One engraving, titled *Notion Company's Works, California* [FIG. 6], is based on a whole-plate daguerreotype by Johnson [36]. In this view of an extensive river mining operation at Barton's Bar on the Yuba River, miners are clustered around the pumps used to drain water from the newly exposed streambed. The two owners stand to the right proudly displaying a pan full of gold. The engraver has taken some liberties and removed a few of the miners from his picture, but most of the key elements like the pumps, paddle wheel, and rock-strewn surface remain unchanged. Another engraving from this periodical titled *North Fork, American River, California* [FIG. 7] is based on a variant of an existing half plate—an unattributed view that may well have been made by Johnson [30]. This daguerreotype also depicts a river mining operation, but instead of focusing on the newly revealed rocky streambed, it emphasizes the paddlewheel used to pump water into awaiting sluices. The engraving is based on a more encompassing view of this subject; this half-plate daguerreotype may be one of several original variants.[101]

Johnson was the preeminent daguerreotypist of gold mining views in California, especially in the early years. Unlike most daguerreotypists, he maker-marked a number of his plates, providing a unique opportunity to study a monographic set of views for stylistic tendencies and aesthetic style. When photographing in the gold fields, Johnson utilized the working method that he had started early in his California career, making multiple views of individual subjects from different vantage points.

One prime example of this method—Johnson's series of views made in El Dorado County at Grizzly Flats—reveals a remarkably thorough body of work.[102] Working over the course of several hours or days, Johnson made at least seven views of the river mining operations in this location, most likely on the Cosumnes River.[103] Two similar half-plate views were made of the river mining operation with the town of Grizzly Flats just behind [37]. In both views, men (presumably the owners of the claim) are positioned just downhill from the camera. Johnson incorporates several picturesque conventions:

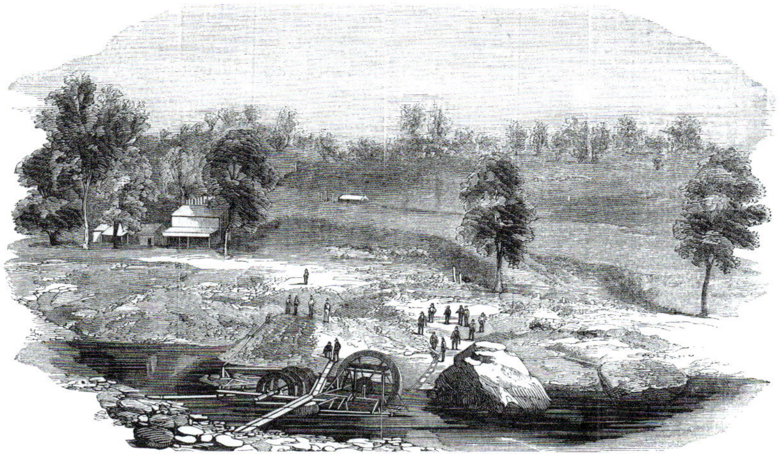

FIG. 7 *North Fork, American River, California*, from *Gleason's Pictorial, Scenes in California*, 6, no. 12 (March 25, 1854). California History Room, California State Library, Sacramento.

a tree in the foreground to frame his composition, the river in the middle ground, and the rolling forested hills in the distance, just behind the town. Another half-plate view [38], taken from the same general vantage point but moving slightly farther downstream, minimizes the river mining operation and instead emphasizes the surrounding scenery of wooded hillside and the horizon beyond. Repositioning his camera closer to the settlement, Johnson then focused on a few buildings scattered on the hillside where a distant water sluice is just visible atop trestlework.

Johnson's other images at Grizzly Flats focus exclusively on the river mining apparatus. Positioning his camera on a ledge just to one side of the diverted waterway, Johnson daguerreotyped the newly revealed riverbed in the process of draining. The final two images in this series are both quarter plates and may have been taken on a different day from the half-plate views. In these two almost identical images, Johnson places his camera just above and to the side of the massive paddlewheels [39–40]. This sight line provides a sense of the succession of mining equipment down the diverted river. Two men are pictured, one standing on a platform by the paddlewheel and the other in the rocky streambed. Although these views are almost identical, in one, there is a slight bend in the knee of the man in the foreground. Exploring all the possibilities offered by the location, Johnson's views reveal a thorough and exacting technique indicative of a thoughtful artist. More than merely "property records intended to accurately document the settlement and mining operations," Johnson's daguerreotypes allow for more than one "correct" view.[104]

Johnson made multiple views when depicting groups of people. In two ambitious whole-plate daguerreotypes of mining on the North Fork of the American River, Johnson daguerreotyped a large river diversion operation.[105] With just a glimpse of the diverted river in the background, this image [41] shows draining pumps (located on the left); canvas hoses carrying water from the pump that allow miners with rockers and pans to efficiently wash

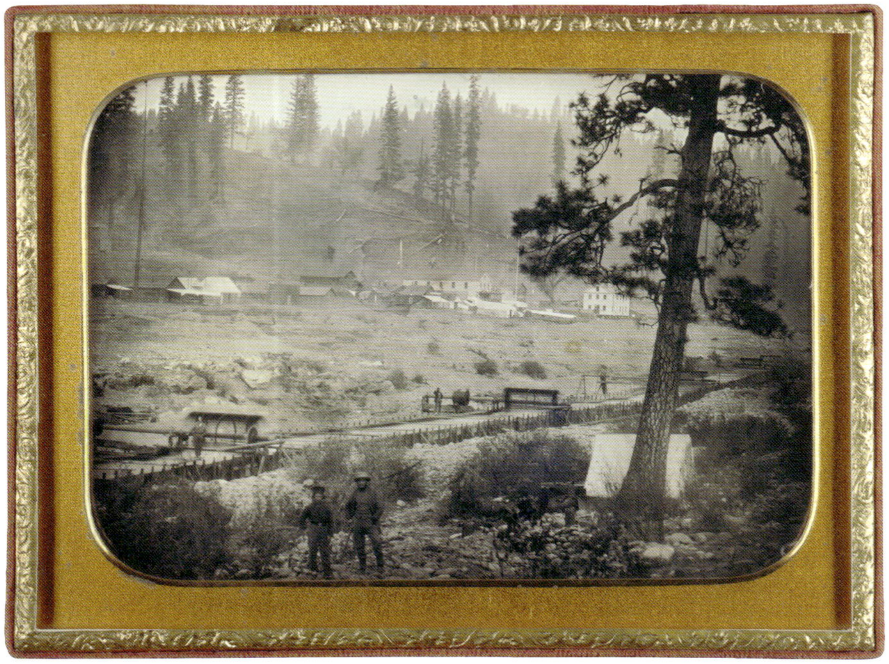

37 **George H. Johnson**, American (1823–ca. 1880s). *Diggings at Grizzly Flats, El Dorado County, California*, ca. 1851–52. Half-plate daguerreotype. Bancroft Library, University of California, Berkeley.

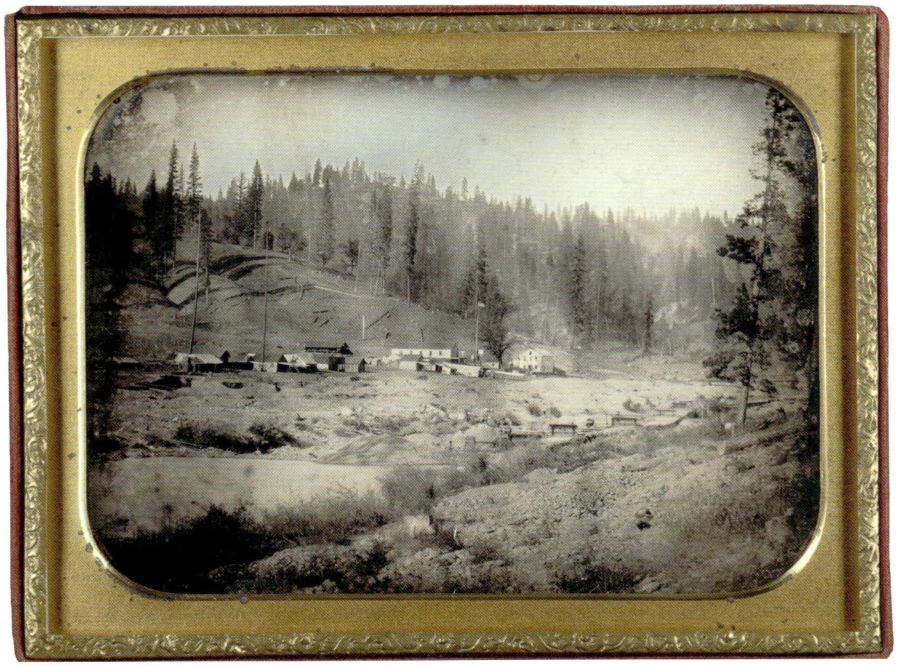

38 **George H. Johnson**, American (1823–ca. 1880s). *Settlement and mining operation in Grizzly Flats, El Dorado County, California*, ca. 1851–52. Half-plate daguerreotype. Bancroft Library, University of California, Berkeley.

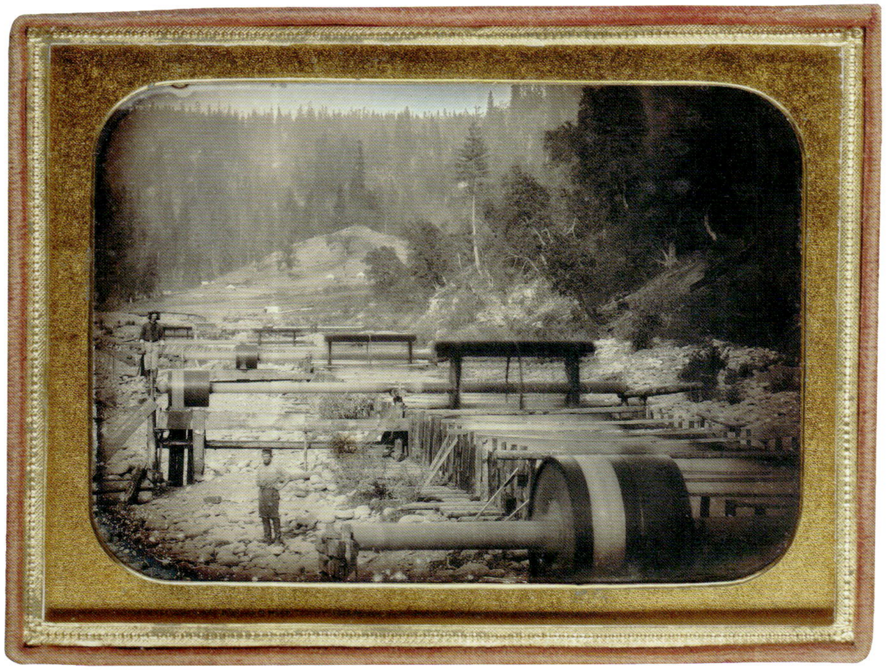

39 **George H. Johnson**, American (1823–ca. 1880s). *Riverbed mining, Grizzly Flats, El Dorado County, California, showing mining apparatus*, ca. 1851–52. Quarter-plate daguerreotype. Bancroft Library, University of California, Berkeley.

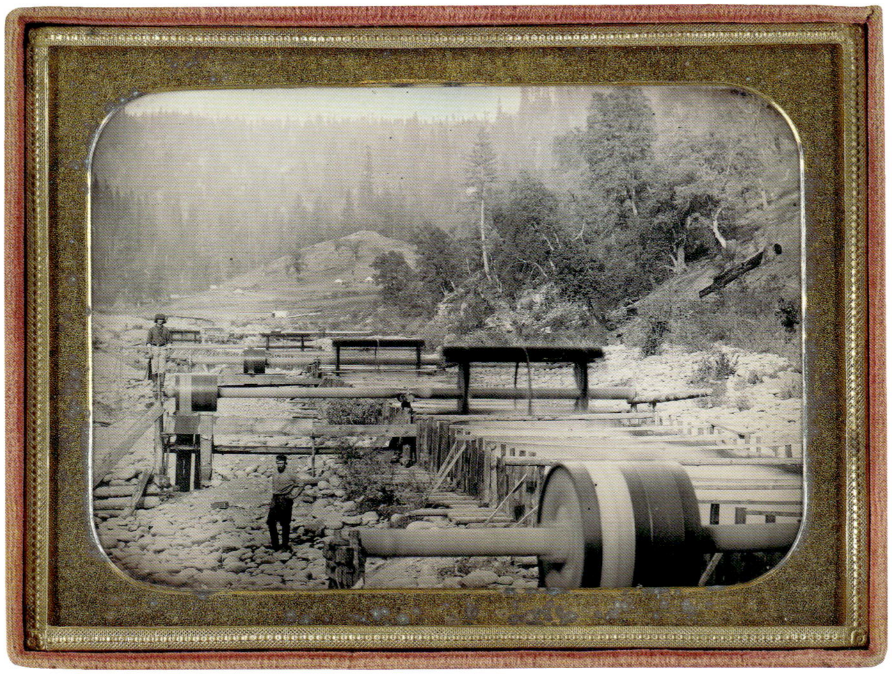

40 **George H. Johnson**, American (1823–ca. 1880s). *Riverbed mining, Grizzly Flats, El Dorado County, California*, ca. 1851–52. Quarter-plate daguerreotype. National Gallery of Canada, Ottawa.

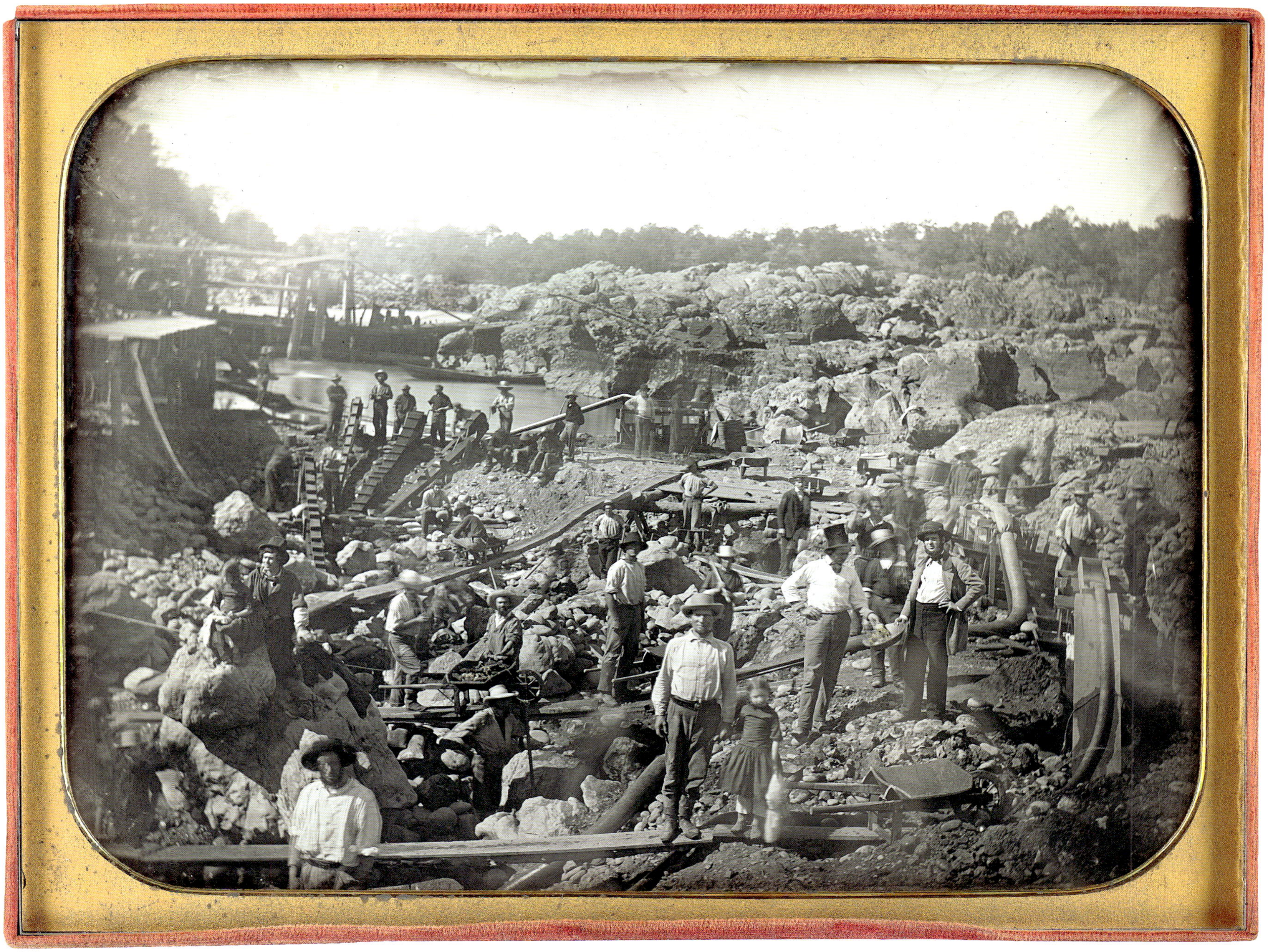

41 **George H. Johnson**, American (1823–ca. 1880s). *Large mining operation at North Fork of American River*, ca. 1852. Whole-plate daguerreotype. National Gallery of Canada, Ottawa.

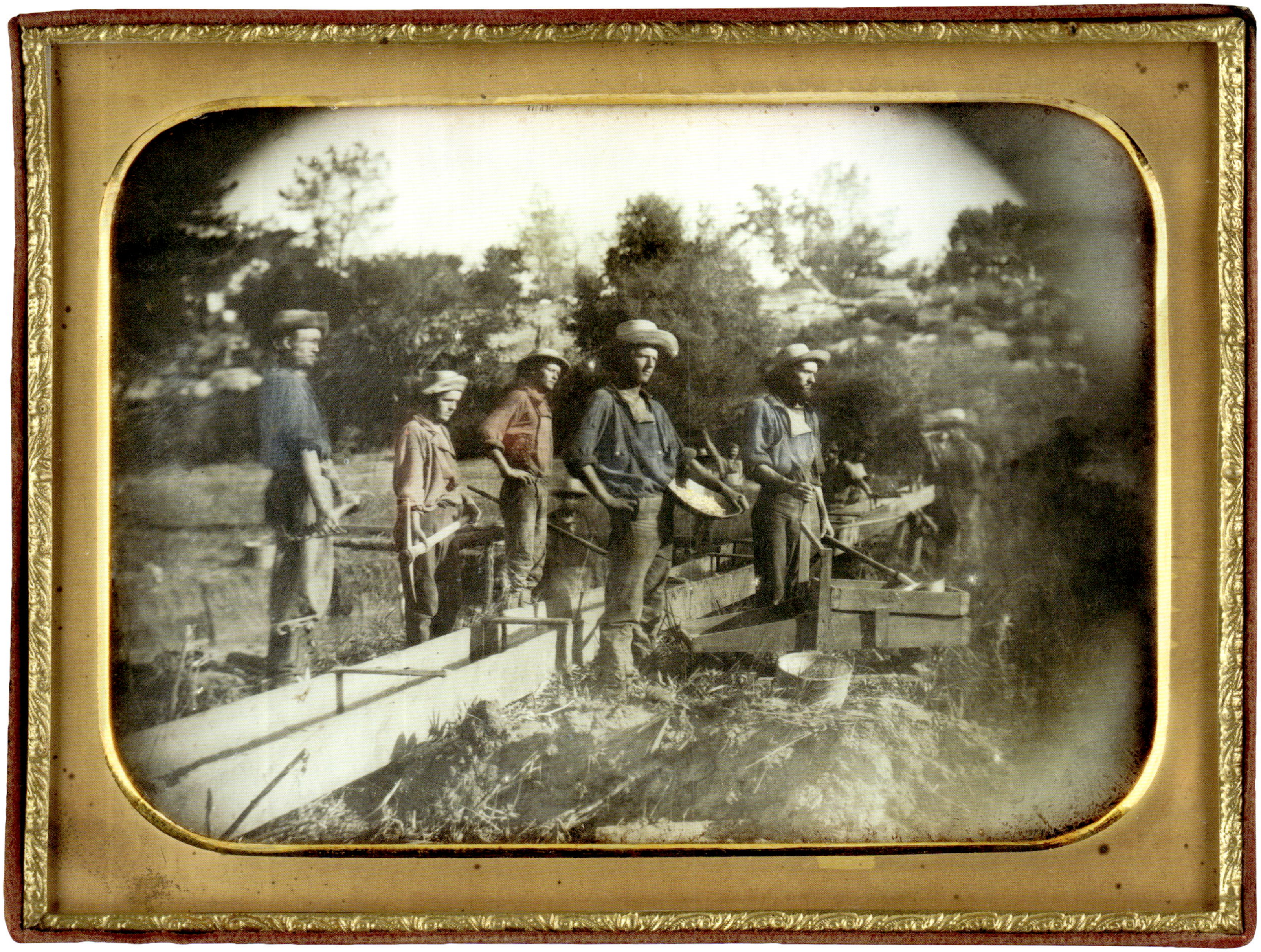

42 **George H. Johnson**, American (1823–ca. 1880s). *California gold miners with rocker and sluice*, ca. 1850. Half-plate daguerreotype.

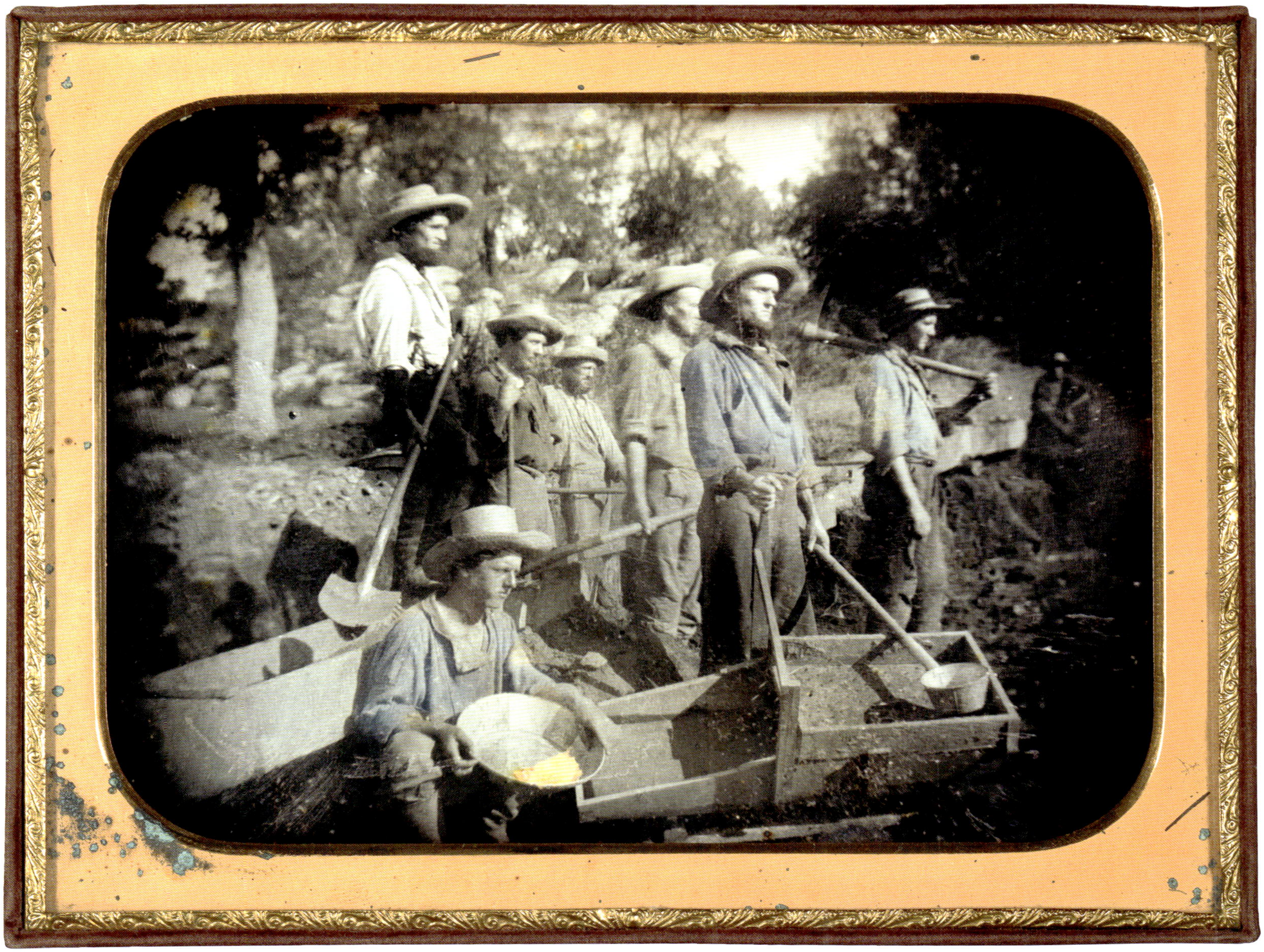

43 Attributed to **George H. Johnson**, American (1823–ca. 1880s). *California gold miners with rocker and sluice*, ca. 1850. Half-plate daguerreotype. The Art Institute of Chicago, The W. Bruce and Delaney H. Lundberg Collection, restricted gift of The Phillip Leonian and Edith Rosenbaum Leonian Charitable Trust.

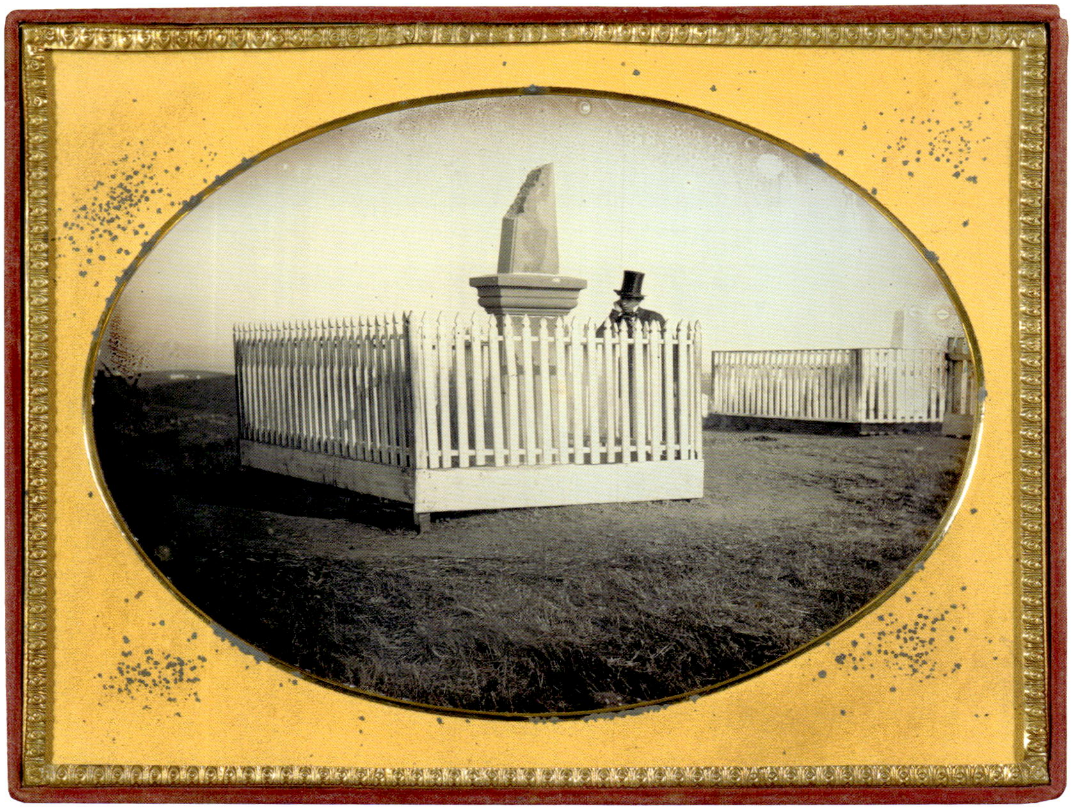

44 **George H. Johnson**, American (1823–ca. 1880s). *Grave of Richard Gulick, Benicia, California*, 1852. Half-plate daguerreotype.

dirt; and temporary scaffolding placed strategically around the crowded streambed to facilitate the moving of wheelbarrows full of dirt and rock. Two well-dressed men, presumably the owners of the claim, stand side by side carefully fingering a pan full of gold. Two little girls — one standing in front possibly holding a doll and the other sitting on a rock on the left — are a very unusual sight in a mining view.

In [42], Johnson daguerreotyped a smaller group standing around a sluice with shovels, pans, and rocker. He positioned his camera very close to one side of the sluice, which created a dramatic angle, emphasizing the profiles of the miners. The shirts of several miners have been hand-tinted red or blue. A peek inside of the pan reveals gold, underscoring a successful day at the claim. A second half-plate view shows most of this same group of miners from the same angle, but a little further down the claim [43]. Several workers have changed positions, and there are no longer any red-shirted miners. Only one view is maker-marked by Johnson—perhaps suggesting that one was purchased by the miners and the other was intended for his studio display wall.

Johnson also made several commissioned views for the Gulick brothers of Benicia, California.[106] During the gold rush, many of the people who struck it rich were not miners but the astute merchants who sold them food and supplies. The three Gulick brothers — James, Richard, and John — were bankers who chose the deepwater port in Benicia as the place to build a wharf in 1851–52. Johnson made half-plate views of both Gulick's Wharf and the Knickerbocker Emporium, which was built on the wharf to house and sell imported goods. The brothers amassed a fortune, but sadly, Richard died in 1852. Johnson daguerreotyped John at the side of his brother's grave [44]. The composition of this somber half-plate daguerreotype — a sole figure before the grave of a loved one — was done in the tradition of the early nineteenth-century mourning portrait.[107]

Some of Johnson's outdoor views are characterized by a distinctive posing style and application of hand-coloring.[108] This half plate [45] depicts a group of eight men: two well-dressed owners and six laborers. The miners have paused in their work at the long tom; several men hold shovels and one holds a pan tilted to reveal the gold inside. Most of the men are positioned in a pronounced profile, facing either right or left — this unusual posing is found in both maker-marked Johnson plates and non-marked plates. Since Johnson did not always include his name on the brass mat or velvet liner, this profile style may be indicative of his authorship. Another of Johnson's stylistic traits was the use of relatively heavy hand-tinting, also seen in this plate. Although hand-coloring was often used by daguerreotypists to highlight gold in a pan or to suggest the color of a flannel work shirt, Johnson's colorists were heavier handed, applying nearly opaque layers of vivid hues.

After operating on his own from January 1854 to November 1855, Johnson went into partnership with his brother, Bryan. Johnson Brothers

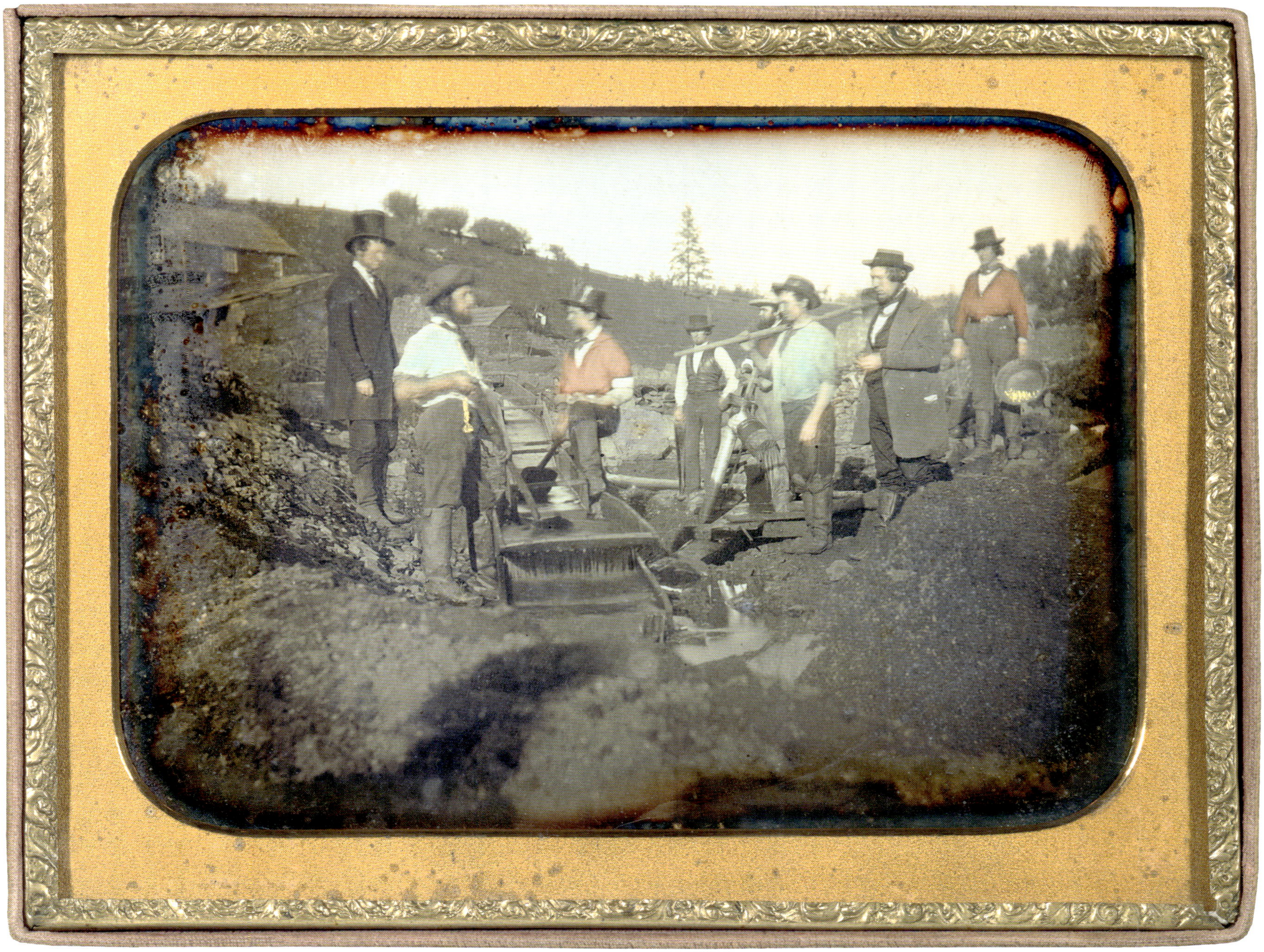

45 **George H. Johnson**, American (1823–ca. 1880s). *California gold miners with long tom,* ca. 1850–52. Half-plate daguerreotype.

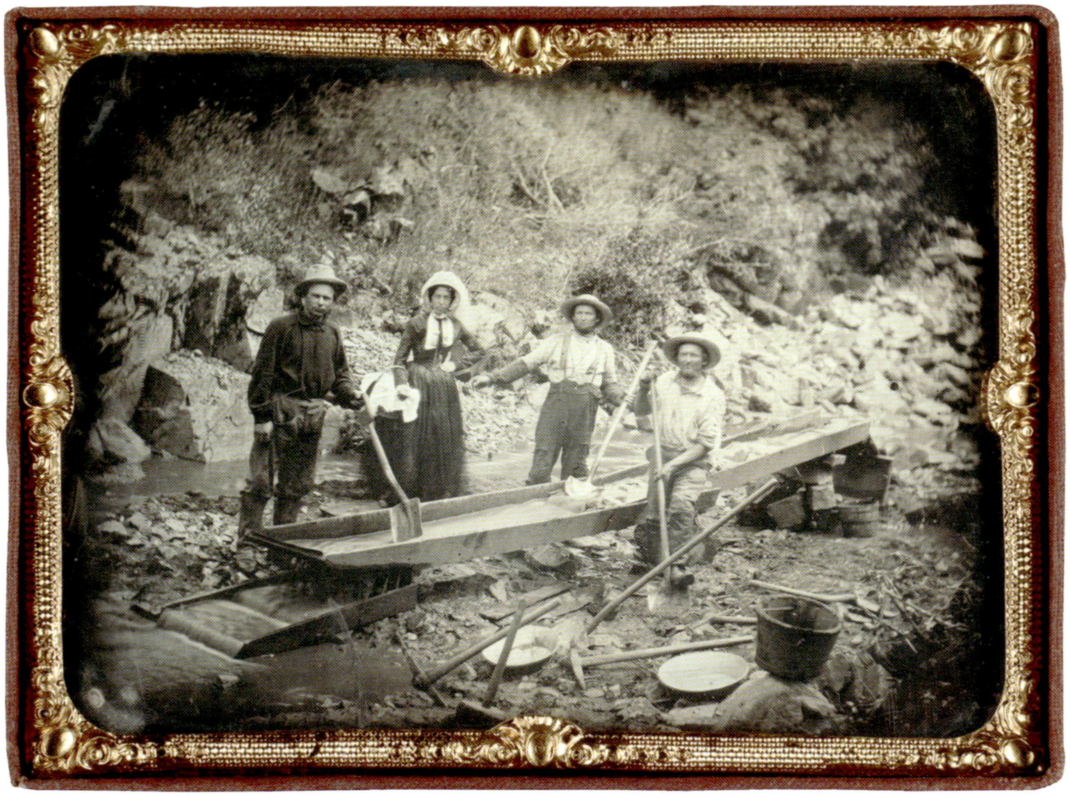

46 **Joseph Starkweather**, American (1822–ca. 1905). *In Auburn Ravine*, ca. 1852. Quarter-plate daguerreotype. California History Room, California State Library, Sacramento.

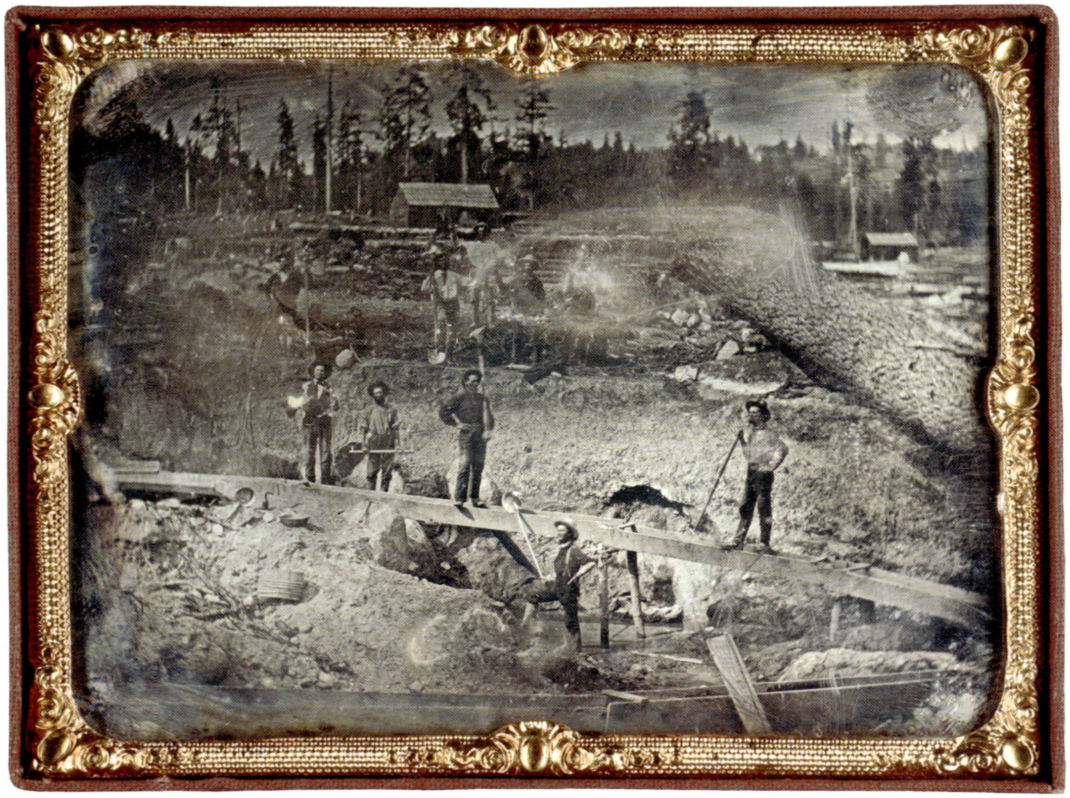

47 **Joseph Starkweather**, American (1822–ca. 1905). *Near Nevada City*, 1852. Quarter-plate daguerreotype. California History Room, California State Library, Sacramento.

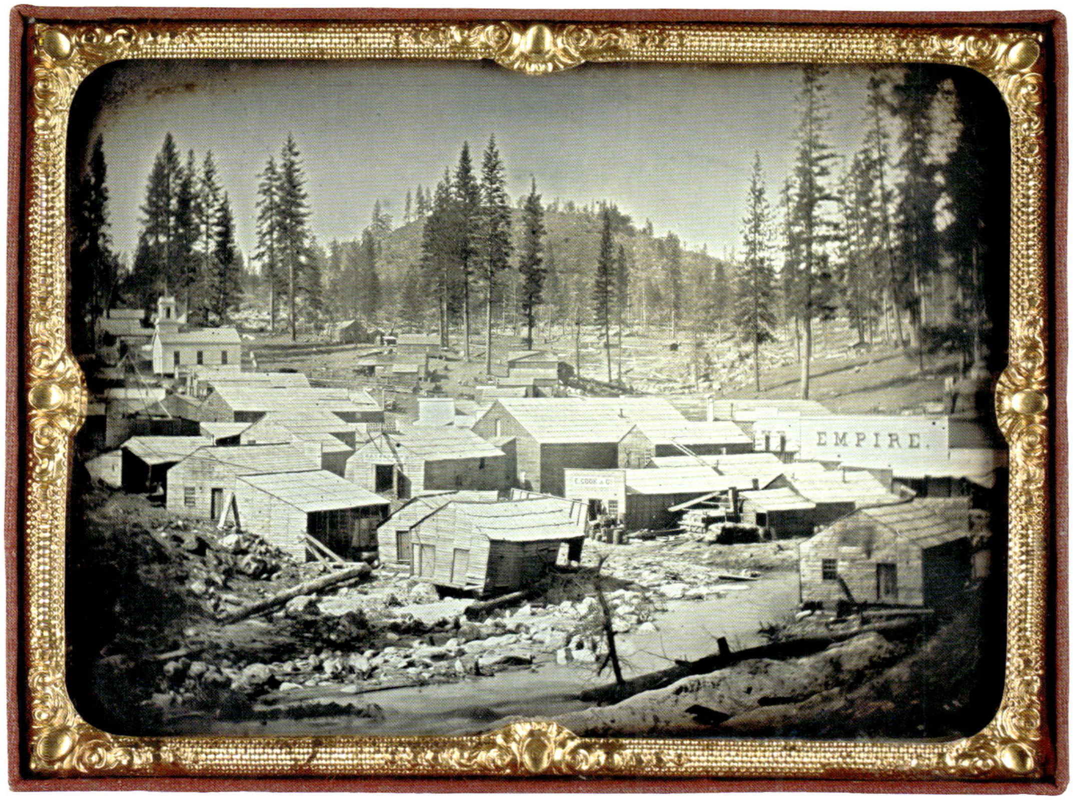

48 **Joseph Starkweather**, American (1822–ca. 1905). *Nevada City*, ca. 1852. Quarter-plate daguerreotype. California History Room, California State Library, Sacramento.

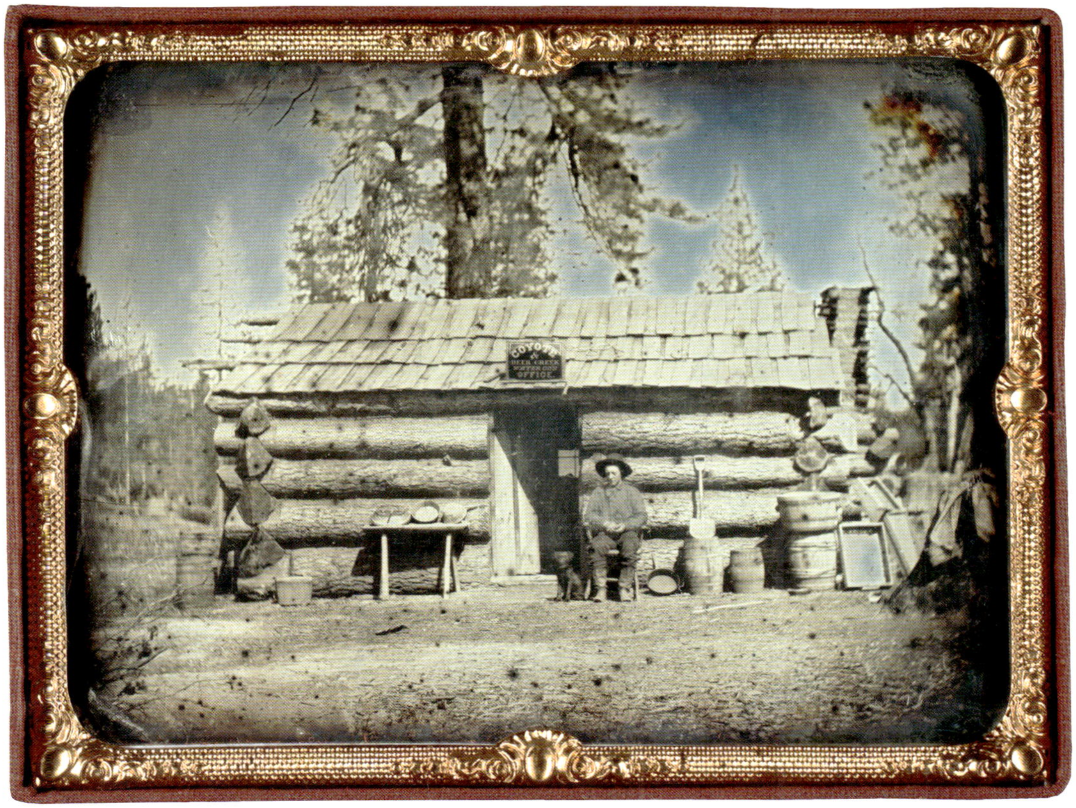

49 **Joseph Starkweather**, American (1822–ca. 1905). *Coyote & Deer Creek Water Co. Office, near Nevada City*, ca. 1352. Quarter-plate daguerreotype. California History Room, California State Library, Sacramento.

operated with mixed success. Their focus remained on portraiture, but a scathing review of their work in the ambrotype process, in 1857, revealed some shortcomings:

> The Messrs. Johnson Brothers . . . have some fine daguerreotypes. . . . Their ambrotypes are very inferior in quality, and are no doubt made by unskilful [*sic*] hands, and they are free to admit that such Ambrotypes are not wanted by their customers.[109]

For George, as proprietor of one of California's oldest photographic businesses, this review must have stung. By June 1857, the Johnson Brothers partnership was no more. More characteristically, George Johnson won bronze medals for his work at the Mechanics' Institute in San Francisco in both 1857 and 1858. Johnson continued to operate a studio in San Francisco, moving into paper photography by 1860. By 1877, he had left California and returned to New York City.

During the height of Johnson's career, his daguerreotypes were favorably reviewed by the press. As they did with Robert Vance, the reviews extolled Johnson's character, his technical prowess, and his ability to provide a "living-like impress."[110] An "accomplished artist," Johnson showed "a graceful disposition of figures" in his daguerreotypes, capturing the "most advantageous point of view."[111]

Joseph Starkweather

Listed on the passenger list of the steamer *Oregon* from Panama, Joseph Starkweather arrived in San Francisco in February 1852.[112] Already a practicing daguerreotypist, he photographed for several months in 1852–53 in the northern mining region of Nevada and Placer Counties.[113] With no known studio location or newspaper advertisements, Starkweather remains a mysterious character. In 1880, he exhibited ten daguerreotypes titled in the exhibitor listing *"49ers* or *Photographic Views of Old Times in California"* at the Fifteenth Industrial Exhibition of the Mechanics' Institute of San Francisco.[114] Starkweather's daguerreotypes were individually titled and on display in Room 2 of the exhibition.[115] Noting the views as "very interesting reminiscences of Pioneer days," the jurors ultimately awarded them a silver medal.[116]

Starkweather's daguerreotypes are a sophisticated union of composition and subject matter. He was one of the only daguerreotypists to prominently feature black and Chinese miners, whom he daguerreotyped in the area around Auburn Ravine.[117] There, he also recorded women living in the gold field region. In [46], three miners in a streambed use a long tom to wash gold, while a woman brings their midday meal.

Starkweather also daguerreotyped further north. For his view of the ramshackle town of Nevada City, he elevated his vantage point in order to include the stream in the foreground and the jumble of wooden structures (including a church and Empire Hotel) in the middle ground [48]. From this angle, it is difficult to discern any sort of organization to the main street or business district. Making the short trek to the mining area just outside Nevada City, Starkweather daguerreotyped a small mining claim near Sugar Loaf Hill as well as an extensive sluicing operation [47]. In this image, sluices crisscross the composition while miners stand holding shovels and rakes. Since no mining operation was viable without a supply of water, Starkweather daguerreotyped the field office of the short-lived Coyote & Deer Creek Water Company [49]. In 1853, Starkweather returned to Massachusetts, effectively ending his California daguerreian career.[118]

George Dornin

George Dornin arrived in San Francisco in August 1849 at the age of nineteen. He spent little time mining for gold, instead taking a series of jobs in San Francisco. After relocating north to Nevada County in 1852, he opened a mercantile in Nevada City, downstairs from George Kilbourne's daguerreian studio. Unable to compete as a grocer, Dornin resolved to pay "close attention to the manipulation of the daguerreotype process." He continued: "I became proficient in the art, and in the early summer of 1853, disposed of my interest in the [grocery] and removed to Grass Valley. . . . There I put out my sign as daguerreotypist."[119] Establishing a studio known as Dornin's Sky-light Gallery, he was amply prepared to provide residents with daguerreotype portraits. Dornin apparently did venture outside his studio occasionally, as other daguerreotypists had previously done.[120] The *Sacramento Union* published excerpts from the *Grass Valley Telegraph*, including "a large and excellent cut of the village of Grass Valley, taken from a daguerreotype by Dornin."[121]

After a fire ravaged Grass Valley in September 1855, Dornin became an itinerant daguerreotypist, spending "a few months . . . with a blue tent among the mining camps, as a traveling 'artist.'"[122] In January 1856, he relocated to North San Juan.[123] Running his studio out of the back room of a grocery store, Dornin reported that "between hanging wall paper, taking daguerreotypes and painting signs [he] soon acquired enough to purchase . . . a home and operating room."[124]

One half-plate daguerreotype view exists from Dornin's time in North San Juan [50]. In 1855, a flume extension was built by the Middle Yuba Canal Company and "the waters of the Yuba were introduced into the mines at San Juan in 1856, crossing the town in a substantially built flume, or aqueduct, 1200 feet long, at a height of 48 feet, and supplying the diggings at North San Juan."[125] To capture the impressive sight of this engineering feat, Dornin positioned his camera above the aqueduct and daguerreotyped the intricate trestlework as it entered and crossed North San Juan.

Shortly after this view was taken, Dornin left the daguerreian trade to pursue other interests. He continued to photograph, however, and at the

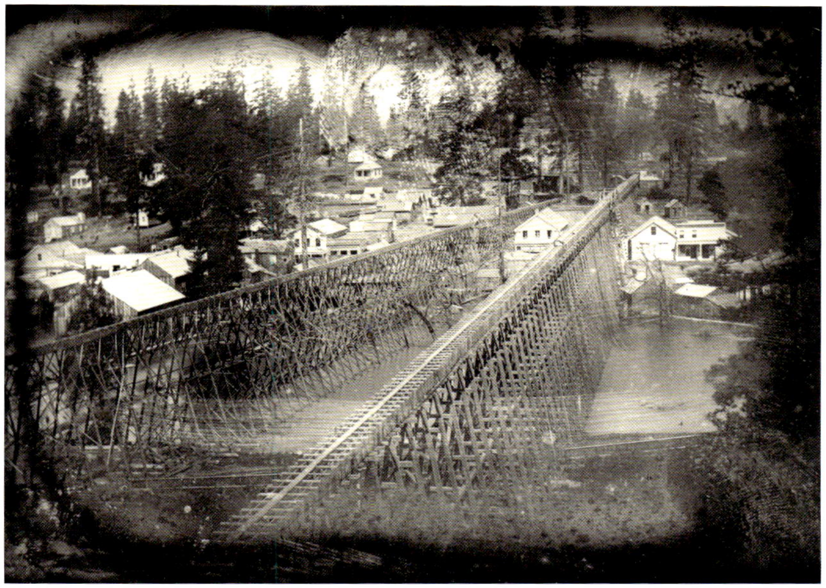

50 **George Dornin**, American (1830–1904). *North San Juan*, 1857. Half-plate daguerreotype. Nevada County Historical Society.

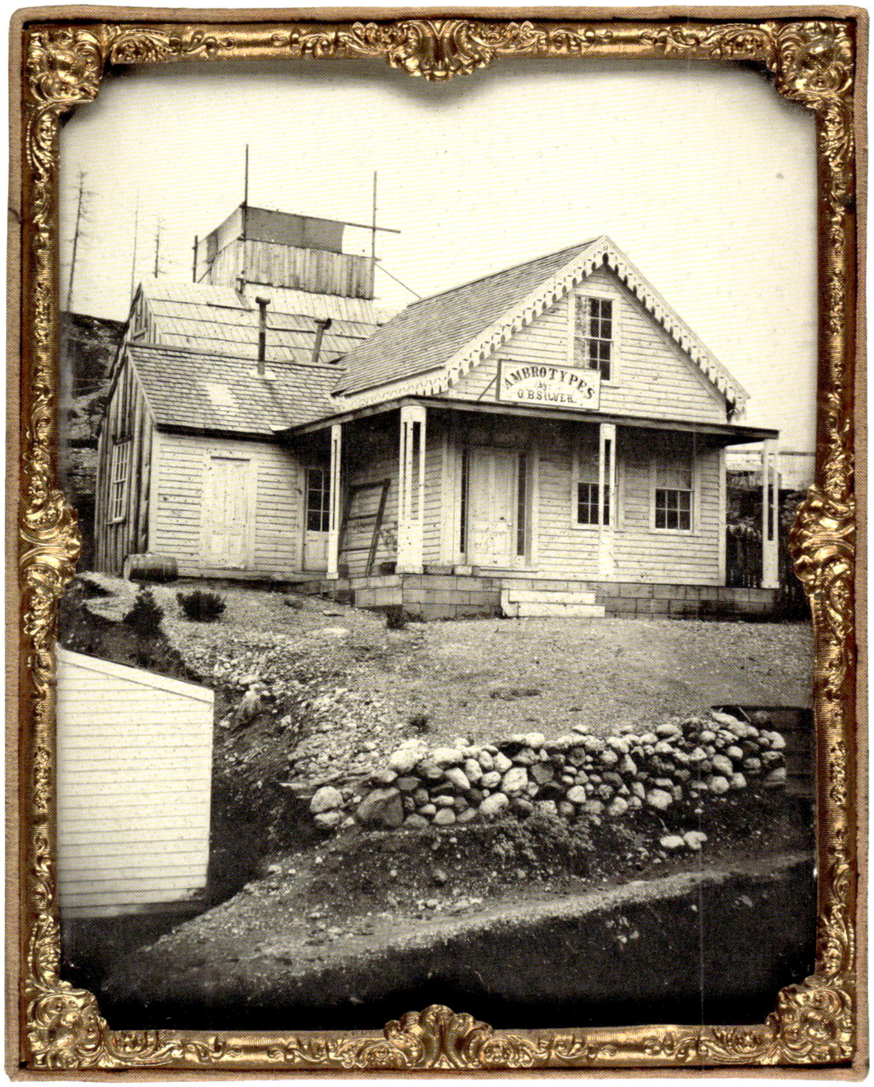

51 **O. B. Silver**, American (active 1860s). *O. B. Silver's Ambrotype Gallery*, ca. 1863. Half-plate ambrotype. California History Room, California State Library, Sacramento.

annual meeting of the Pacific Coast Amateur Photographic Association in 1890, he gave a demonstration of the daguerreotype process. He exhibited "some specimens of his work, nearly forty years old," and many attendees were astonished to find the daguerreotypes were "still perfectly preserved."[126]

O. B. Silver

One of the most elusive photographers of the California gold rush era was O. B. Silver. Very little is known about this gifted ambrotypist, although he produced at least six extant views of the town of Dutch Flat in Placer County.[127] Established in a studio by 1863, Silver may have been operating in this town much earlier.[128] A major hydraulic mining area, Dutch Flat had "an unlimited supply of water from pure mountain springs."[129] While Silver does not appear to have ventured out to the nearby hydraulic mines, he did photograph the town itself.

From the top of a hill, Silver ambrotyped one of the picket-fence-lined residential streets and the undulating hills of the surrounding landscape. Silver's own studio—with wood columns, gingerbread trim, and hand-painted sign—was ambrotyped from street level [51]. Two unusual half-plate ambrotypes depict fenced areas of the countryside, one in summer and one in winter [52, 53]. The ambrotypes were made from an elevated vantage point, the winter view shifted slightly to the right of the summer view. Situated in the mountains, Dutch Flat had a seasonal climate that made "a pleasant place for summer residence. . . . Snow falls at times to considerable depth in the winter and spring months, but the summers are warm and exceedingly pleasant."[130]

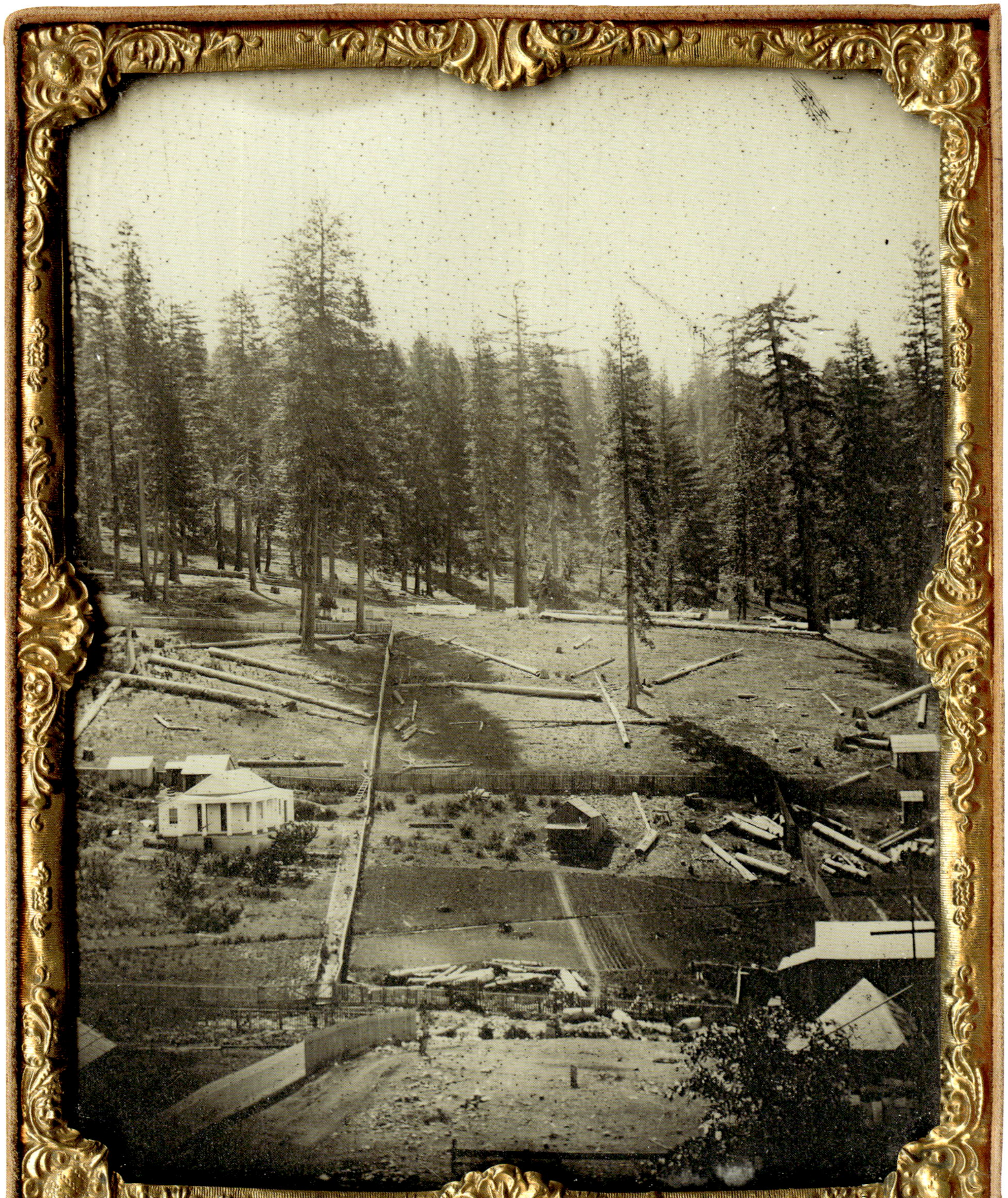

52 **O. B. Silver**, American (active 1860s). *Dutch Flat, summer scene*, ca. 1863. Half-plate ambrotype. California History Room, California State Library, Sacramento.

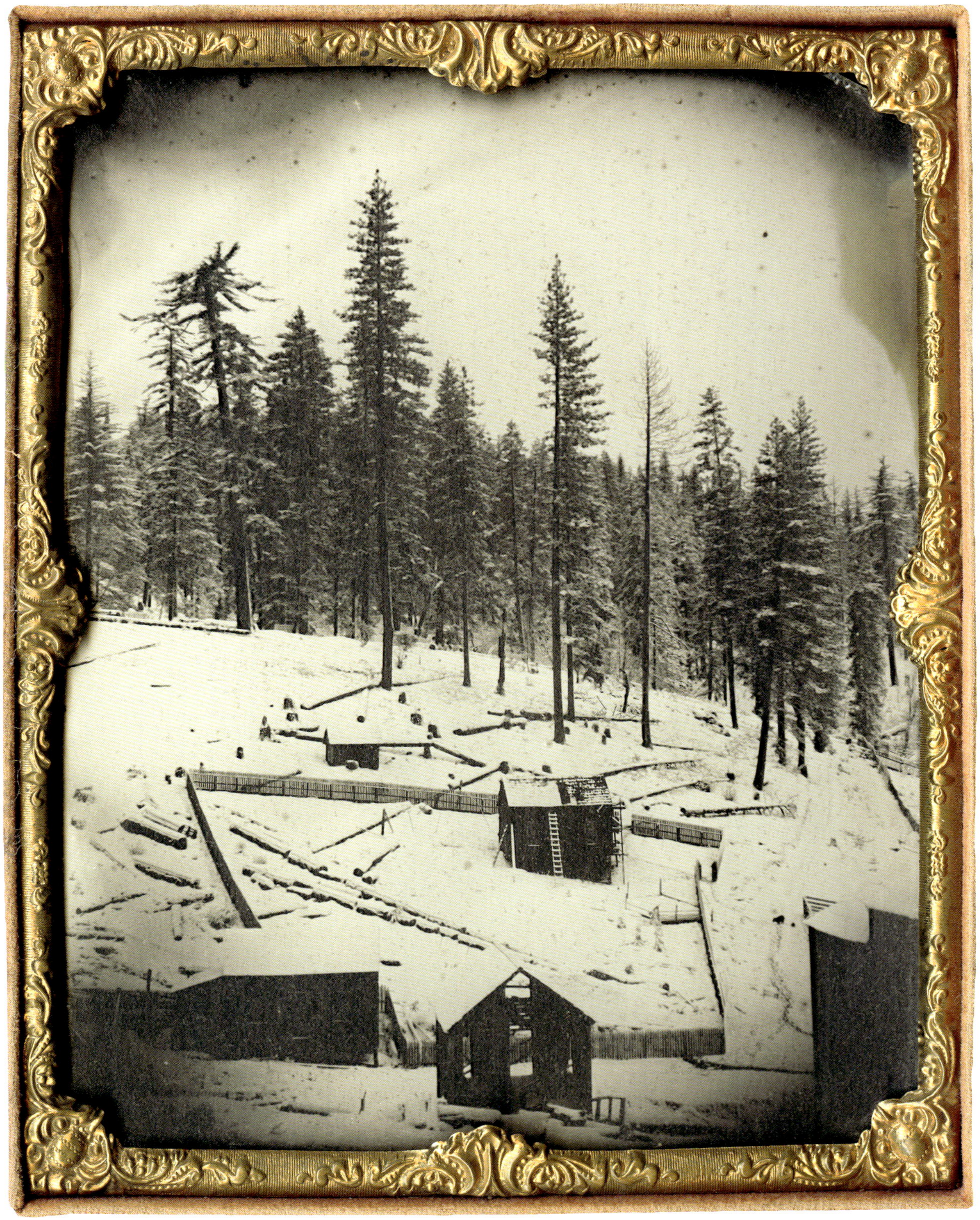

53 **O. B. Silver**, American (active 1860s). *Dutch Flat, winter scene*, ca. 1863. Half-plate ambrotype. California History Room, California State Library, Sacramento.

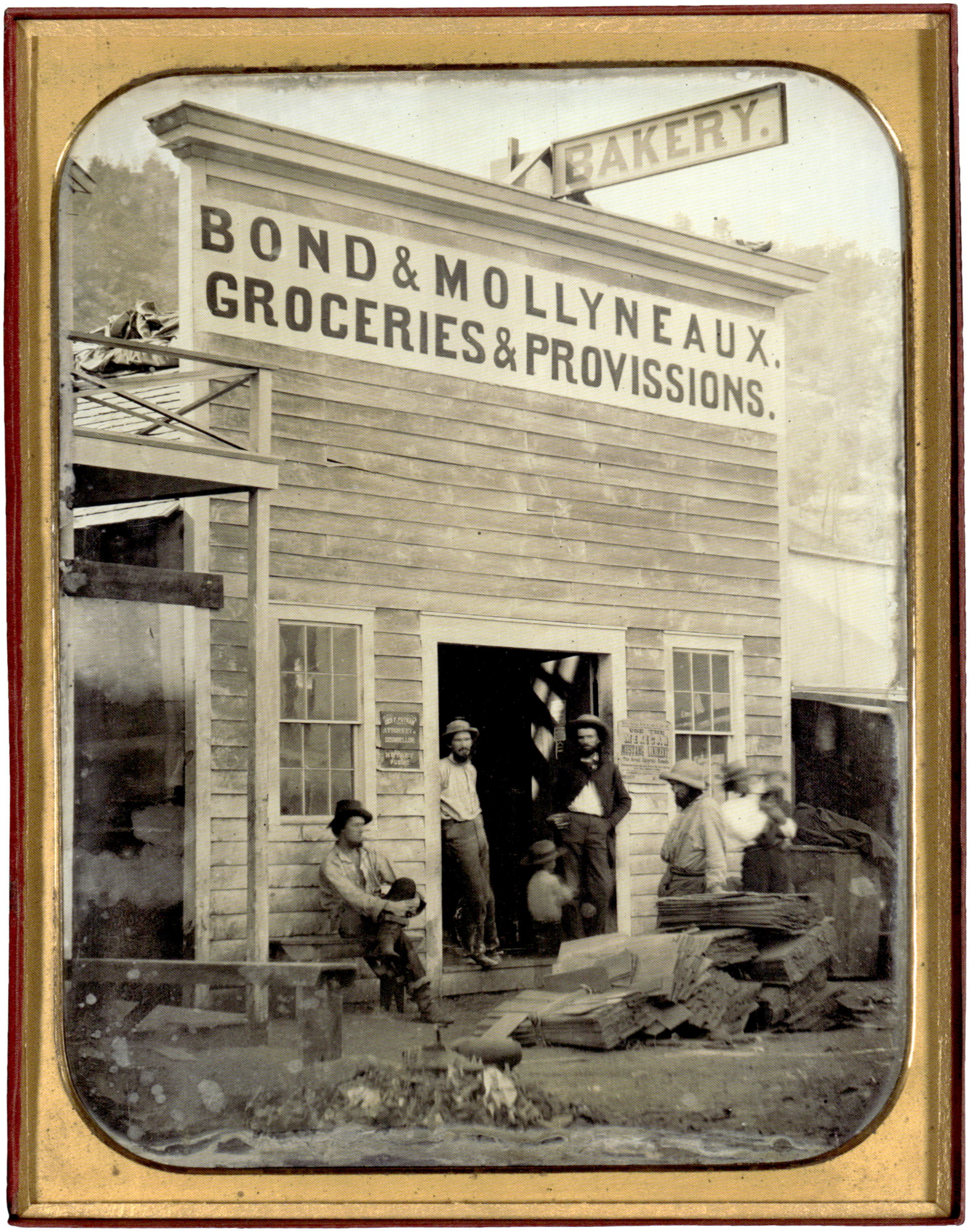

54 **Unknown maker**, American. *Bond & Mollyneaux Groceries and Provisions, Jacksonville, California*, 1852.
Whole-plate daguerreotype.

CHAPTER 4 *"Where but a few weeks since a wilderness was only visible": Life and Work in the Gold Towns*

Upon arrival in California, freshly outfitted miners were especially eager to have their likenesses taken. In most miner portraits, great emphasis was placed on "looking the part"—wearing the clothing and holding the tools associated with gold mining. The California studios reported that on days just before a ship was to return east, "the gallery would be filled with miners in rough suits carrying their mining tools and a pair of pistols in the belt," and that the studio would make "several sittings before [a sitter] left the chair and usually sold them all."[1] It seemed remarkable that

> Californians were so anxious that their friends in civilized countries should see just how they looked in their mining dress, with their terrible revolver, the handle protruding menacingly from the holster, somehow, twisted in front, when sitting for a daguerreotype to send to the States! They were proud of their curling mustaches and flowing beards.[2]

Daguerreotypists like George Johnson encouraged this desire to be photographed in mining attire. Capitalizing on a prime opportunity, Johnson advertised that all interested in "sending their miniatures home, or of being 'preserved' in the *recherche* costume of this latitude to give him a call."[3]

To be daguerreotyped as a miner had larger social and cultural implications. From the beginning, the gold rush was considered an historic adventure of mythic proportions. As historian J. S. Holliday has noted, "1849 will ever be a memorable epoch in the history of our country. Neither the Crusades nor Alexander's expedition to India (all things considered) can equal this emigration to California."[4] Miner portraits were made to confirm and commemorate participation in this once-in-a-lifetime experience. As these portraits were sent to loved ones left behind, even those who had not directly participated could establish a personal connection to this great event.

The personal separations caused by the gold rush were difficult. Because the journey to California involved months of arduous travel, miners were not only separated from, but for a time unreachable by, their loved ones. Once in California, a miner faced the realities of brutal labor, likely disappointment, and fear of the unknown. To fill the void of separation, a daguerreotype portrait preserved the appearance of a missing son, brother, or husband, unchanged through time and distance. Letters and daguerreotypes helped families back home reinforce emotional ties and participate vicariously in the miner's distant experience. The miner pictured here [55] acutely felt the loneliness of separation. Holding a letter from home in one hand and a daguerreotype portrait of a woman and child in the other, he peers forlornly into the camera lens, willing his sadness onto the plate. In this moment, the man cares nothing about the activity of mining, of financial success, or of participation in an historical event. He simply longs for home.

Miner portraits were a part of the larger narrative that was the "gold rush myth." For the first time in American history, it seemed possible through hard work and determination for a "common man and woman, the most ordinary individual, a person without even the money to get to California, the lowly peasant of centuries of European society" to rise to a higher class in society.[5] The gold rush presented the possibility of a new democratic society based on initiative, luck, and quick wealth. The fact that most participants never struck it rich was irrelevant; the tantalizing chance that the incredible was possible perpetuated the myth.

Miner Portraits

In a typical miner portrait, the subject was seated in a chair, in a three-quarter or bust length view. Space around the sitter was often required to accommodate various tools or artifacts; in a few rare examples, full-length views were necessary. Here, for example [56], the full view conveys the subject's disheveled state—the wrinkled and torn clothing and unkempt beard signaling a long and arduous life in the mines. The facial expression of most miners was solemn. However, this miner [57] is seated in an unconventional pose, with his hand placed defiantly on his hip. Legs apart, he looks directly

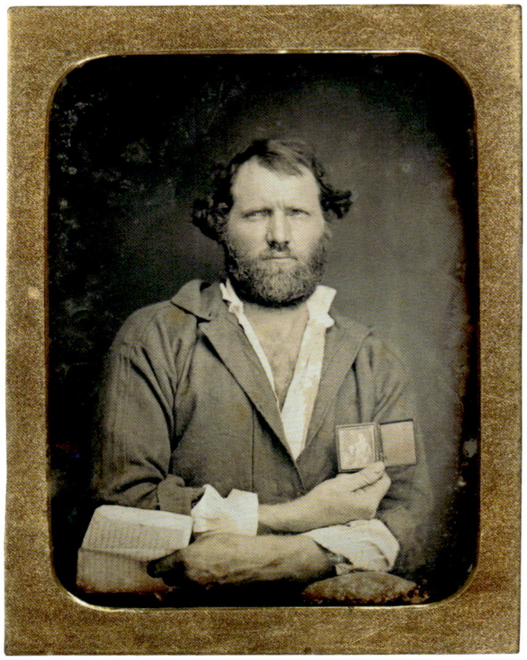

55 Unknown maker, American. *Portrait of a California gold miner with daguerreotype and letter*, ca. 1852. Quarter-plate daguerreotype.

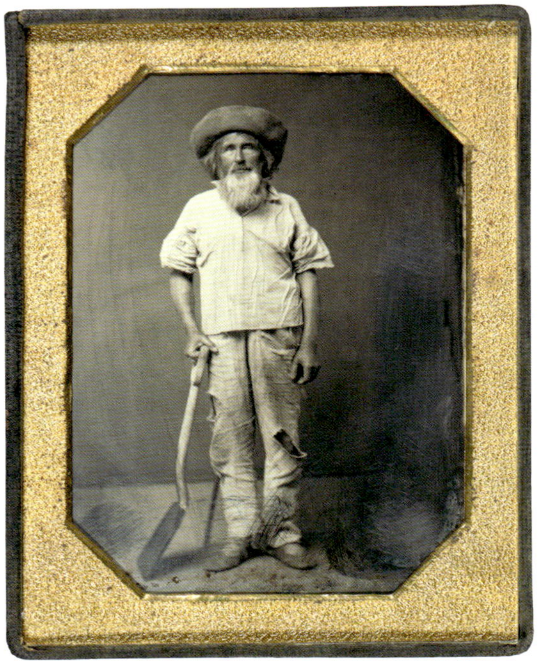

56 Unknown maker, American. *Portrait of Seth Boyden, California gold miner*, ca. 1850. Quarter-plate daguerreotype.

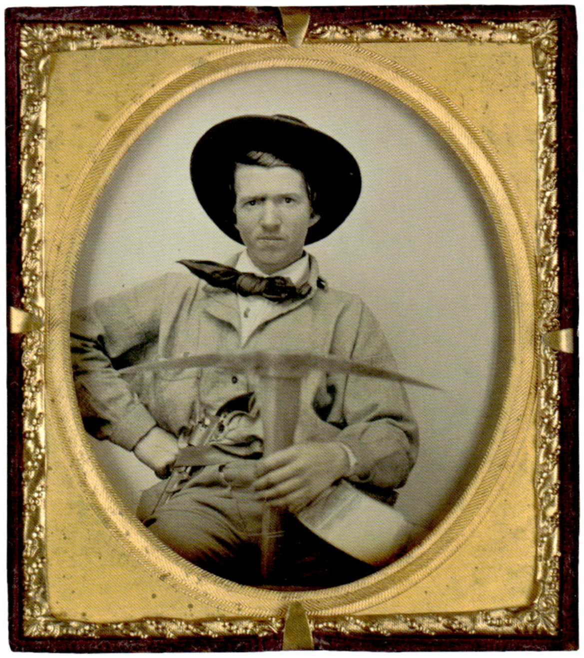

57 Unknown maker, American. *Joseph Sharp, with a pick axe, pan, and gun*, ca. 1855. Sixth-plate ambrotype. Bancroft Library, University of California, Berkeley.

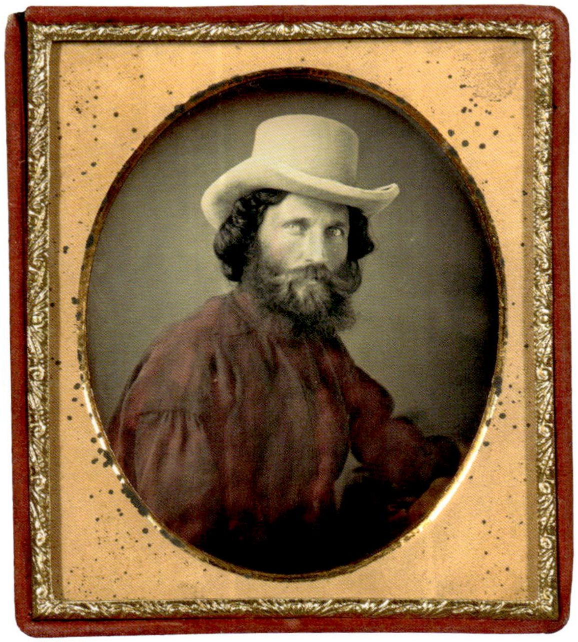

58 Unknown maker, American. *Portrait of George Boyden*, ca. 1852. Sixth-plate daguerreotype.

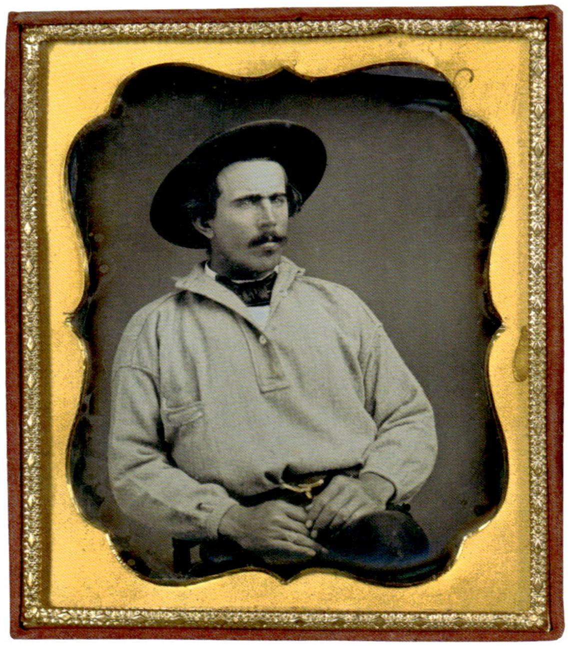

59 Unknown maker, American. *Portrait of a California gold miner*, ca. 1850. Sixth-plate daguerreotype.

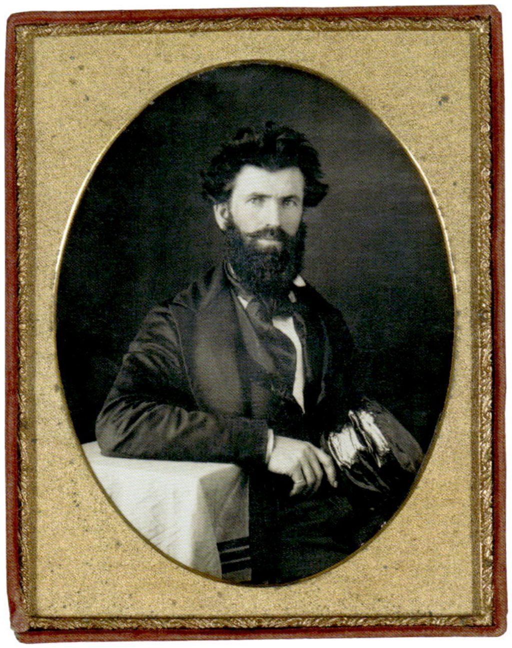

60 Unknown maker, American. *Portrait of a California gold miner*, 1852. Quarter-plate daguerreotype.

at the camera, exuding a spirit of fierceness and determination. With a gun tucked into his belt, he holds an inverted gold pan. A pickaxe is featured prominently in the foreground, thrust so far in front of him that it falls beyond the focus of the lens. The pickaxe, the pan, and the gun allude to the system of belief widely held by white male miners—that hard work would be rewarded with riches, that profits would be staunchly defended, and that the gold rush experience signified the fulfillment of the American dream. On close examination, the objects he holds and the shirt he is wearing appear unused. One suspects that this miner has not been involved in any actual mining activity, at least not in these clothes. The fact that he may not yet have done any real mining work is of little significance, however; the *image* of "the miner" was every bit as important as the reality. The larger message here is one of American determination. Not simply records of fact, such portraits conveyed a sense of ambition and expectation.

Miners were typically daguerreotyped in work shirts, often tinted in the traditional mining color of red [58, 121]. A few men, interested in looking their best, wore nicer shirts with ties [57, 59, 60]. Clothing with holes or patched knees were not the result of a dire financial circumstance but rather an indication of the time miners had spent in the field. Miners of 1849 were humorously described as having "ragged clothes covering lots of gold, and long hair and whiskers, springing from piles of dirt, in faces that perhaps lately adorned the walks of civilized life."[6] Regardless of prior societal standing, participants in the gold rush—assuming they were white males—were all considered equal in the field. The miner in [61] sports a bushy beard and well-worn clothes, suggesting a long stint in the mines. His pan and tools show evidence of use and his hat is mangled and torn. Recognizing the experience of these old-timers, the *Marysville Herald* commented that a miner's "soiled and way-worn garments, red shirt and ancient beard betoken him no greenhorn."[7] In rare instances, miners wore custom patterned shirts emblazoned with hand-stenciled gold mining designs (pick and shovel). This miner [66] wears a particularly spectacular custom-made shirt. To emphasize his mining success, he also wears a gold watch chain and his pocket bulges with the spoils of his mining efforts.

Most men proudly wore beards—sometimes quite unruly and long—indicating a dedication to work (they could not be bothered to shave) [63]. For some, the choice was predetermined; these men were too young to grow whiskers [64]. The essential miner's hat, also known as a wideawake, was meant to be worn straight on the head to protect from the heat and glare of the sun.[8] In the comfort of the studio, however, miners often tilted their hats back at a rakish angle to reveal their entire face [57, 59]. Most miners wore their hats in their portraits; those that did not often set them on a nearby table. For those choosing not to wear a hat, their wild, uncontrolled hair became the focal point of the composition [65]. The two-piece metal belt buckle [62] was another distinctive accessory.[9] The disk, which slid into the

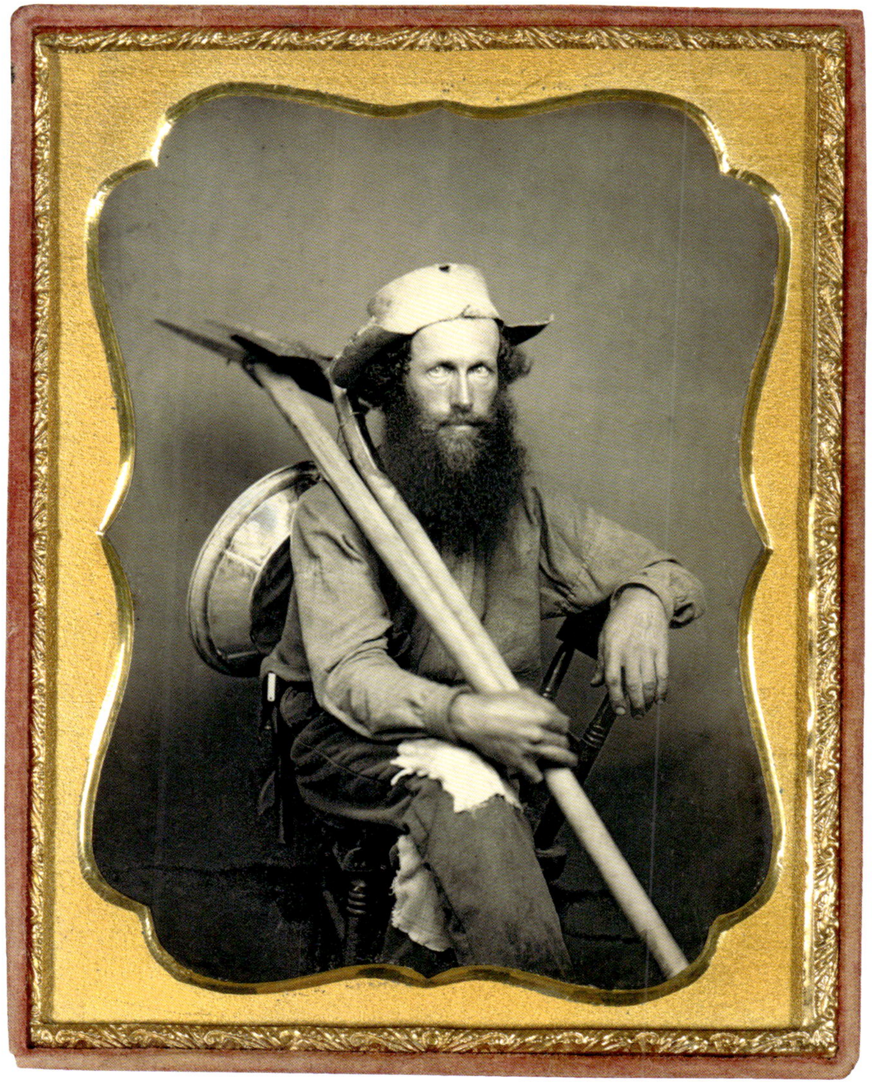

61 **Unknown maker**, American. *Portrait of a California gold miner with tools*, ca. 1850. Quarter-plate daguerreotype.

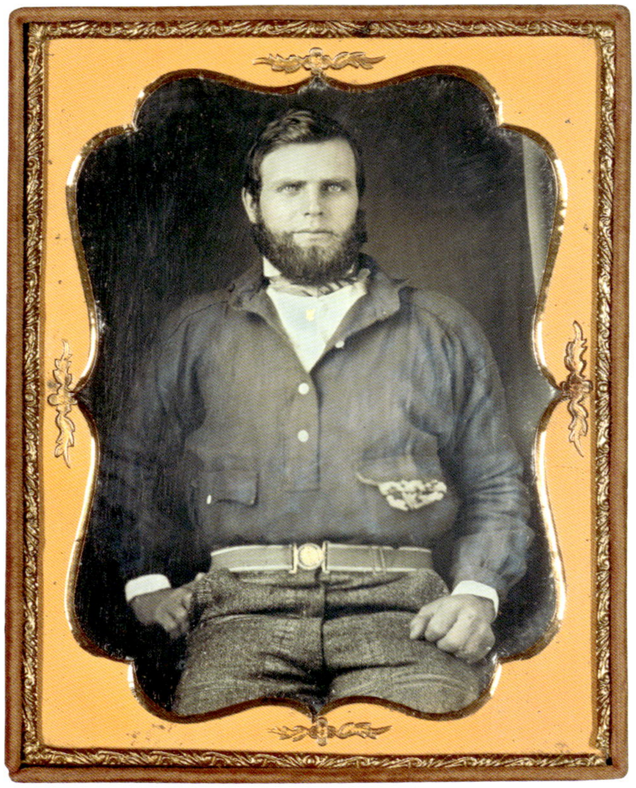

62 **Unknown maker**, American. *Portrait of miner with belt buckle*, ca. 1855. Sixth-plate daguerreotype. The Art Institute of Chicago, The W. Bruce and Delaney H. Lundberg Collection, restricted gift of The Phillip Leonian and Edith Rosenbaum Leonian Charitable Trust.

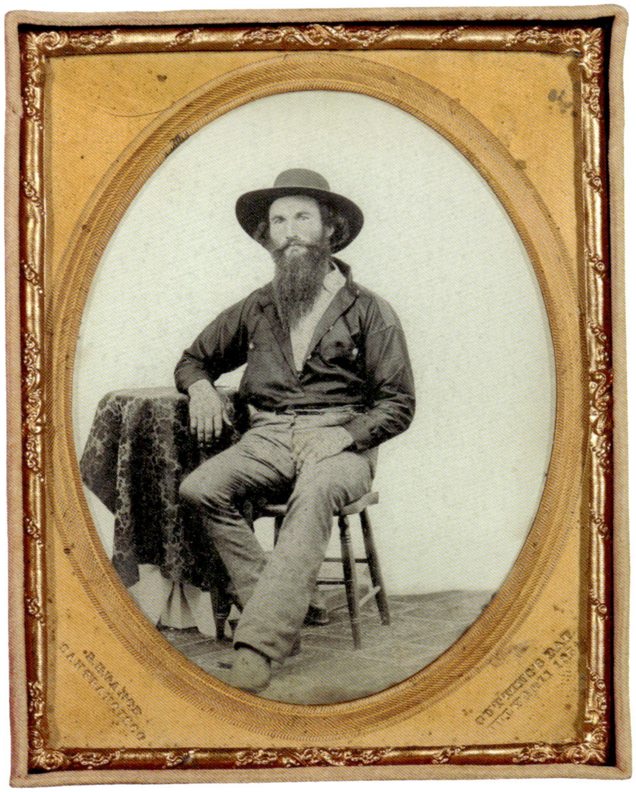

63 **Robert H. Vance**, American (1825–1876). *Portrait of a California gold miner*, ca. 1854. Quarter-plate ambrotype.

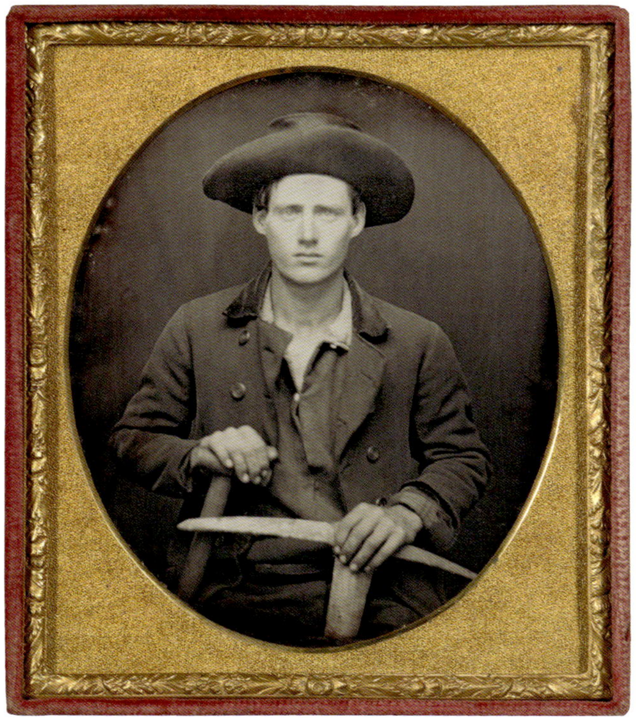

64 **Unknown maker**, American. *Portrait of a California gold miner with pick and shovel*, ca. 1850. Sixth-plate daguerreotype.

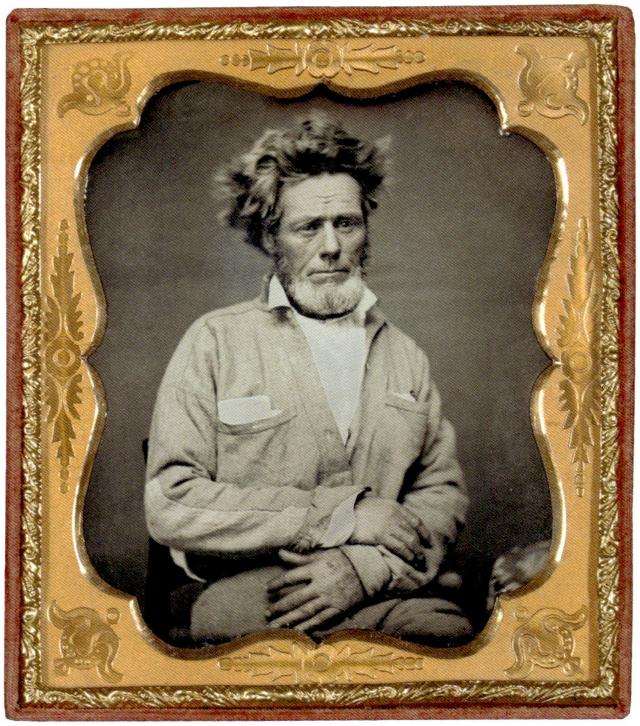

65 **Unknown maker**, American. *Portrait of California gold miner with tousled hair*, ca. 1850–55. Sixth-plate daguerreotype. The Art Institute of Chicago, The W. Bruce and Delaney H. Lundberg Collection, restricted gift of The Phillip Leonian and Edith Rosenbaum Leonian Charitable Trust.

tongue to provide a secure clasp, was often stamped with a design—an eagle, a ship, or another symbol meaningful to the wearer.

The most common tools pictured in miner portraits were the pan, the pickaxe, and the shovel. The miner here [67] stands in order to showcase his tools, pickaxe in one hand and shovel in the other. In other cases [68], the pickaxe was held across the lap. It could be challenging to hold multiple tools, but these portraits could appear effortlessly done [61]. These tools stood as emblems for the idea of the "lone miner" with individual determinism and the willingness to work, the traits necessary to become a wealthy man.

Of course, any suggestion of a romantic, easygoing life was greatly at odds with reality. Gold was easily gathered only in the earliest years of the rush, before most Americans arrived. More typically, mining was back-breaking work that barely covered the cost of necessities. Huge windfalls were few and far between. As a result, individual efforts inevitably gave way to organized, corporate mining operations. Nevertheless, the ideal of the lone, successful miner persisted well beyond his actual existence.

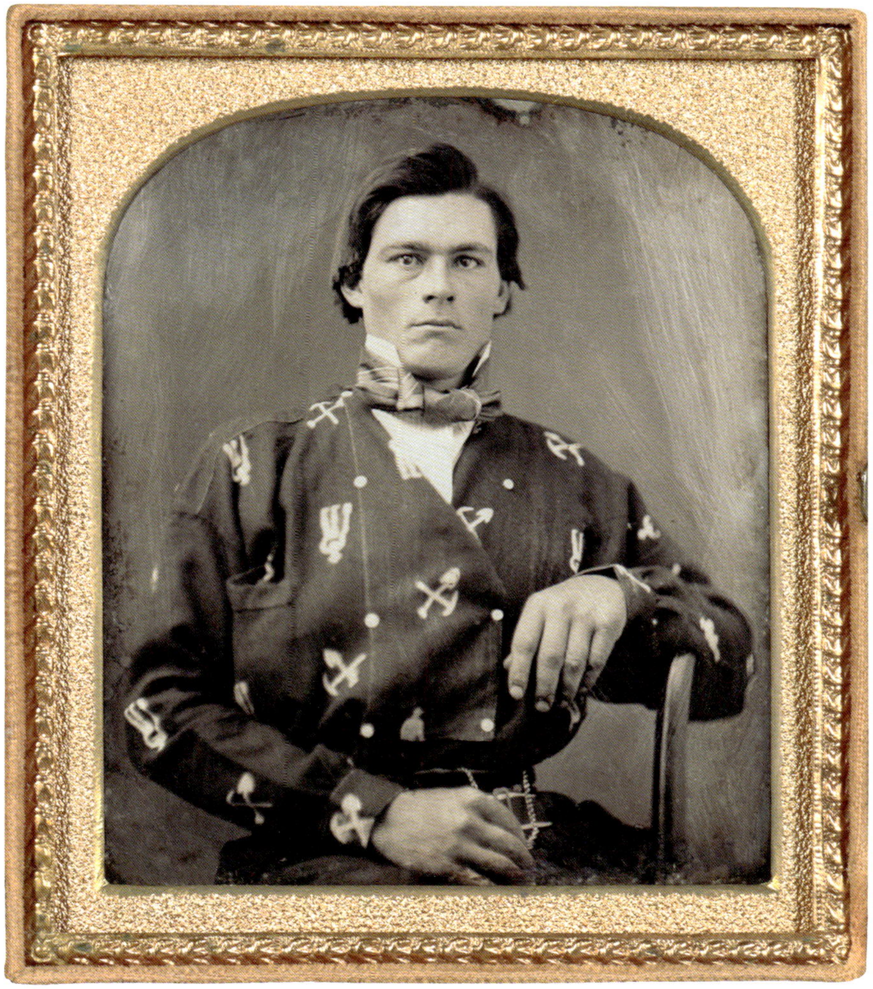

66 **Unknown maker**, American. *Portrait of Lyman Alvinson Rundell in mining-themed shirt*, ca. 1855 Sixth-plate daguerreotype.

Miners wearing pistols and large knives in daguerreotype portraits referenced the image of lawlessness in 1850s California. For many miners, part of the lure of the quest for gold was participation in the exciting adventure, including outfoxing fellow miners, thwarting cheats and robbers, and adapting to unpredictable weather conditions. Although danger was real, many used guns only for hunting and knives only for digging in crevices for particles of gold.

Some lucky miners were daguerreotyped with gold nuggets, gold dust, or gold jewelry. These objects were hand-gilded directly on the daguerreotype surface, giving an otherwise monochromatic plate an unexpected sparkle. Miners also proudly displayed stickpins, watch chains, and rings with gold [69]. Bags of gold dust [70, 71], instantly recognizable by all Californians, were balanced on studio pedestals or stuffed conspicuously in bulging shirt pockets. (This bag was sometimes referred to as "poke.") One young miner was daguerreotyped with his arm protectively cradling a large chunk of gold-veined quartz [72]. Upturned mining pans filled with gold [73, 74] directly connected the earliest gold mining technology with the hoped-for result. These gold-laden portraits signified the ultimate success, in terms that every viewer understood.

Gold Towns

In 1845, the Western explorer and later politician William Gilpin proclaimed, "The untransacted destiny of the American people is to subdue the continent . . . to rush over this vast field to the Pacific Ocean, to confirm the destiny of the human race."[10] Because of its location at the far edge of the continent, the state of California served as a potent symbol of cultural conquest. The establishment of gold towns throughout the mining region helped fulfill the

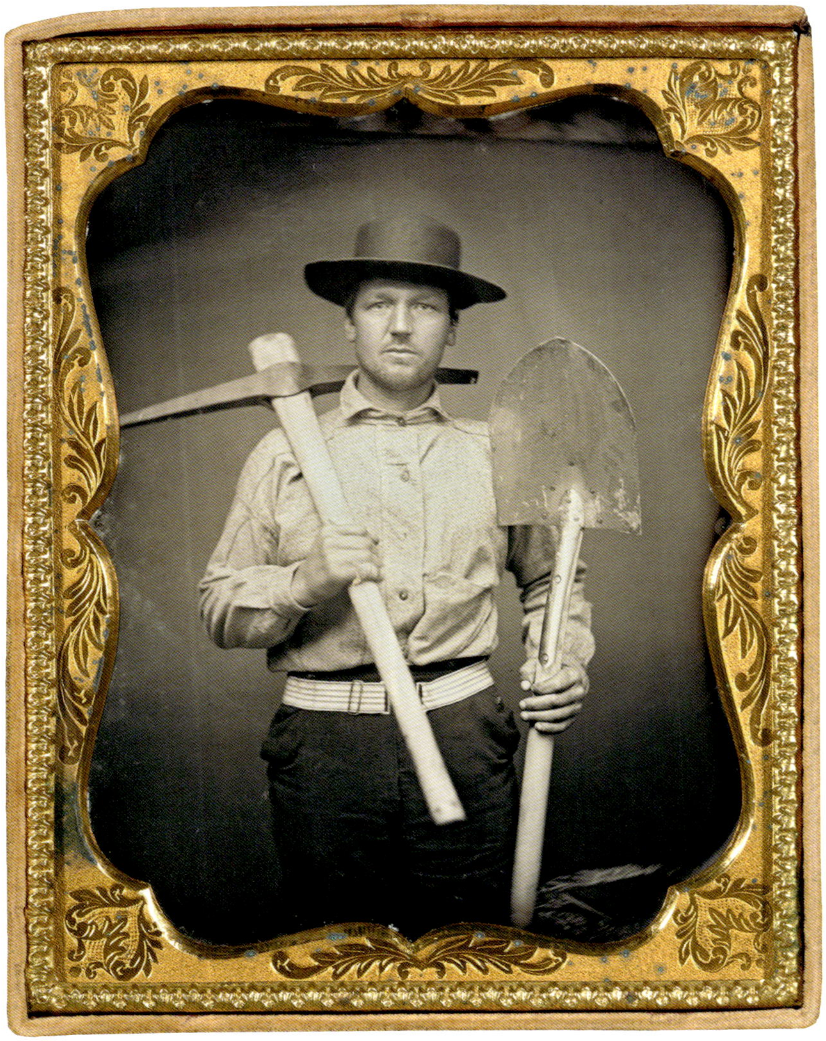

67 **Unknown maker**, American. *Portrait of a California gold miner with pick and shovel,* ca. 1855. Quarter-plate daguerreotype.

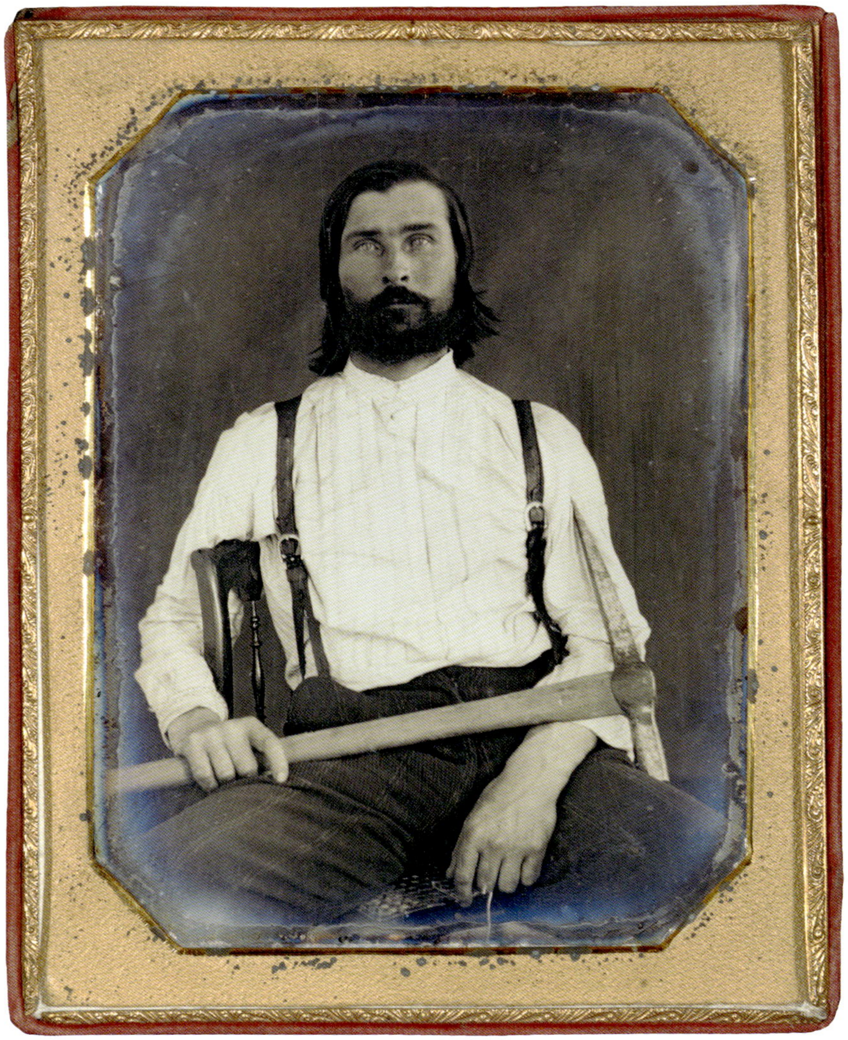

68 **Unknown maker**, American. *Miner holding pickaxe,* ca. 1855. Half-plate daguerreotype. The Art Institute of Chicago, The W. Bruce and Delaney H. Lundberg Collection, restricted gift of The Phillip Leonian and Edith Rosenbaum Leonian Charitable Trust.

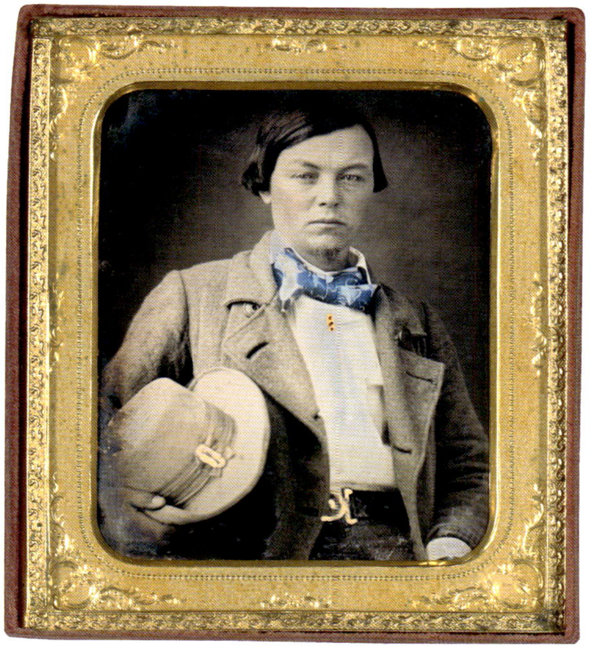

69 **George H. Johnson**, American (1823–ca. 1880s). *Portrait of miner*, ca. 1850. Sixth-plate daguerreotype. The Art Institute of Chicago, The W. Bruce and Delaney H. Lundberg Collection, restricted gift of The Phillip Leonian and Edith Rosenbaum Leonian Charitable Trust.

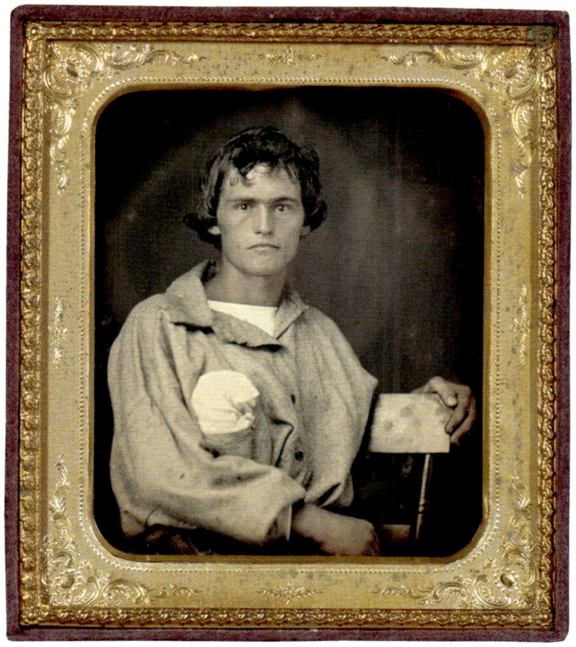

70 **Unknown maker**, American. *Portrait of a California gold miner with poke in pocket*, ca. 1854. Sixth-plate daguerreotype.

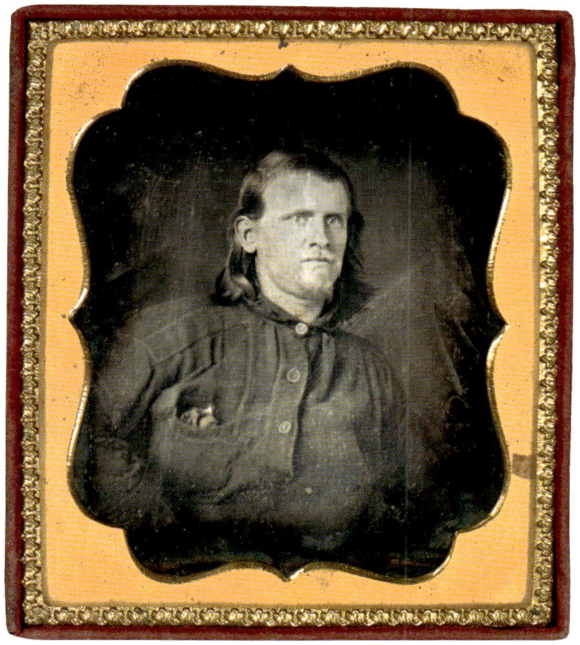

71 **Unknown maker**, American. *Portrait of miner with poke in pocket*, ca. 1850–55. Sixth-plate daguerreotype. Collection of Bruce Lundberg.

goals of Manifest Destiny, the nation's seemingly divine right to appropriate and to exploit. The editors of the *Alta California* newspaper commended the local populations for doing their part in this great national effort:

> We are glad to hear of the prosperity of our inland towns. There can be no surer evidence of the rapid development of the resources of our State, than the building up of towns in different parts of the country. It will . . . lay the foundation of flourishing colonies, which, by the time the mines are entirely exhausted, will be amply able to sustain themselves without the assistance now requisite and supplied by the gold country.[11]

Gold mining towns were an integral part of the cycle of progress outlined in Frederick Jackson Turner's famous paper, "The Significance of the Frontier in American History." Moving in an unrelenting arc from wilderness to civilization, Turner defined urban development as an inevitable and unstoppable series of steps. Samuel Colville, in his preface to an early San Francisco directory, delineated these stages in the development of California:

> To see dark forests open to the sunlight . . . to see the clipper supersede the canoe . . . to mark the resolute landing of hale, adventurous, thinking, civilized men on shores hitherto trod only by the listless aborigine . . . to hear the war whoop give way to the saw, hammer, and ribbon-stripping plane, and note the cabin follow the original hut, the handsome dwelling succeed the squalid hearth-fire of the native; to observe how habitations advance upon the hill sides and out upon the ocean's verge; lumber, brick and stone supplanting sticks, bark and brush . . . the frowning face of nature changed by the wooing touch of human industry and intellect into a picture which greets the visitor with a smile and lives in the minds of the absent a pleasant memory.[12]

In California, therefore, the sight of a debris-filled, muddy street, or a few rickety structures was seen to symbolize man's "triumph" over the wilderness, and a promise of civilization to come. In accepting the logic of patriotic "divine ordination," miners moved into previously unsettled areas throughout the gold region, claiming territory in a quest for gold and aggressively pushing the American empire westward.

Historian Robert Phelps has described the urban growth of gold rush California as a rank-order system that developed as "an expanding population's increasing distance from initial points of convergence generat[ing] the establishment of additional central places."[13] At the top of this system was the metropolis of San Francisco, the point of entry for most traveling to the gold region, and the place where virtually any item available in an eastern port city could be purchased. After San Francisco, the cities of Marysville, Stockton, and Sacramento served as commercial and transport centers for smaller towns farther away.[14] Marysville and Stockton supplied towns in the northern and southern mining districts, respectively. Sacramento was especially significant for its proximity to the central mining region and as a common point of entry to both the northern and southern regions. Located

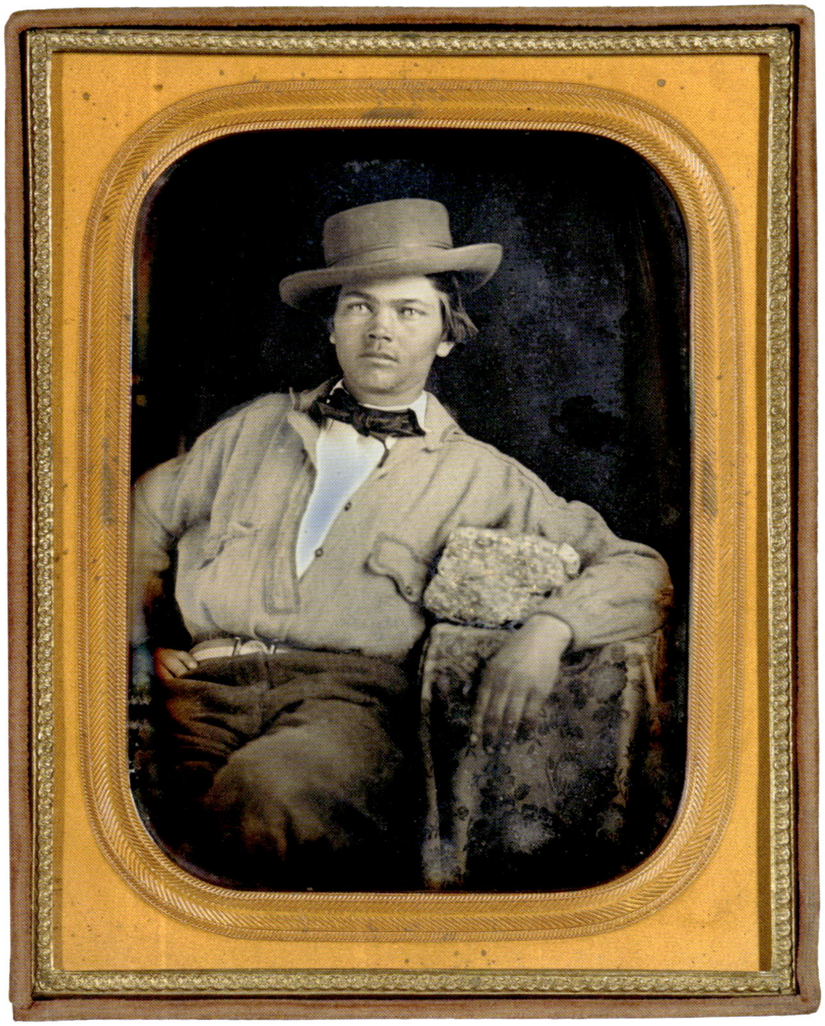

72 **James M. Ford**, American (1827–1887). *California gold miner with gold ore*, ca. 1855. Quarter-plate daguerreotype.

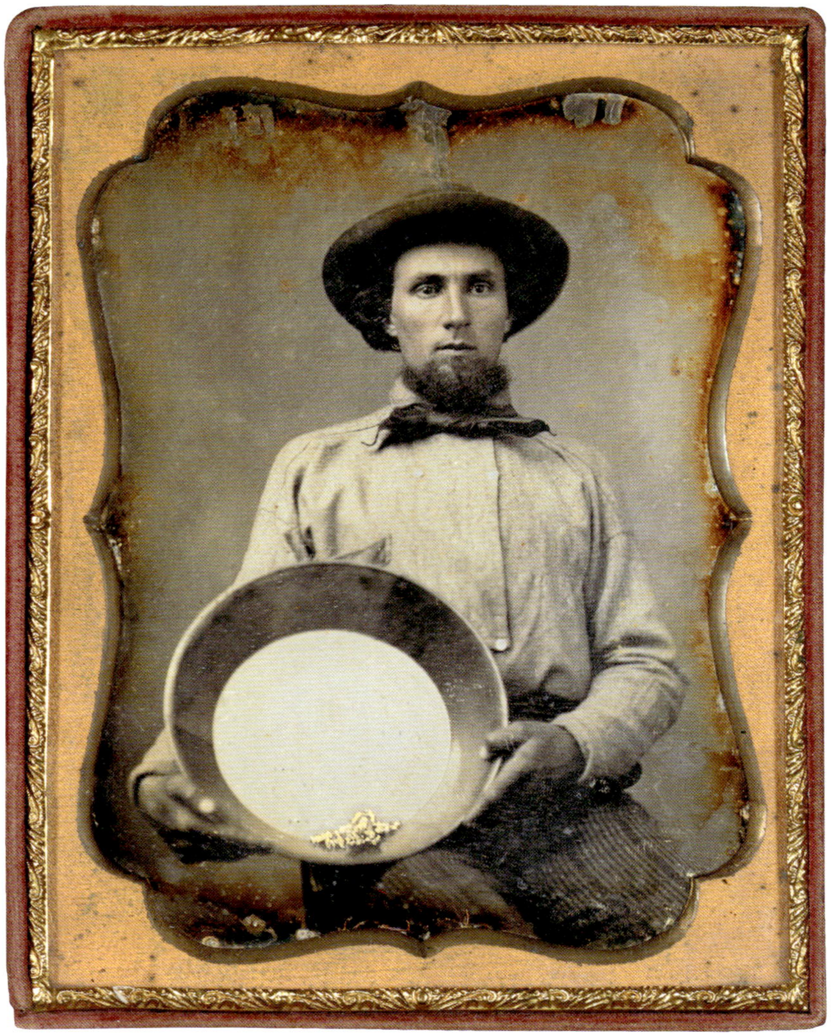

73 **Unknown maker**, American. *Miner with pan of gold*, ca. 1852. Quarter-plate daguerreotype. The Art Institute of Chicago, The W. Bruce and Delaney H. Lundberg Collection, restricted gift of The Phillip Leonian and Edith Rosenbaum Leonian Charitable Trust.

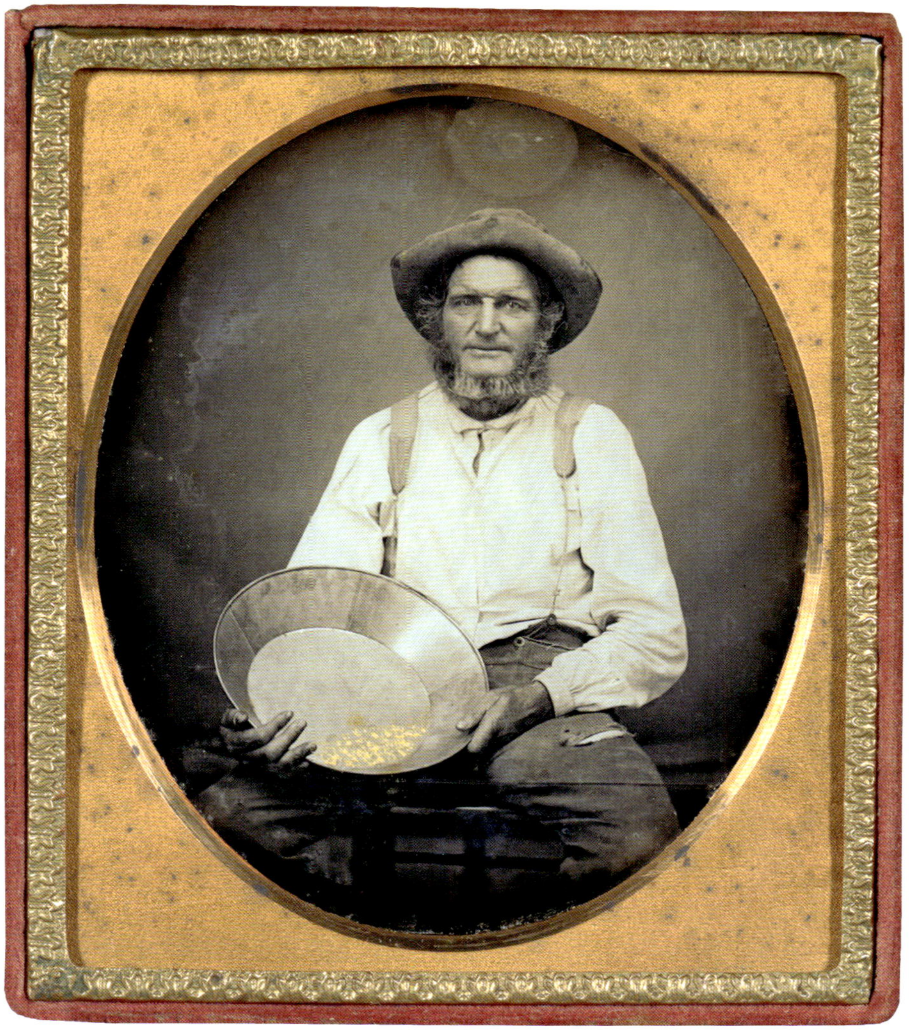

74 **Unknown maker**, American. *Portrait of a California miner with pan of gold*, ca. 1852. Sixth-plate daguerreotype.

throughout the mining regions, gold rush towns served the immediate needs of those living nearby. The miners' environs, the last of the rank-order system, were almost exclusively residential. When available, stores were typically primitive, small, and specialized.

Following an historical geographical approach, Randall Rohe noted that mining towns, which emphasized commercial before residential development, evolved differently from towns in the eastern United States. With occupational demographics decidedly skewed toward mining (in 1850 in Nevada City, eight out of ten residents were miners; in Grass Valley, seven out of ten), a large segment of the population had need for specific goods and services.[15] To meet these demands, merchants appeared almost simultaneously with the miners. Towns took shape around the commercial hubs, sometimes consisting of little more than a tightly constructed business district on a single street. Typically serving large unincorporated mining areas, trade in these centers "assumed an importance all out of proportion with their size."[16] In 1850, the town of Nevada City had one merchant to every nine miners; Grass Valley had one to every four.[17]

Because of the large influx of miners and merchants, towns grew quickly and haphazardly with little thought to organized development. Wooden sidewalks and ungraded dirt streets wound up slopes along existing foot and cattle paths. Perplexed by the layout of Mokelumne Hill, one resident described "the city . . . not only built on a hill but in the ravines also. The streets run in all directions, horizontally, perpendicularly and circularly. The buildings, with a few exceptions, are of a very inferior order indeed, being constructed chiefly of canvas."[18] Similarly, the appearance of Nevada City spurred this disgusted observation:

> I must give you description of Nevada City, as it is called, for there is a great many such cities in California. The town has actually got a street in it (though to be sure it is crocked and not very safe for the ox carts which occasionally pass through it) . . . The houses are either made of canvas or of cedar boards split out instead of sawed and put on rough in the same way clapboards are at home. There are five round tents as large almost as a circus tent occupied entirely as gambling shops and nine out of every ten doors on the street open the way to a liquor bar. There are several tents, camps, and cabins scattered around in the woods. Such is the city of Nevada.[19]

For settlements such as these, some residents alleged, "the fire was a benefit to the town, for better buildings and straighter streets resulted from it."[20] As a result of both fire and population growth, successful mining towns evolved quickly. One miner's repeat visit to Placerville was met with wonder at the speedy transformation:

> Where but a few weeks since a wilderness was only visible, now can be seen the stars and stripes floating in the breeze over the sumptuous gambling saloons, commodious stores, and hotels thronged with customers.[21]

Although canvas was initially a common building material, most mining areas had some access to timber from nearby forests. Log buildings were

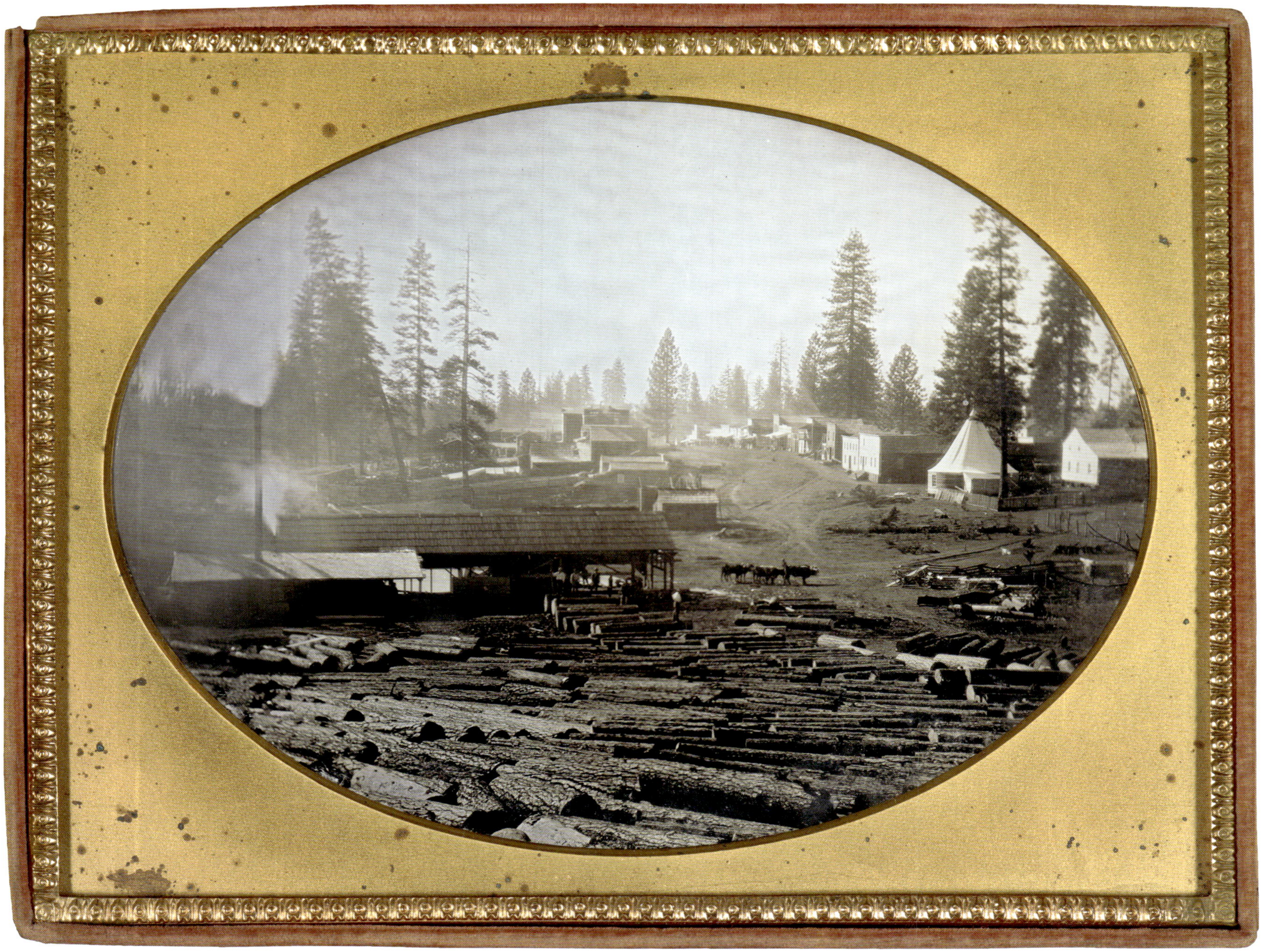

75 Unknown maker, American. *Georgetown, California,* ca. 1850–54.
Half-plate daguerreotype.

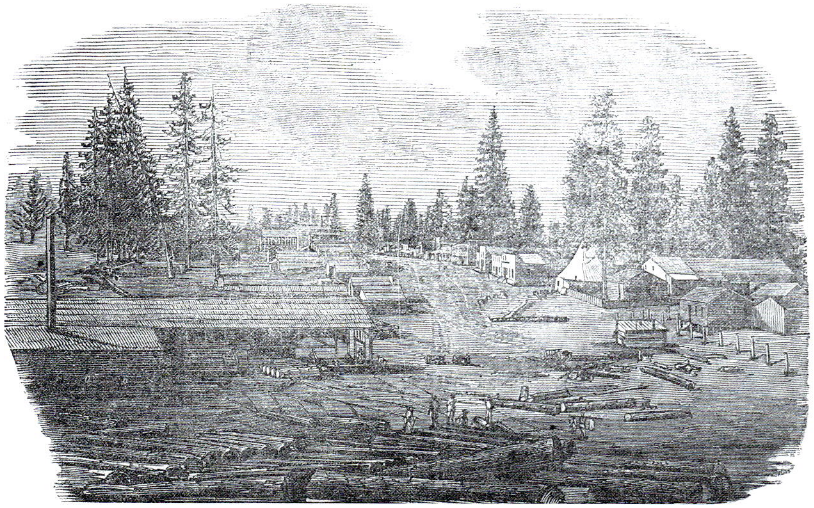

FIG. 8 *View of Georgetown*, from *The Pictorial Union* (April 1854).

erected and later, in many towns, "wooden false fronts distinguished the log structures that served as business houses."[22] Prior to 1850, with little developed industry in California, most lumber had to be imported at great cost. The scarcity of building materials was a real concern. Established sawmills, like Sutter's Mill in Coloma, operated at full capacity, but with buildings "going up about as fast as the mill can saw out the lumber," it was difficult to keep up with the demand.[23] Recognizing an opportunity for profit, savvy entrepreneurs built sawmills powered by steam and water in the more heavily forested areas of the gold region [75]. These ventures were highly lucrative. By 1849, in cities like Sacramento, "carpenters are in demand. . . . Lumber and building materials are much wanted and bring high prices."[24]

To alleviate the shortage of lumber, some California merchants imported prefabricated housing. Architectural historian Charles Peterson claimed that by fall 1849, "an estimated five thousand houses had been sent out or were under contract" from New York City alone, one of the country's largest suppliers of prefabricated housing.[25] Most of these structures were wooden, but iron houses were also shipped.[26] As historian Harold Kirker has observed, these "imported New England houses were significant in extending American building standards to the most isolated areas of the state."[27]

As soon as lap siding was available, log buildings were completely covered, expanded, or replaced with frame structures, usually within the first year or two of a town's founding. Early stores were often a single story, while hotels were two-story structures with large, wide balconies. Continued expansion and frequent destruction by fires left many gold towns with "examples of each stage and a variety of architectural styles side-by-side."[28] Overlooking canvas-covered stores and other detritus, newly arrived visitors recognized similarities to towns they had left behind. Relieving the fear of the unknown, the mere existence of these new towns offered reassurance of California's civility.[29]

As miners and merchants rushed into the gold regions, daguerreotypists followed close behind. Indeed, by 1852, fearing that too many daguerreotypists were headed to California, the editors of the *Daguerreian Journal* cautioned, "Several daguerreotypists of this city [New York] have left for California. We wish them success in the land of gold, and for fear that too many may go there, we would say to all, go prepared to work in the mines."[30] This fear was unfounded, and most skilled practitioners found a ready market of potential customers.

In and around the gold towns, daguerreotypists typically focused on individual businesses, main streets, merchant and miner residences, and overviews. Many daguerreotype images present human settlement and commerce within a hospitable natural setting, furthering the tenets of Manifest Destiny. Images not only convey the facts of geography, but also further the ideas of growth, prosperity, and the relentless march of civilization. Nature appears at once accommodating and generous.

When making town views, daguerreotypists usually corrected the process's inherent image reversal. While this reversal was easily accepted in portraiture (conforming, as it does, to our self-image in a mirror), it was much more objectionable for signs on storefronts. Daguerreian suppliers provided simple devices—small mirrors or prisms, placed in front of the camera lens—to create correct, right-reading images. As writer and editor Samuel Humphrey asserted, "Views are always most desirable when taken in right position; that is, without being reversed in the camera."[31] While these devices sometimes required slightly longer exposure times, they were routinely used for views of gold mining towns.[32]

Miners' Environs

The population of most gold rush towns was split between the town proper—businesses and merchant residences—and the outlying areas where miners worked and lived. Ralph Mann's study of the mining towns of Grass Valley and Nevada City revealed that "a sharp obvious dichotomy existed between the commercial area identified with the name, and its environs." The town had a clearly defined business district; beyond that were "scatterings of cabins and small trading posts located by whim or for convenience to claims."[33]

Located near claims, miner housing included canvas tents, semipermanent log cabins, and barracks. The variety of these accommodations reflected the length of stay, materials available, and the time and labor needed for construction. Some miners lived in temporary housing in the summer months but retired to more permanent cabins for the winter. The cheapest, quickest, and most portable structure was the canvas tent. Tents

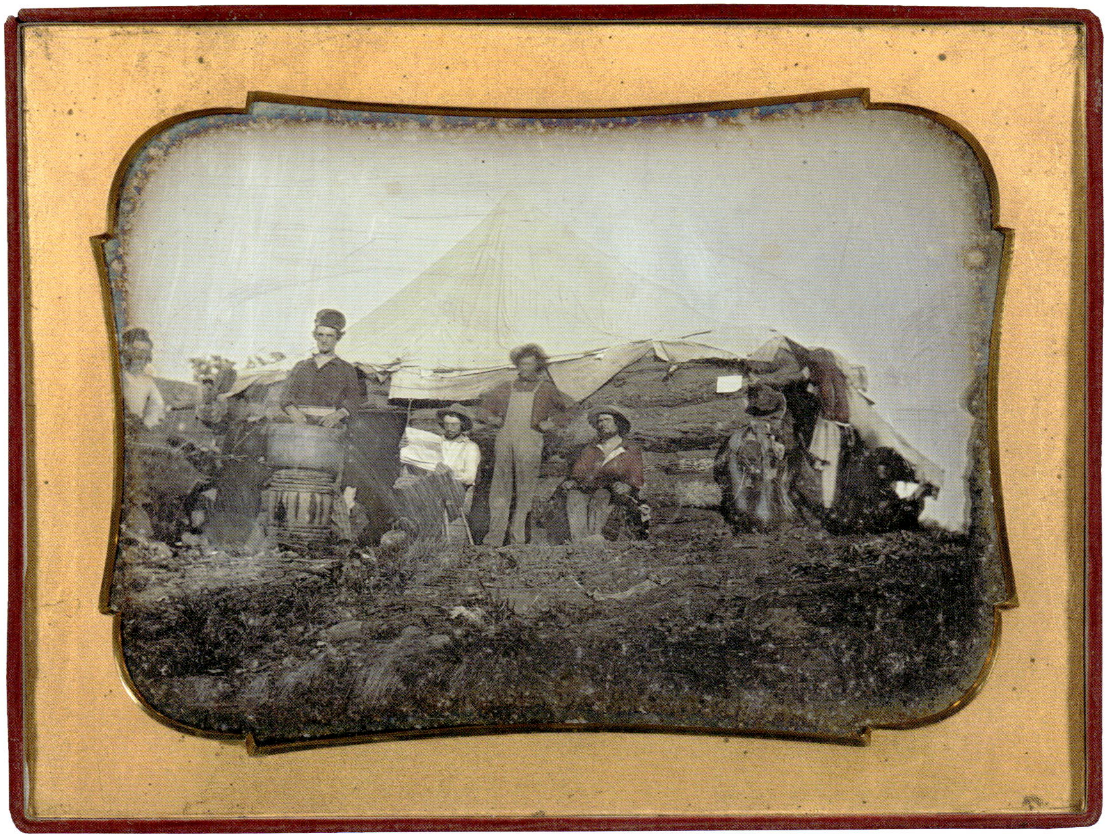

76 **Unknown maker**, American. *California gold miners in camp*, ca. 1853. Half-plate daguerreotype.

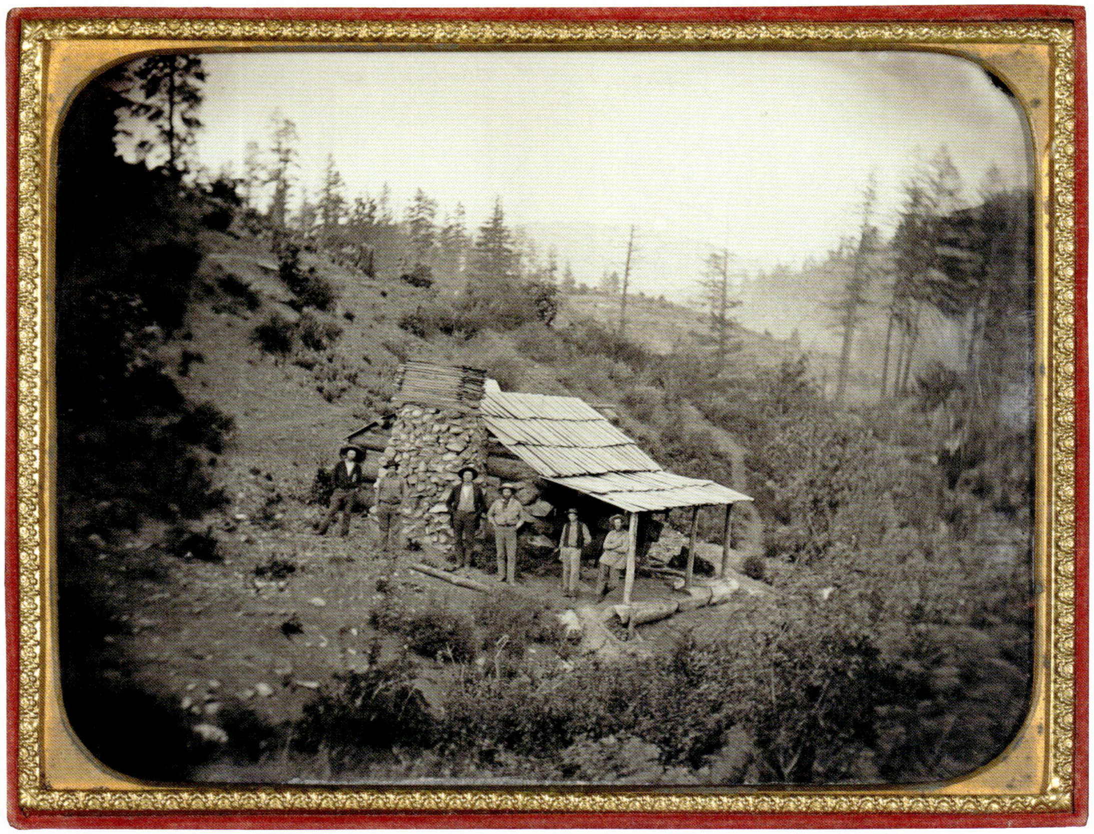

77 **Unknown maker**, American. *Six miners in front of their log cabin*, ca. 1854–56. Half-plate ambrotype. The Art Institute of Chicago, The W. Bruce and Delaney H. Lundberg Collection, restricted gift of The Phillip Leonian and Edith Rosenbaum Leonian Charitable Trust.

were considered temporary, erected while waiting for confirmation of a successful strike or to house new arrivals when boardinghouse rooms were unavailable. Larger tents were reinforced with wood framing to improve stability and longevity.

Many of the structures built by the miners were tenuous at best. One miner described typically haphazard residences near Jacksonville:

> As in every other settlement, the houses are of every possible variety, according to the taste or means of the miner. Most of these, even in winter, are tents. Some throw up logs a few feet high, filling up with clay between the logs. The tent is then stretched above, forming a roof. . . . Those who have more regard to their own comfort or health, erect log or stone houses, covering them with thatch or shingles. . . . Many only spread a piece of canvas, or a blanket, over some stakes above them, while not a few make holes in the ground, where they burrow like foxes.[34]

Architectural historian Harold Kirker puts it plainly: "This is obviously not architecture; it is hardly even housing."[35] But these flimsy structures were ubiquitous in the California landscape, given that more than seventy-five percent of the state's population was engaged in mining. When trees were available, miners sometimes constructed cabins with a base six to eight logs high and a canvas-covered roof [76].[36] On the other hand, some made log cabins with wood-shingled roofs complete with stone or wood chimneys. Here [77], six miners stand proudly in front of such a structure, precariously located on a sloping hillside.

Log homes located near productive mining areas were sold and resold, often for staggering amounts. One mining group looking for a residence at Weaver's Creek in 1849 discovered that "the day after our arrival . . . we determined to build a log house . . . when we received an offer for the sale of one. We examined it, and found a little box of unhewn logs, about twenty feet long by ten wide, which was offered us at the moderate price of five hundred dollars." It was an admittedly large sum, but the group made the purchase "with the reasonable expectation that we could pay for our house by gold-digging in a less time than it would require to build one."[37] According to Ralph Mann's social-structure study of Nevada City and Grass Valley, most cabins were shared by two to five inhabitants—usually related to each other or originating from the same region or state. Few miners working in the field brought their entire families to California and few lived alone.[38] The two miners sharing a cabin in [78] have even built a small framed structure to house their dog.

Harold Kirker objects to the term "log cabin" for many of the log-constructed buildings in the gold fields. Although "genuine log houses with notched ends and mud-chinked walls were erected occasionally among the frame and cloth dwellings that made up the typical mining communities of the early fifties . . . sometimes the 'log cabins' proved to be nothing more than timbered lean-tos . . . with walls and roofs of rough slabs with the bark left on

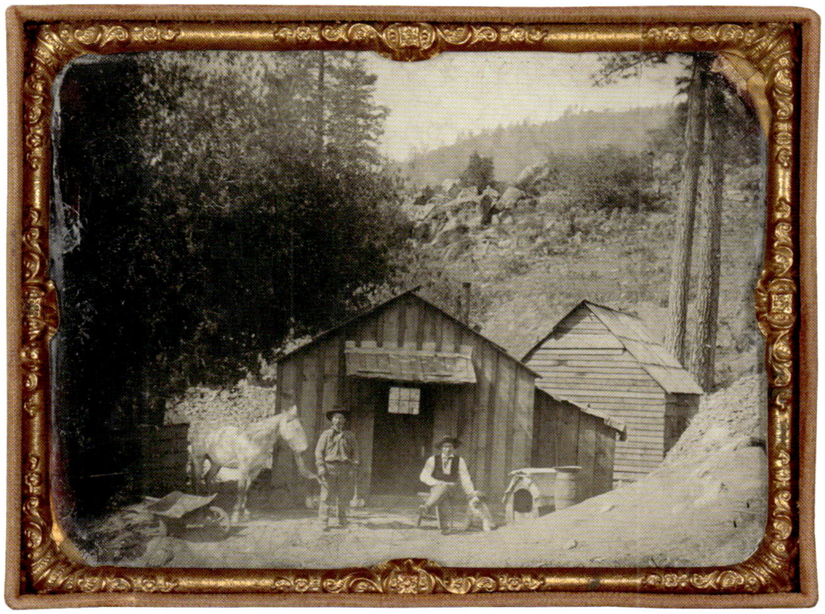

78 **Unknown maker**, American. *Miners in front of cabin with dog*, ca. 1857–60. Quarter-plate ambrotype. The Art Institute of Chicago, The W. Bruce and Delaney H. Lundberg Collection, restricted gift of The Phillip Leonian and Edith Rosenbaum Leonian Charitable Trust.

the outer side."[39] Although predominantly free of bark, the structure built by this large mining crew [79] is a good example of this primitive building style. This view also demonstrates the difficulties faced by daguerreotypists working in the field. With this residence perched at the top of a hill, there appears to have been no "good spot" from which to make this image.

As lumber became increasingly available, "miners constructed their dwellings in the frame manner and covered them with rough boarding and hand-split shingles."[40] Some of these houses were still roughly constructed, with dirt floors and without chimneys. When a woman was living in the house, structures appear more refined. In front of a home with curtains in the windows, a woman stands between two men, one most likely her husband [80]. They are pictured with the tools of their trades—the men with mining shovels, one upright and one on the ground, and the woman holding a plate and wash rag.

For labor-intensive operations requiring a large workforce, companies erected larger and more permanent buildings to serve as miners' barracks. In [81], miners stand on the front porch of a two-story dwelling with the owners (or foremen) on horseback in front. The long diagonal of the building is at odds with the framing of the image; the terrain appears to have forced the daguerreotypist to use a vantage point well below the eye-level of the subjects. In another image capturing an inclusive view of various miner dwellings scattered on a steep hillside [82], the daguerreotypist has

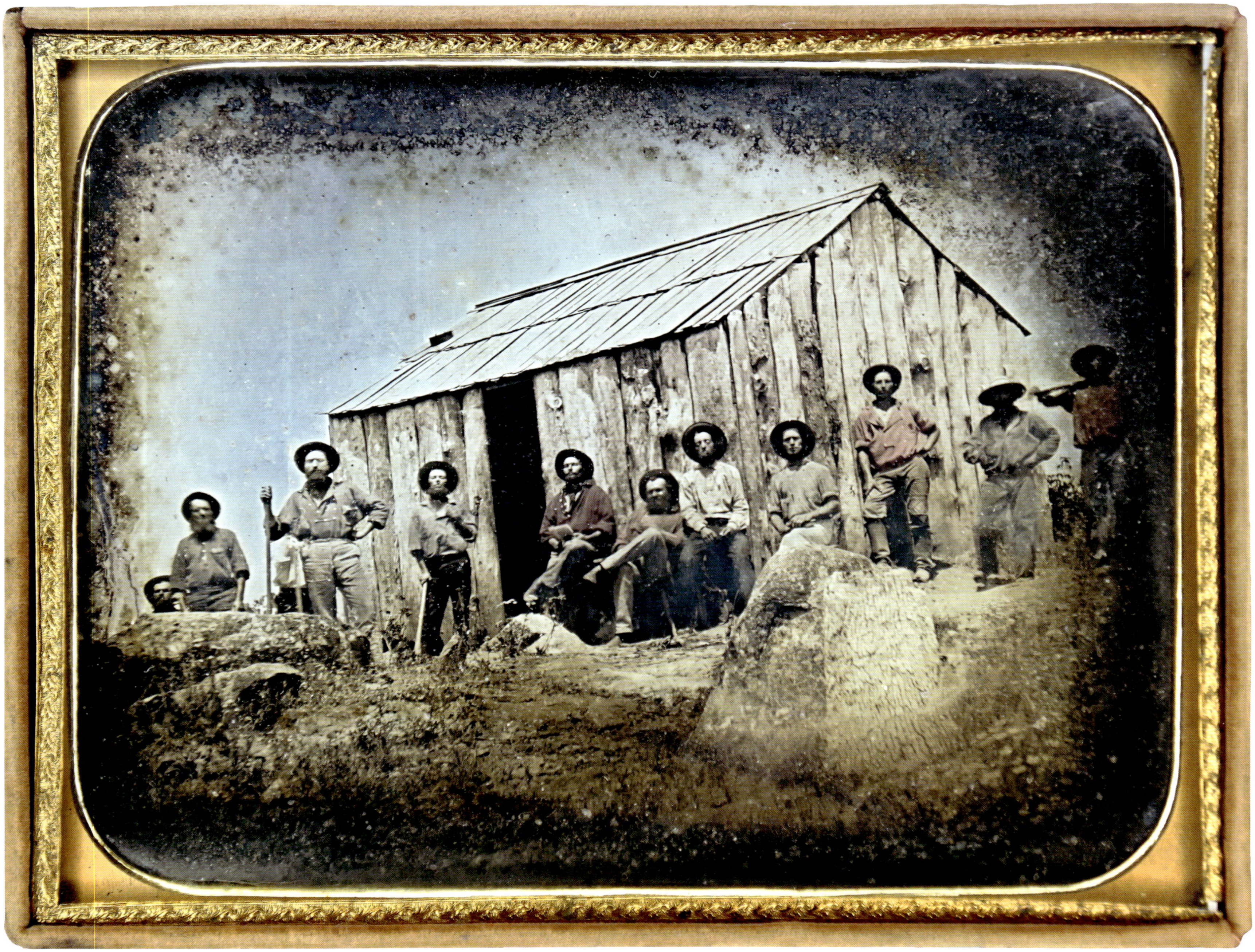

79 **Unknown maker**, American. *Eleven miners at their cabin*, ca. 1850–55. Half-plate daguerreotype. Collection of Michael Peterson.

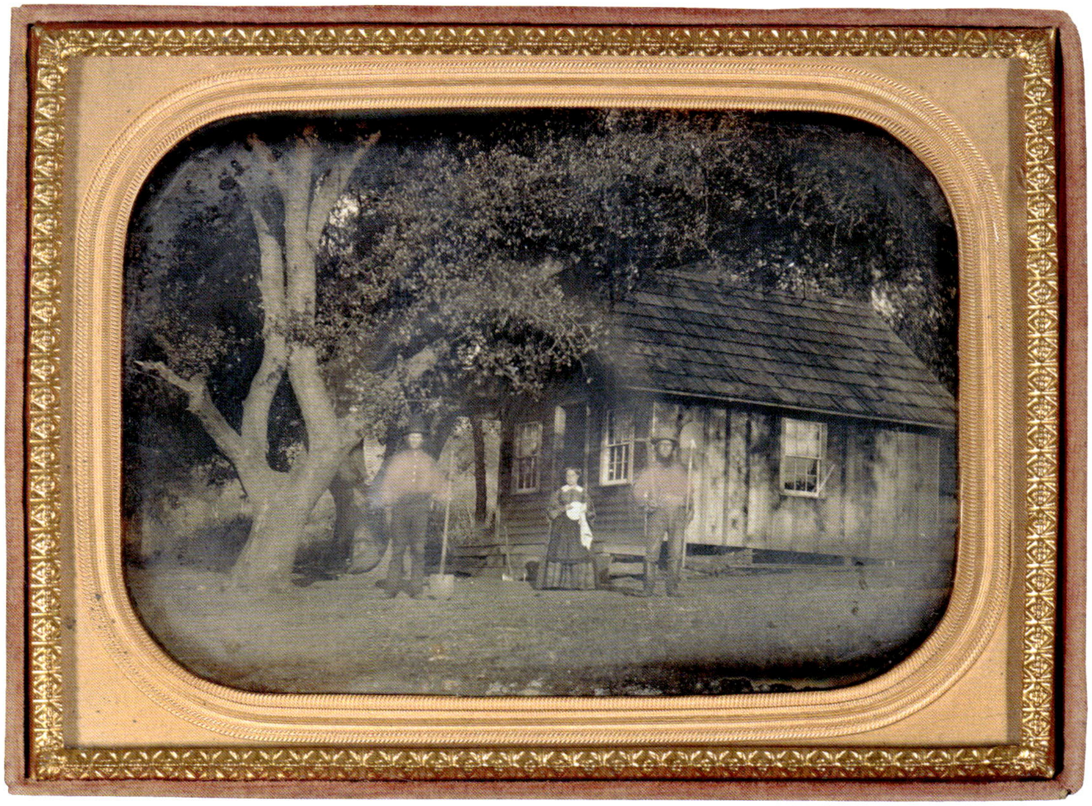

80 **Unknown maker**, American. *California gold miners with cabin*, ca. 1852. Quarter-plate daguerreotype.

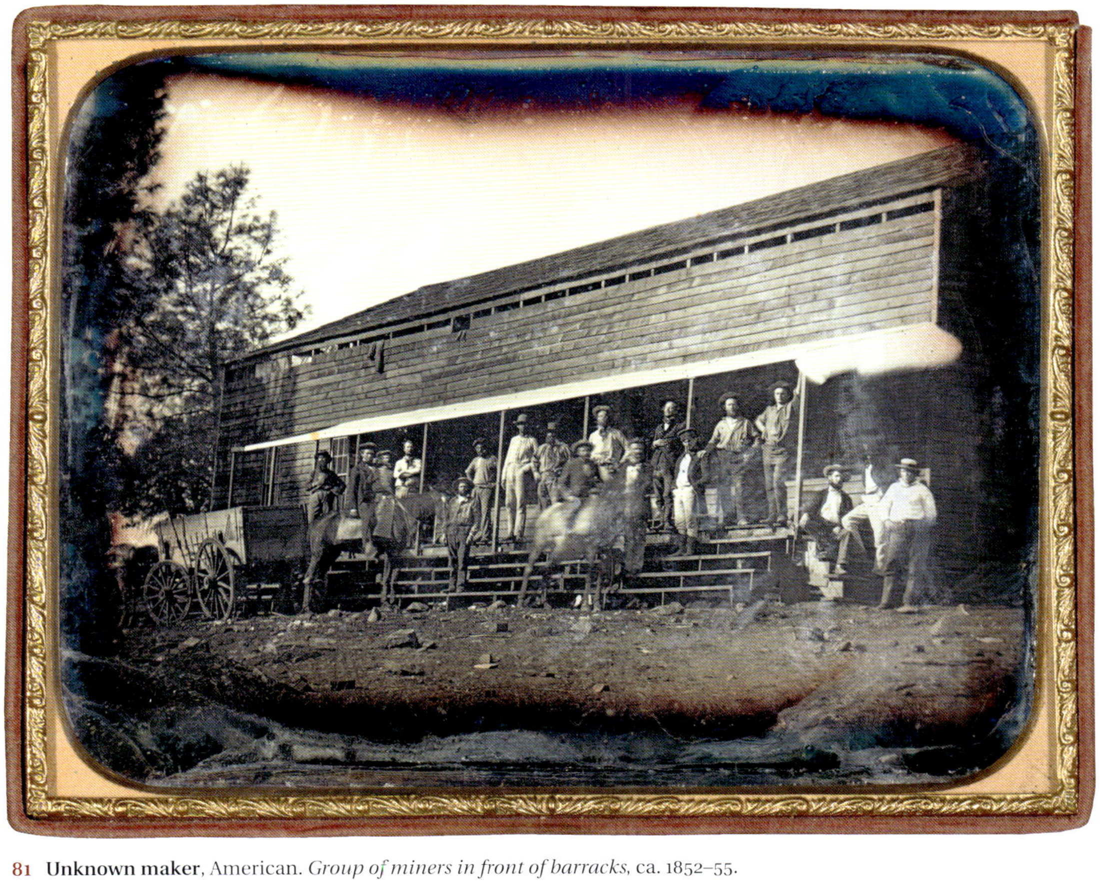

81 **Unknown maker**, American. *Group of miners in front of barracks*, ca. 1852–55. Half-plate daguerreotype. Collection of Bruce Lundberg.

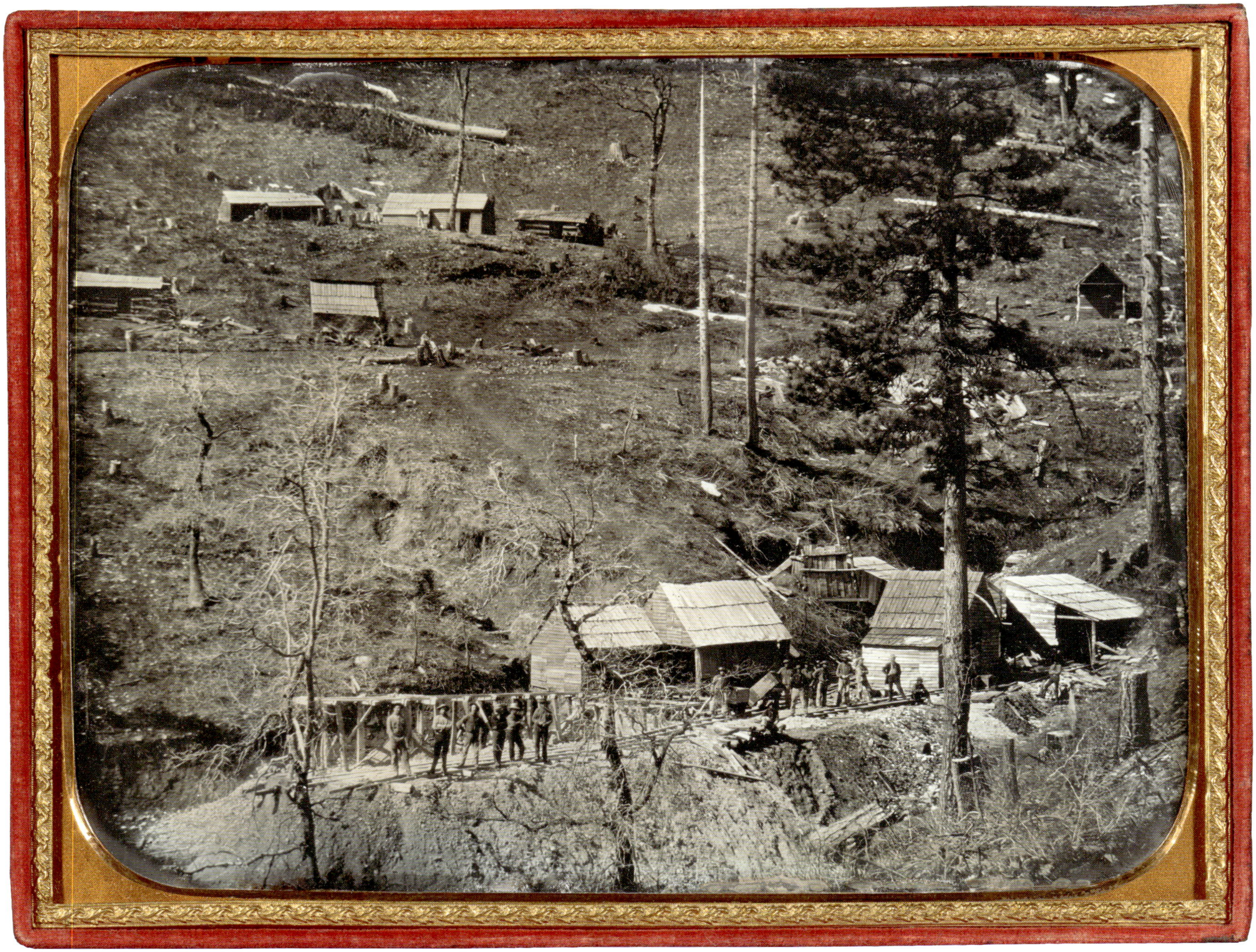

82 Unknown maker, American. *Gold mining camp, California,* ca. 1850–55. Half-plate daguerreotype.

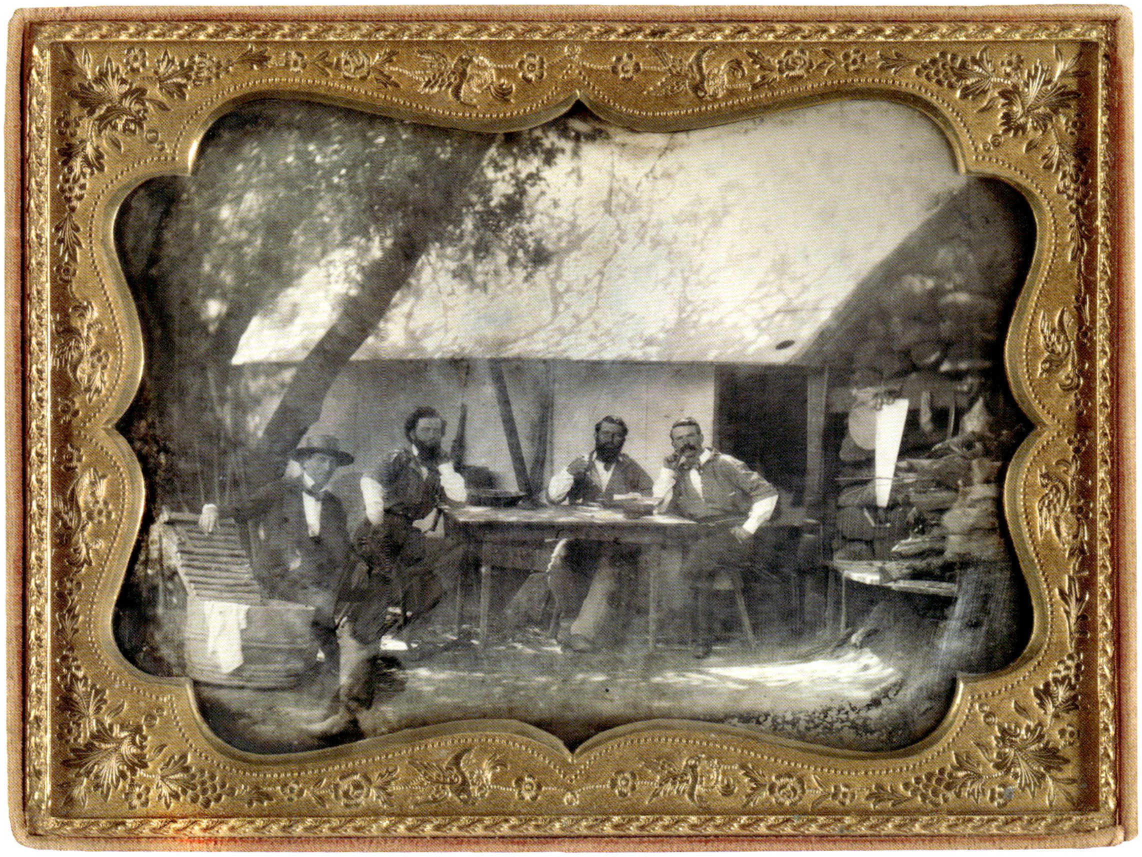

83 **Unknown maker**, American. *Four gold miners seated in front of their house*, ca. 1852. Half-plate daguerreotype. Metropolitan Museum of Art, New York, Gilman Collection, Museum Purchase, 2005.

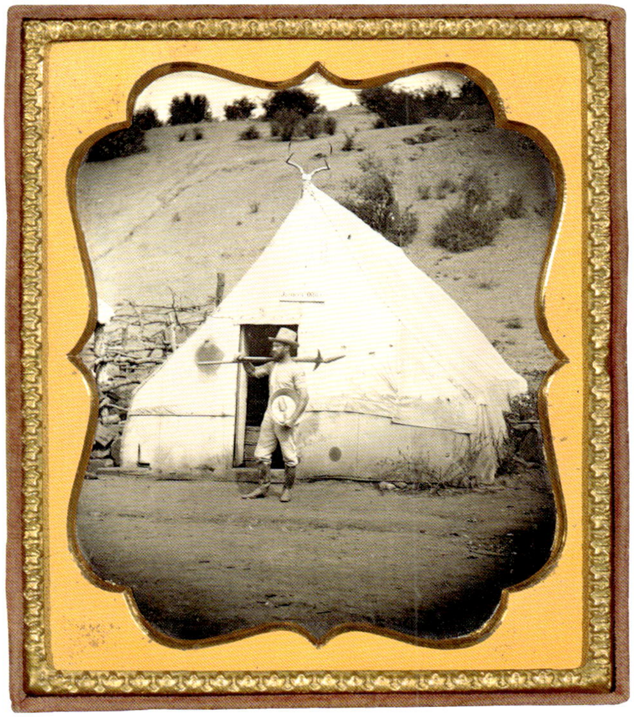

84 **Unknown maker**, American. *California gold miner in front of Justices Office tent*, ca. 1850–55. Sixth-plate daguerreotype.

conquered the difficult topography by positioning himself on a nearby hill. The trestled track at the bottom of the hill may be part of a larger mining claim.

Miners rarely rested after their evening return to the cabin. Diaries are full of accounts of the uncomfortable nature of domestic tasks such as cooking and washing (widely regarded as "women's work"). The miners in this image [76] are alternately at rest and at work. One miner reads the newspaper (one source for information on new gold discoveries) while his roommate washes clothes. In another image [83], three miners relax at a wooden table set up in front of their residence. A fourth miner rests his arm on the washboard sitting in the tub next to him; his gesture suggests a familiarity with the task at hand.

Supplies in the gold field were expensive. One miner advised: "Purchase no provisions in San Francisco. The expenses of transportation are so great . . . that your provisions will cost more in money and time than they would if purchased in the mines."[41] Catering to miners located away from towns, merchants sold essential supplies from retail stores made of canvas. With so many miners vying to stake claims, these temporary structures were also set up to provide legal services, like this one [84] advertising "Justices Office." The community of Sandy Gulch, identified as a makeshift trading center in 1849, appears to have successfully transitioned into a small gold town.[42] In this image [85], the daguerreotypist has distanced himself in order to provide a complete view of the town, which he has framed with trees in the left foreground.[43]

To accommodate travelers, lodging houses were established throughout the region. Comanche House was a primitive lodging structure, catering either to travelers or to large mining crews [86]. The canvas covering appears to be sectioned by flaps that follow one after the other down a long, low roofline. Instead of showing a frontal view, the camera was situated to best capture the horizontal length of the structure and the line of seated residents. The most prominent position is occupied by a man in suit and hat, sporting a distinctive pair of pants (perhaps military or Californio-style), accompanied by his trusty canine companion.[44]

A few cased images emphasize miners positioned within the larger landscape—shifting focus from the miners' pursuit of wealth to the transcendent California environment. Rarely, as in this unusual quarter-plate daguerreotype [87], the subject appears exclusively devoted to the landscape—here a

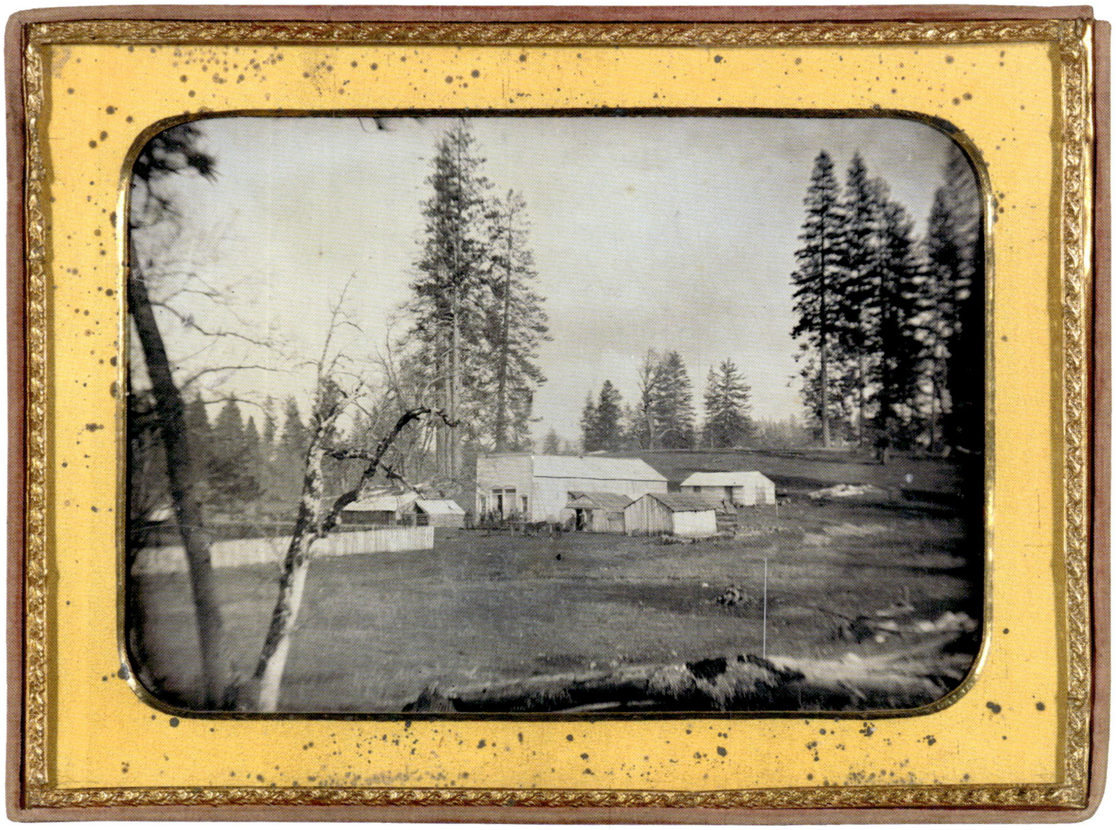

85 **Unknown maker**, American. *Sandy Gulch, California*, ca. 1854. Half-plate daguerreotype.

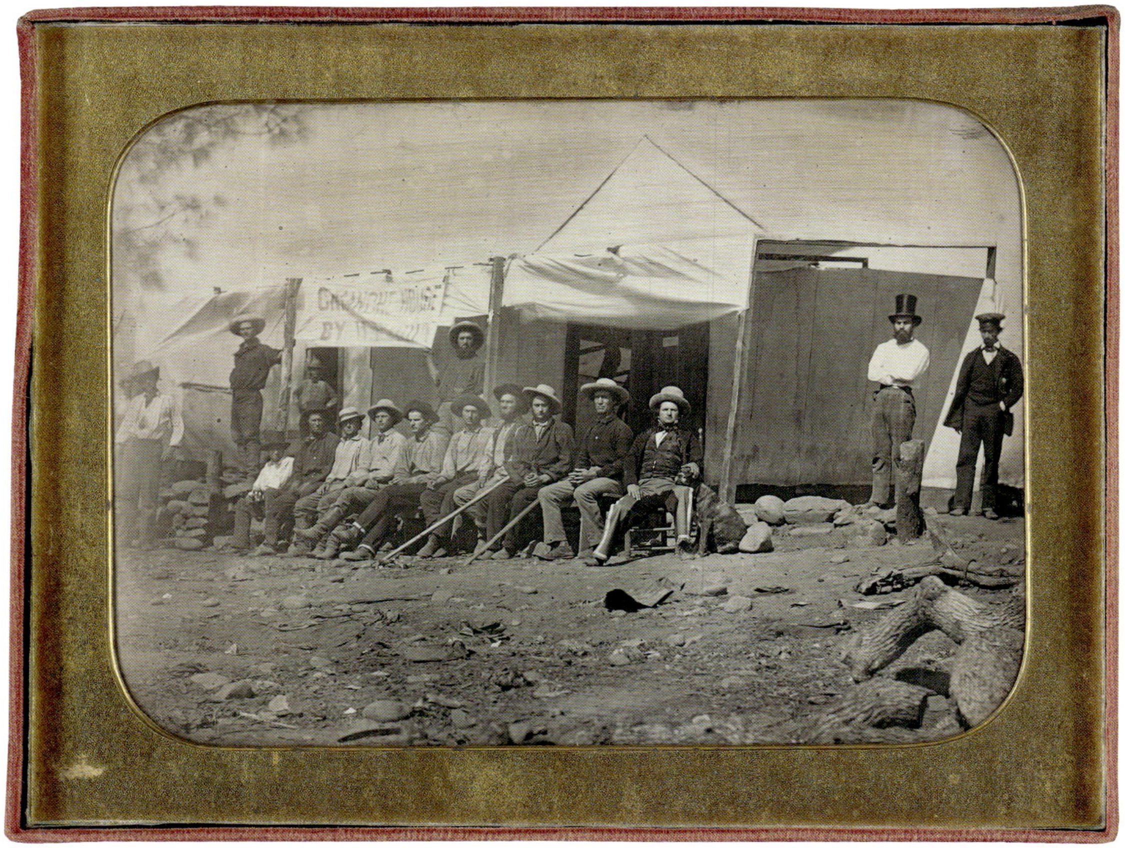

86 **Unknown maker**, American. *Group of unidentified men and dog in front of Camanche House*, ca. 1850. Half-plate daguerreotype. National Gallery of Canada, Ottawa.

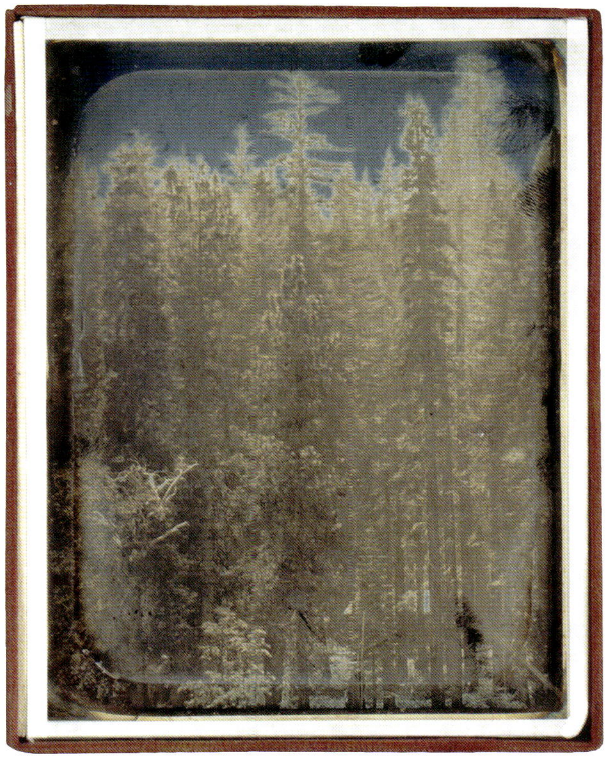

87 **Unknown maker**, American. *Big trees*, ca. 1852–55. Quarter-plate daguerreotype. Bancroft Library, University of California, Berkeley.

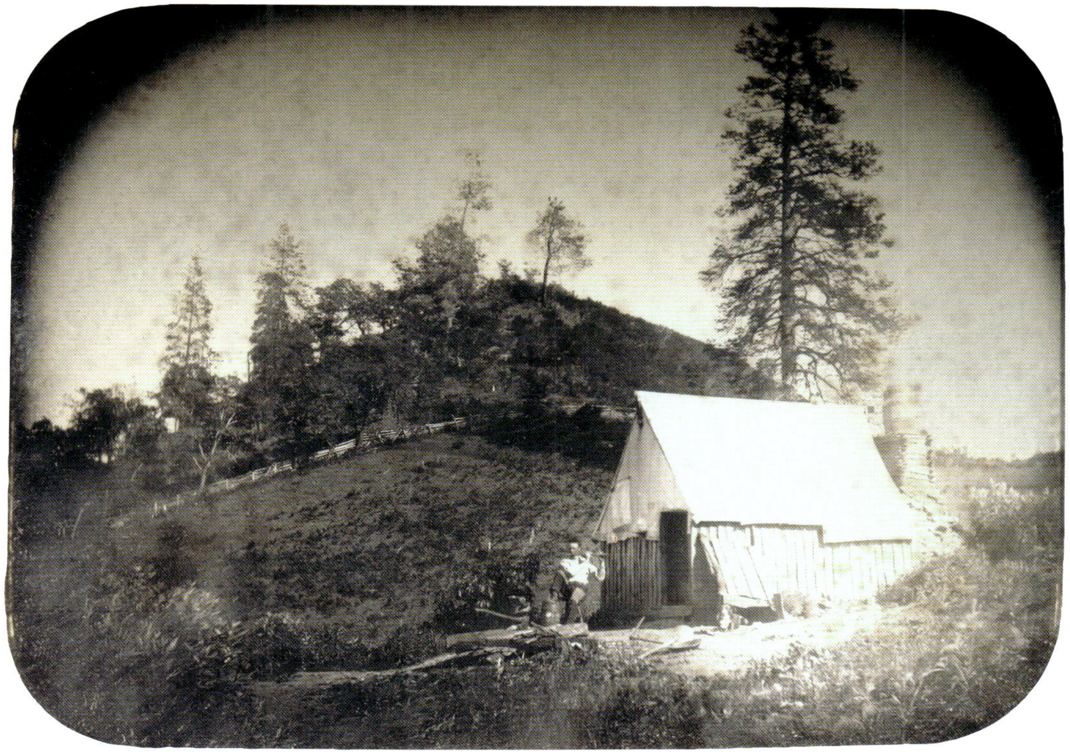

88 **H. M. Bacon**, American (active 1850s–1860s). *An Evening Scene, Boston Flat, Calaveras County [miner playing flute by cabin]*, ca. 1857. Half-plate daguerreotype. Society of California Pioneers, San Francisco.

thick grove of evergreens.[45] In *An Evening Scene, Boston Flat, Calaveras County*, a miner sits outside his canvas-roofed cabin, dwarfed by the majesty of the landscape [88]. Unfazed by the largeness of his surroundings, the miner peacefully plays music. Daguerreotyped by H. M. Bacon, this image was reproduced as a laterally reversed engraving in *Hutchings' California Magazine* [FIG. 9] with accompanying text:

> This picture is intended to represent the Miner at home, after his day's work is done. To the man who rises early, that he may cook his breakfast and be at work by sunrise; and sits down by his claim . . . when the sun has sunk beneath the distant hill, hies him to his cabin to chop his wood, kindle his fire . . . there is a luxury in taking a seat outside the door, while his supper is cooking; and in the cool and quiet of the evening . . . to take his flute . . . and play any favorite air.[46]

Bucolic scenes like this celebrated the romantic notion of the miner, but of course did not tell the full story. In the heedless quest for gold, nature did not stand a chance. Hubert Bancroft reminded the readers of his *History of California* (1888) that "the picturesque faded fast as the foliage fringe round the white-peaked tents was reduced to shorn stumps, midst unsightly mounds of earth, despoiled river-beds, and denuded slopes."[47]

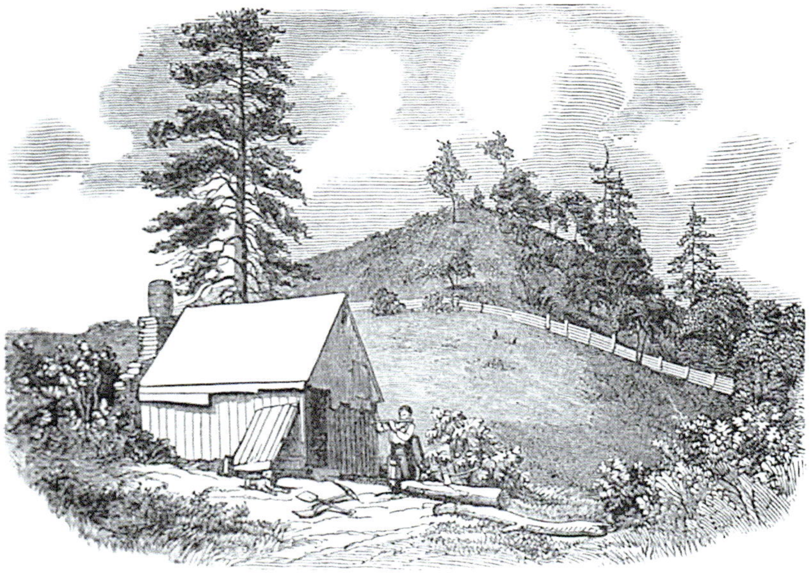

FIG. 9 *An Evening Scene—Boston Flat, Calaveras County*, from *Hutchings' California Magazine*, 2 (1857–1858).

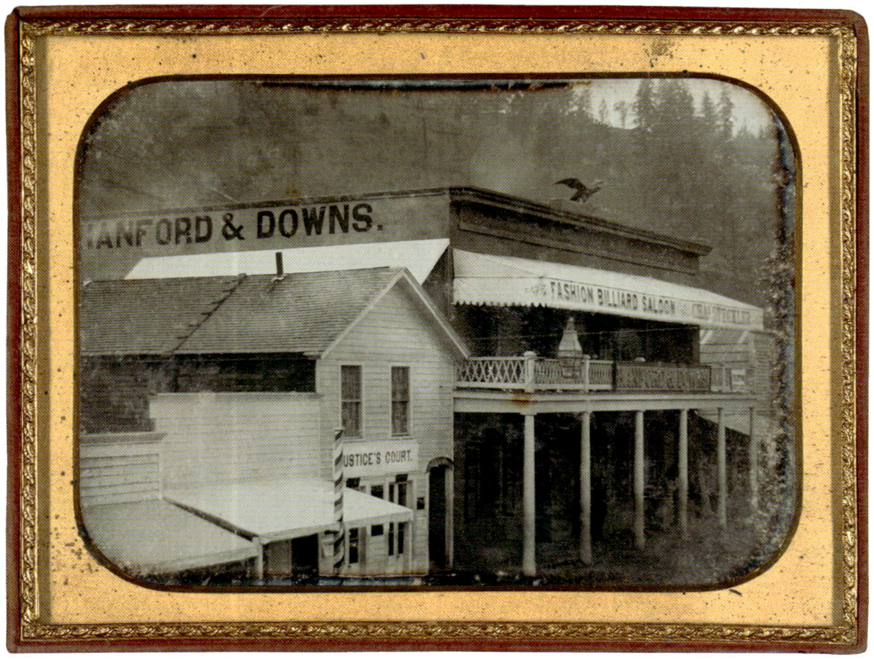

89 **Unknown maker**, American. *Hanford & Downs store, Volcano, California*, ca. 1850–55. Half-plate daguerreotype. The Art Institute of Chicago, The W. Bruce and Delaney H. Lundberg Collection, restricted gift of The Phillip Leonian and Edith Rosenbaum Leonian Charitable Trust.

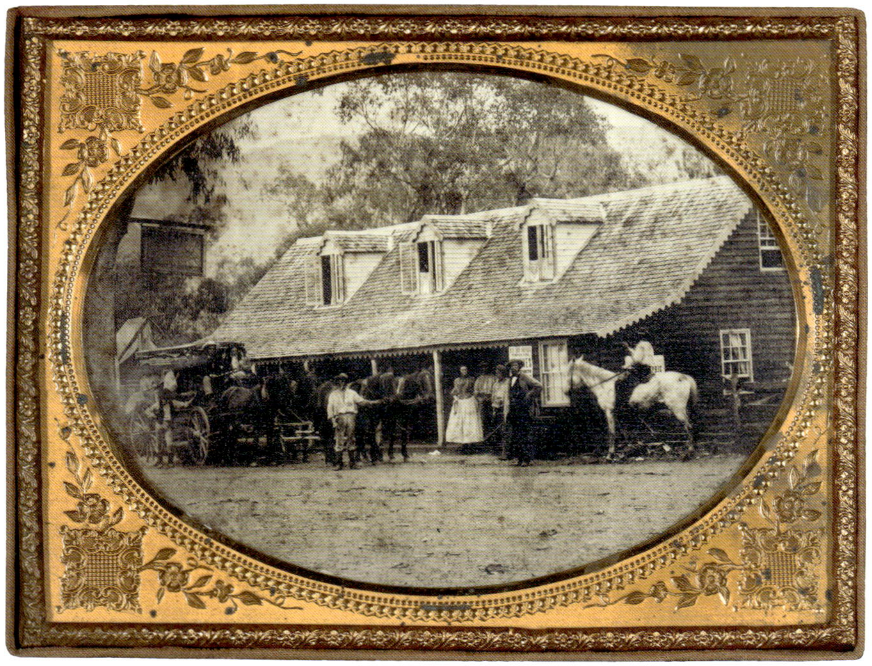

90 **Unknown maker**, American. *Stagecoach stop*, ca. 1857–60. Half-plate ambrotype. Collection of Bruce Lundberg.

Individual Businesses in the Gold Towns

For miners, success was commemorated by daguerreotypes of their diggings. With a similar desire to memorialize their prosperity, business owners commissioned daguerreotypes of their storefronts. Hotels, express and banking services, and retail merchants were frequently pictured. Many of these tightly cropped views focused on one building, excluding adjacent structures. The owner, oftentimes indistinguishable from other passersby, positioned himself out front with a group of friends or customers. Some merchants included their family members, signifying an increased sense of permanence and commitment to the community. Two residents of Volcano, Levi Hanford and R. C. Downs, were miners turned merchants: after a successful stint in mining, the partners became "engaged in merchandising at Amador, Rancheria, Sutter Creek and Volcano . . . having establishments at each of those places." A daguerreotype view of their store in Volcano [89] is evidence that they were "eminently successful" and "well known over the State."[48] Similarly, daguerreotypists documented their own successes by photographing both permanent and temporary studio locations and, in at least one instance, a traveling daguerreian wagon [33]. Collectively, these images broaden our understanding of the meaning of success in the California gold rush.

During the winter months, many miners retreated to hotels or barracks in towns to wait out inclement weather.[49] Stagecoaches, essential for travel between gold towns, had stops that doubled as lodging locations [90]. A rising tourism industry also brought curious visitors to the region for a glimpse of the gold fields and the state's spectacular scenery. At Murderer's Bar near the Middle Fork of the American River, at least one hardworking miner described the locale as an eminently worthy tourist destination, noting that "the mountains and green hills—the large waterfalls, formed by enormous ledges of rock, over which the river courses—the pleasant valleys between the hills, covered with rich grass—make the environs of this place really romantic."[50]

Many of the larger hotels shared a similar architectural style: two-story buildings with wide porches spanning the full width of the structure on both the downstairs and upstairs levels. In Mariposa, the Oso Hotel [91] was the picture of success—busy with visitors arriving by wagon, on horseback, or on foot. Outside the larger gold towns, hotels were not typically big but were central to the social life of the region.[51] In Bidwell's Bar, the Union House Hotel dominates most of this daguerreotype [92]. The image was likely taken on a warm day; curtains billow out of the open second-floor windows. Curiously, a man standing in the far left foreground was partially captured in the view, giving this image a spontaneous feeling.

Auburn was one of the oldest mining towns in Placer County. Located near the gold fields, it was established as "a good trading-point and a good place to pass the winter."[52] Taken from an unusually high level, this sixth-plate daguerreotype [93] of the Empire Hotel and stagecoach office emphasizes the

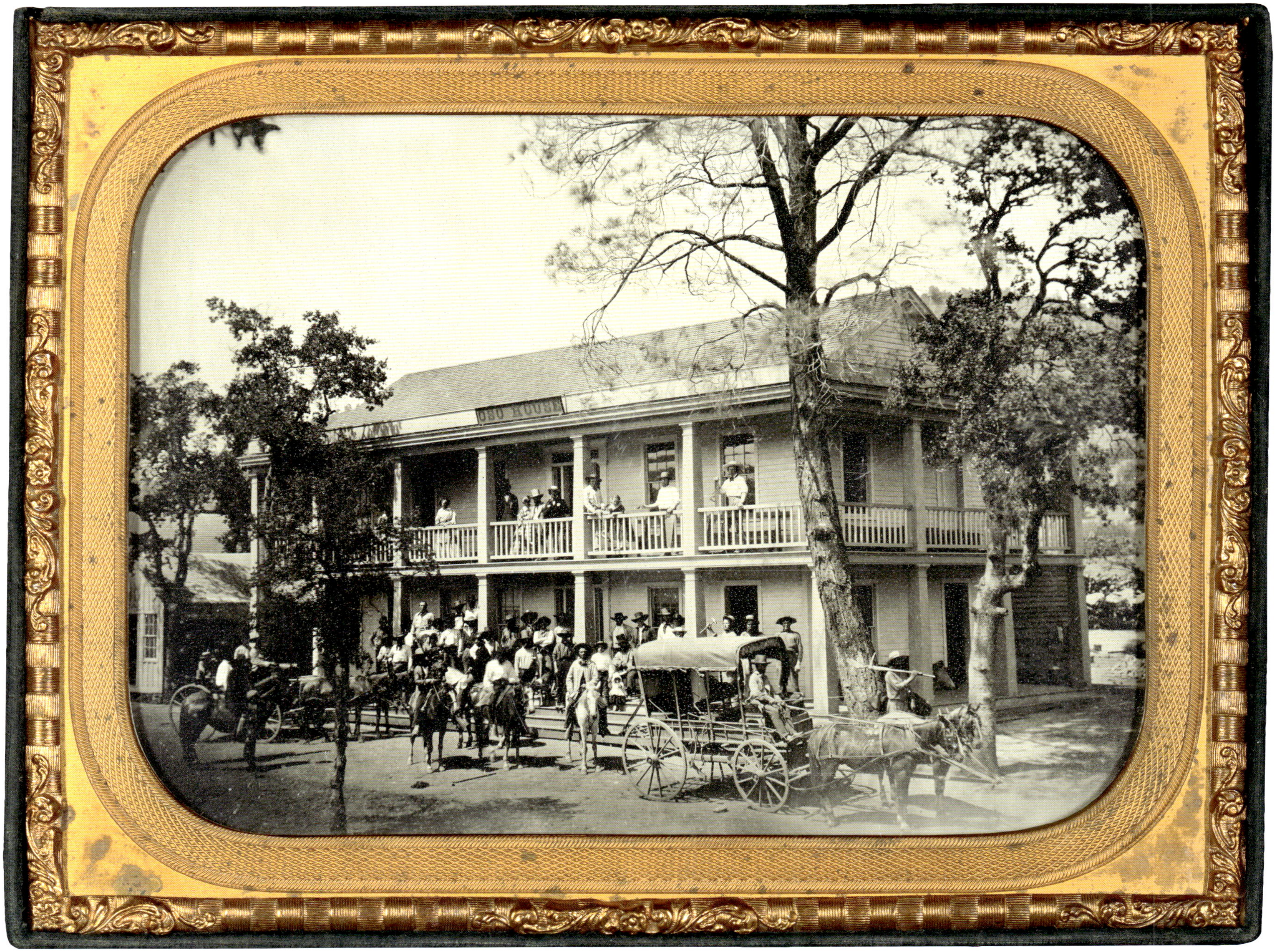

91 **Unknown maker**, American. *John Fremont's Oso Hotel, near Mariposa*, ca. 1861. Half-plate ambrotype. The Art Institute of Chicago, The W. Bruce and Delaney H. Lundberg Collection, restricted gift of The Phillip Leonian and Edith Rosenbaum Leonian Charitable Trust.

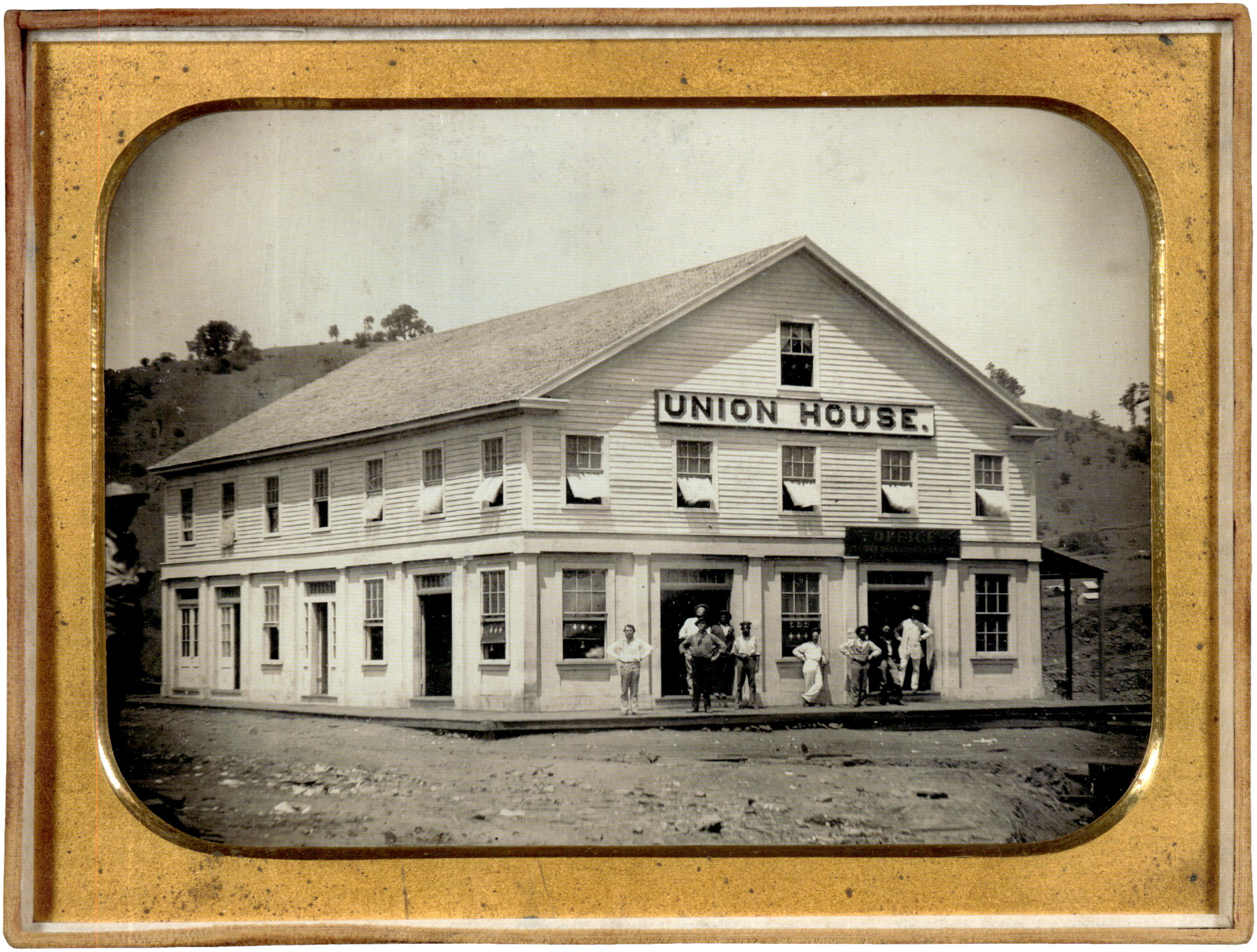

92 **Unknown maker**, American. *The Union House Hotel, Bidwell's Bar, California*, ca. 1855.
Half-plate daguerreotype.

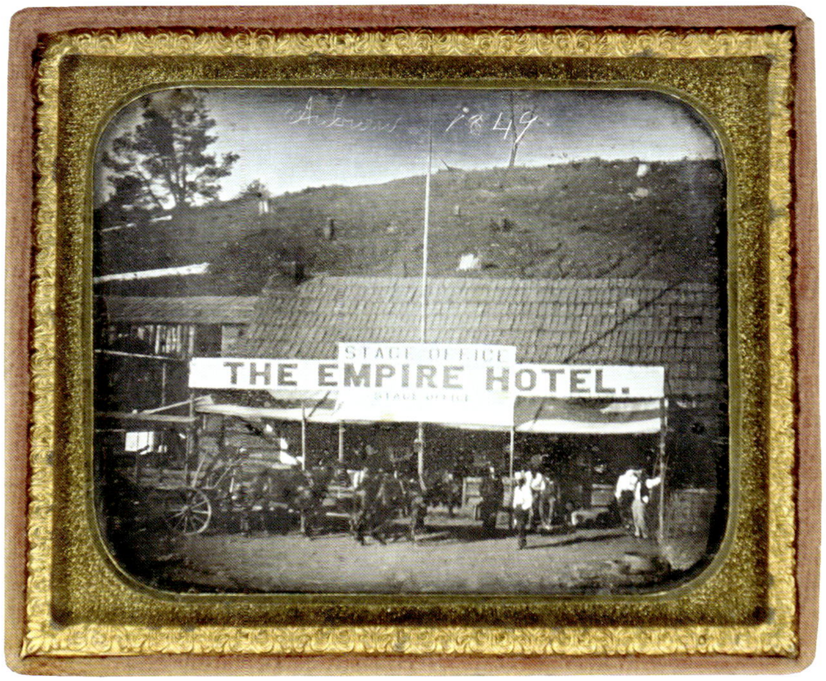

93 **Unknown maker**, American. *The Empire Hotel, Auburn, California*, 1849. Sixth-plate daguerreotype. Collection of Michael Peterson.

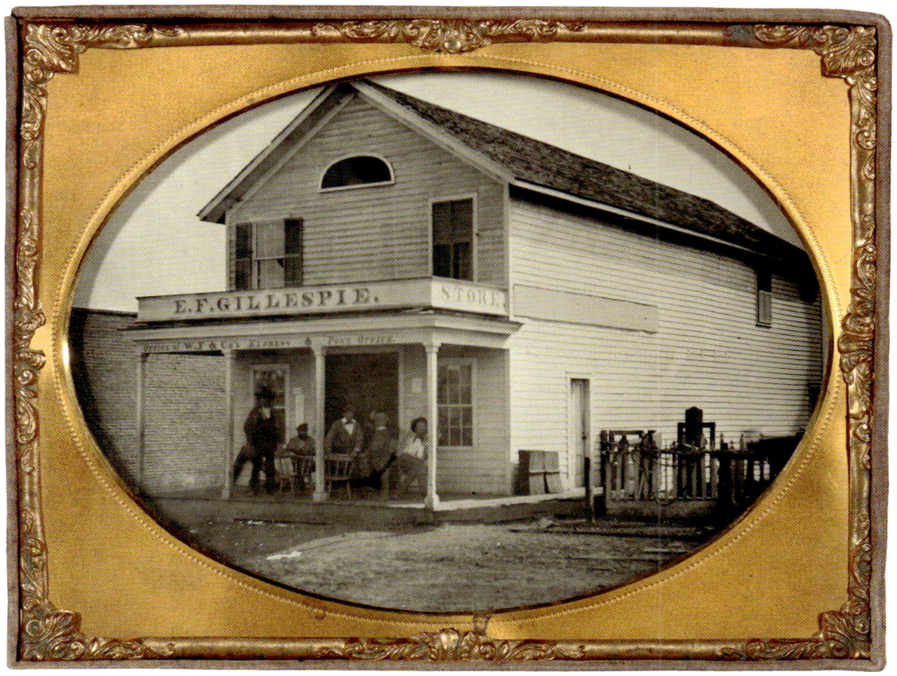

94 **Unknown maker**, American. *Wells Fargo & Co. Express Stop and Post Office, Vacaville, California*, ca. 1855. Half-plate ambrotype.

split shake roof and dramatic incline of the hillside behind. Very unusually, it is flamboyantly inscribed directly on the plate "Auburn 1849". Only two daguerreotypists known to make outdoor views were in California when this was made, in November or December 1849—Jacob Shew and George Johnson.[53] Although both used the sixth-plate format for portraiture, neither was known to use it for outdoor views.

With miners accumulating gold dust, express services were needed to transport gold from the smaller towns to banks in the larger cities and beyond. In 1849, the West Coast branch of Adams & Co. Express was established in San Francisco. Providing mostly banking and exchange services, Adams & Co. expanded by purchasing smaller independently owned companies. In turn, the company was purchased by Wells Fargo in 1855. In that year, Wells Fargo boasted 55 offices; by 1860, it had almost 150.[54] There was hardly a town in the gold mining region of California that did not contain a Wells Fargo express office. Whether humble [94] or grand, these offices quickly "became the center of the town's activities and often among [its] most impressive structures."[55]

Many daguerreotypists who traveled to gold towns established either temporary facilities in hotels or permanent studio locations. For example, this hotel [32] housed "Hendee's Daguerrean Rooms," and was possibly located in Sonora or Auburn. Most likely taken by Edwin or Denny Hendee, this daguerreotype may include members of their family—a woman and child stand just inside the open front window. Another daguerreian operation, located in Mokelumne Hill [95], has several daguerreotype plates hanging on a pillar outside the studio to entice prospective customers to step inside. This view focuses tightly on the facades of the studio and the adjacent horse stable; one could hardly tell that these structures are part of a much larger, thriving community.

Women

Gold town views include images of residents—business owners, customers, and passersby. Most were white men, but sometimes women (and even children) were pictured. For decades, there was a general misperception that the California gold region was practically void of women. Although the male to female ratio was extremely skewed toward males, American Indian women, women of African descent, Chinese women, and white women were continuously present in gold rush California.[56]

From the earliest days, women mined. American Indian women traveled with their tribes throughout the gold fields, as noted by Jean-Nicolas Perlot in September 1854:

> The Indians had worked constantly around us. All the companies let them go freely . . . even in our ditches, to gather the paydirt in their pans, carry it on their heads and go to wash it at the river. The women especially did this work . . . however, I have never seen an Indian woman cede to her husband the gold she gathered, which made me suppose that each one worked for herself.[57]

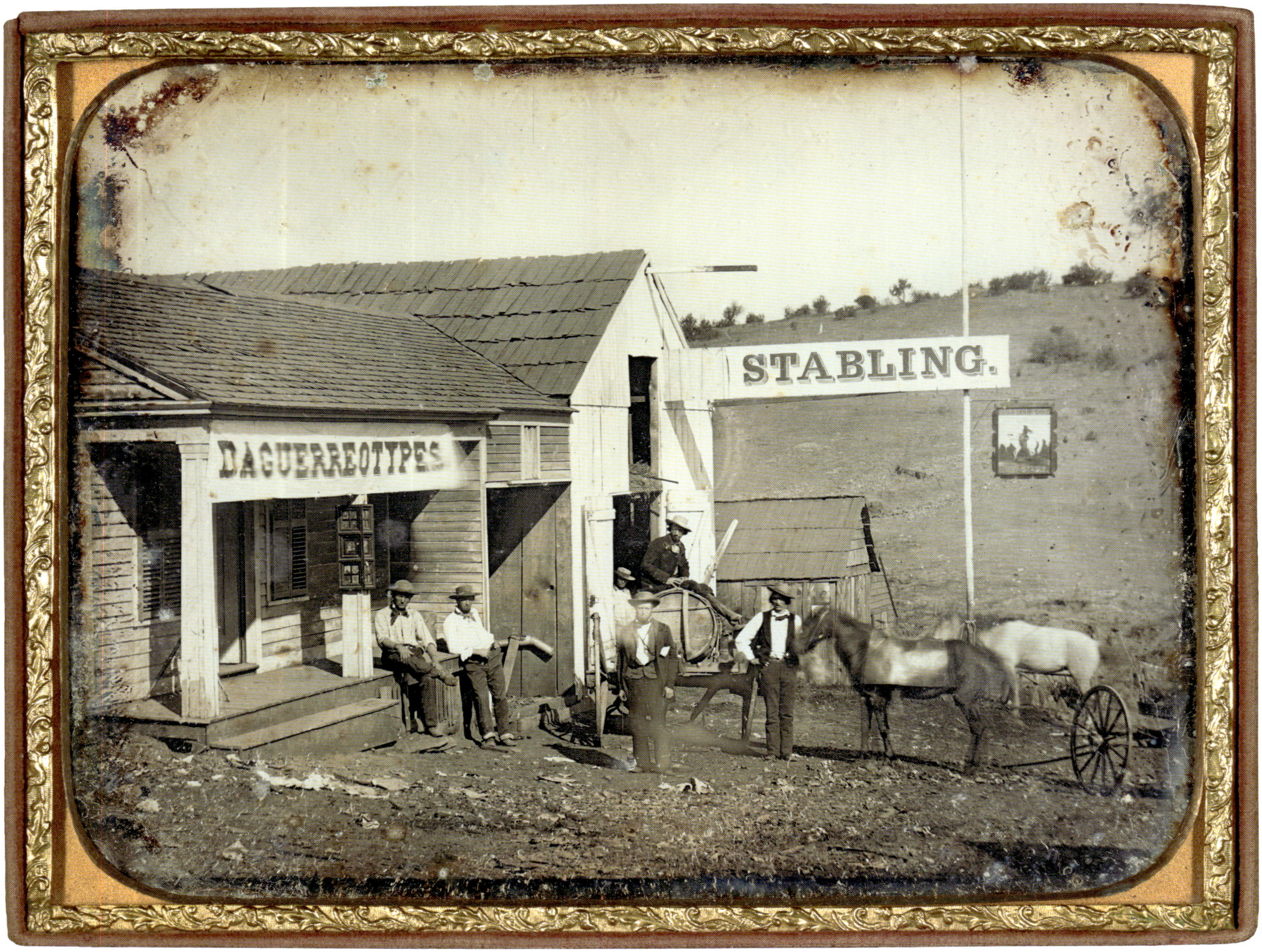

95 **Unknown maker**, American. *Daguerreotype studio, Mokelumne Hill, Calavaras County, California*, ca. 1850–55. Half-plate daguerreotype. The Art Institute of Chicago, The W. Bruce and Delaney H. Lundberg Collection, restricted gift of The Phillip Leonian and Edith Rosenbaum Leonian Charitable Trust.

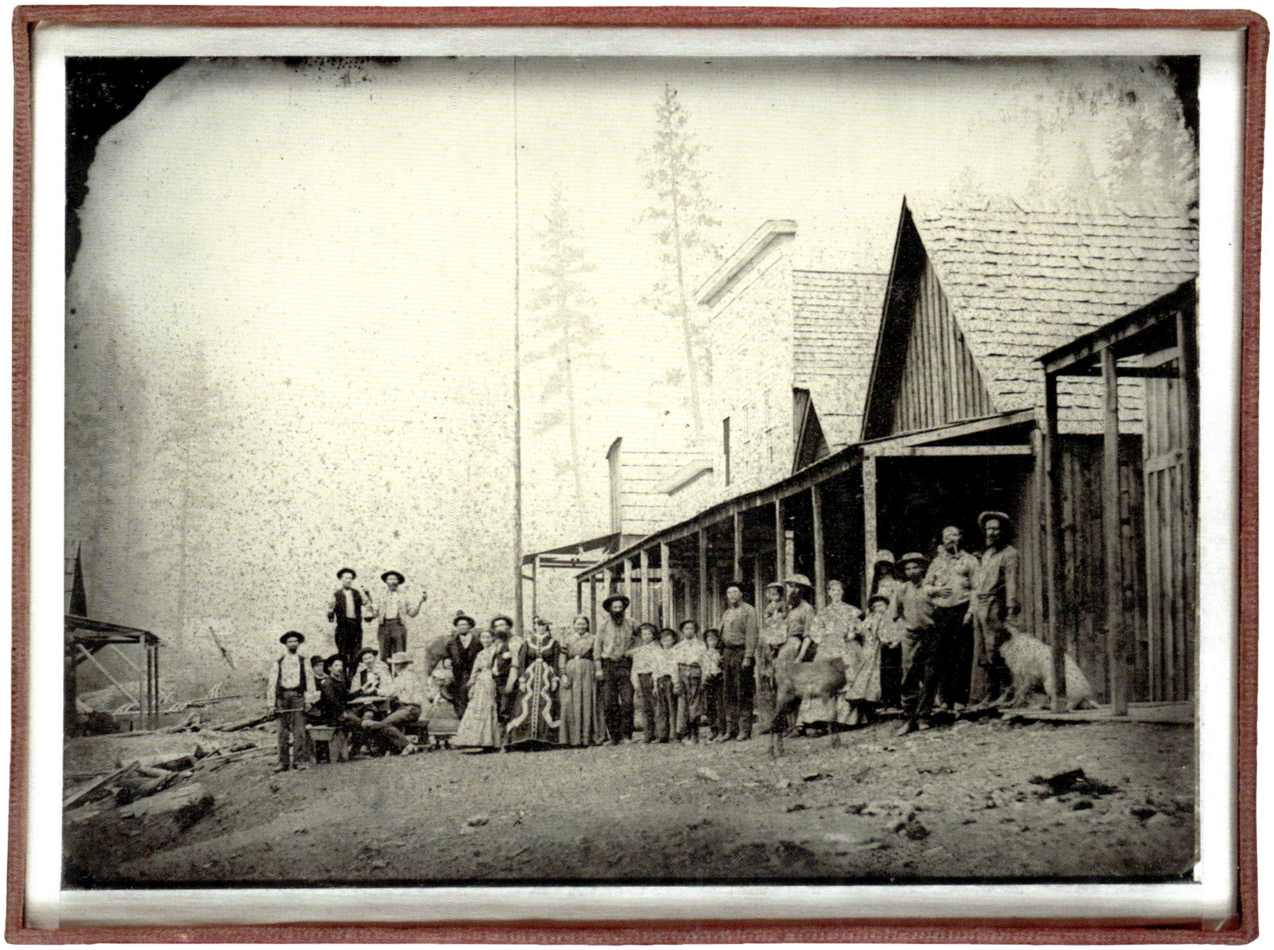

96 **Unknown maker**, American. *Street with large crowd of miners, women, children and animals in Sierraville, California*, ca. 1855. Half-plate ambrotype. Bancroft Library, University of California, Berkeley.

American Indian women were noted as exceptional miners: "On the rivers they obtain gold by scraping out the crevices that have been abandoned by the whites. The mining is done almost exclusively by the squaws. I have known a company of four or five squaws to obtain as much as $8 in one day."[58] Tasked with essential responsibilities, American Indian women harvested acorns, gathered fruit and seeds, sewed clothing, and wove baskets used to pan for gold. When white women mined, they usually worked in tandem with their husbands. In one instance, near Placerville,

> a woman, who had been assisting her husband to wash out the gold . . . took it into her head to scratch round a little in a ravine with a case-knife on her own hook, when she soon dug out a lump weighing just *thirteen* pounds. As some fifty persons have seen this specimen weighed, we think there is no occasion for doubting the story.[59]

Women miners were rarely mentioned in contemporary accounts. In 1852, a report about two women mining with a man near Forman's ranch prompted the editors of the *Alta California* to call for an increase in women's mining and a decrease in women's activism:

> While the gent picks and shovels, one of the ladies—whose costume is a silk dress covered with a man's coat, as near, we suppose, as she can imitate the *Bloomer* in the mines—carries the dirt to the rocker, where the other lady sits working with all the assiduity of an old miner. We wish California were well supplied with such ladies as these, who instead of harassing their husbands about "Women's Rights" . . . would wash as well as rock the *cradle*.[60]

Most of the women pictured in daguerreotype views were wives and mothers, and not miners themselves. At Auburn Ravine [46], Joseph Starkweather daguerreotyped three miners in a streambed using a long tom to wash gold. A woman carrying a cloth-covered basket (presumably the midday meal) stands alongside a man, whose outstretched arm beckons as if to claim her. Responsible for all domestic duties, women in the gold fields enabled men to work longer hours on their claims.

In a few rare cases, women disguised themselves as men in order to mine alongside their husbands or to establish independent claims. Marie Suize (also known as Marie Pantalon) was a Parisian woman who lived and worked near Gold Hill where "she got along very well." She was known as "the woman who was allowed to keep herself dressed in men's clothing," but after she moved to San Francisco in 1871, she encountered a less tolerant community and was arrested.[61] The idea of a woman masquerading as a man was a tantalizing one that fueled imaginative—but completely fabricated—stories which were often later debunked.[62]

California gold towns provided a variety of economic opportunities for enterprising white women. Entrepreneurial women commodified domestic chores—laundry, ironing, sewing, cooking, and cleaning—for which there was great demand.[63] One woman, noted for her successful bakery business, was astonished at the situation: "There is no labor so well paid as women's labor in California. It is hard work to apply one's self incessantly to toil, but a few years will place you above want with a handsome independency."[64] Working alone, this woman stated the she had baked

> about $18,000 worth of pies—about one-third of this has been clear profit. . . . Now I bake about 1,200 pies per month, and clear $200. . . . I have been informed there are some women in town clearing $50 per week at washing, and I cannot doubt it.[65]

Women with an aptitude for cooking could also find employment in restaurants, hotels, and boardinghouses. While much of this was stereotypical "women's work," these entrepreneurs operated outside the traditional domestic economy. In the new social experiment of the gold towns, both men and women were at once customers, creditors, and employees.[66]

As early as October 1849, white women owned and ran boardinghouses for miners and general travelers alike. Proprietorship required juggling a multitude of tasks, including negotiating the price of goods, collecting rent, managing staff, and, occasionally, tending to the sick. Although it could be a profitable venture, running a boardinghouse was clearly difficult work. In a letter dated October 6, 1849, from a proprietor to her children back in Portland, Maine, one woman relayed the cost of success:

> I have ten boarders, two of which we board for the rent. We have one hundred and eighty-nine dollars per week for the whole. We think we can make seventy-five of it clear of all expenses but I assure you I have to work mighty hard—I have to do all my cooking by a very small fire place, no oven, bake all my pies and bread in a dutch oven.[67]

Saloon owners actively pursued women to work as monte dealers and barmaids. With most male miners far from their families, the employment of a barmaid could easily double business profits. A visitor to one such establishment commented: "The population flock in crowds and receive drinks from the fair hands of the female dispenser, whilst the fortunate proprietor of the saloon realizes a fortune in a week."[68] Daguerreotype views of female employees working in saloons and gambling establishments are rare. However, in this street view of Sierraville [96], one woman on the left wears an unusually fancy dress, which may indicate bar employment.

Laundry services were regularly provided by women. Outside San Francisco, a body of water was affectionately dubbed "Washerwoman's Bay,"

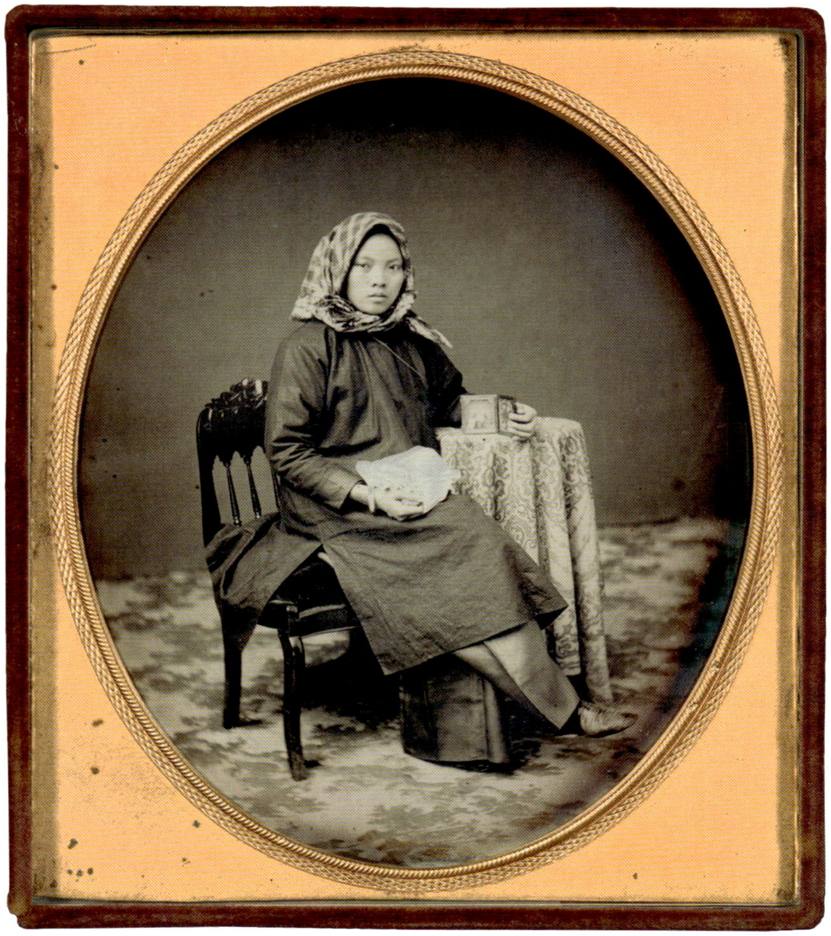

97 **Unknown maker**, American. *Portrait of a Chinese woman with daguerreotype*, ca. 1850. Sixth-plate daguerreotype.

due to its regular and consistent use for washing. The editors of the *Alta California* noted, "women of every clime and color are kneeling down upon the bank engaged in the pious work of washing, beneath the shade of their drying clothes."[69] By the end of the 1860s, Chinese men had largely supplanted women in this line of work.[70]

Women of African ancestry were employed in the gold towns primarily in the domestic realm. Black women served in the same duties as black men, as household servants, cooks, laundry workers, and housekeepers. Some women with light complexions were employed in saloons. One visitor to a Sonora bar remarked on the young woman behind the counter:

> In one of the saloons, a very interesting and well-looking young girl was attending at a part of the bar where confectionary was sold. I should not have supposed her to have had black blood in her veins; but J. B. assured me that she had been a slave, and had been once sold at New Orleans at a very high price. . . . She was free now."[71]

Chinese women were hardly mentioned in nineteenth-century accounts of California, though they were undoubtedly there. By 1857, *Hutchings' California Magazine* reported "the Chinese have sent hither swarms of their females."[72] Most Chinese women immigrated as a part of a husband-wife economic unit and assisted as agricultural workers, seamstresses, cooks, and laundrywomen [97]. Chinese women were also miners:

> Women very frequently accompany the men to the scenes of their labor, and while the men prosecute the work of coyoting, and bringing to the surface the pay dirt, the women not unfrequently do the panning out, separating or washing the dirt from the "oro" in some adjacent pool.[73]

While some Chinese women did engage in prostitution, many white Americans mistakenly viewed all Chinese women to be prostitutes—a misperception perpetuated by some later historians.[74]

Gold rush California provided an atypical set of circumstances that resulted in a shift in traditional gender roles. Historian Susan Lee Johnson noted that historians have applied "poststructuralist analyses of language [to] show how oppositions work . . . such as the one between productive and reproductive labor."[75] In most areas of the country, productive labor (men's work) took primacy over reproductive work (women's work), paralleling social relations of dominance and subordination based on gender. In California, however, reproductive labor (domestic services) was often financially more successful than productive labor (mining). In some cases, women (American Indian) performed productive labor more successfully than men. Opportunities varied, however; some groups of women (non-white) were marginalized, while others (white) arrived to take advantage of financial opportunities. Ultimately, all shared some economic benefits derived from performing the routine but essential tasks of "women's work."

Gold Town Residences

Less transitory than the average miner, merchants (and their families) contributed strongly to the respectability and relative permanence of gold mining communities. They typically lived in residences behind the business district. Wooden structures—both businesses and homes—transformed temporary camps into more organized towns.[76] One visitor to Rough and Ready, a town located a few miles east of Nevada City, was charmed by the residential area:

> When I first saw the place . . . the only sign of a town, visible, were some ten or twelve canvas houses. . . . Two months afterwards, I passed through the town, along a street nearly three-fourths of a mile in length, compactly built up on both sides with frame houses, many of them two stories high, with handsome exteriors.[77]

Many of these town residences were not unlike their counterparts in the eastern United States. Clapboard siding, paned windows, and stone chimneys were typical of many of these dwellings. A sign of home life, a picket fence separated private space from public street [98]. Secured with a stone foundation, these houses were clearly not temporary dwellings.

After a visit to Robert Vance's studio, where "the great and most successful artist of Daguerre" exhibited "some of the finest specimens" of architectural views, the editors of the *California Farmer and Journal of Useful Sciences* urged readers to "have their 'homestead' taken by this artist so as to preserve them and pass them down to their children and children's children."[78] A home was seen as an extension of character and keeping a neat and orderly residence in deference to the larger community was an owner's ethical responsibility. As the editors wrote, daguerreotypes of homes "do not represent the face, but [the homeowner's] character. They exhibit to every one, his ability as a cultivator, his taste for neatness and order, and in some degree his moral character. . . . Every landowner or resident is in some degree pictured by the external appearance of his premises."[79]

Stressing the importance of eastern architecture in California, Harold Kirker noted that although "one-half of the Americans came from the northeastern states, 85 percent of the emigrant-architects were from New England."[80] Because of this, "the New England frame house, and not the log cabin, was the typical American dwelling on the California frontier at the time of the gold rush."[81] The predominance of New England architecture signified to Kirker "one of the first victories in the struggle between the mutually antagonistic Spanish-Mexican and American cultures" with "the triumph of Yankee building standards over those of the adobe builders."[82] Yet another example of Manifest Destiny, this was seen as a necessary step toward a perceived cultural refinement. Establishing this "American" architectural standard fulfilled Harvard president Edward Everett's directive to New England gold seekers to go to California with the "Bible in one hand and your New England civilization in the other and make your mark upon the people and the country."[83]

Main Street

In addition to photographing individual businesses and merchant residences, daguerreotypists documented towns from within—on the main street. The smallest towns had only a single street, with stores located on either side of the thoroughfare. Business structures ranged from primitive canvas tents and log cabins to finished structures with painted clapboard siding. Most main streets included a general store, saloon, hotel, restaurant, express office, blacksmith shop, and livery stable, with schools and churches located away from the commercial district.

Views of a main street were challenging to make—streets were often narrow, muddy, and rough. In order to capture the most inclusive view, daguerreotypists sometimes positioned themselves directly in the middle of the roadway. Other times, it was easier to photograph from one side of the street diagonally across to the other, as in this view of Fiddletown [99]. The daguerreotypist's effort to capture both sides of the street results in an awkward camera position that makes the building on the left appear

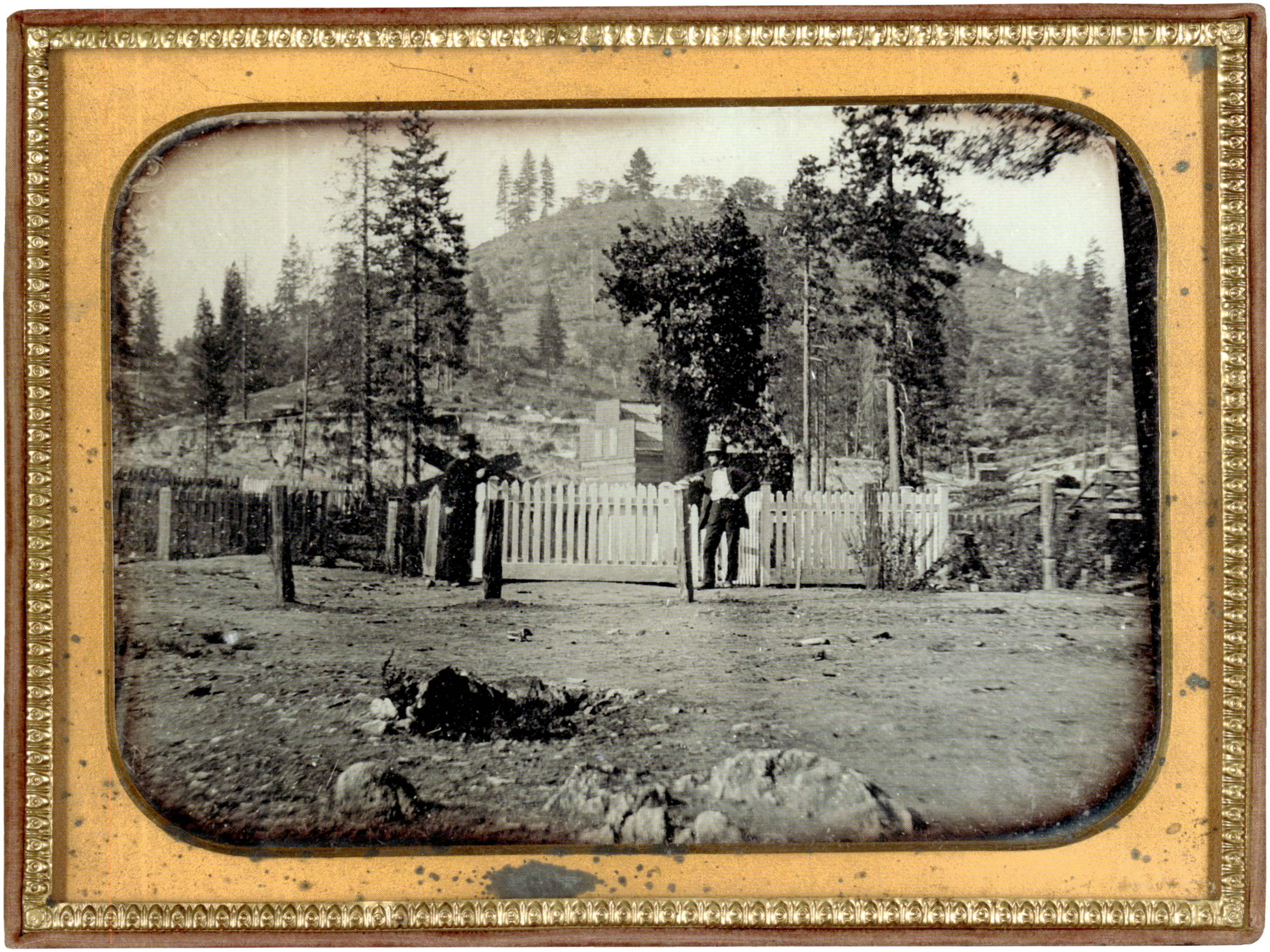

98 **Unknown maker**, American. *Men at fence outside a California town*, ca. 1850–55. Half-plate daguerreotype. The Art Institute of Chicago, The W. Bruce and Delaney H. Lundberg Collection, restricted gift of The Phillip Leonian and Edith Rosenbaum Leonian Charitable Trust.

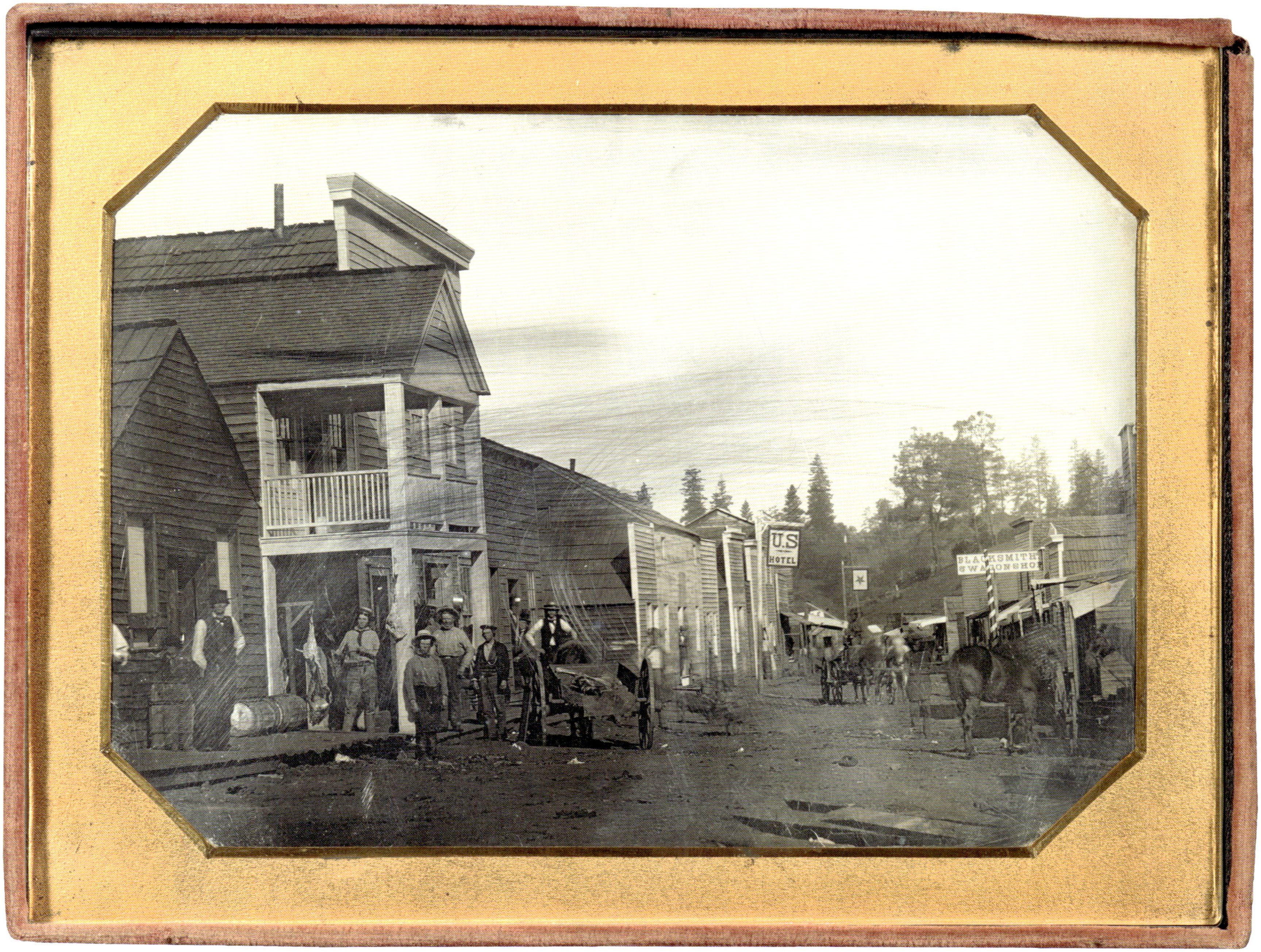

99 Unknown maker, American. *Main Street, Fiddletown, California*, ca. 1850.
Half-plate daguerreotype.

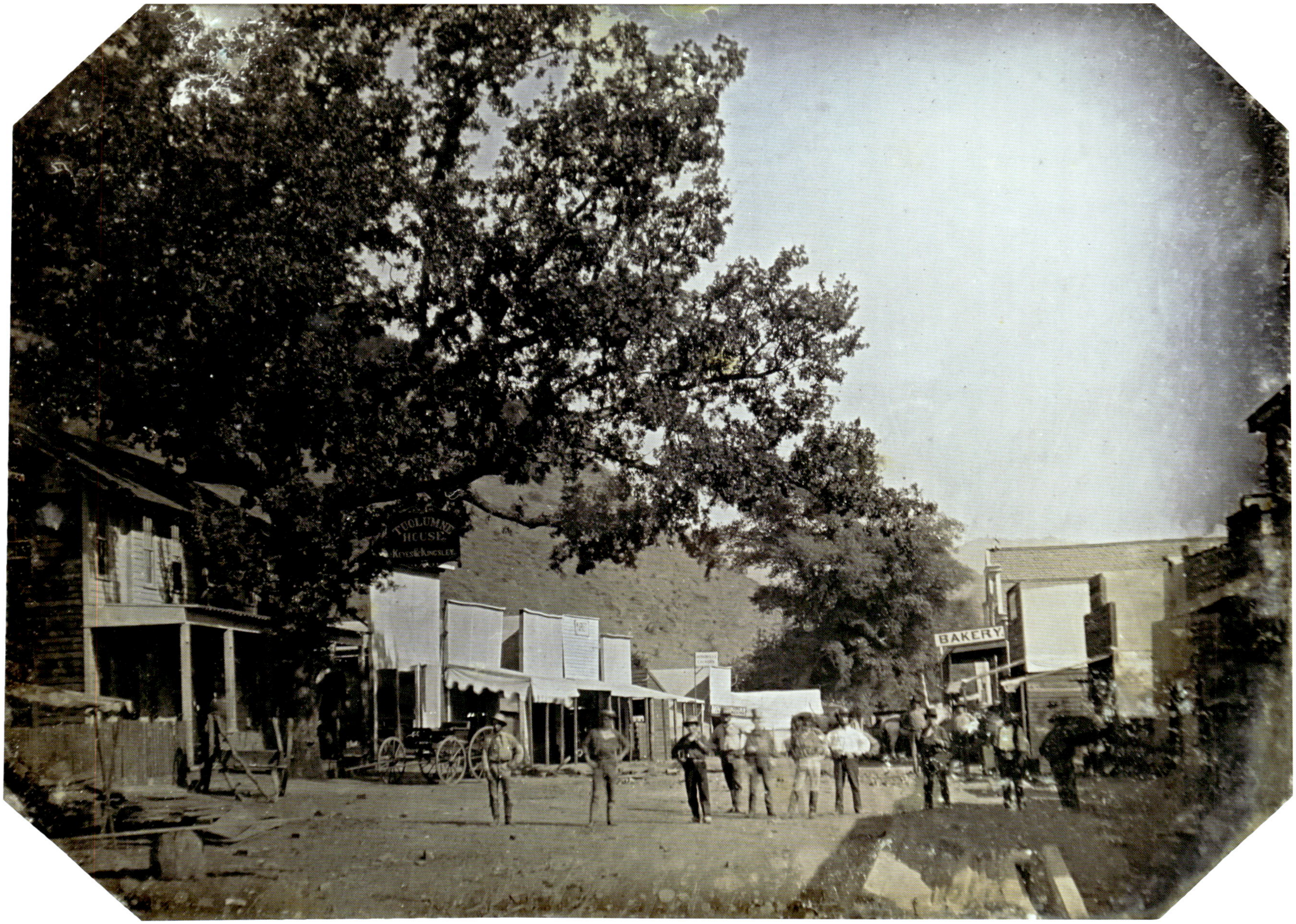

100 **Unknown maker**, American. *Street view of Jacksonville, California*, ca. 1852–55.
Half-plate daguerreotype. Collection of Michael Peterson.

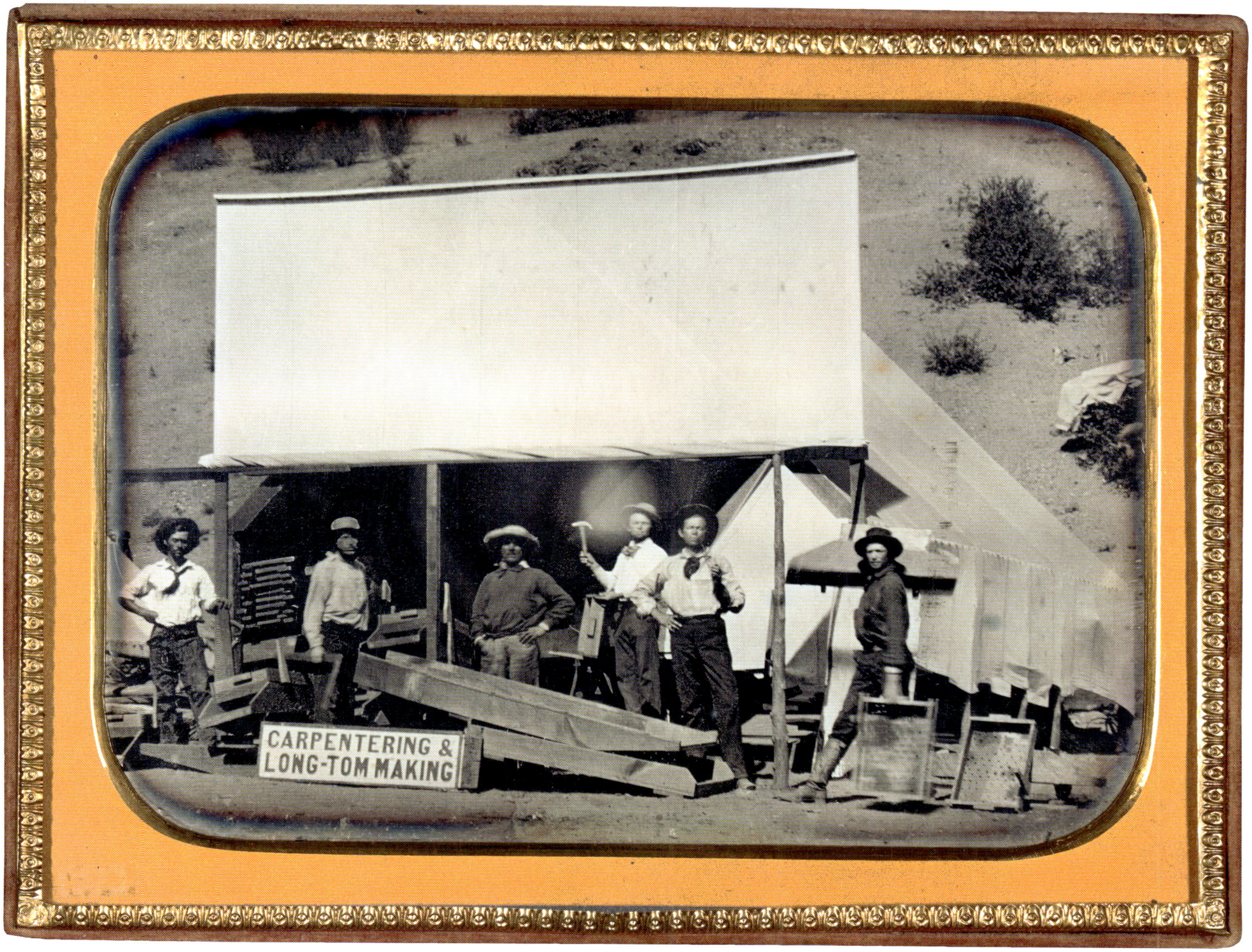

101 **Unknown maker**, American. *Carpentering and long tom making business, Jacksonville, California*, ca. 1852–55. Half-plate daguerreotype. The Art Institute of Chicago, The W. Bruce and Delaney H. Lundberg Collection, restricted gift of The Phillip Leonian and Edith Rosenbaum Leonian Charitable Trust.

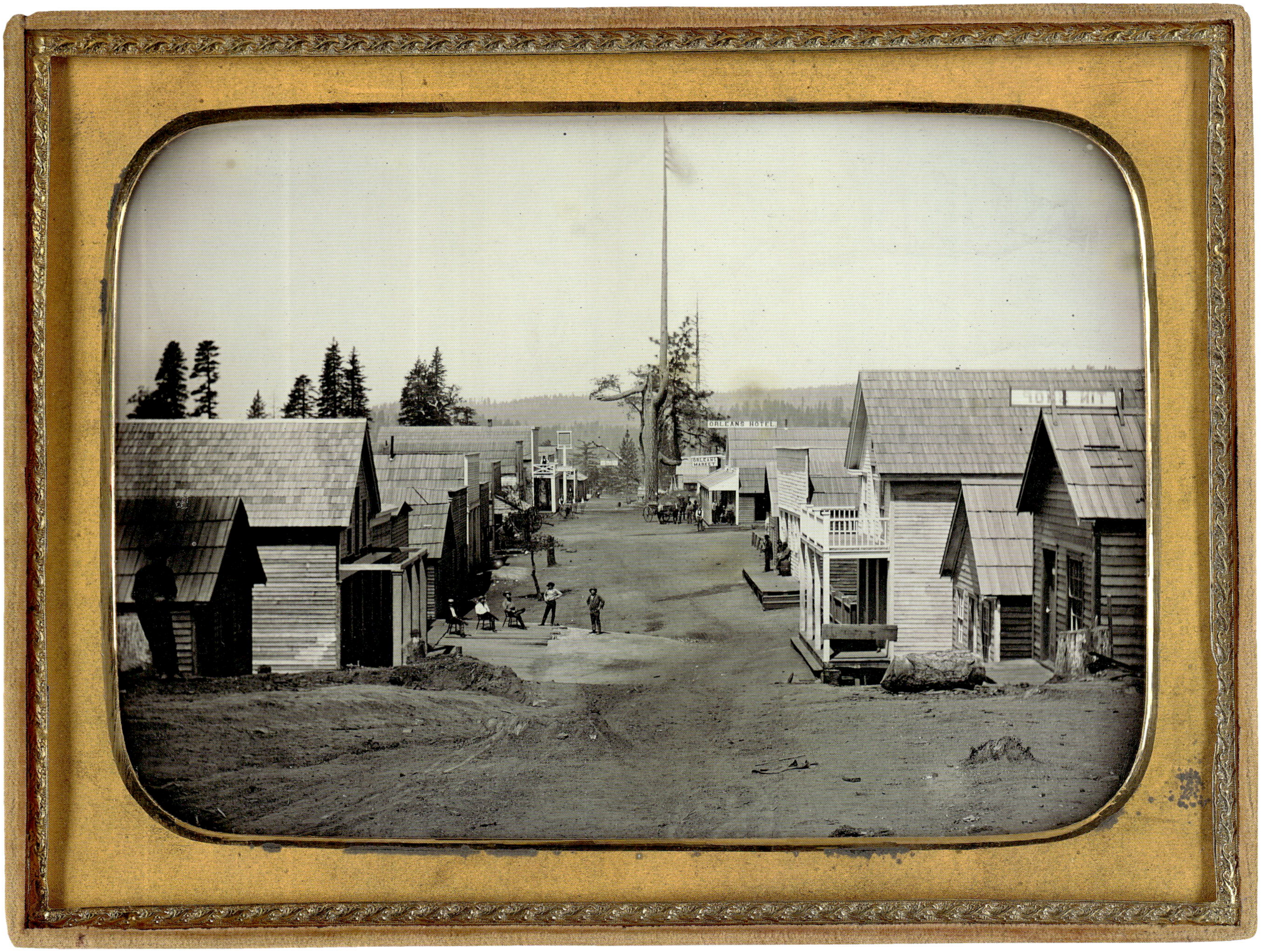

102 Unknown maker, American. *Street in mining town with American flag,* ca. 1852. Half-plate daguerreotype. National Gallery of Canada, Ottawa.

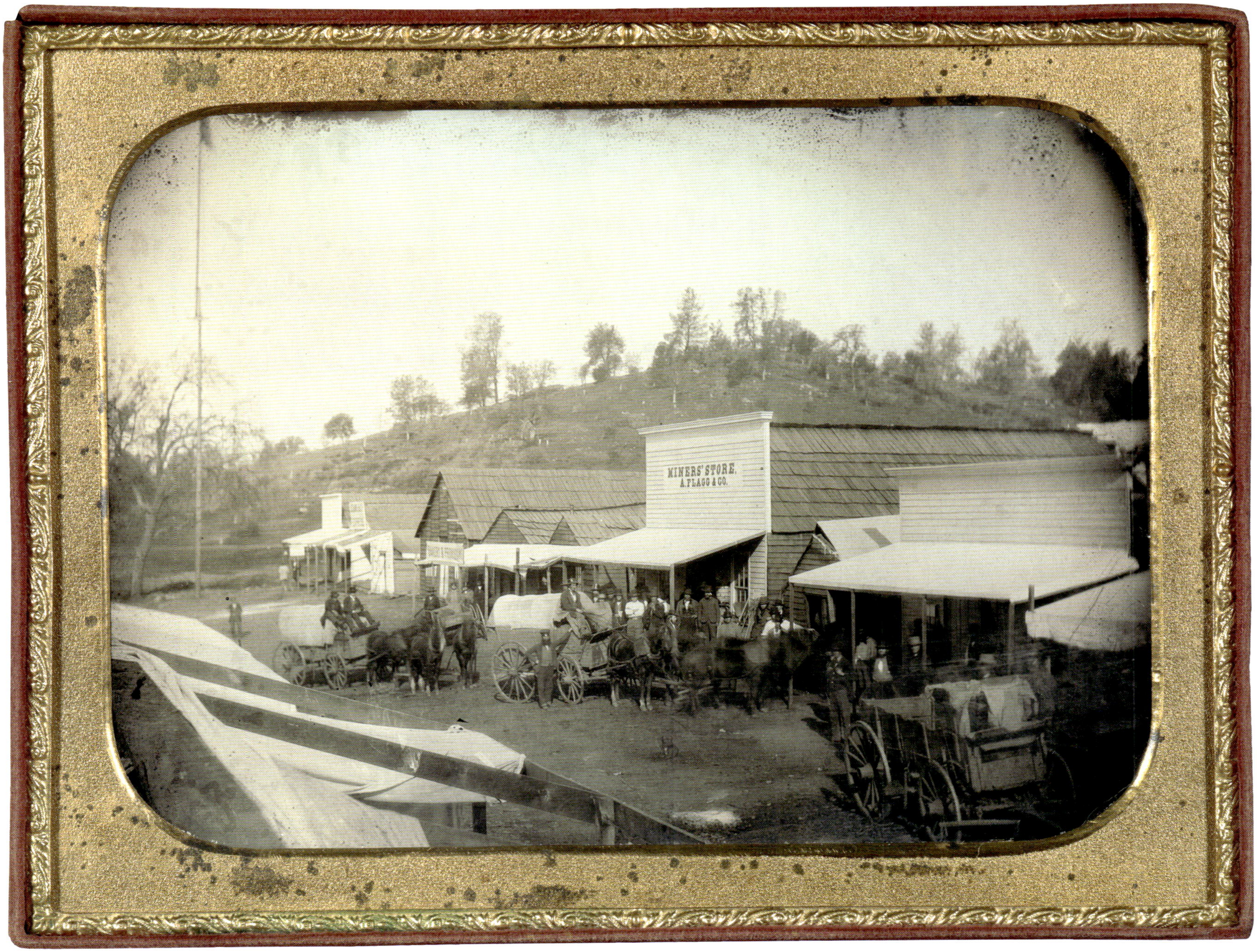

103 **George H. Johnson**, American (1823–ca. 1880s). *Mining town, California*, ca. 1850–52.
Half-plate daguerreotype.

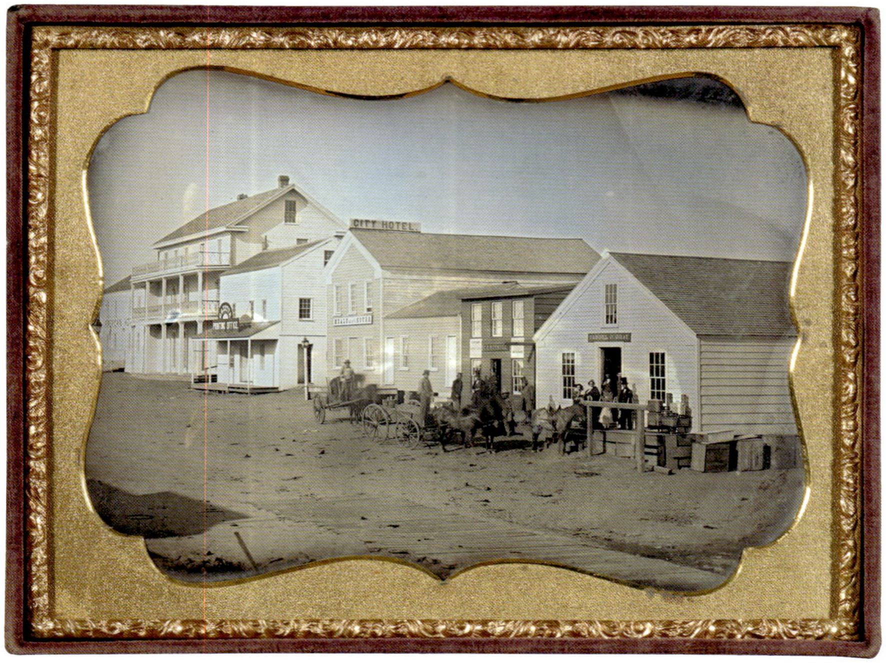

104 **Robert H. Vance**, American (1825–1876). *Benecia, California*, ca 1851. Quarter-plate daguerreotype.

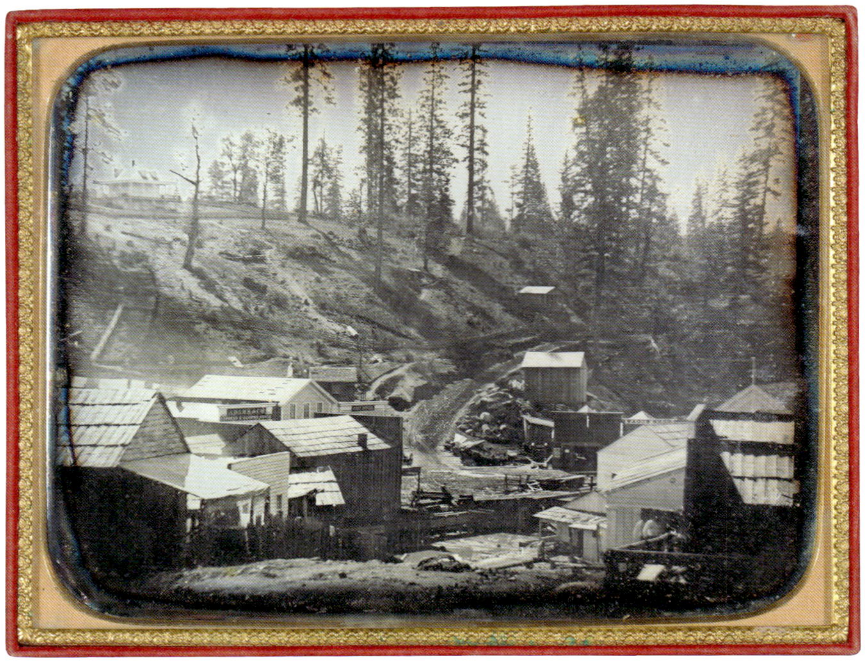

105 **Unknown maker**, American. *Mining town (possibly Rough and Ready), Nevada County, California*, ca. 1850–55. Half-plate daguerreotype. The Art Institute of Chicago, The W. Bruce and Delaney H. Lundberg Collection, restricted gift of The Phillip Leonian and Edith Rosenbaum Leonian Charitable Trust.

to pitch dramatically backward while the buildings in the background recede from view.

The town of Jacksonville, located in Tuolumne County, was founded in 1849 when gold was discovered in a tributary to the Tuolumne River. By 1851, the town had a population of about 400.[84] Around this same time, a daguerreotypist made a view [100] of the main street with canvas-fronted businesses, including a hotel and bakery.[85] At the far end of the street, just visible with the aid of a magnifying glass, a long-tom and carpentering business [101] highlights the persistent demand for mining equipment. H. E. Bond and Robert Mollyneaux, immigrants from Ohio, established a grocery store to provide for the needs of the growing town.[86] In this whole-plate view [54], the store dominates the composition with, we presume, Bond and Mollyneaux standing at the entrance. Children in motion are only partially captured on the plate. Shingles piled outside the store may indicate a newly constructed roof.

Located east of the mining region in the Sierra Nevada, Sierraville was settled in 1857. At 5,000 feet above sea level, the town was mainly devoted to agriculture. Probably taken close to the time the city was founded, this ambrotype view [96] pictures a varied grouping of town residents posing for the camera. Women are dressed in their finest, a group of men plays cards at a table at far left, and two men holding liquor bottles stand behind them. Children, a dog, and a small mule round out the lively ensemble.

When an elevated camera position was available and strategically located at the end of the street, as in this image of Orleans [102], a superior view resulted. This vantage point reveals the entire street, on both sides, creating a well-balanced composition. Some men recline in chairs in the foreground, and another stands on the top balcony of a hotel at the rear. A flagpole, topped by an American flag, has been fashioned from an existing evergreen tree.

George Johnson understood the importance of elevation in securing a successful town view [103]. Positioned on a roof or balcony, he managed to capture a remarkable amount of activity in this street scene. Three wagons, each pulled by a team of four horses, line up for their turn at the Miner's Store. The elevated vantage point also allows the viewer a glimpse of the hill with sparse foliage behind the main street. Although unidentified, this town is probably not in the Sierra Nevada northeastern region, which is characterized by evergreen forests. Robert Vance made similar choices when daguerreotyping Benicia [104].[87] Positioned on an upper floor of a business across the street, Vance secured a lively view of hotels, businesses, and townspeople. Here, Samuel Gray, one of the first board members of the Young Ladies' Seminary, stands with his wife and daughter in front of his business.[88]

Views taken from hillsides sometimes resulted in untidy overviews of the town. In this daguerreotype of an unknown mining town (possibly Rough and Ready) [105], the main street view is off-center, but many of the signs are visible and readable. Perched on a hillside above the town is a neatly painted home with a fenced yard—the residential area is located above and away from the commercial district, a common feature in town development. The place feels remote; the access road into town is steep and muddy. The forest,

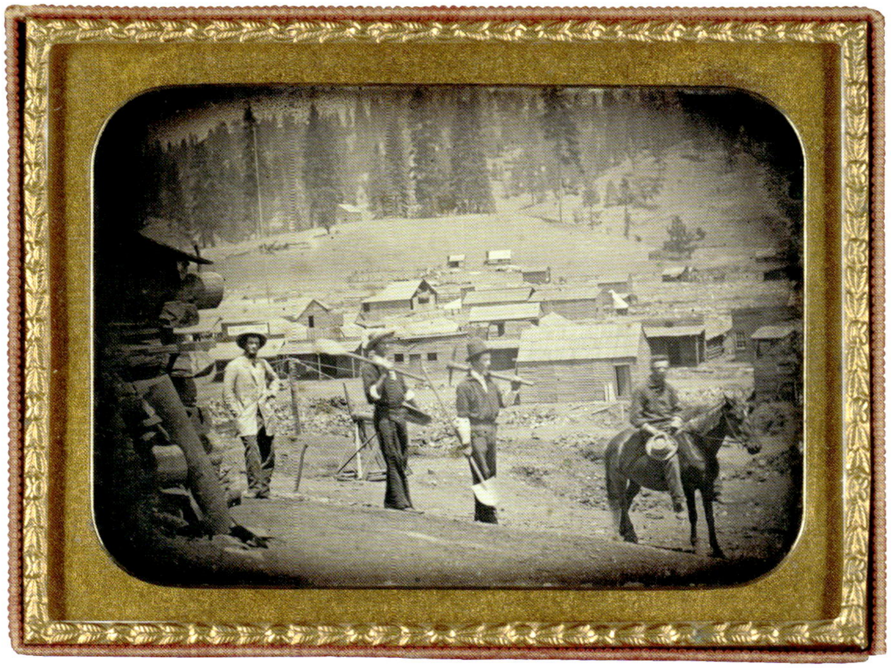

106 **Unknown maker**, American. *View of the town of Volcano, California*, ca. 1854. Quarter-plate daguerreotype. Bancroft Library, University of California, Berkeley.

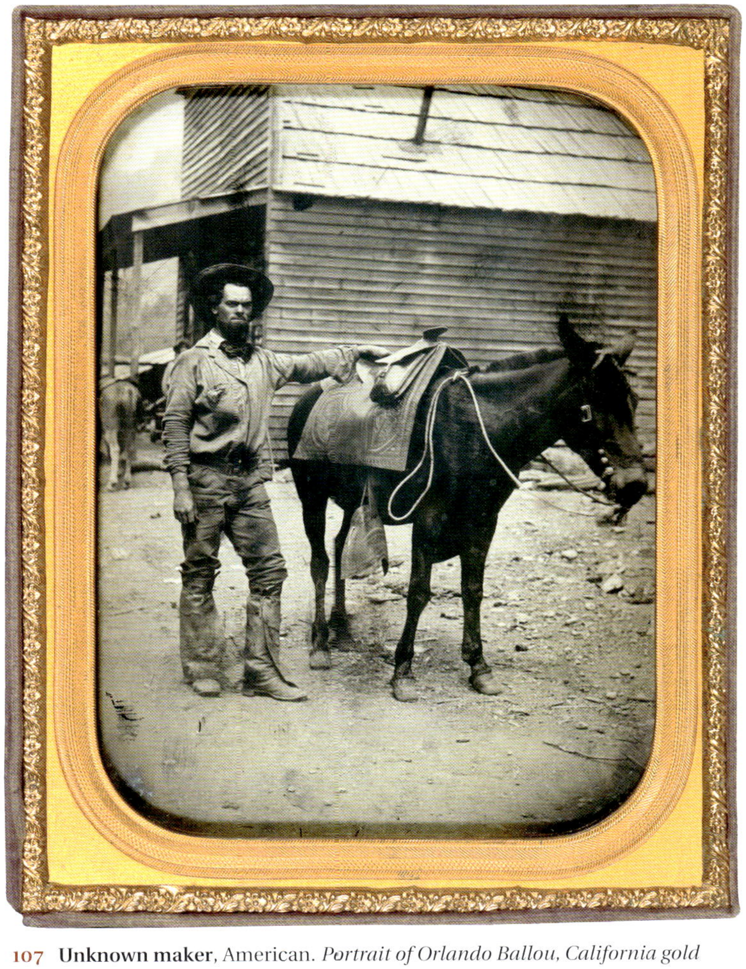

107 **Unknown maker**, American. *Portrait of Orlando Ballou, California gold miner*, ca. 1854. Half-plate ambrotype.

although partially cleared for the town, dominates the overall landscape. In other hillside views, like this one of Volcano [106], the focus is divided between the town and a group of miners readying themselves for a day's work. Horses and mules were frequently the only mode of transport able to navigate the treacherous roads [107].

In towns made of canvas and wood, fires were frequent and deadly. Newly rebuilt towns like Georgetown were ideal subject matter for daguerreotypists traveling through the region.

> Founded in 1849, [Georgetown] was destroyed by fire on the 14th of July, 1852. After this afflicting event, its site was changed, and it now occupies a prominent position on a level and picturesque ridge, about two miles from the Middle Fork of the American River.[89]

In a bold image of Georgetown [75], the daguerreotypist, positioned behind an expanse of logs, underscores the importance of the lumber industry to the rebuilding of the town.[90] Half the composition is devoted to the sawmill and lumber yard. This daguerreotype view was used as the basis for an engraving in the April 1854 issue of the *Pictorial Union* [FIG. 8]. A year later, the *Sacramento Union* emphasized the town's building frenzy: "In many places where but a few months since the ground remained in its primeval state, are now seen and heard the busy strokes of the carpenters, who are erecting beautiful and neat cottages that would be an ornament to any village in the Union."[91]

The Distant View

At their greatest remove, daguerreotypists emphasized the place of gold rush towns within the overall landscape. Photographing from a distance rendered individual characteristics indiscernible, as one gold town could be easily confused with another. However, distance also obscured shortcomings—muddy, littered streets and canvas structures were much less obvious. It was a delicate balancing act: daguerreotypists faced the challenge of representing the actual city while simultaneously signaling the ideal. Although the town may have been flawed, the promise of a prosperous future was understood to compensate for any number of present-day limitations. The significance of these towns, particularly in the earliest and roughest stages, lay not in what they were, but in what they would become.

The elevated view had a well-known artistic history and significance. A precursor to the bird's eye view, the elevated perspective was key to the aesthetic of panorama paintings.[92] Invented in the late eighteenth century by Robert Barker, the first large-scale painted panorama was exhibited in London in 1788.[93] The viewer would ascend a stairway to a platform located at the center of a specially designed rotunda in which the panorama was displayed. This viewing platform was positioned to roughly align the painting's horizon line with the eye level of the spectator, giving a powerful

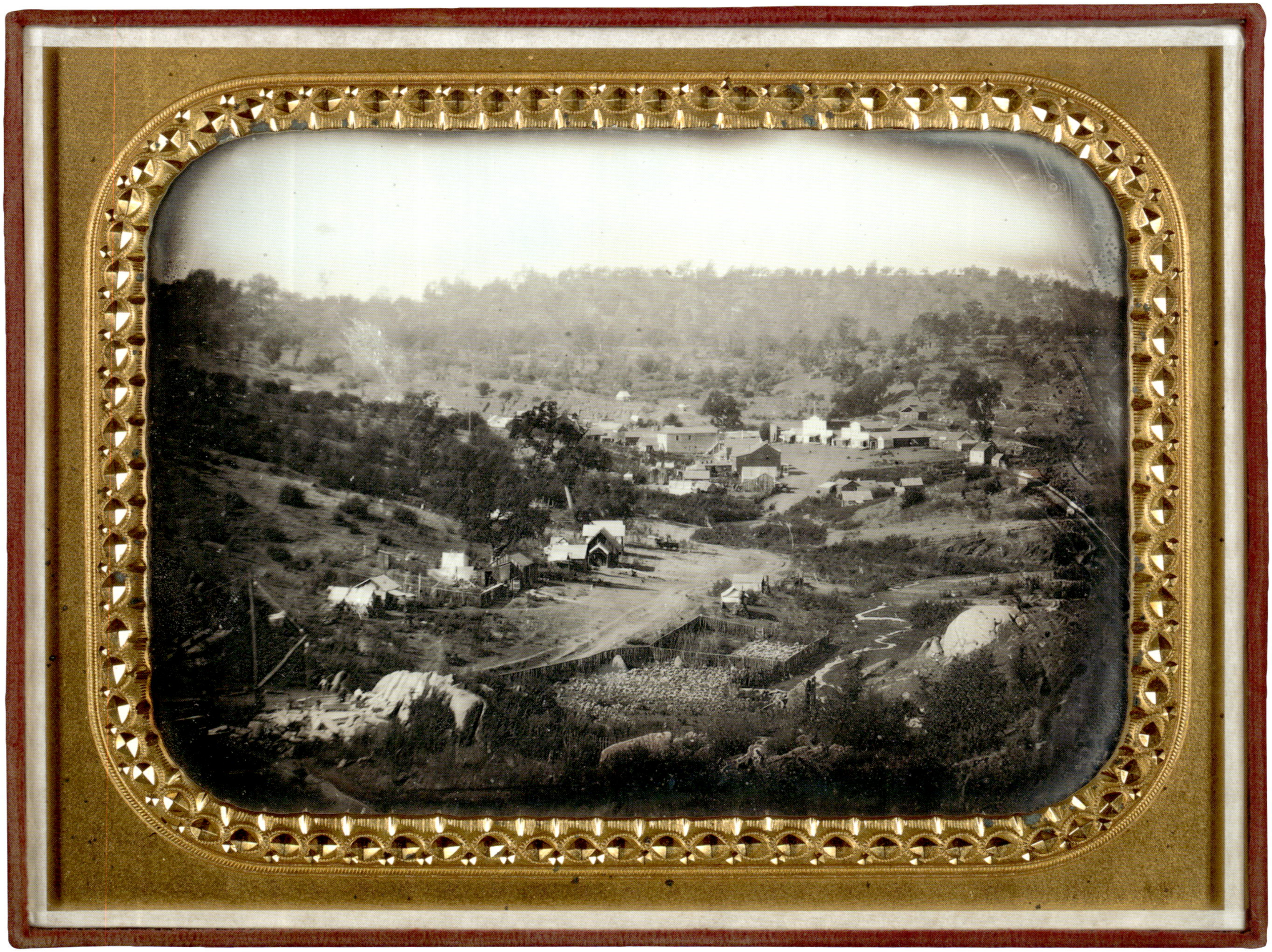

108 **Unknown maker**, American. *Mormon Island: gold rush town view among hills*, ca. 1854. Half-plate daguerreotype. Bancroft Library, University of California, Berkeley.

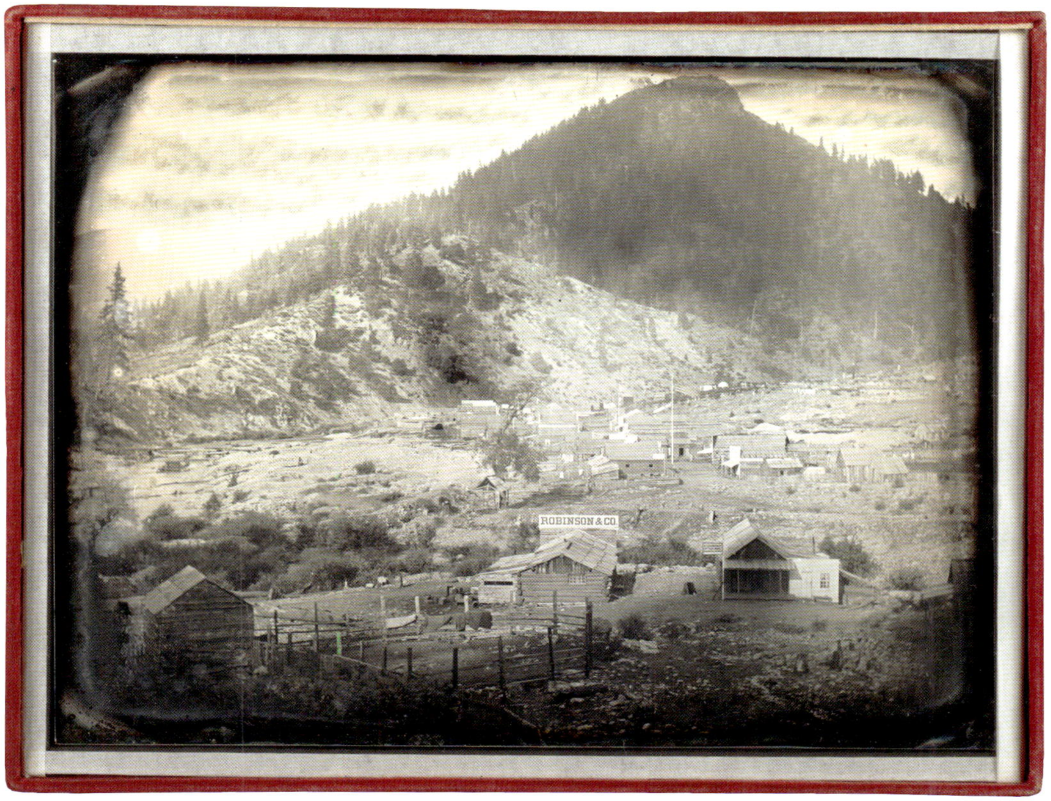

109 **Unknown maker**, American. *Henry Robinson's store in a California mining town*, ca. 1855. Half-plate daguerreotype. Bancroft Library, University of California, Berkeley.

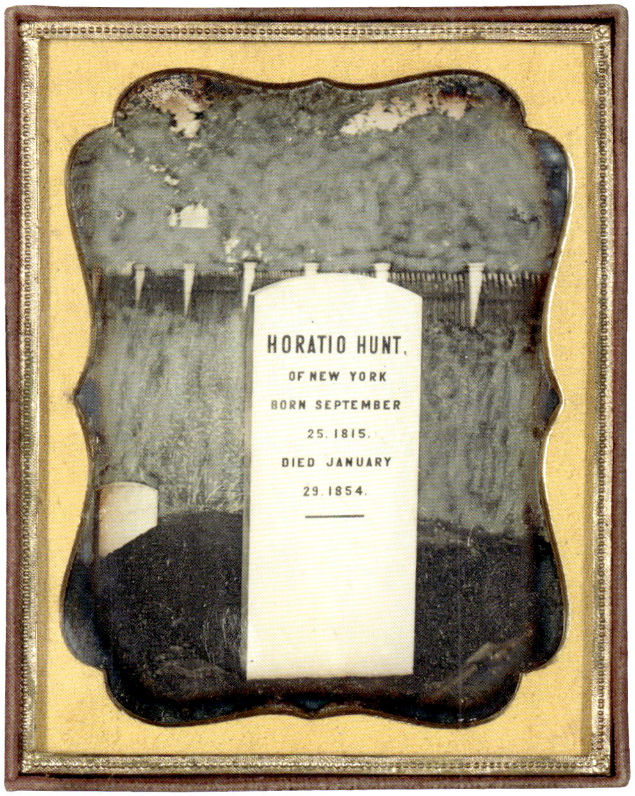

110 **Unknown maker**, American. *Grave of Horatio Hunt*, ca. 1854. Quarter-plate daguerreotype. The Art Institute of Chicago, The W. Bruce and Delaney H. Lundberg Collection, restricted gift of The Phillip Leonian and Edith Rosenbaum Leonian Charitable Trust.

sensation of elevation over the scene. According to Alan Wallach, the panorama "disguised the fact . . . that what was being produced was not only a spectacle but a spectator with a particular relation to reality."[94] The elevated panoramic view suggested a perspective of privilege and dominion. Coining the term "panoptic sublime," Wallach argues that "having reached the topmost point in an optical hierarchy, the tourist experienced a sudden access of power, a dizzying sense of having suddenly come into possession of a terrain stretching as far as the eye could see."[95]

Unfortunately, no pictorial tradition existed in the eighteenth century to precisely re-create the panoramic viewing sensation in two-dimensional terms. Art critic William Gilpin remarked on "the absurdity of carrying a painter to the top of a high hill to take a view. He cannot do it. Extension alone, though amusing in nature, will never make a picture."[96] Thomas Cole agreed. After climbing a mountain in October 1828, Cole remarked that he saw "on every side prospects mighty and sublime opened upon the vision." But for "all its beauty the scene was one too extended and map-like for the canvass."[97] Captain Basil Hall, a retired British naval officer touring the United States in 1827–28, created sketches of his subjects of interest using the camera lucida, which he called a "magical secret for recording the features of Nature with ease and fidelity."[98] One sketch, drawn while perched on a promontory point high above a river, caught the eye of Cole, who later used it as the basis for one of his most significant paintings. The photographically oriented "machine of sight" had provided the means by which the elevated view was successfully transformed onto a two-dimensional surface, helping to establish the elevated perspective as appropriate subject matter for all artists.[99]

In California, physical ascension was linked to the cultural idea that everyone had the opportunity to rise and achieve visual or economic mastery, reinforcing the values of liberty and democracy. A view once reserved for the elite was now widely available; anyone from any background could transcend their given circumstances through hard work and dedication. The "view from the top" was about possibility, power, and dominion.

Lithographers of the day specialized in producing elevated views of towns and landscapes, exposing their audiences to this new and strange perspective. Several elevated daguerreotype views were used as the basis for engravings, but it is unclear whether these views were commissioned by lithographers to be used exclusively in this way. Scholars have long acknowledged the shared legacy of lithographs and daguerreotypes: both were democratic and affordable reproductive mediums that thrived in early urban centers. In parallel ways, both provided idealized views imbued with the visual rhetoric of western expansion and Manifest Destiny.

This elevated long view of Mormon Island [108] was the basis of a wood engraving for a pictorial letter sheet. Mormon Island was one of the oldest of

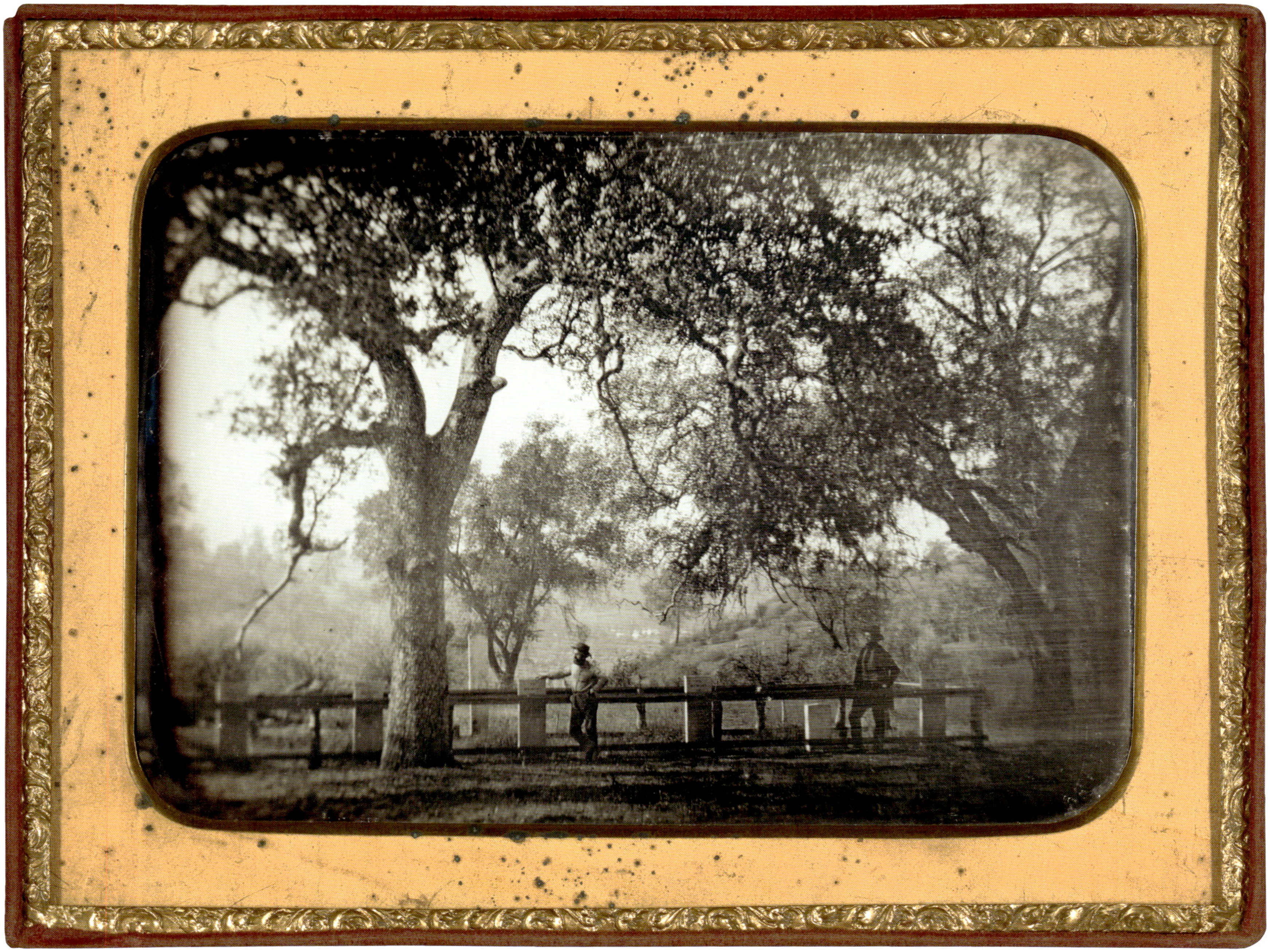

111 **Unknown maker**, American. *California mining cemetery*, ca. 1850–55. Half-plate daguerreotype. The Art Institute of Chicago, The W. Bruce and Delaney H. Lundberg Collection, restricted gift of The Phillip Leonian and Edith Rosenbaum Leonian Charitable Trust.

the California gold towns; gold was discovered there in March 1848, three months after the find at Sutter's Mill. An all-encompassing view, this vantage point includes three distinct areas of the town: the commercial district in the rear, the residential area in the middle, and a glimpse of a mining enterprise at bottom left. Although the river is not visible in this daguerreotype, it is presumably nearby, as the miners appear to be using a jack, a tool used to move large boulders from an exposed river bed.

In this view [109], reputed to be of Henry Robinson's store in Marysville, the scenic beauty of the location is undeniable. The daguerreotypist was as interested in picturing the hill itself as he was in the town at the foot of the hillside. A close inspection reveals many signs: "Robinson & Co.," "R. Barnes & Co.," and "Exchange Hotel." The "Sierra Hotel" may indicate that this is instead a town located in Sierra County, in the northeastern gold mining region. A hilly and densely forested area, the Sierra Nevada foothills have a very similar topography to the geographic region pictured here.[100]

One of the largest of the California gold towns, Nevada City was frequently photographed.[101] While working on their early projects, both J. Wesley Jones and Robert Vance spent time in and around this town, daguerreotyping the main street and miners at work on nearby claims. Vance was especially intrigued; he made a multi-plate panorama from a hill, highlighting the surrounding landscape. Awed by the "surrounding forest," Vance noted "the enormous size to which the trees attain in this region, some of them three hundred feet in height, and twenty-seven feet in circumference."[102] Joseph Starkweather's view of the same city [48], taken in 1852, is very different from the one described by Vance just the year before. Starkweather's daguerreotype reveals a town where building standards were clearly secondary to the primary occupation of mining. The rocky main street looks impassable for wagon traffic. Buildings speedily constructed are held upright by wooden braces while others pitch precariously sideways. The trees are significantly thinned out; the few that remain tower over the city.

Cemeteries

Death was a real and regular part of life in gold rush California. Rudimentary living and mining conditions promoted the spread of diseases such as cholera and tuberculosis. Additional causes of death included mining accidents, physical conflict, and weather-related disasters. Remarkably, it was estimated that one in five people who arrived in California in 1849 were dead within six months.[103]

In San Francisco, the Yerba Buena Cemetery was established in 1850 with "enough town property in that locality to make a cemetery sufficient to accommodate the dead . . . for the next half century."[104] By 1850 in Placerville, the first gold town encountered by those making the overland journey to California, "the cemetery on the hill is fast filling up with many who left their homes under cheering auspices and with glowing hopes for the future. Their deaths are attributable to the enervating effects of travel over the plains."[105]

Daguerreotypists were often commissioned to commemorate deaths in the gold mining region. A familiar genre of this work featured one or more mourners at a gravesite [44]. Some images were undoubtedly made for evidentiary purposes to send to family members back home [110]. Inside many California cemeteries, individual graves were surrounded with white fencing and the entire area was enclosed "with a substantial fence, [laid] out in a style becoming a people who have been educated in a civilized and christian land."[106] With so many people "widely separated from those intimately connected with them," it was the responsibility of local communities to show a "reverence for the departed."[107] In this daguerreotype [111], two men stand under large graceful trees surrounded by a lush landscape; their profiles reflect deep contemplation. The moral lesson was particularly relevant in California: "The effect will not be unbeneficial to a community "so peculiarly constituted as ours, when, in the midst of their wild struggle after gold, they may see the cold tombstone rearing its head with its solemn admonition . . ."[108]

After the Gold Rush

The life cycle of many of these gold rush towns was brief. The initial influx of people caused by gold discovery "proved short, never more than six years, usually no more than half that, and not uncommonly, only a season."[109] Miners were itinerant, moving from location to location on a quest for gold. One study of miners residing in Nevada City in 1850 showed that only seven out of one hundred were still residents just six years later.[110] Population changes were tied to mining successes or developments, leading to boom-and-bust economic cycles. Conversely, a town's longevity depended on more permanent and sustainable mining technologies. For those finding long-term mining work, it was "a new era in the history of this district; for [the] hitherto wandering population [would] become permanent settlers, . . . enabled to surround themselves with comforts which were supposed to be utterly incompatible with a miner's life."[111]

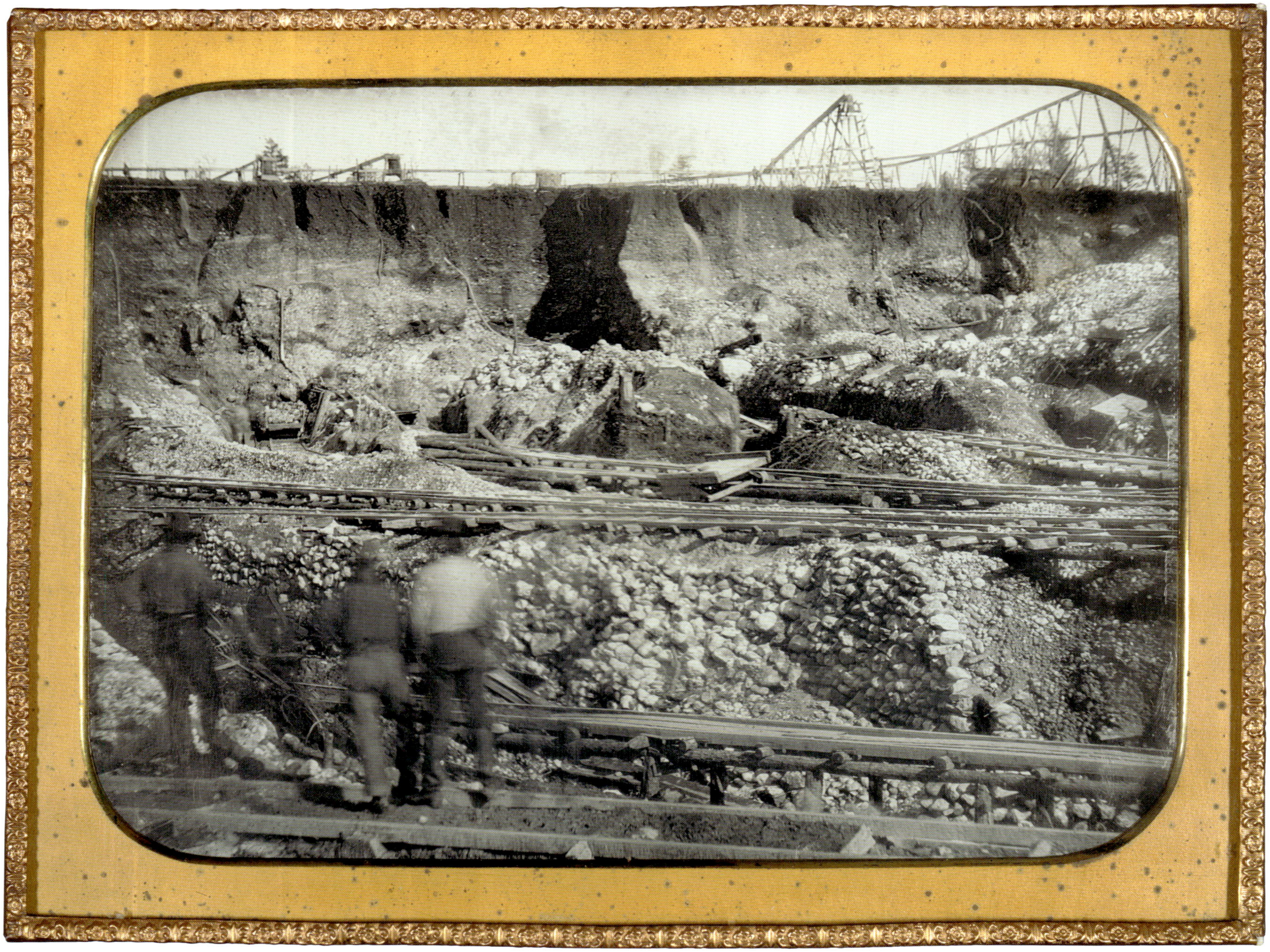

112 William Shew, American (1820–1903). *Hydraulic mining, Michigan Bluff, Placer County, California,* ca. 1852. Whole-plate daguerreotype.

CHAPTER 5 *"Finding the color": The Evolution of Mining Technologies*

Mining processes pictured in daguerreotypes of gold fields often are not identified.[1] Vague titles like *Gold Mining Scene* or *Miners with Sluice* are repeatedly used, yielding little information on what is pictured. Similarly, dates and locations of these views are often best guesses. Visual analysis of the mining technologies pictured in these images can help to fill in some of these blanks. Miners used several distinct processes, all based on one or both of two fundamental principles: gold is heavy, and in fluid mixtures with other materials will inevitably sink to the bottom; and it bonds, or amalgamates, with the element mercury (quicksilver). Understanding the evolution of mining technologies is a first step toward determining population demographics, as well as time periods and locations.

In the July 1857 issue of *Hutchings' California Magazine*, James Hutchings published a detailed synopsis of mining technologies. He later reprinted much of the text and accompanying illustrations in *The Miners' Own Book* (1858), intended to be used by miners in the field. Hutchings covered the following tools and processes: the pan, the rocker/cradle, the long tom, the sluice, ground sluicing, sinking a shaft, drifting, tunneling, the water flume, and hydraulic mining. Later articles covered the technologies of river diversion and quartz mining. Hutchings' definitions are extremely useful in identifying mining techniques and are used throughout the following discussion.[2]

The earliest gold miners of 1848 did not require special equipment; a pickaxe, shovel, and knife were often sufficient. Before heading to the rivers, miners sometimes concentrated on "dry diggings"—ravines and gorges located at the bottom of the hills through which a river once flowed. "At that [early] period the precious metal was supposed to be found only in rivers, canons [*sic*], gulches, or ravines; and as the latter were the readiest prospected, and the easiest worked and often paid very well . . . they were the first places sought after and tested."[3] Dry digging (as opposed to "wet digging" which was done directly in the streams) was especially relevant in places where water was not readily available. To dry dig, the miner first removed loose stones from an area and "the digging continued until the bottom rock of the ravine was reached, commonly at a depth of from one to six feet."[4] The surface of this rock contained small crevices from which gold could be scraped with a sharp knife. This was a popular technique in the early years of the gold rush—when gold was relatively easy to find, there was little competition, and an individual miner could work a claim.

Pan

The earliest tool of mining, the pan, was used throughout all the years of the gold rush. Panning was an easy technique, but it required practice to master. As described in *Hutchings' California Magazine*, for "panning out," a miner,

> having placed his pan by the edge of a pool or stream, takes hold of the sides with both hands, and squatting down lowers it into the water, then, with a kind of oscillating and slightly rotary motion, he moves it about beneath the surface for a few moments, then after drawing it to the edge of the pool, he throws out the largest of the stones, and assists to dissolve the dirt by rubbing it between his hands; the washing is then repeated; and, while the muddy water and sand are floated out of the pan into the pool, the gold, if there is any, settles gradually to the bottom of the pan and is there saved.[5]

Any gold sighted in the pan was called "finding the color." One to three cents of gold was called "good pay dirt" and ten to twenty-five cents was "a good prospect."[6]

The first panning devices were made by indigenous people of California: American Indians and Mexicans.[7] Most of the early miners new to the region learned the panning technique by imitating these groups. Americans Indians used reeds and grasses to create tightly woven, watertight baskets used for panning. In March 1849, Chilean miner Vincente Pérez Rosales made the following observation of an American Indian tribe panning for gold:

> The division of labor they followed was this: the men dug and gave the mud to the children, who then carried it in baskets to the women. The women, lined up along the stream, then washed it in grass baskets of the most perfect construction. The gold was tied in rags, in amounts more or less equal.[8]

When panning near a stream, Mexican miners used broad wooden bowls (bateas) in a similar way to the American Indians' use of baskets. Bateas were handcrafted "out of solid block[s] of wood" to specific dimensions: twelve to twenty-four inches in diameter and two to four inches deep. The batea was popular in the southern mines (south of the Mokelumne River), where most Mexican miners were located.[9] In areas of water scarcity, the batea was used for "dry washing," a difficult technique used exclusively among the Mexican population. In 1849, American miner William Ryan observed several Mexicans working at the bottom of a ravine:

> One was shoveling up the sand into a large cloth, stretched out upon the ground, and which, when it was tolerably well covered, he took up by the corners, and shook until the pebbles and larger particles of stone and dirt came to the surface. These he brushed away carefully with his hand, repeating the process of shaking and clearing until the residue was sufficiently fine for the next operation.[10]

The residue was then deposited in large bateas and the contents thrown high into the air, with the lighter material progressively blown out as it descended. This arduous process was repeated until the gold could be seen and retrieved.

Although early miners used the batea, metal pans were more common.[11] Many American miners used a sheet iron pan measuring sixteen to eighteen inches in diameter, two-and-a-quarter to four inches deep, and with sides angled at thirty-seven to fifty degrees [73, 74]. Most of the pans were made and purchased in the United States, but some immigrant groups, such as the Chileans, brought their own.[12]

Rocker

The pan was unmatched for its simplicity and portability, but it was laboriously slow and unsuitable for larger-scale mining. In July 1848, Colonel Richard Barnes Mason, the military commander of California, reported that miners at work at Mormon Diggings on the American River were washing gold "with tin pans, some with close woven Indian baskets, but the greater part had a rude machine known as the cradle."[13] This tool [FIG. 10], also called a rocker, consisted of

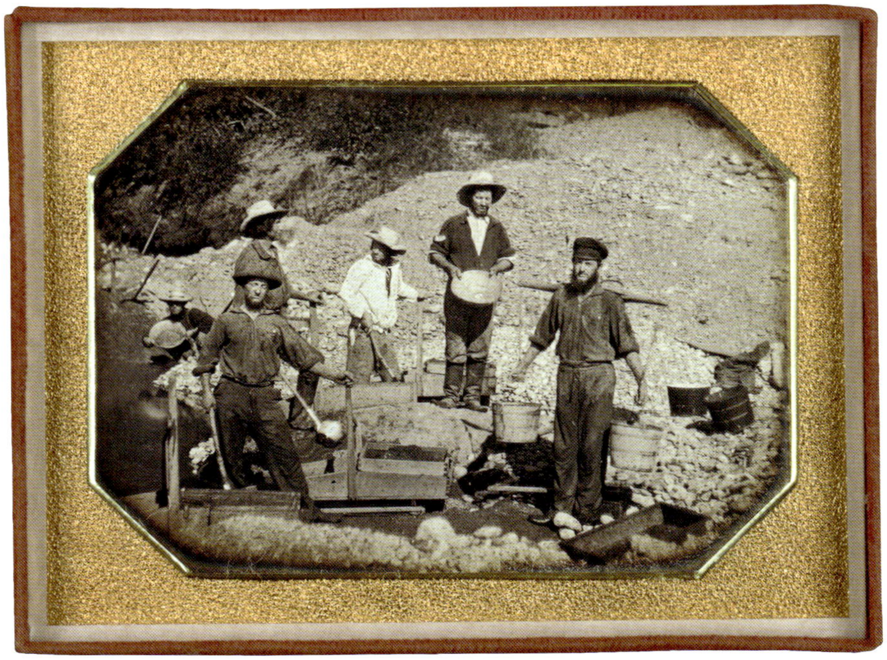

113 **Unknown maker**, American. *Six miners with rocker, wheel barrows, picks, shovels, and gold pans*, ca. 1850. Quarter-plate daguerreotype. Bancroft Library, University of California, Berkeley.

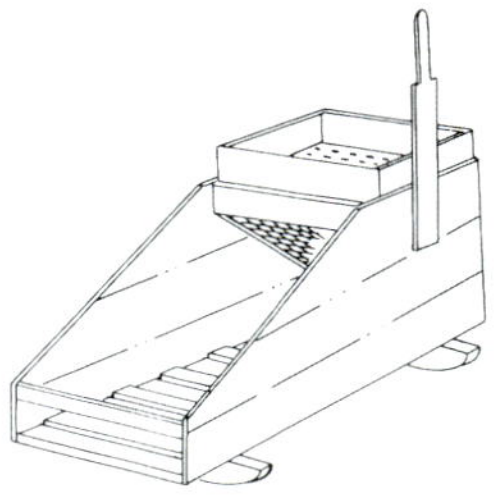

FIG. 10 *Rocker*, from Jeffrey M. LaLande, "Sojourners in Search of Gold: Hydraulic Mining Techniques of the Chinese on the Oregon Frontier," in *Journal of the Society for Industrial Archeology* 11, no. 1 (1985).

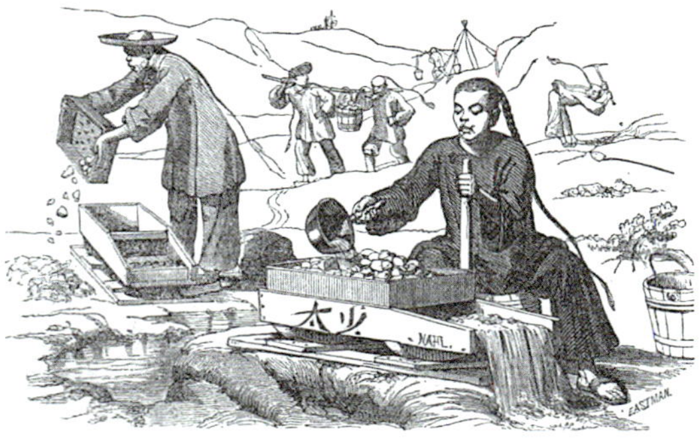

FIG. 11 *The Cradle and Manner of Using It*, from "Mining for Gold in California," in *Hutchings' California Magazine* 2 (1857–58).

> an oblong box from three to three and a half feet in length, eighteen to twenty-two inches in width, and about nine inches in depth at the upper end with a bar across the middle; one end of the box is left open or has no end board. . . . A separate box, sieve, or hopper, is made to fit into and occupy the half of the cradle. . . . This hopper is about four inches in depth; the bottom is of sheet iron, perforated with holes. . . . Rockers are attached to the under side of the whole, quite similar to those of a child's cradle; near the middle an upright handle is attached, by which motion is given to it. The hopper being nearly filled with auriferous earth, the operator being seated by its side, while rocking the cradle with one hand, he dips and pours on water with the other. . . . The water dissolving the earth, it falls through the sieve . . . a "riffle-bar" placed crosswise. . . . While the lighter sand and dirt passes over with the water, the gold, by its greater weight, is retained.[14]

By the spring of 1849, most miners had adopted this new tool, which was faster, more efficient, and could be worked by an individual or a small group. Some miners used the pan and rocker in tandem. In [113], the miner at far left squats next to a stream with his pan in hand while a standing miner, at center, displays the contents of his batea. Three of the miners hold rockers in one hand and tin dippers in the other while a fourth carries buckets of water on a yoke around his shoulders. Because the rocker held only one bucketful of water at a time, this time-consuming method of water retrieval was perfectly adequate.

Rocker technology was quickly adopted in the northern mining region where men "rocked the cradle to the tune of chunks of gold, instead of chunky babies."[15] A correspondent to the *Alta California* newspaper reported on the quick dissemination of this method along the Stanislaus River, noting that when he first arrived in mid-April "some five weeks since, there were but two machines within two miles; at the present, rocking 'cradles' are as plentiful as they ought to be in any healthy district."[16] By the end of May 1849, they were also in use in the southern region at the Mokelumne River diggings.[17]

Some American miners who had made their way to California by ship brought "newfangled machines" that had been manufactured in the eastern United States. Noting the absurdity of many of them, gold miner E. Gould Buffum reported, "They were of all imaginable shapes and sizes, some of them appearing most admirably adapted to the churning of butter. I saw, last spring, hundreds of huge bulky machines, which had been brought round Cape Horn." Quickly found to be insufficient, these machines were "invariably abandoned for the common rocker . . . the best machine to be used in connection with mere manual labour."[18]

The pan and the rocker were essentially the only technologies used in California in 1848 and early 1849. The rocker was most effective in rich, easily worked areas where gold was readily accessible.[19] As these richer deposits were depleted and the water supply became more reliable, the usage of the rocker declined in the northern mining region. In an 1852 letter from Indian Bar, Louise Clapp wrote: "As to the rockers, so often mentioned in story and song . . . I have seldom seen them used, though hundreds are lying ownerless along the banks of the river."[20]

By April 1854, "a striking contrast [was] observable" between the cities of Sonora (in the south) and Mariposa (farther south). In Sonora, "the operatives are Americans and North Europeans" and "the old familiar rocker is seldom seen" because an "abundant supply of water enables the miner to wash vast amounts of earth." In Mariposa, however, because of the scarcity of water, "the rocker is the principal 'medium' of washing and fully one half of the operatives are Chinese and Mexicans."[21]

Chinese miners were adept at the rocker and used it extensively when reworking smaller abandoned claims. In fact, the miner illustrating the use of the rocker in *Hutchings California Magazine* was Chinese [FIG. 11].[22] Nineteenth-century observers reported that the Chinese used the rocker for a much longer time than other cultural groups even though more efficient technologies were available.[23] Historians from past generations have suggested that the Chinese miners were content to use the rocker because they were "willing to work for much smaller returns than white miners" and were "simple peasants and laborers accustomed to a limited standard of living in their overcrowded native land."[24] Contemporary historians have

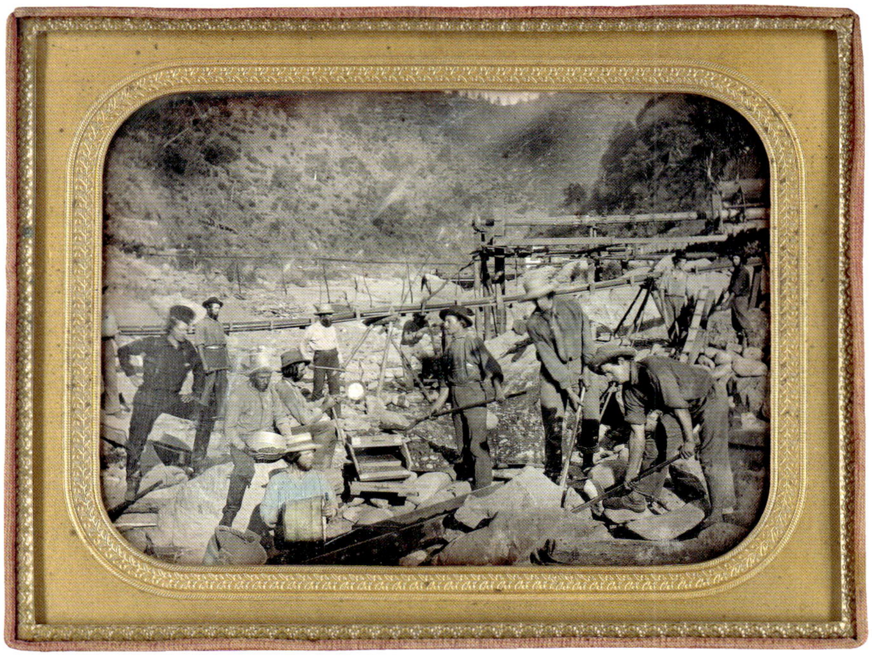

114 **Unknown maker**, American. *Scene with miners*, ca. 1853. Half-plate daguerreotype. National Gallery of Canada, Ottawa.

moved beyond such stereotypes to highlight the significant technological contributions of Chinese immigrants.

Even after it was deemed obsolete, the rocker remained in limited use in all mining districts. It was simple and inexpensive to construct, easy to use, and appropriate for working deposits with a limited water supply. Rockers continued to be used when other methods were impractical or expensive, during times of the year when other methods could not be worked, or in geographic areas not suitable for more advanced techniques.

River Diversion

Differing from the small-scale work of a few men by the river's edge, river mining or turning was a massive undertaking, involving the use of dams, ditches, flumes, and canals to divert streams from their natural beds. After the water was diverted, miners worked the gravel of the drained streambed with pans and rockers, and later with long toms and sluices [114]. Potholes provided rich sources of accumulated gold. An inherently risky endeavor, river mining required a significant investment of time, money, and human resources. It could be attempted only when the streams were at their lowest—typically from September through December. Once winter/spring rains were imminent, the river mining season was over. It was difficult to test the richness of the bed before mining began, and there was no way of ensuring that the weather would cooperate. Many of these operations failed, and miners viewed the process "as a sort of gambling."[25]

When beginning a river mining operation, a company of men first constructed a "race" substantial enough to carry the full volume of river flow.

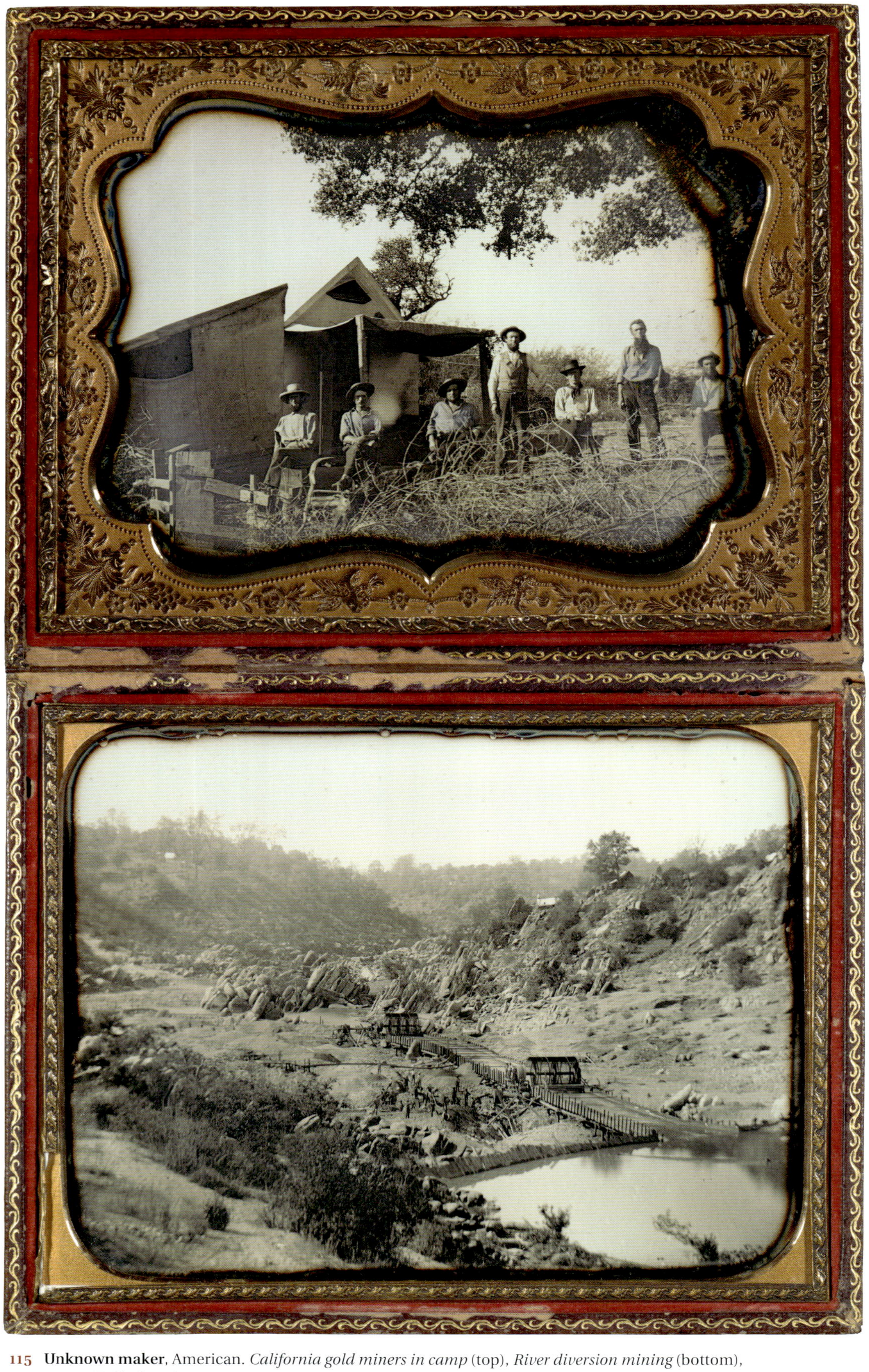

115 Unknown maker, American. *California gold miners in camp* (top), *River diversion mining* (bottom), ca. 1850–55. Half-plate daguerreotypes.

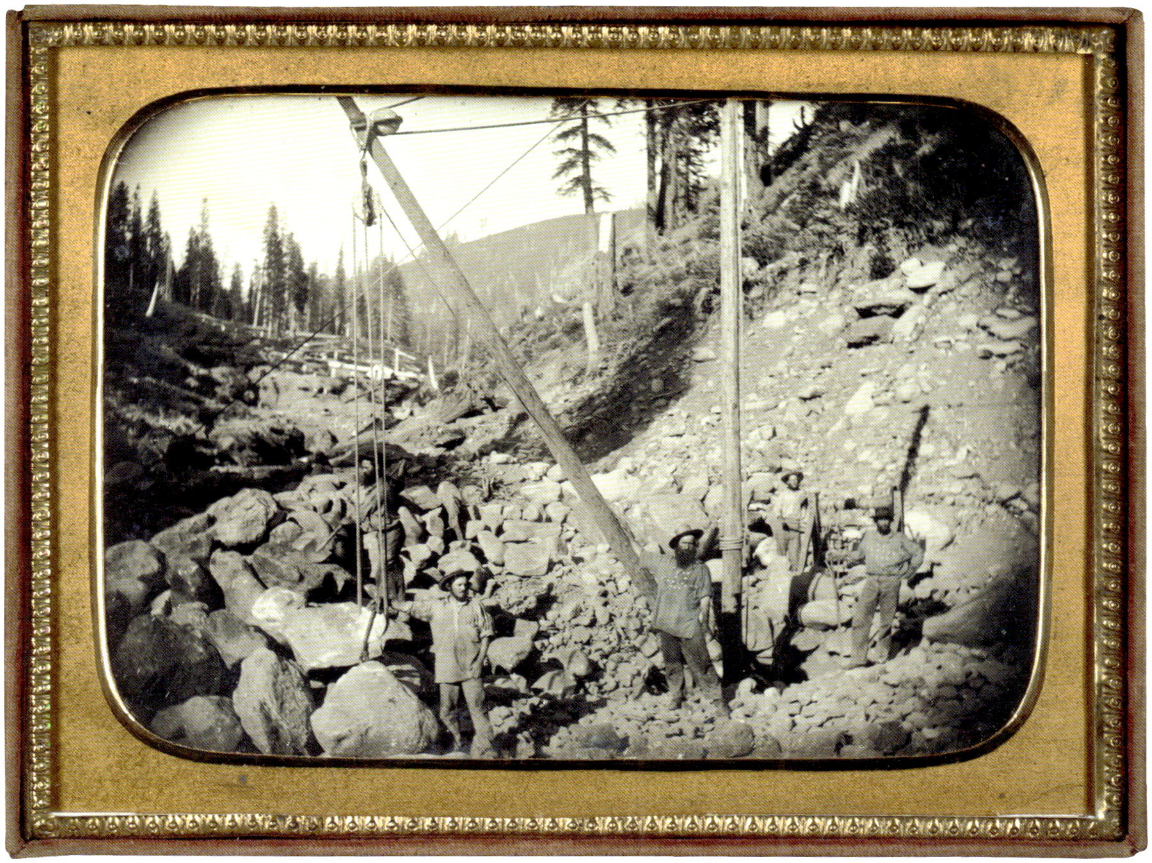

116 **Unknown maker**, American. *Five riverbed miners in a rocky gulch in the Motherlode*, ca. 1850–53. Half-plate daguerreotype. Bancroft Library, University of California, Berkeley.

When the river level was at a low point, a dam was

> constructed across the river. . . . By rolling up large boulders into a line building a wall, they turn the water from the one side towards the flume on the other and when one wall is thus rudely but substantially constructed, another is built behind it. . . . A clayey soil is then filled in and well tramped until the dam is tight; and the water is running through the race or flume. Sometimes a tree or log is felled across the stream . . . split timbers are put in, in an inclined position and nailed to the log, when the whole space in front is filled up with clayey soil and fine boughs of trees until it is made water tight.[26]

In the bottom image of this double half plate [115], the dammed portion of the river can be seen at bottom right. The flume or canal carries the water across the riverbed, where it is released back into its normal course on the other side. The riverbed to the left of the canal has been drained of water, and workers are digging into the underbelly of the stream bed.

As the river flowed through the newly constructed channel, large waterwheels were erected across the race. Pumps attached to the waterwheels helped remove remaining water in the riverbed. In this river mining operation [30], located on the North Fork of the American River at Horse Shoe Bar, the wheel is "for pumping out water on back claims."[27] For the largest boulders, men used a "jack"—a long pole with a pulley at its top that was held in an almost upright position by two or more cables or ropes [116].[28] After boulders were removed and rocks wheeled out, long toms or sluices were put in place to sift the golden-laden gravel.

In this double half-plate view of a river mining operation [117], the massive scope of the undertaking is obvious. In one plate, the river's exposed rocky underbelly is littered with heavy mining machinery, miner accommodations, and other outbuildings; the second plate reveals a closer look at the fluming operation.

Many river mining operations began modestly with the construction of wing dams.[29] Extending a short distance into a river, the dam consisted of stone and brush packed with clay. Wing dams were first run "half-way across the river, then down the river, and back again to the same side, thus damming off a portion of its bed without the necessity of the more expensive operation of lifting up the whole river bodily in a 'flume.'"[30] In 1852, British journalist J. D. Borthwick marveled at the wing dam built by a company of 150 Chinese miners at Mississippi Bar. It was "two or three hundred yards in length, and was built of large pine-trees laid one on the top of the other. [The miners] must have had great difficulty in handling such immense logs in such a place; but they are exceedingly ingenious in applying mechanical power."[31]

The first attempt "familiar to the chronicles of gold gathering in California, to drain and dig the beds of rivers" occurred in the fall of 1848 at

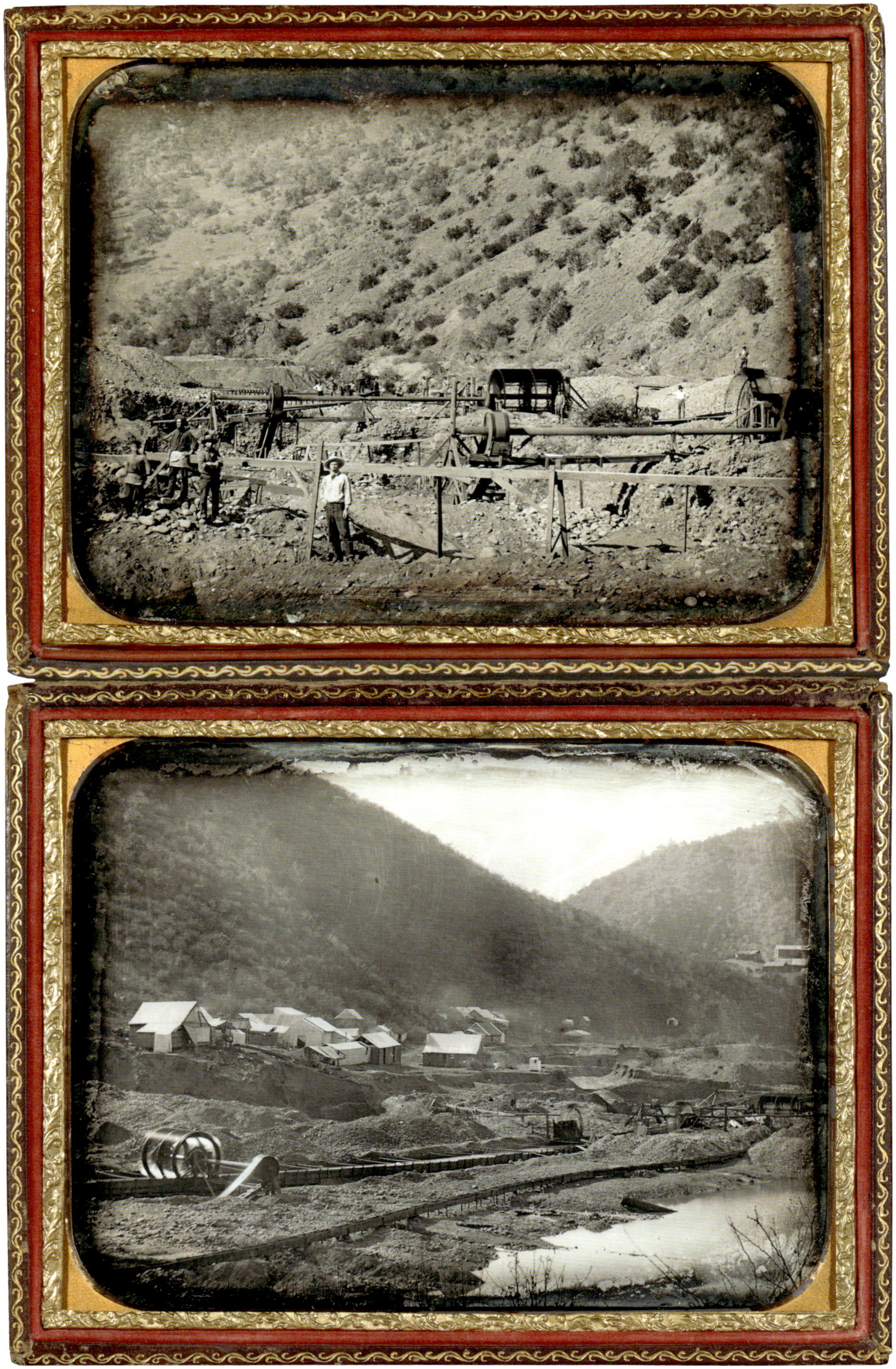

117 **Unknown maker**, American. *River diversion mining operation, California* (top), *Riverbed mining operation with camp, California* (bottom), ca. 1852. Half-plate daguerreotypes.

Mormon Island on the American River.[32] Progress was interrupted by winter rains, but a company of miners "renewed their operations in the spring and after expending a large amount of capital finally abandoned the project, foreseeing that their labors were not to be crowned with the success anticipated."[33] By August 1849, the Mormon Island Mining Association had taken over the abandoned claim and had nearly completed the dam. Unfortunately, as of October, the company had "not yet overcome the obstacle presented by hidden springs" stubbornly refilling the riverbed.[34]

When a profitable spot was chosen and the weather cooperative, the effort was well worth the risk. In August 1849, the North Fork Dam and Mining Association completed a lateral canal at Beal's Bar. Three days after the drainage of the riverbed was complete, the company of thirty men found $15,000 in gold.[35] On the Middle Fork of the American River, another company operating with "submarine armor"—early wetsuits—bypassed the need to divert the stream and ingeniously used underwater equipment to pluck gold from the streambed.[36] The following year in the southern mining region, the beds of the Tuolumne and Stanislaus Rivers were also extensively mined.[37]

Throughout 1850, river mining companies used canals as the primary means to drain water from dammed sections of rivers. On the South Fork of the American River, near Coloma, however, there was a "stupendous plan" for the "construction of a tunnel through a bank, about fifty feet high from the river's edge . . . 700 feet in length . . . to divert the course of the stream for a space of two miles." Requiring the company to cut through solid granite, the project carried an estimated cost of $40,000 for excavation alone.[38] North of Coloma, the North Yuba Tunnel Company also cut a tunnel on the North Yuba River at Goodyear's Bar in 1853.[39]

By 1851, most river mining companies had transitioned to wooden flumes instead of earthen canals as the primary means to drain water from a dammed section of river.[40] Although the size varied, wooden flumes were usually between eighteen to forty feet wide and six feet high. Described by one observer as "a plank race with water wheels and pumps rigged like the chain pumps of ships," the flumes had "a style most astonishing, when you consider the means employed, green hands, and imperfect tools."[41]

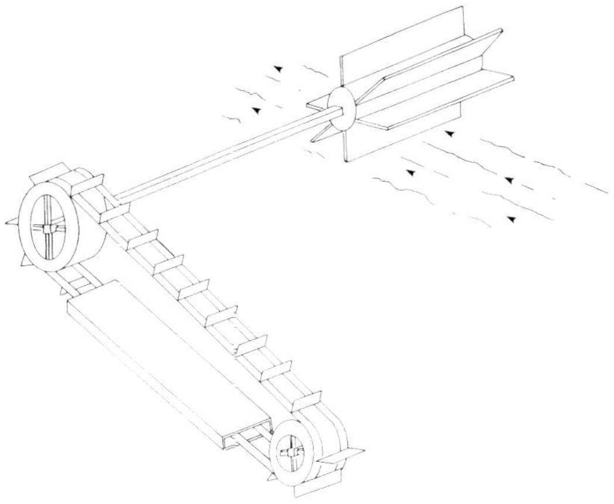

FIG. 12 *Chinese pump*, from Jeffrey M. LaLande, "Sojourners in Search of Gold: Hydraulic Mining Techniques of the Chinese on the Oregon Frontier," in *Journal of the Society for Industrial Archeology* 11, no. 1 (1985).

On the Middle Fork of the American River at Murderer's Bar and on the North Fork at New York Bar, the water was flumed for considerable distances. To build a flume over seven miles long, the North Fork Water Company had an ingenious way to raise the $50,000 in needed capital. Selling $200 worth of water per day to surrounding claims, presumably pumped by the waterwheels on the river, the company would reinvest those earnings to pay for the further extension of the flume down the river. It was a win-win situation: not only would the water company be providing "water at less expense than any other company in the country" but the remaining "water in the river [would] be diminished by one half, enabling the owners of [smaller] claims to work with less than half the expense." The company further predicted that this massive project would "add one third to the value of all the leads on the line of the flume" and make "valuable hundreds of claims perfectly worthless before."[42]

The Chinese made significant contributions to the evolution of river mining technology.[43] While they had mined for gold and diamonds in China since the early eighteenth century, their greatest contribution lay in their skill in water management. Many of the early Chinese miners were from Canton, an agricultural rice region in southern China renowned for its sophisticated systems of collecting and directing water. They were engaged with large-scale river mining soon after their arrival in California.

J. D. Borthwick noted Chinese miners working on the Yuba River in the northern mining region in 1852.[44] Circumventing the need to build a flume system, the Chinese miners instead constructed wing dams.[45] To drain the remaining water from behind the dam, the miners used a pump design imported from the rice fields. This worked on the principle of a chain-pump:

> The chain [was] formed of pieces of wood about six inches long, hingeing [*sic*] on each other, with cross-pieces in the middle for buckets, having about six square inches of surface. The hinges fitted exactly to the spokes of a small wheel, which was turned by a Chinaman at each side of it working a miniature treadmill of four spokes on the same axle.[46]

"An American miner at the expenditure of one-tenth part of the labour," Borthwick pontificated, "would have set a water-wheel in the river to work an elevating pump."[47] Lacking financial capital, the Chinese miners substituted human labor. The Chinese may have had an advantage, however. In years of drought, when the waters ran exceptionally low and claim owners found it "impossible to pump them out because the current of water running is too weak to turn a wheel to work a pump . . . Chinamen remedy the want of water by using Chinese power, in the form of a tread mill."[48] Regardless of the power source—human or river current—the "Chinese chain pump" [FIG. 12] was widely adopted by most river mining companies.[49]

Many observers were impressed with the Chinese cost-effective use of labor: "these people prosecute their mining operations with much neatness and at little cost, substituting labor for capital. The reason for their success, some speculated, was because "these Chinamen are very fond of working in the river, and had rather be in the water than on dry land."[50] Others assigned insect-like qualities to the Chinese workers, in a backhanded attempt at a compliment: "The claims appeared rich and well worked. It is remarkable how scientific and systematic the Asiatics [*sic*] work . . . none of their labor manifests a slovenly appearance; neatness and industry, like the labor of the ant, is the ruling feature in all they do."[51]

By 1856, the Chinese were successfully mining on both rivers in the north, dominating the Middle Fork of the American River and the Middle and South Forks of the Yuba.[52] Many times, American fluming companies built flumes and then sold them to the Chinese at a per-foot price, allowing American companies the means to recoup the construction expense.[53] Preferring to work alone, Chinese river mining companies did occasionally work in tandem with American companies to extend a flume. On the North Fork of the American River, in an especially congested area, one miner noted "a company of Celestials have two hundred feet of flume attached to ours, and John is busy in making preparations to take out the oro."[54] On the Fresno River in the south, a Chinese company and two non-Chinese companies agreed to construct canals on the same side "to bare the river only once." Although each company initially built their own sections, as the river level dropped, "the three companies for greater speed united to execute in common the work of diverting the stream."[55] Whether operating their own claims or working for or with others, the Chinese had an undeniable dominance in river mining.

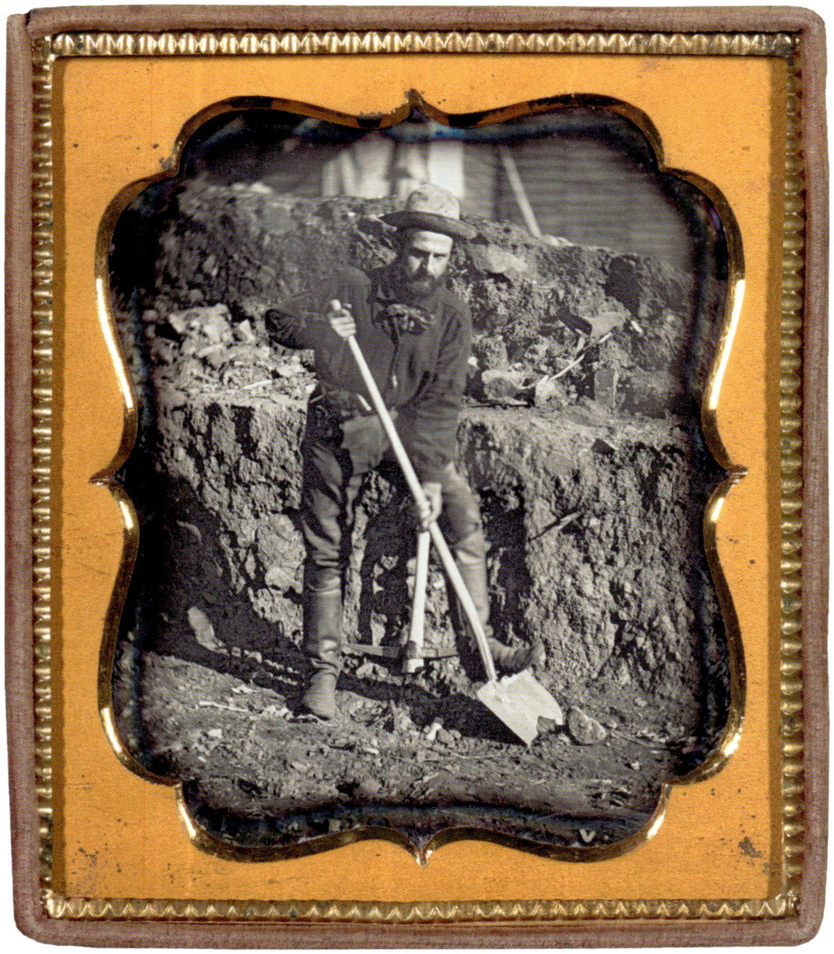

118 **Unknown maker**, American. *California gold miner digging*, ca. 1851. Sixth-plate daguerreotype.

Long Tom

By the spring of 1850, the miner population in California had increased dramatically and easily accessible gold had become more difficult to locate. As a result, miners began digging into the riverbanks to extract gold from the soil [118]. By August 1850, miners were "aware of the inexhaustible richness of the innumerable ravines, gulches, and canons [*sic*]," of dry ancient streambeds.[56] The gold in this "tertiary gravel" was not nearly as rich as in the beds of the streams the miners had been working; while in the streams gold was concentrated by millions of years of erosion and accumulation, in the hills it was finely dispersed throughout tons of dirt and gravel.[57]

The shift to lower-grade deposits necessitated a new form of technology—one that could efficiently process large amounts of dirt. Although it required a constant source of running water and a team of three to five men, the long tom was essentially an adaptation of the rocker to larger-scale operations. First employed in the northern mining region, the long tom was easily used in the river, where the strong current forced the cleaning of gravel, or away from the river, where a flow of water could be provided by a hose or ditch. Sometimes, as in [FRONTIS], miners using a long tom were forced to supply water by manual means—a bucketful at a time.

The long tom [FIGS. 13, 14] was

> an oblong box or trough about twelve feet in length, open at the top and usually at both ends. . . . It is about eight inches in depth, and at the upper end from one foot to two feet in width; but increasing to nearly double that width at the middle from thence its sides are parallel to the lower end. . . . The tom is not straight upon its bottom the whole length; but the sheet iron portion is turned upward as it approaches the lower end so that the depth of the tom is diminished at that end to less than three inches. The object of this is that the water may all pass through the sieve or tom-iron without running over the top. Under this perforated iron portion is placed a riffle box. . . . Water is now let on . . . which by its force, carries the dirt when put in, down the tom; and while two or more men are employed shoveling the dirt into the tom at the upper end,

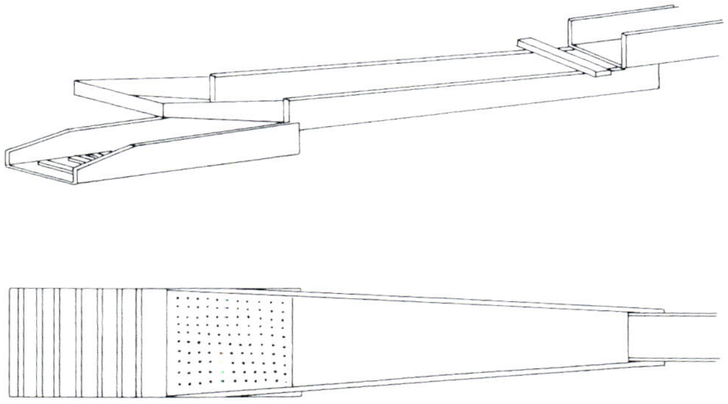

FIG. 13 *Long tom*, from Jeffrey M. LaLande, "Sojourners in Search of Gold: Hydraulic Mining Techniques of the Chinese on the Oregon Frontier," in *Journal of the Society for Industrial Archeology* 11, no. 1 (1985).

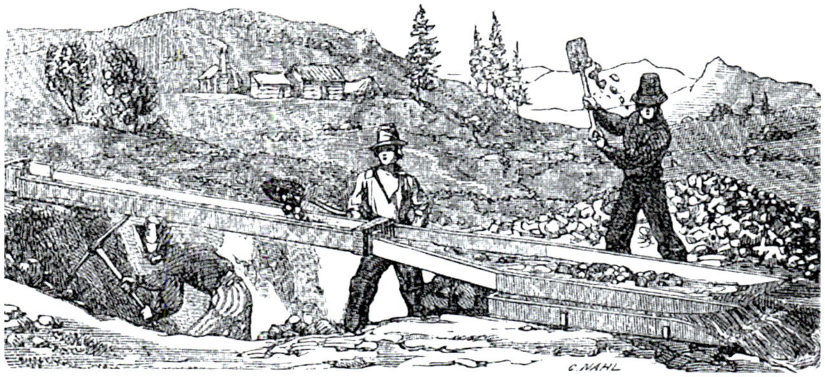

FIG. 14 *Mining with the Long-tom*, from "Mining for Gold in California," in *Hutchings' California Magazine* 2 (1857–58).

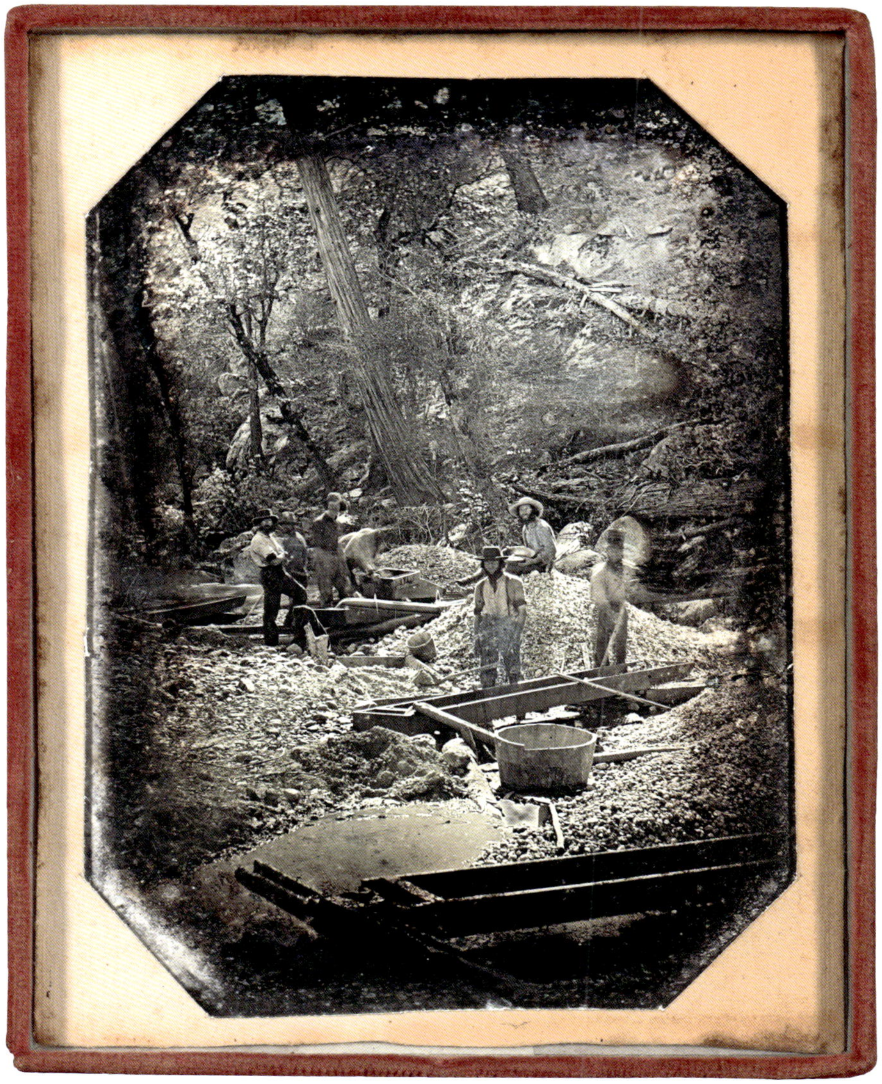

119 **Unknown maker**, American. *California gold miners with long toms*, ca. 1851. Quarter-plate daguerreotype.

> one man at the side of the lower end, with hoe or shovel in hand receives the dirt as brought down by the water; and after being violently stirred and moved about upon the perforated iron bottom until all has passed through it. . . . The manner of saving the gold by the riffle box, is precisely the same in principle as that of the cradle.[58]

Miners were quick to acknowledge the advantages afforded by this new technology: "Some wash with cradles, some with what is called a tom. . . . But I like the tom best of any thing that I have seen."[59] [121] Transitioning to the new technology, many miners used the long tom and rocker (cradle) at the same time [119]. In [120], six miners work a long tom while the overseer stands behind, with one hand resting on a rocker. Very unusually, this daguerreotype was inscribed at the bottom of the plate ("Dresser & Co., June 7th, 1852").[60]

At Gold Run, the miners were pleased to find that the long tom captured the small, "fine particles, not flakes" of gold that mixed with topsoil anywhere from "two inches to two feet below the surface."[61] By 1851, the long tom was used sparingly in the southern mining region. Near Sonora, one miner reported that the new device "will wash as much dirt as four cradles. It is generally used in old diggings, and then every particle of dirt can be put through." This technology had one significant drawback, however: "it requires plenty of water."[62] In the water-challenged southernmost mines of Mariposa County, long toms were not introduced until 1852.[63]

Mining operations in the hills could access water from mountain streams through a system of ditches. Enterprising water companies created "dams on the creeks and turned the water down a ditch dug on the sides of the hills. . . . One ditch runs 1100 yards long."[64] Louise Clapp gave a detailed description of the working water ditch at Indian Bar in a letter to a friend back home:

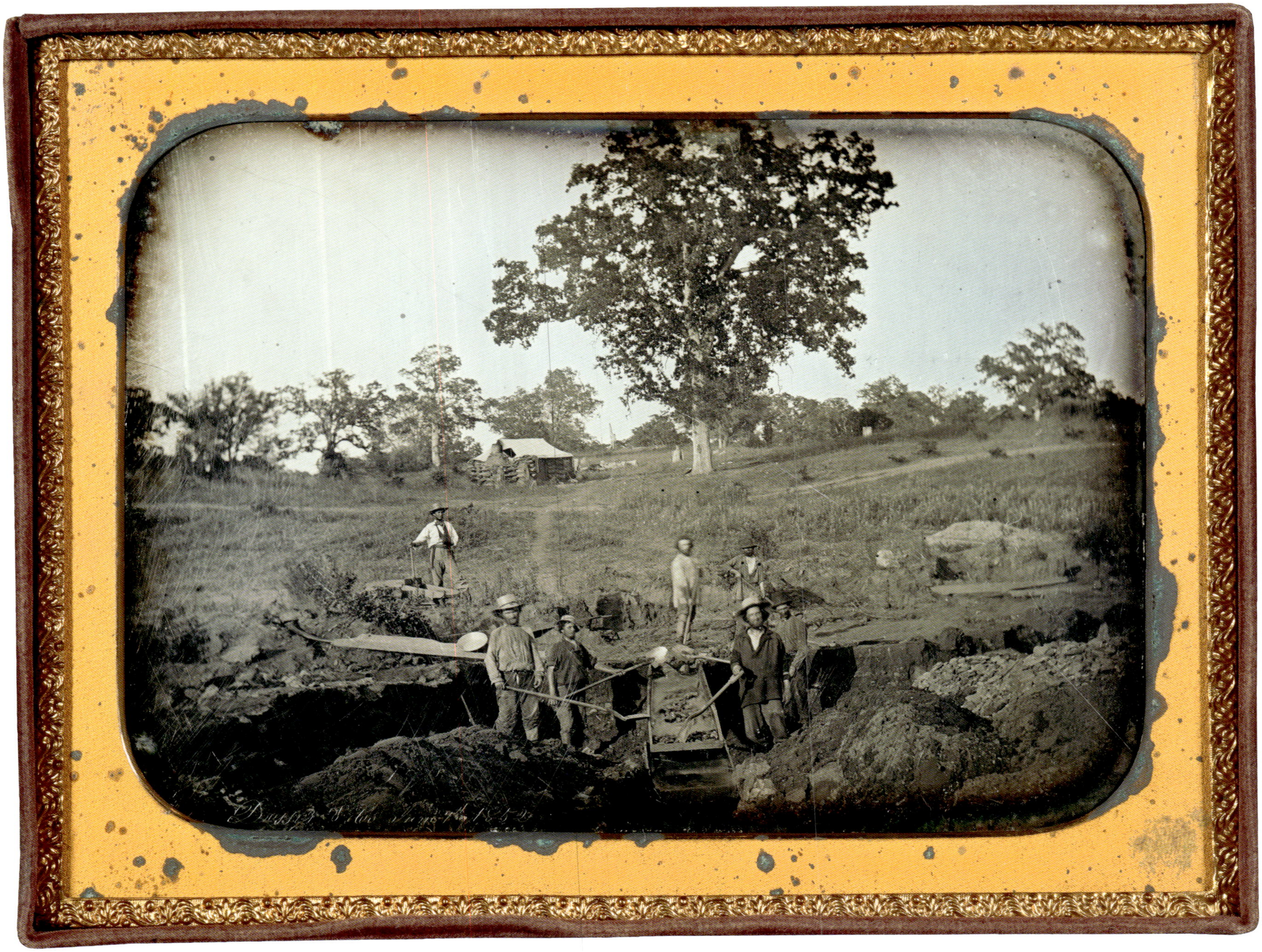

120 **Unknown maker**, American. *Dresser & Co., California gold miners*, June 7, 1852.
Half-plate daguerreotype.

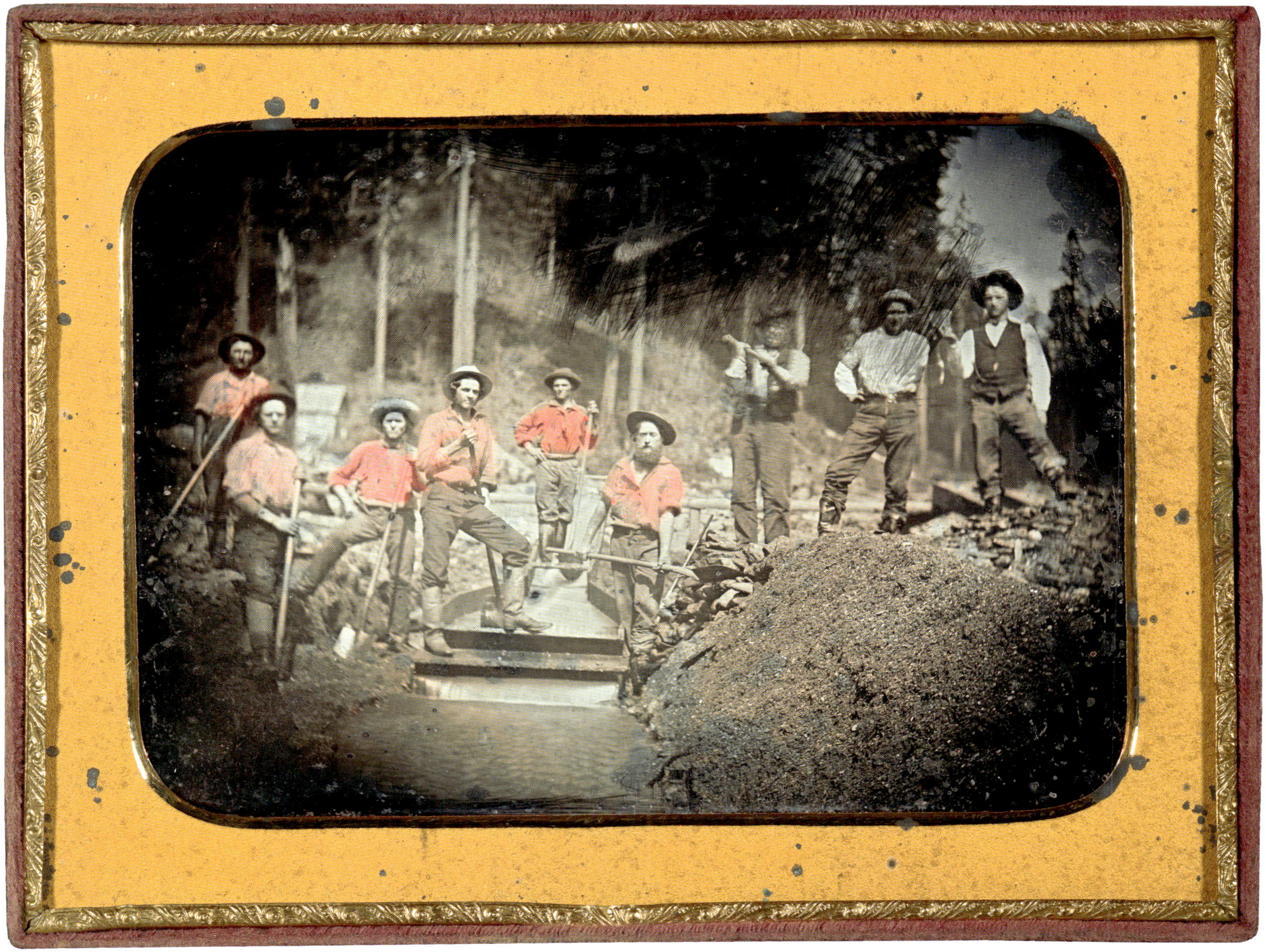

121 Unknown maker, American. *Nine California gold miners with long tom*, ca. 1853. Half-plate daguerreotype.

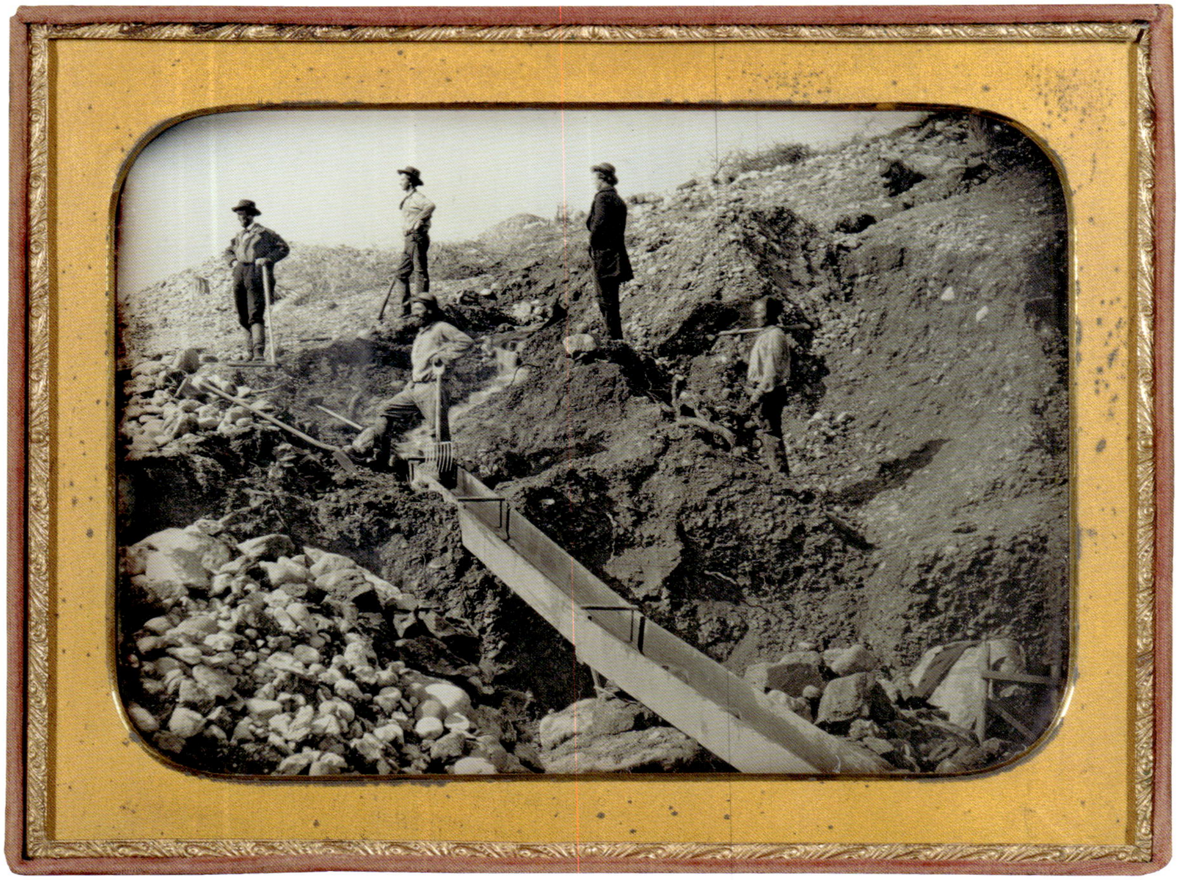

122 **Unknown maker**, American. *California gold miners with sluice*, ca. 1850. Half-plate daguerreotype.

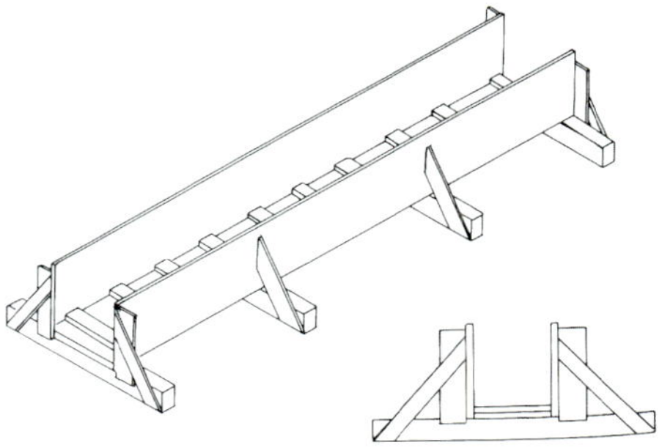

FIG. 15 *Sluice*, from Jeffrey M. LaLande, "Sojourners in Search of Gold: Hydraulic Mining Techniques of the Chinese on the Oregon Frontier," in *Journal of the Society for Industrial Archeology* 11, no. 1 (1985).

> [Water] is brought from ravines in the mountains. A company, to which a friend of ours belongs, has dug a ditch about a foot in width and depth, and more than three miles in length, which is fed in this way. . . . It undulates over the mossy roots, and the gray, old rocks, like a capricious snake. . . . When it reaches the top of the hill, the sparkling thing is divided into five or six branches, each one of which supplies one, two, or three "long toms."[65]

Sluice

By the spring of 1851, the long tom was already being superseded by its close cousin, the board sluice. Useful for processing large quantities of dirt, the sluice worked especially well on hillsides where gravity and a strong flow of water made quick work of gravel washing, as seen in [122]. Multiple sluices could also be attached end to end and run long distances [123, 124]. In instances where the ground was too level for sluicing, the tom might still be the tool of choice. Once the sluice was introduced, however, it tended to overwhelm virtually every other mining technology used in California.

The board sluice [FIGS. 15, 16] was

> an open trough, usually made of three inch boards—a bottom, and two sides; twelve or fourteen feet in length and from twelve inches to forty in width. . . . A continuous line of these troughs or sluice boxes the smaller and lower end of each, inserted for three or four inches into the larger end of the next one below,

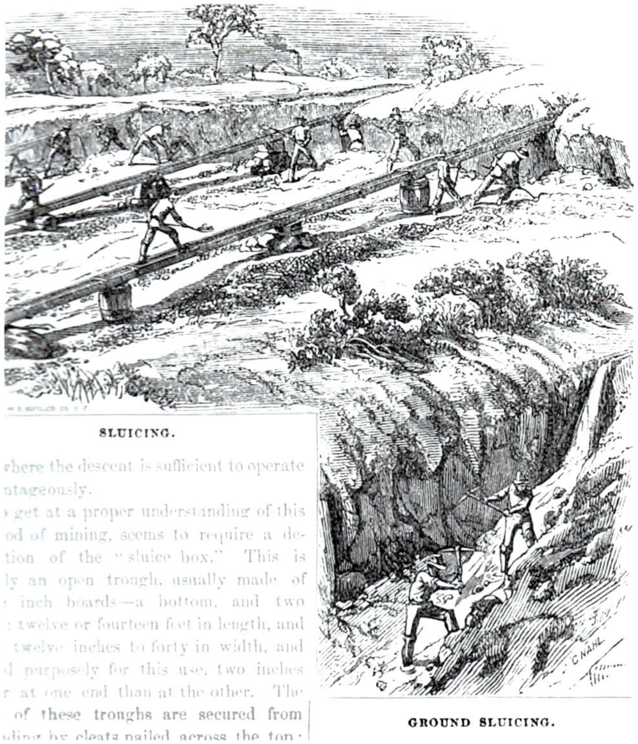

FIG. 16 *Sluicing* and *Ground Sluicing*, from "Mining for Gold in California," in *Hutchings' California Magazine* 2 (1857–58).

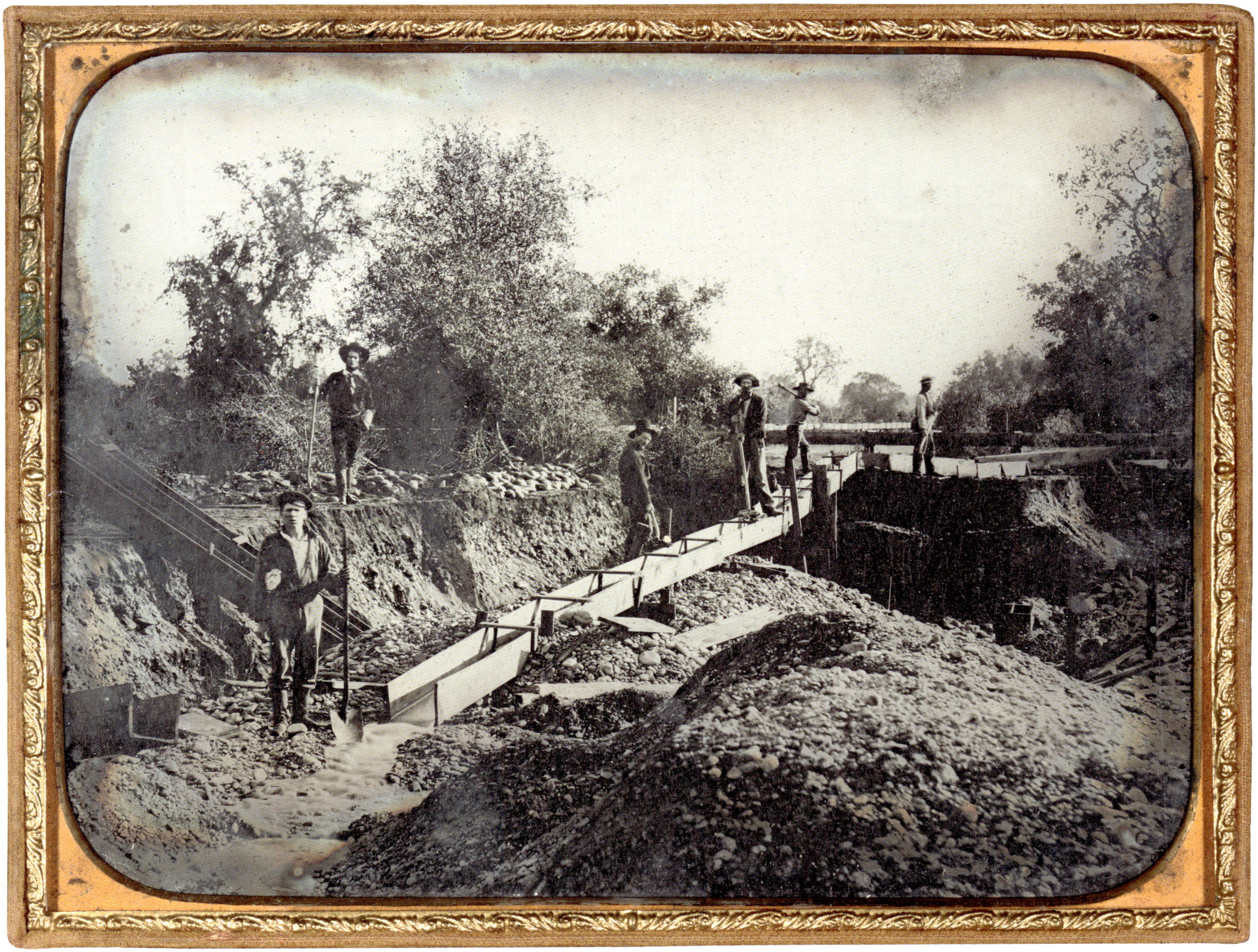

123 **Unknown maker**, American. *California gold miners with sluices*, ca. 1854–58. Half-plate ambrotype. The Art Institute of Chicago, The W. Bruce and Delaney H. Lundberg Collection, restricted gift of The Phillip Leonian and Edith Rosenbaum Leonian Charitable Trust.

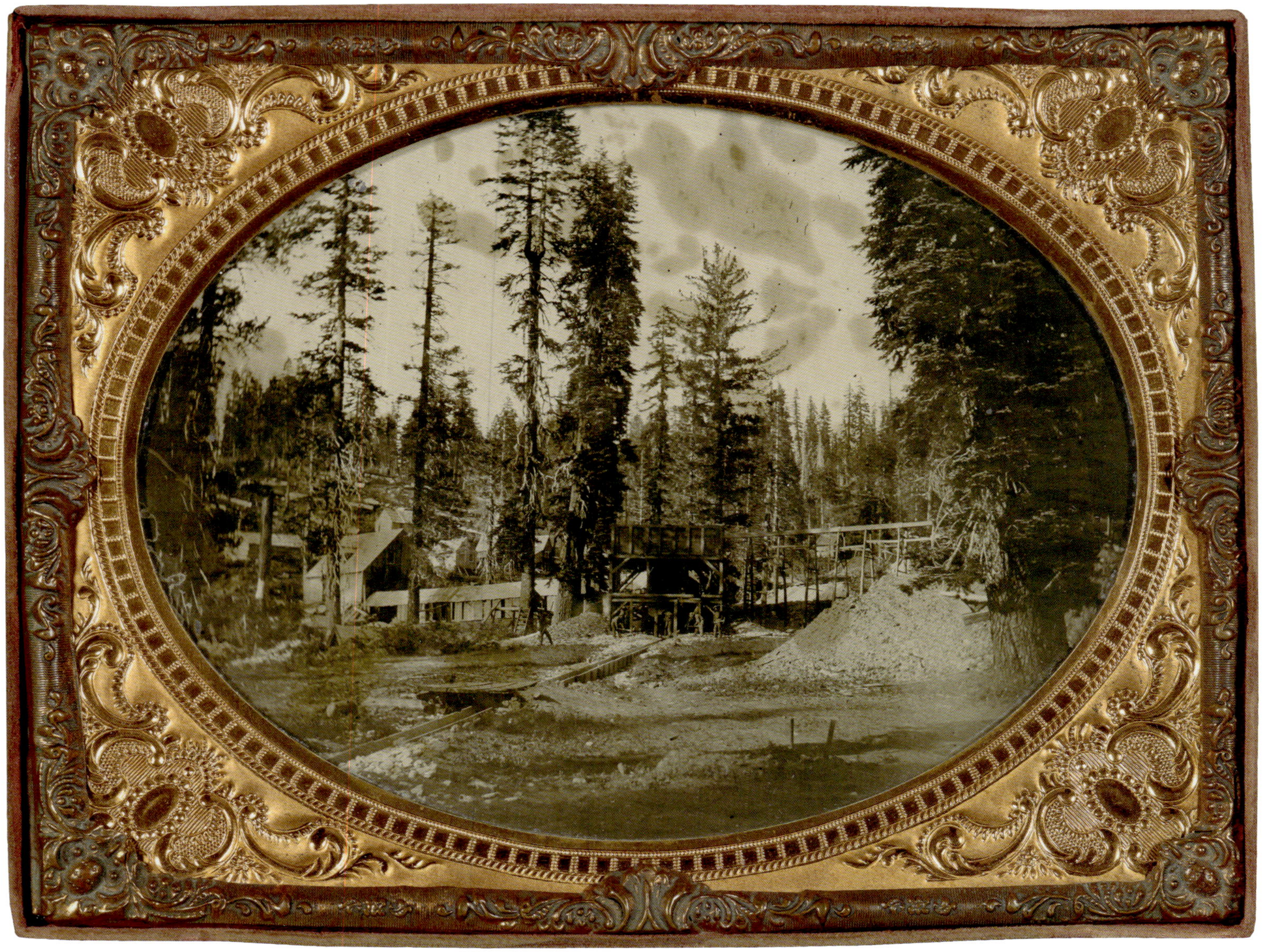

124 **Unknown maker**, American. *Mining camp, California*, ca. 1856. Half-plate ambrotype.

> form the sluice. . . . The dirt [is shoveled] into the sluice. . . . The whole mass of dirt, from the finest particles, to stones and boulders of four or five inches in diameter, go rattling down by their own gravity and the force of the water, the entire length of the sluice. . . . There are different appliances attached to the bottoms of these sluices, inside, for the purpose of saving or catching the gold in its passage down the sluice, such as riffles.[66]

Sluices could be run for several days and then washed down—the false bottoms removed, and gold caught at the bottom "panned" to remove any extraneous particles. After mercury (quicksilver) became available, it was added to the sluice to amalgamate the finer gold particles. The amalgam was then scraped up and heated over a fire to separate mercury from gold.

Although it is unclear whether the sluice was of European or Californian origin, most historians agree that it was first introduced in late 1850 or early 1851 at Nevada City. In April 1851, the *Nevada (CA) Journal* noted, "this new method of washing . . . was first introduced here and has been in operation some three months."[67] In the southern mining region, the sluice did not immediately supplant the tom: there simply was not enough water available to make sluicing viable.[68] A great advantage of sluice technology was that it enabled miners to rework old claims:

> Dirt which will not pay more than two dollars to the hand with the rocker, will yield, where it can be readily obtained, from twelve to sixteen dollars by sluicing. This is decidedly the greatest improvement which has been introduced into mining in this country, and will render valuable, acres of ground when the "rocker" or "tom" would not pay the board bills of those who might engage in washing it.[69]

Fluming

"Water is the great want of all kinds of surface mining" was the lament of James Hutchings and, indeed, of most of the gold miners working in the region.[70] After the invention of the long tom and the sluice, a consistent and plentiful supply of water was essential to fully engage the next generation of gold mining technology. At claims located far from rivers, a sudden lack of water could bring operations to an immediate halt. Early miners working in dry ravines adapted to this lack of water by digging and saving "the earth in which the gold is found . . . until the rainy season affords a supply of water for washing it."[71] There were times when an unexpected shower might pop up—like the one in Columbia at Christmastime 1851—and produce a stream "fed only by the rains, [which] was flowing through the streets." In this case, "fifty 'toms' intercepted its progress, and not a drop of the precious fluid but was made to do its work over and again, in separating the yellow particles from the gravel."[72] These occurrences, though welcome, were infrequent and unpredictable.

In the mountains, where gravity assisted the flow of water, miners sought a permanent solution. Streams were dammed, reservoirs created, and water was directed by means of earthen and stone ditches. Soon, starter water companies were organized by groups of miners needing water for their own claims. The Coyote & Deer Creek Water Company [49] and other small water businesses such as the Sonora Water Company, Seco Water Company, and Sullivan's Creek Company were "in operation for a time, while the height of water in the respective streams admitted of it. . . . The above companies were all small in numbers, their races affording but a 20 or 30 tom stream, when at the fullest, and that only for a few days. Their operations were stopped simply by giving out of the water."[73]

Streams were dammed in the mountains to create repositories for the melting spring snow [126]. Transporting water from mountain reservoirs to the mining regions was a difficult and often treacherous undertaking. Mountain ranges rose to heights of 7,000 to 9,000 feet and were transected by deep gorges and canyons. At the upper end of a water course, it was not unusual to build three to ten miles of flume solely to navigate out of a deep canyon [125]. To carry water over this rugged landscape,

> many miles of flume [were] constructed entirely of wood, because the steep sides have not, in many places, a single inch of earth in which to excavate a ditch. The flume [was] constructed upon trestle work, a hundred or more feet in height; and even in some instances actually suspended by iron work.[74]

To convey the water at "a fall from five to twenty feet to the mile," surveyors were required to take accurate measurements of the terrain, carefully positioning the structure high enough to span the distance [127].[75] These wooden flumes were spectacular feats of engineering and soon became ubiquitous fixtures in the northern gold mining landscape.

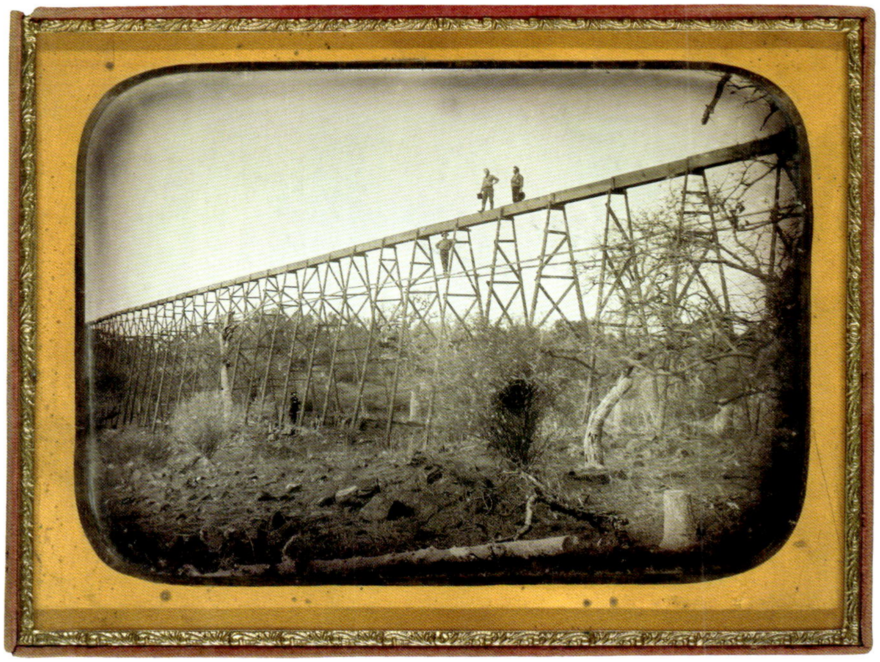

125 **Unknown maker**, American. *Flume near the North Fork of the American River*, ca. 1850. Quarter-plate daguerreotype. The J. Paul Getty Museum, Los Angeles, Open Content Program.

The earliest gold miners settled close to water sources. As population density increased, later miners lived farther and farther away from primary water sources. As miners jockeyed for position in the water-ownership hierarchy, major conflicts occurred over water rights.[76] Miners located directly on or adjacent to streams claimed riparian rights—the right to undiminished water flow past their property. Riparian owners could divert the stream temporarily, as with river mining, but were required to return the water to its original course, unchanged in quantity and quality, for the sake of other riparian owners downstream. Riparian rights were considered a common law principle before California achieved statehood in 1850.

The frequent scarcity of water, and water's necessity to mining, resulted in the rejection of riparian rights in the mining districts in favor of appropriative rights. Under this system, emphasis was placed on the use of water: miners who were the first to use water in a stream for mining activities were entitled to divert it, regardless of whether it diminished the flow to others. After California became a state, the California Practice Act (1851) enforced the customs and regulations already in use in the mines, validating both riparian and appropriative rights. California was in an unusual and unprecedented position. Because mining claims were on public land, miners were essentially trespassers, not truly entitled to any ownership rights, and although the federal government had regulations covering navigable water sources, the authority over non-navigable sources was debatable. This ambiguity led to liberal interpretations of the law as it pertained to water rights.

The first water ditches were built by miners with no outside capital. These miners clearly saw water as their basic mining right, but larger

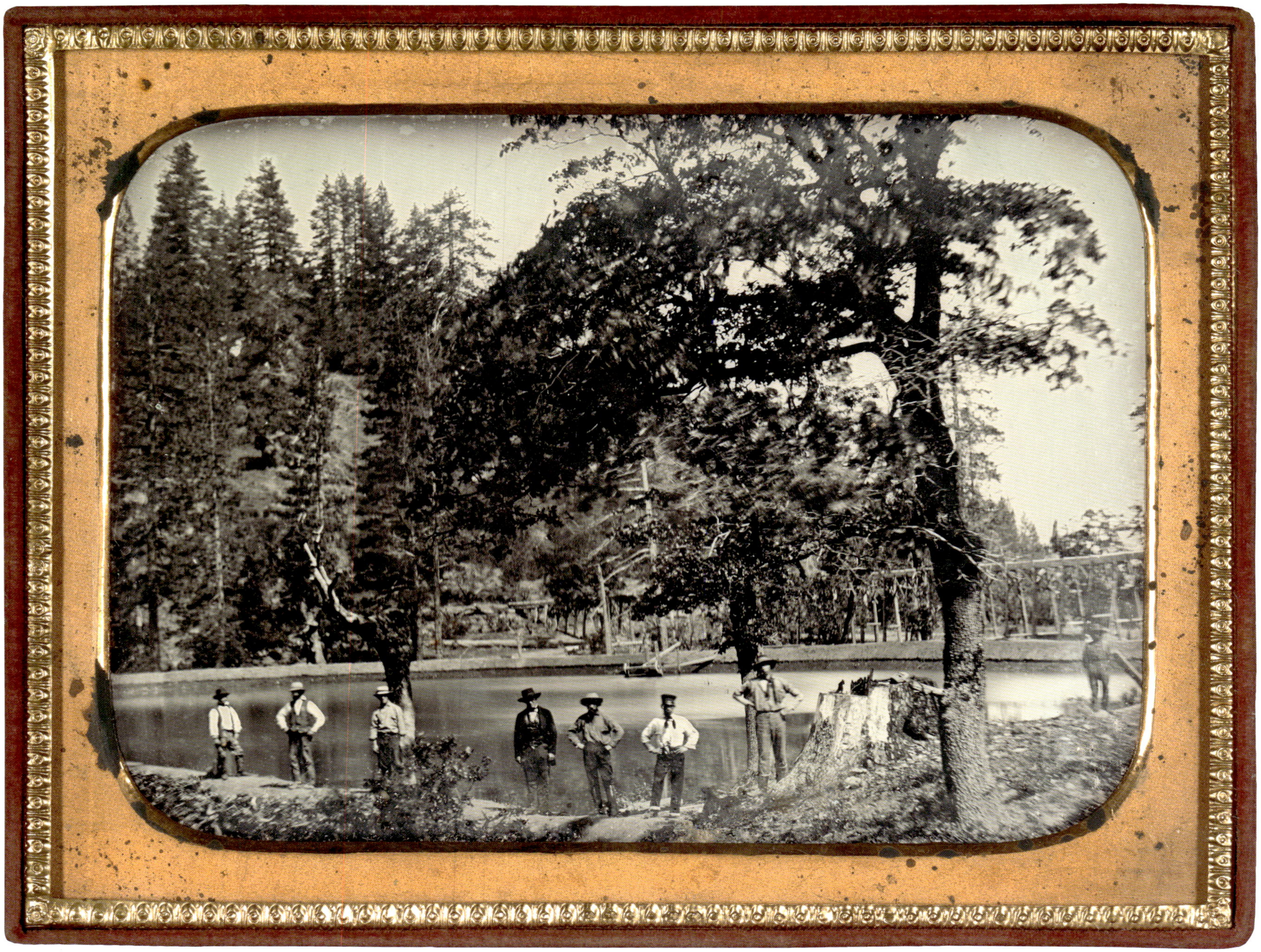

126 Unknown maker, American. *Dammed water reservoir with water flume*, ca. 1854–58. Half-plate daguerreotype. The Art Institute of Chicago, The W. Bruce and Delaney H. Lundberg Collection, restricted gift of The Phillip Leonian and Edith Rosenbaum Leonian Charitable Trust.

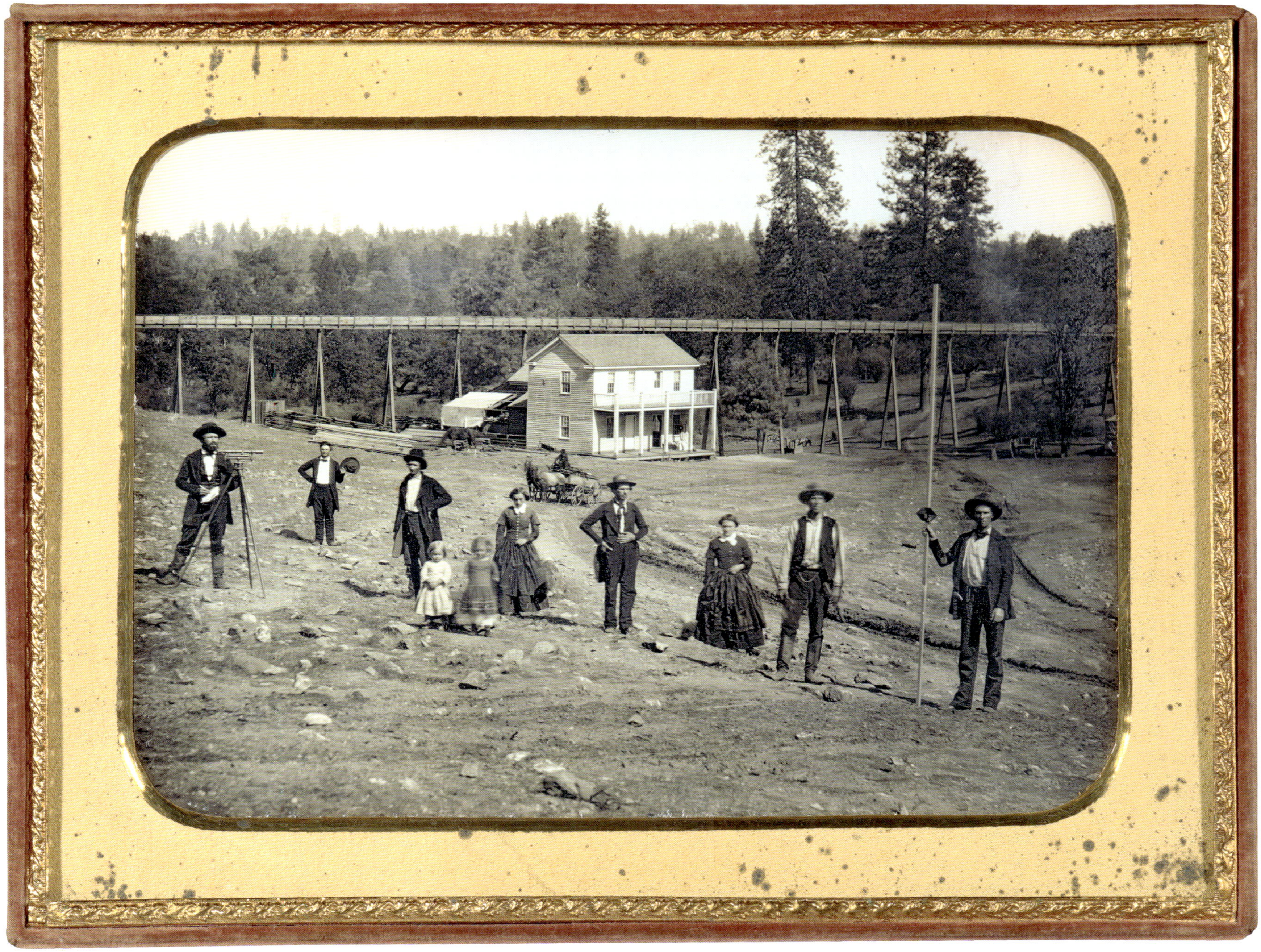

127 **Unknown maker**, American. *Water flume and surveyors, El Dorado County, California*, ca. 1855.
Half-plate daguerreotype.

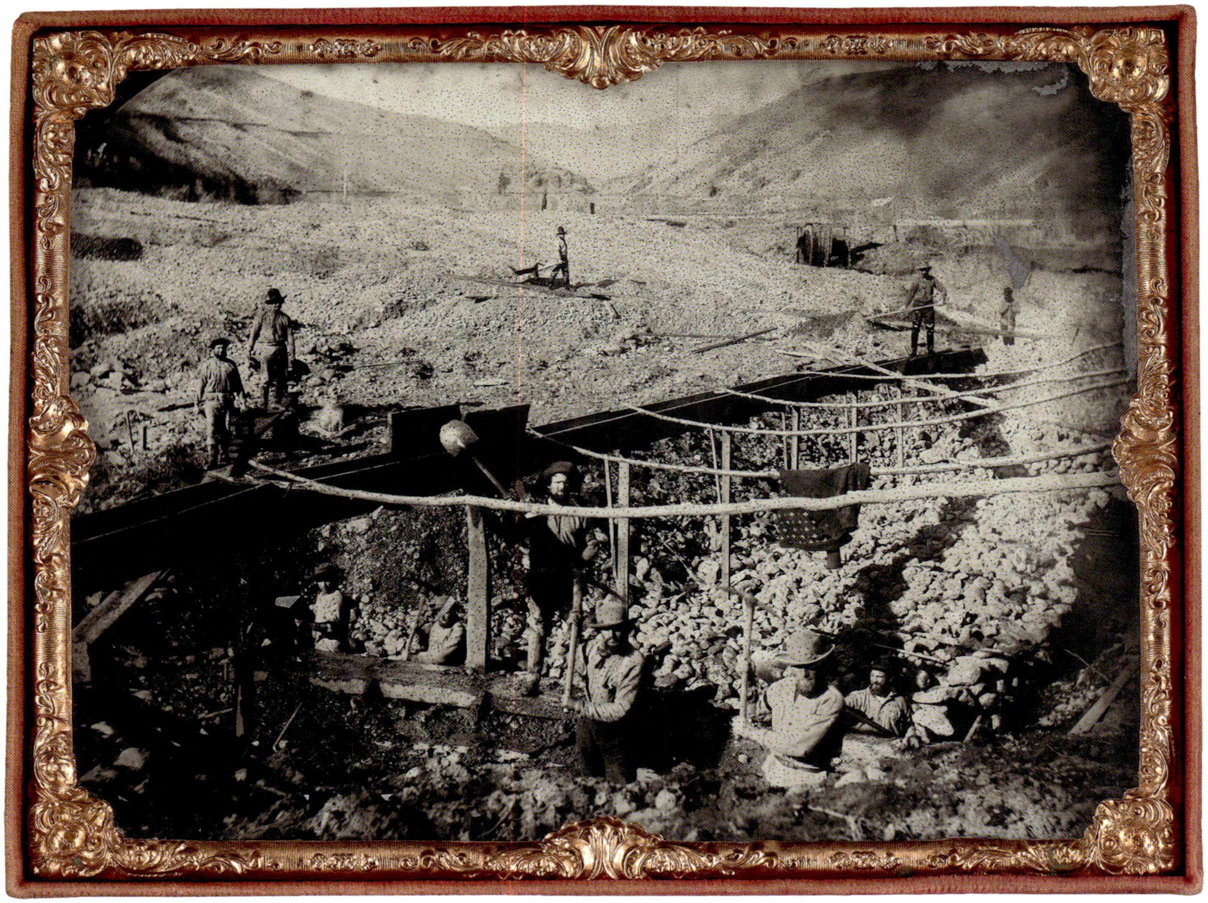

128 **Unknown maker**, American. *Gold mining operation*, ca. 1857. Half-plate ambrotype. National Gallery of Canada, Ottawa.

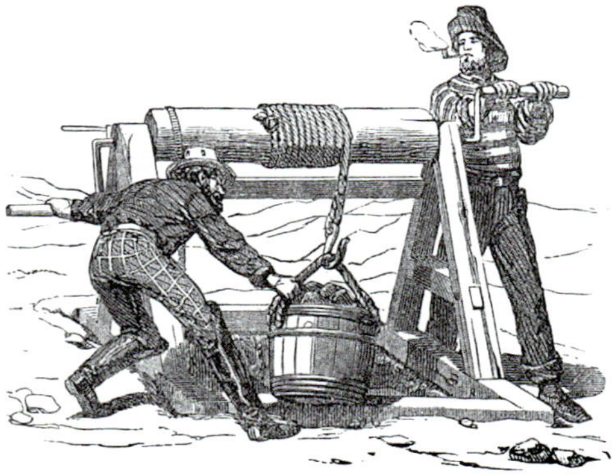

FIG. 17 *Sinking a Shaft*, from "Mining for Gold in California," in *Hutchings' California Magazine* 2 (1857–58).

companies saw it as a commodity, as providing water to miners became increasingly big business. In June 1851, two bankers from Columbia, California, raised over $250,000 from within the city, including resident miners, to cover the expense of an extensive fluming system.[77] The success of this operation, the Tuolumne County Water Company, led to the development of other water systems. As capital for projects shifted from local to outside sources, however, control was effectively passed from miners to capitalists and investors. As a result, the *act* of mining was irrevocably separated from the *business* of mining. This set the groundwork for generations of hotly contested battles over water rights that would eventually become the basis for water law in most western states.

Excavation Methods

As miners turned their attention from streams to the surrounding landscape, some worked from the theory that "below the junction of the gulches and ravines that descend from the mountain sides to the river, the very heaviest and richest deposits of gold washed down through such ravines would lie nearest to the original beds of the river" deep beneath the earth's surface [31, 128].[78] New modes of underground excavation were needed, to be used with the existing technologies of rocker, long tom, and sluice.

Drift mining involved the excavation of deep tertiary gravel by means of holes, shafts, or tunnels.[79] By July 1850, miners had devised an excavation technique called "sinking a shaft" [FIG. 17] to determine the presence of gold in underlying bedrock.[80] The shaft was

> a perpendicular opening in the earth usually from four to six feet in diameter. . . . The pay dirt is raised to the surface by the same means that are used in sinking the shaft, the principal of which is, the windlass and bucket, or tub.[81]

Sometimes a stratum of gold was intersected while sinking the shaft; miners traced that vein horizontally from a ravine or dry gulch back into a mountain. Sinking a shaft was often used in prospecting as a cheap and effective way of determining the presence of gold.[82]

The western slope of the Sierra Nevada from Mariposa to Siskiyou, through Plumas, Butte, El Dorado, Amador, Calaveras, and Tuolumne Counties was found to be geologically ideal for underlying veins of gold. Finding that "gold [was] not confined to those deep canons [*sic*] and on running streams in which it [had] been generally located heretofore," miners sunk multiple shafts until the hills were "literally covered with holes and piles of

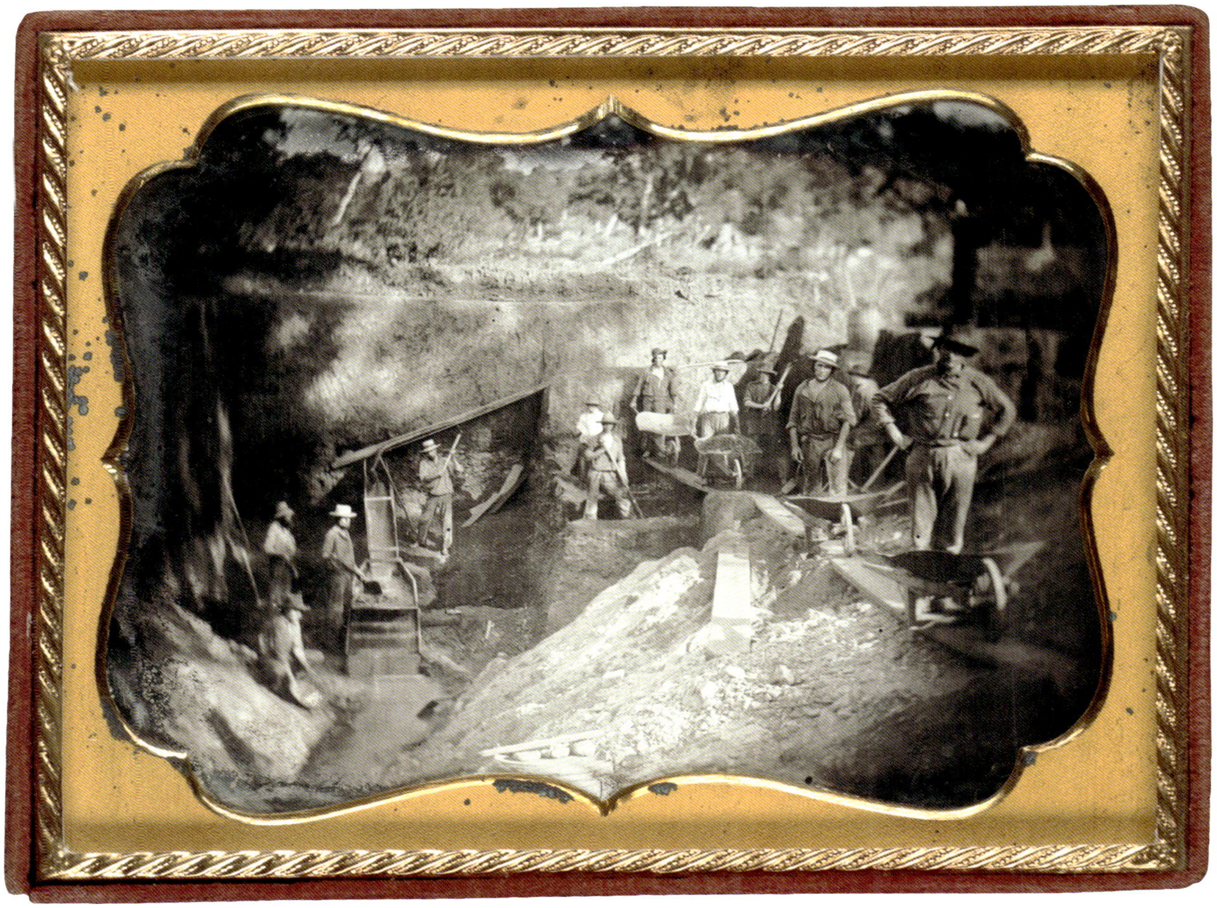

129 **Unknown maker**, American. *View of the Anable Placer Mine, Auburn, California*, ca. 1853. Quarter-plate daguerreotype. Bancroft Library, University of California, Berkeley.

earth."[83] As miner Lorenzo Sawyer noted, this work was a high-stakes gamble: "I am told that not more than one shaft in fifteen or twenty pays. But occasionally one turns out a fortune."[84] In a letter home, Louise Clapp recounted that after striking bedrock by sinking a shaft,

> they then commence "drifting coyote holes" (as they call them) in search of "crevices" which . . . often pay immensely. These "coyote holes" sometimes extend hundreds of feet into the side of the hill. . . . When they think that "coyote hole" has been faithfully "worked," they "clean it up" which is done by scraping the surface of the "bed rock" with a knife, lest by chance they have overlooked a "crevice," and they are often richly rewarded for this precaution.[85]

In some areas, the sight of these pockmarked hills was so striking that towns were named Coyoteville and Coyote Diggings.[86]

Tunneling was another excavation method related to the shaft-sinking process:

> Tunnels are usually commenced upon hillsides, or near the bottom of gulches and ravines and are run in nearly horizontal. . . . When the basin of the hill or pay dirt is reached, an open cut is first made into the hill, until a sufficient depth is attained to enable the tunnel to be commenced. . . . When only earth and detached stones or boulders are met with, it often becomes necessary to "timber up" as the tunnel progresses.[87]

A wheelbarrow was often used to remove dirt and rocks from the tunnel. For larger operations, a narrow railroad was constructed with cars pushed by hand. Once the pay dirt was extracted, it was sluiced in the usual manner to retrieve the gold. In [129] miners push empty wheelbarrows back to the mouth of the mine, ready to haul out another load of rock. An even larger operation is shown here [130], with multiple sluices working at once.

By 1854, tunnel mining was considered "the most important and productive of any branch of mining in the State."[88] With a better understanding of the technology and of the geological characteristics of the mountains, miners were reworking tunnels that had been created and abandoned in 1851 in El Dorado County, "extending them farther into the hill and in a downward direction."[89] Instead of the slow and methodical work of the pickaxe and shovel, miners in Diamond Springs used dynamite to blast their way through rock. By 1857, a small team of five to six men could effectively work a drift mining claim.

Encouraged by the results of these smaller operations, some miners formed companies to drift mine on a large scale. In the northern mines, this began at Forest Hill in 1852; in the southern region, the area around Sonora, it began in 1853.[90] By 1859, the size of drift mining operations had increased

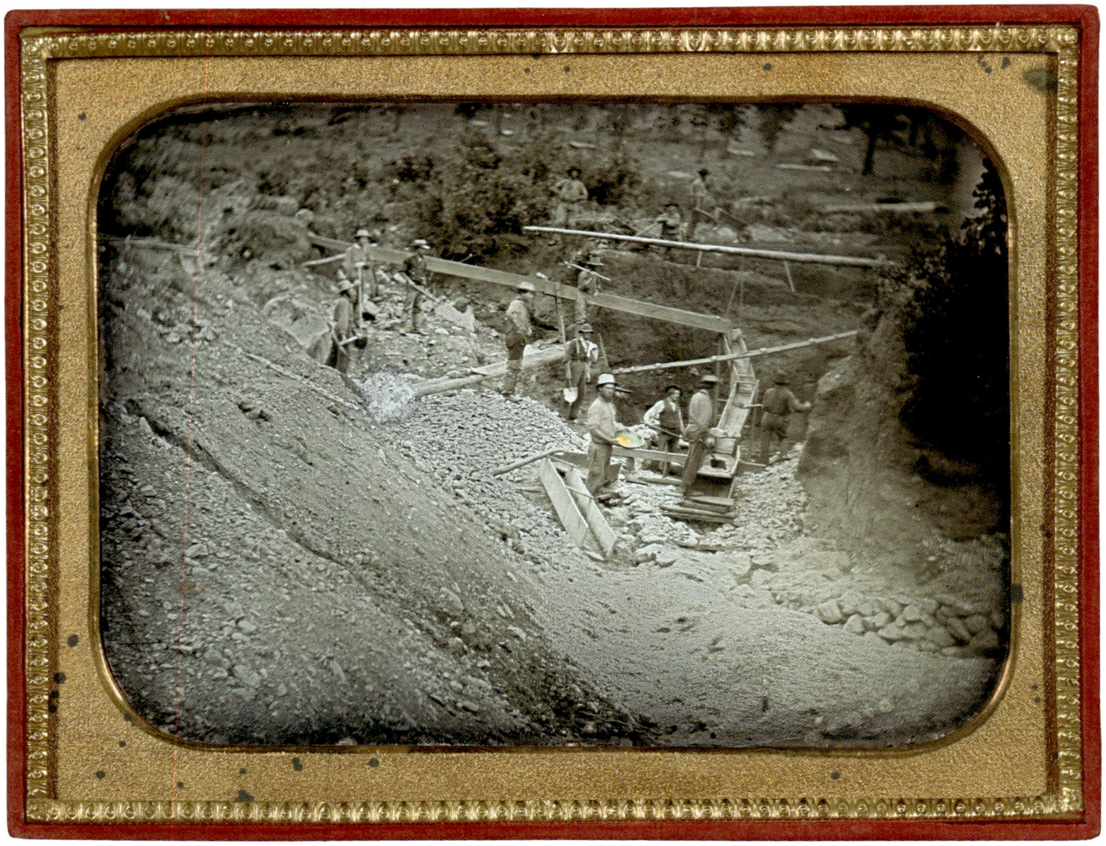

130 **Unknown maker**, American. *California gold miners drift mining*, ca. 1853. Half-plate daguerreotype.

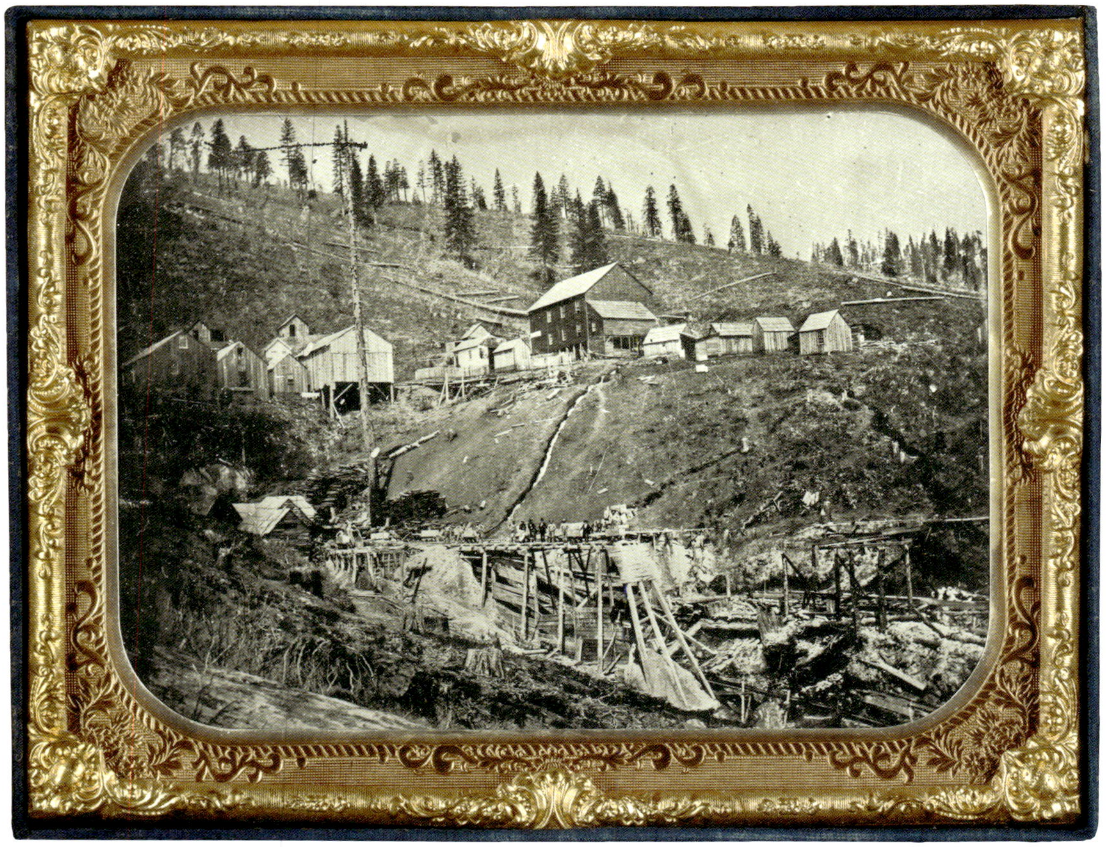

131 **Unknown maker**, American. *Mines at Forest City, in gully below main street, with miners pausing near trestles, and ore carts*, ca. 1855–60. Half-plate ambrotype. Bancroft Library, University of California, Berkeley.

considerably. The Masonic Company, located at Wet Ravine near Forest City, had dug a 375-foot-deep shaft in which two elevator cars were operated by steam engines [131]. The company spent over $100,000 but was completely without debt due to the richness of the claim.[91]

Hydraulic Methods

Ground sluicing was an excavation method developed to reach pay dirt lying many feet below non-gold-bearing soil.[92] Introduced as early as the summer of 1850 in Nevada City and achieving general use in the northern mines by 1851–52, ground sluicing was effective in hilly areas with abundant water [FIG. 16]. In this process, "the surface soil, being loosened up or thrown into a trench cut in the bed rock, was washed away by a stream of water, leaving only the heavy gravel at the bottom."[93] The miners would select a bank of earth,

> which it is desired to reduce or wash away, down to the pay dirt; a stream of water is conducted thereto, at so high a level as to command it; a small ditch is then cut along the portion to be found sluiced, the water turned on and then any number of hands with picks and shovels either upon the edges of the ditch or by getting directly into the stream of water, pick away and work down the banks and bottom, to be dissolved and carried away by the water while the gold that may be contained in it, settles down without being conveyed or lost.[94]

In many instances, the cracks in the rocky underlay of the ditch acted as natural riffle bars for capturing gold.

In April 1852, while ground sluicing, Anthony Chabot used a canvas hose to direct water onto a hill, breaking up the ground and washing it into his sluice. This early application of hydraulic power allowed him to work a large area very quickly.[95] This ground sluicing method, employing water to do most of the work, greatly affected the nature of mining. Hydraulic mining was a further extension of ground sluicing. Building upon Chabot's adaptation of the canvas hose, the team of Edward Matteson and Eli Miller had the simple but brilliant idea of enlarging the hose and adding a nozzle.[96] Hydraulic mining quickly became the most efficient system for large-scale hill diggings.

According to Hutchings's description of the hydraulic mining process, water was

> run from the small ditch into a trough fixed upon tressel [*sic*] work, which is often technically termed the "Hydraulic Telegraph," . . . or, run in heavy duck hose upon the ground, to the edge of the claim thence over the edge and down the almost perpendicular bank to the bed rock, or bottom of the claim, where it lies coiled about on the rock and dirt like a huge serpent. As the upper end of the hose is much larger than the lower end, the water running in, keeps it full to the very top; and the weight of this water, escaping through a pipe attached to the lower end of the hose plays upon the bank with great force and effect, washing it rapidly away. . . . A stream of water runs over the bank which is often required effectually to cleanse and remove the large quantities of earth and rocks washed down by the pipe, and convey them to the sluice, down which they pass, and in which the gold is principally saved.[97]

The riffles on the bottom of the sluices broke up gravel and captured the small gold particles. To enhance gold recovery, the riffles were submerged in mercury, which amalgamated with the gold. Gold was then separated from the mercury by the same procedure used in sluice mining.

This operation was clearly an expensive undertaking. In [112], the "Hydraulic Telegraph" sits at the top overhanging the cliff while canvas hoses drop from various locations to miners below. Rail cars haul excess debris away from the primary mining area. In [132], several hoses converge in a wooden box-like structure to maximize the force of the water stream. The water and dirt are then washed down the slope, through a ditch, and out a sluice that empties just in front of the daguerreotypist.

Hydraulic mining required a heavy capital investment, a large workforce, and, most critically, a great quantity of water.[98] Ditches, flumes, and reservoirs were constructed to transport and store water from the mountains. Chinese miners who became proficient at hydraulic mining were hired to construct many of these ditches.[99] After the North Bloomfield Gravel Mining Company built a ditch extension, for example, one journal stated that "without Chinamen, it would not have been attempted."[100] The miles-long ditches required careful surveys so that the water arrived at a sufficient elevation above the area to be mined—this ensured a constant high pressure for the water hoses. Later advancements included an iron pipe replacement for both the hoses and the wooden flumes, and powerful water cannons in place of nozzles.

Upon the introduction of hydraulic mining in Nevada City, a correspondent for the *Alta California* wrote, "The column of water thus produced ranges from twenty to one hundred feet according to the height of the hill" and was of such force that boulders instantly "melt like ice under a midsummer sun."[101] The advantages of the new method included a reduction in manual labor, access to previously inaccessible deposits, and the ability to work at a distance from dangerous overhanging embankments.

Hydraulic mining was powerful but crude. During the late 1850s, the process lost as much as three-fifths of the recoverable gold, as water turbulence through the sluices prevented the capture of finer particles. Two modifications were thus developed: the grizzly and the undercurrent. The grizzly consisted of a grating of parallel iron rails secured in the bottom of the main sluice through which sand and finer gravel could fall. After falling through the grizzly, the finer gold-laden material was dropped into an undercurrent sluice, while the smaller-sized rocks continued down into a tailings sluice and were discarded.[102] The undercurrent, a system of six or seven sluices placed underneath the grizzly, could extend forty feet in length.

Though effective, hydraulic mining was environmentally disastrous. This method left huge, gaping pits in the earth. Because mercury was used, the tailings poisoned the surrounding streams and water supply.[103] In addition to the toxicity, debris clogged the streams and—during periods of

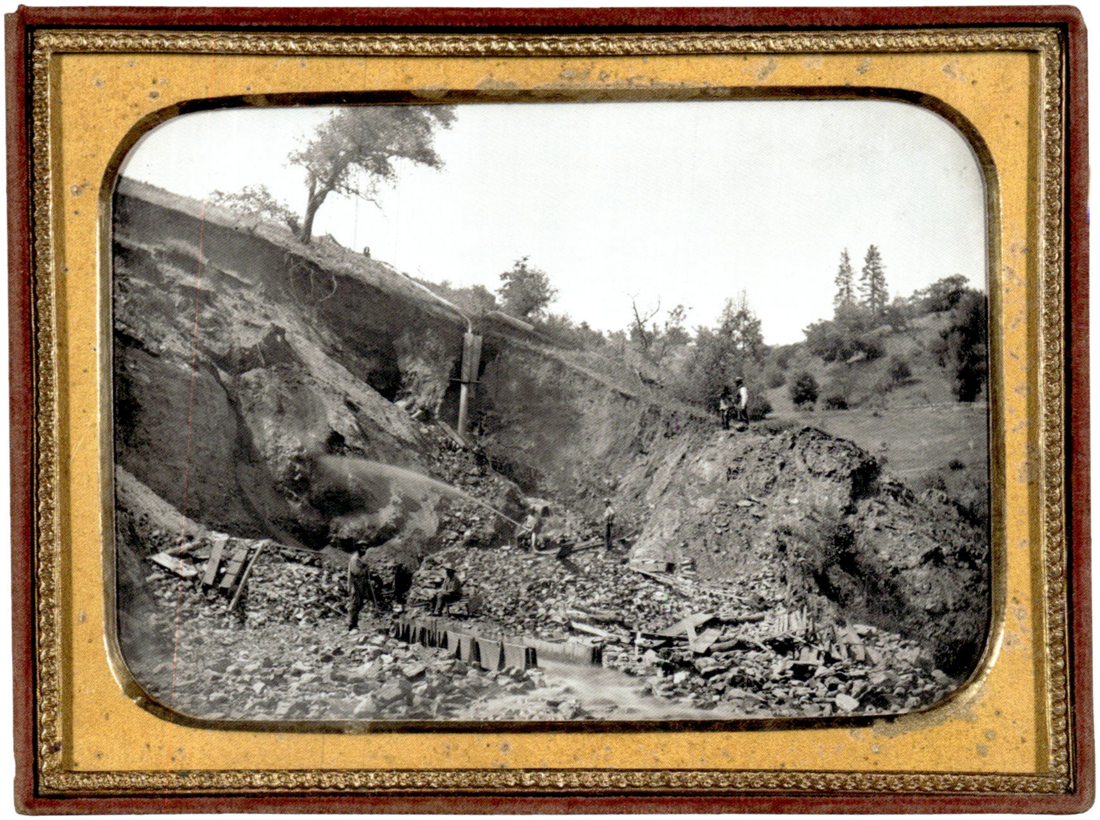

132 **Unknown maker**, American. *Hydraulic mining, California*, ca. 1855. Quarter-plate daguerreotype.

flooding—was washed downstream, smothering towns and farms. By the 1860s, the environmental destruction reached a critical point; many of the hydraulic mines were unable to continue functioning because of the massive accumulation of debris in streams.

Quartz Mining

Placer mining involved retrieving gold from living rivers and ancient riverbeds.[104] These surface deposits of gold were the residue of veins embedded in quartz rock in the mountains that had, over millions of years, been eroded by these rivers. Quartz mining, also known as hard-rock or lode mining, involved locating the gold vein at its source, deep underground in the hills and mountains [FIG. 18].[105] The most common method of retrieving quartz buried deep within a mountain was

> to sink a perpendicular shaft. . . . From this shaft workmen commence removing the quartz along the vein, to form a tunnel. . . . At the bottom of the drift another man was employed to shovel the quartz into a . . . railway car. . . where it was drawn up and taken to the mill. . . . The large pieces are broken by hand to about the size of a man's fist or a little smaller.[106]

In areas where the ore was closer to the surface, miners used a pick and shovel to break off pieces of rock, which were then transported by cart and mule. Although the most productive quartz deposits were found in the northern fields, the initial discovery originated in the southern region, or "Mother Lode." As early as 1849, pockets of high-grade gold ore were found in Mariposa County, on the property of John C. Fremont.[107] This find generated much excitement and the *Placer Times*—in a humorous play on words—noted a reader's confusion that if "gold was found in *quartz*" had any "yet been discovered in *gallons*."[108]

Figuring out exactly how to extract the gold from the quartz remained a major challenge. Simple heat was not enough to capture the gold efficiently, and several new devices were tested to crush the quartz.[109] Seizing a potentially lucrative opportunity, mining promoters secured European funding and imported expensive mining machinery.[110] Caught up in the "wild excitement regarding the immense profits," European investors apparently were duped by questionable field reports prepared by inexperienced operators.[111] By 1852, most of these mines were shut down and the financial capital lost. Commenting on the unfortunate situation of his fellow countrymen, British businessman Thomas Allsop noted, "The character of the country [California] has yet to be ascertained, and it will not be found out by the guesser or mere prospector, but by the man of practice and experience. At present all is guess, and hope, and chance."[112]

Miners in the northern region were similarly vexed by quartz extraction as they hoped to access a quartz vein between Nevada City and Rough and Ready. The northern method of pulverization began as a distinctly primitive,

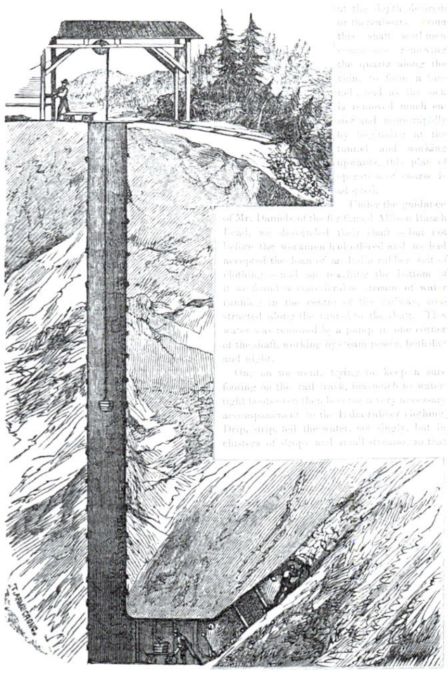

FIG. 18 *Quarrying Quartz at the Vein*, from "Quartz Mining in California," in *Hutchings' California Magazine* 2 (1857–58).

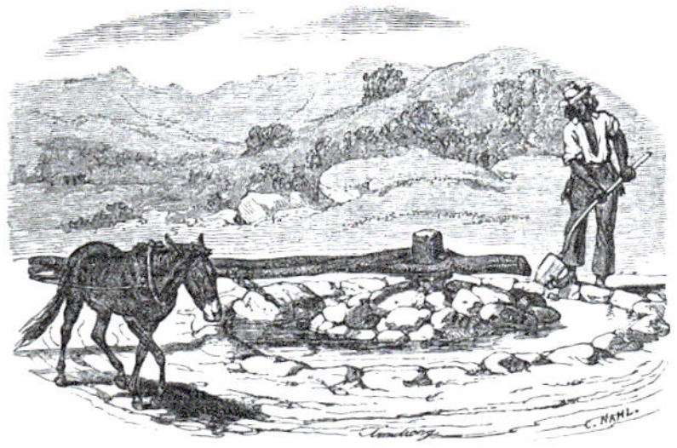

FIG. 19 *The Mexican Rastra*, from "Quartz Mining in California," in *Hutchings' California Magazine* 2 (1857–58).

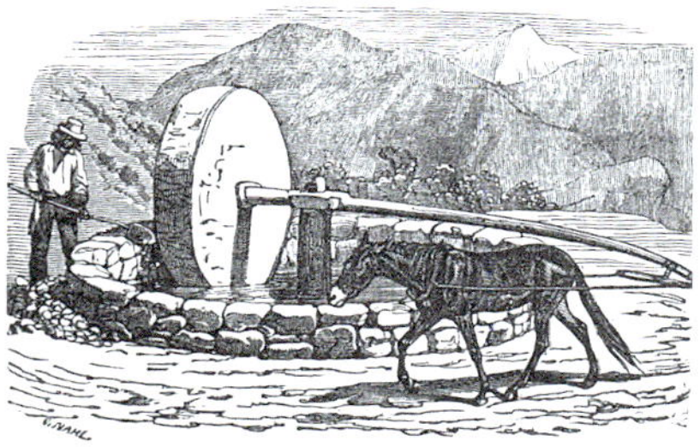

FIG. 20 *The Chili Mill*, from "Quartz Mining in California," in *Hutchings' California Magazine* 2 (1857–58).

labor-intensive process: "Fifteen or twenty men, by mere manual labor, breaking the quartz with hammers."[113] Clearly, an advance in technology was needed. Unlike placer mining, in which gold was plainly visible in a pan, quartz mining was often deceptive: "In many of the richest kinds of rock it has been almost impossible to see gold; while in some . . . considerable has been visible; and yet a sufficient amount has not been taken."[114] It was therefore necessary to pulverize rock to a pulp-like consistency to free the nearly invisible gold from the quartz. When early quartz mining machinery proved inadequate to this task, miners turned to Mexican and Chilean technologies.

Miners from Mexico and Chile had centuries of hard-rock mining experience. For pulverizing rock in Mexico, miners used the arrastra, a shallow, rock-lined circular pit in which large stones were dragged by a horse or mule [FIG. 19]. The mule walked in circles until small pieces of ore were crushed to powder.[115] Water was added with mercury to amalgamate the gold. After the water was drained, the amalgam was scraped from the crevices on the bottom of the arrastra and heated in a furnace [133] to separate quicksilver from gold.[116] Prior to 1860, most miners felt that "the Mexicans with their arrastas were the only successful quartz miners. Experience in their own country enabled them to realize fair profits upon their labors."[117] The Chilean mill worked on much the same "mortar and pestle" principle [FIG. 20].[118] In some areas of the mining region (especially in the south), the Mexican and Chilean methods continued to be used as cost-effective alternatives to the later stamp mills. The mining process in [134] is undoubtedly a version of these crushing methods.

Early quartz mining (before the 1860s) involved underground excavation, though the mines rarely went deeper than 300 feet. Except for the use of mule-pulled ore carts, underground work was done by hand. In the northern gold fields, miners from Cornwall, England, nicknamed "Cousin Jack," brought extensive underground mining experience to California. In Grass Valley, where Cornish influence was strong, the arrastra was replaced by ore crushing machines of Cornish design.[119] Once quartz was pulverized, the finely crushed pulp passed through a series of amalgamation boxes where most of the gold was captured. In the final step, remaining gold was separated by "blanket washing," which had been used for centuries in Cornwall and came to be known as the "Grass Valley system." The process involved laying the quartz pulp in long wooden troughs lined with coarse wool

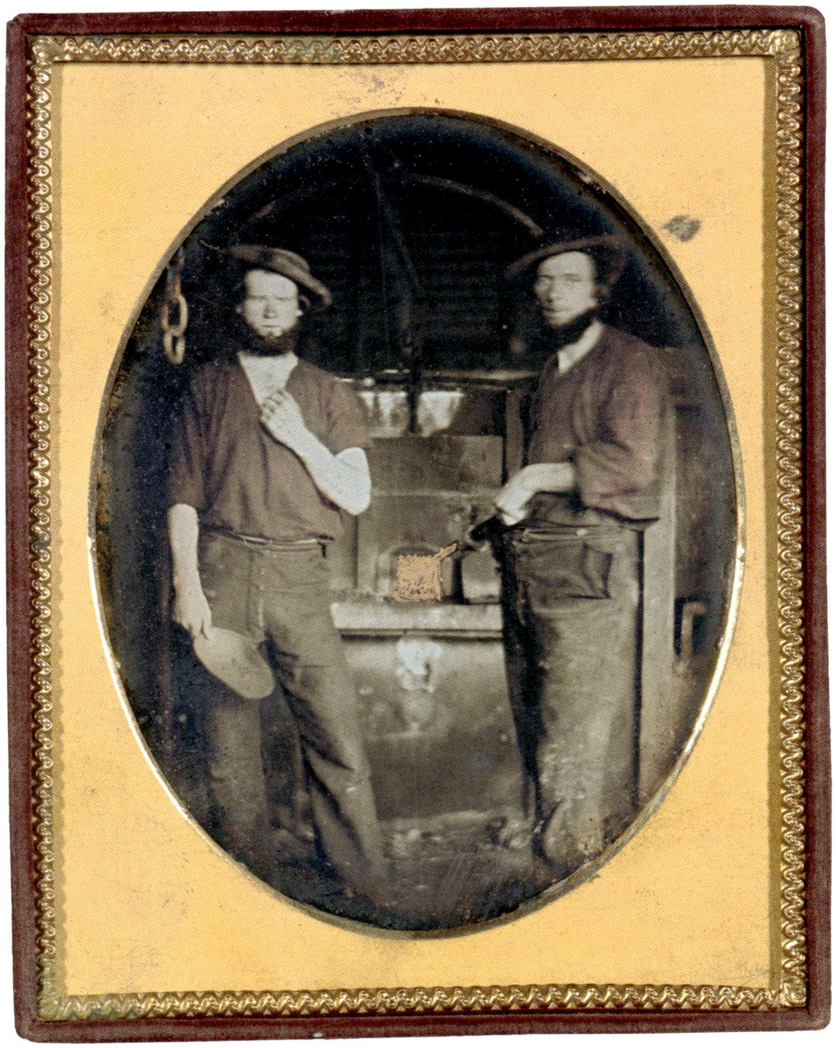

133 **Unknown maker**, American. *Two California miners smelting gold*, ca. 1855. Quarter-plate daguerreotype.

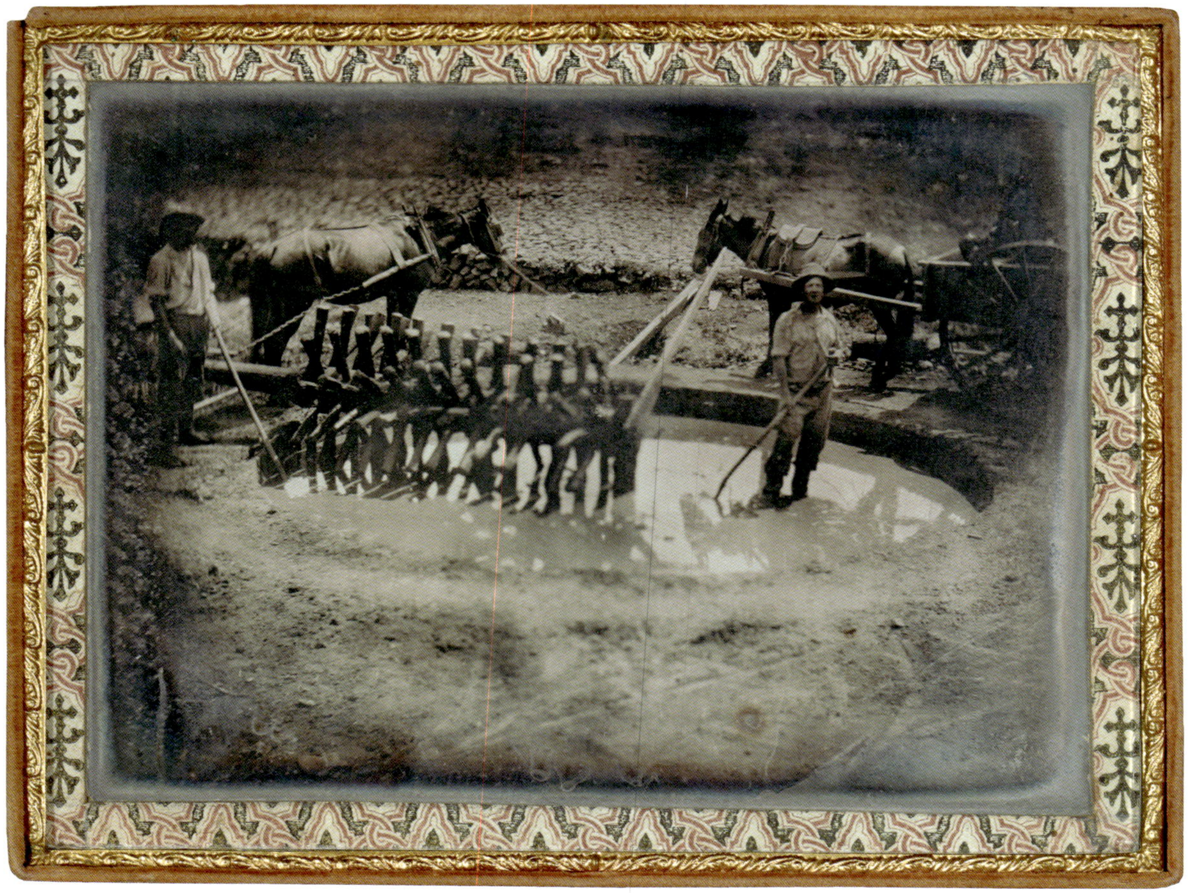

134 **Unknown maker**, American. *California gold miners with ore-crushing mechanism*, ca. 1850–55. Half-plate daguerreotype. The Art Institute of Chicago, The W. Bruce and Delaney H. Lundberg Collection, restricted gift of The Phillip Leonian and Edith Rosenbaum Leonian Charitable Trust.

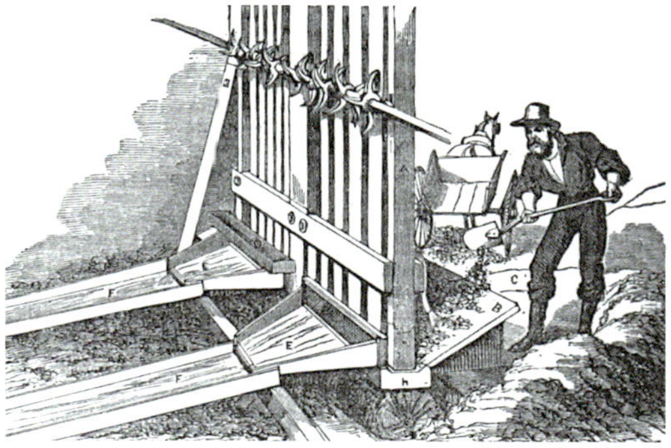

FIG. 21 *Feeding the Mill*, from "Quartz Mining in California," in *Hutchings' California Magazine* 2 (1857–58).

blankets. Every fifteen minutes, the blankets were removed and washed in amalgamation tanks (with mercury) to recover minute particles of gold.[120]

By the late 1850s, it was clear that the California quartz mining industry had outgrown its existing technologies.[121] The California Stamp Mill [FIG. 21], developed by American engineers and designers, was created to fill this gap.[122] The mill was extremely durable, with a mechanical jaw for breaking rock, an automatic feeder, a five-stamp battery, and a heavy iron mortar.[123] The stamping process involved feeding pebble-sized bits of quartz mixed with water into the mortar, where five cast-iron stamps crushed and re-crushed the rock, in the words of Mark Twain, into a kind of "creamy paste."[124] Mercury added during the grinding process aided gold recovery. By the 1860s, the California Stamp Mill was used throughout the gold mining region, north and south.

The Evolution of Mining Processes

Toward the end of the first decade of gold mining in California, it was evident that the basic nature of the work had changed. The days when an individual with little or no capital could use simple tools to earn a living from mining gold were over. New processes required more money, more men, and more expensive machinery—gold mining had become a corporate enterprise. On his trip through the mining region in 1859, Eduard Vischer noted: "The cooperative system of labor has called forth a new era in California's mining industry. Well-organized companies will be able to do work which would have been forever impossible for the individual."[125] Astute observers had seen this coming. Almost ten years earlier, another visitor to the region, E. Gould Buffum, predicted mining's large-scale, corporate future: "The era which follows the present successful gold-washing operations will be one [in which] joint-stock companies will perform what individuals now do. While gold can be found lying within a few inches of the earth's surface . . . there is no need of combination . . . but when hills are torn to their very bases . . . and the streams . . . turned from their channels," collective effort would be required.[126]

The evolution of mining technology was influenced by several factors, including gold ore quality, population growth, water availability, workforce makeup, and access to capital investment. The first miners, who had easy access to higher-grade gold ore, used simple, readily available tools. With the exhaustion of this easy-to-access supply, miners sought gold underground, at the bottom of river channels, and within quartz rock. The inevitable shift to a lower-grade gold ore made technological innovation a necessity.

Mining technology evolved organically. It "came not through sweeping technological changes like a rising tide, but by piecemeal, step-by-step movement, mostly forward but often erratic and sometimes lateral or even backward."[127] The nonlinear nature of this timeline creates some serious categorization challenges. Miners used a variety of tools (pan, rocker, sluice, etc.) at the same time; new tools supplemented, but did not necessarily replace, older ones. Notably, some daguerreotype images exhibit as many as four different technologies in a single view. In other images, technologies appear ambiguous and difficult to analyze accurately.[128] Although it may not be possible to pin a daguerreotype to an exact date based solely on mining technology, understanding the overall complexity offers a wealth of information about cultural, geographic, and environmental conditions, richly informing our understanding beyond the ubiquitous *Gold Mining Scene*.

American Engineering

In the early nineteenth century, significant deposits of gold were found in the South; copper in Michigan; and lead and zinc along the Mississippi River. The technologies used for extraction were crude and dependent on dated European methods. By the 1830s, the loosening of trade barriers with Great Britain allowed for the import of improved mining machinery. But even the earliest mining experiences in the United States were dependent on foreign technology.

When the gold rush began in 1848, the nation was desperate to break from European standards and traditions. Seeking a new national identity, Americans held fast to democratic and nationalistic ideals. Imbued with a strong sense of the Jacksonian democratic spirit, California was seen as a geographically isolated place free from the rigid social structures of Europe. California newspapers were full of accounts praising the equalizing nature of mining:

> Among these miners who wear coarse boots and rough shirts—these miners whose hands are hard and whose faces are tanned—that there are more men of intelligence and education—more men who have occupied honorable and intellectual positions . . . side by side with the gold digger, the man of education and refinement plies the pick and shovel.[129]

In California, all (white) miners were considered equals, regardless of background or community standing.

Most American miners had no prior knowledge of gold mining techniques. Many of the early technologies—pan, rocker, tom, sluice—were not American inventions unique to California mining. The Mexican batea and Native American woven basket were precursors to the tin pan. The chain pumps used to drain the river beds of diverted rivers were of Chinese design. Quartz crushing methods like the arrastra and "Chili" mill were of Mexican and Chilean origin, respectively. Miners used basic principles borrowed from other cultures and adapted them to their needs. With no formal training, these early engineers stressed practice over theory, focusing on application and experience by adapting existing machines and methods to local conditions.

As individual mining gave way to industrial mining, however, American inexperience became apparent and costly. In striking contrast to their highly trained European counterparts, Americans were seat-of-the-pants mechanics with little education. In a scathing summary of American quartz mining ignorance, Rossiter Raymond, the US Commissioner of Mines, found the American mining industry "sadly desultory, incomplete, untrained and unsystemized."[130] Lack of formal training led to unreasonably high production costs and time wasted on processes already tested and discarded in Europe. Raymond's predecessor J. Ross Browne lamented, "Our mines and mills are practically managed by foreign experts; we furnish the labor and mechanical ingenuity, but they furnish the scientific skill." However, he conceded that "without the aid of foreign institutions we could have made but little progress in mining."[131]

The real disappointment was not that the American engineers were untrained but that the United States was once again subordinate to Europe. In his *Report of Mines and Mining*, Raymond understood that "men of science abroad" felt that the US was "totally blundering along . . . in the treatment of our gold . . . ignorant of the experience already gained in older countries." Many in the American scientific community suggested that "somebody should be sent to Europe by our government to study the methods . . . and enlighten us with the results." Instead, Raymond posited that the US was "neither wholly in advance nor wholly in the rear" of other countries, pointing out the "distinctly American processes" of hydraulic mining and the California Stamp Mill. He continued:

> We have employed and improved nearly all the European methods which our economical conditions will admit, and we have invented several of our own. . . . Even now, it is necessary for foreign governments to send agents here to study our methods and report at home. We know the processes of Europe better than Europe knows ours.[132]

In the end, American engineering success stressed ingenuity over originality and invention. European processes and equipment were adapted to meet the unique conditions of the gold mining region. Cultural diversity, often considered a source of conflict, instead became a vital opportunity for innovation. In this technological realm, it was this spirited pragmatism that gave rise to a new and distinctly American identity.

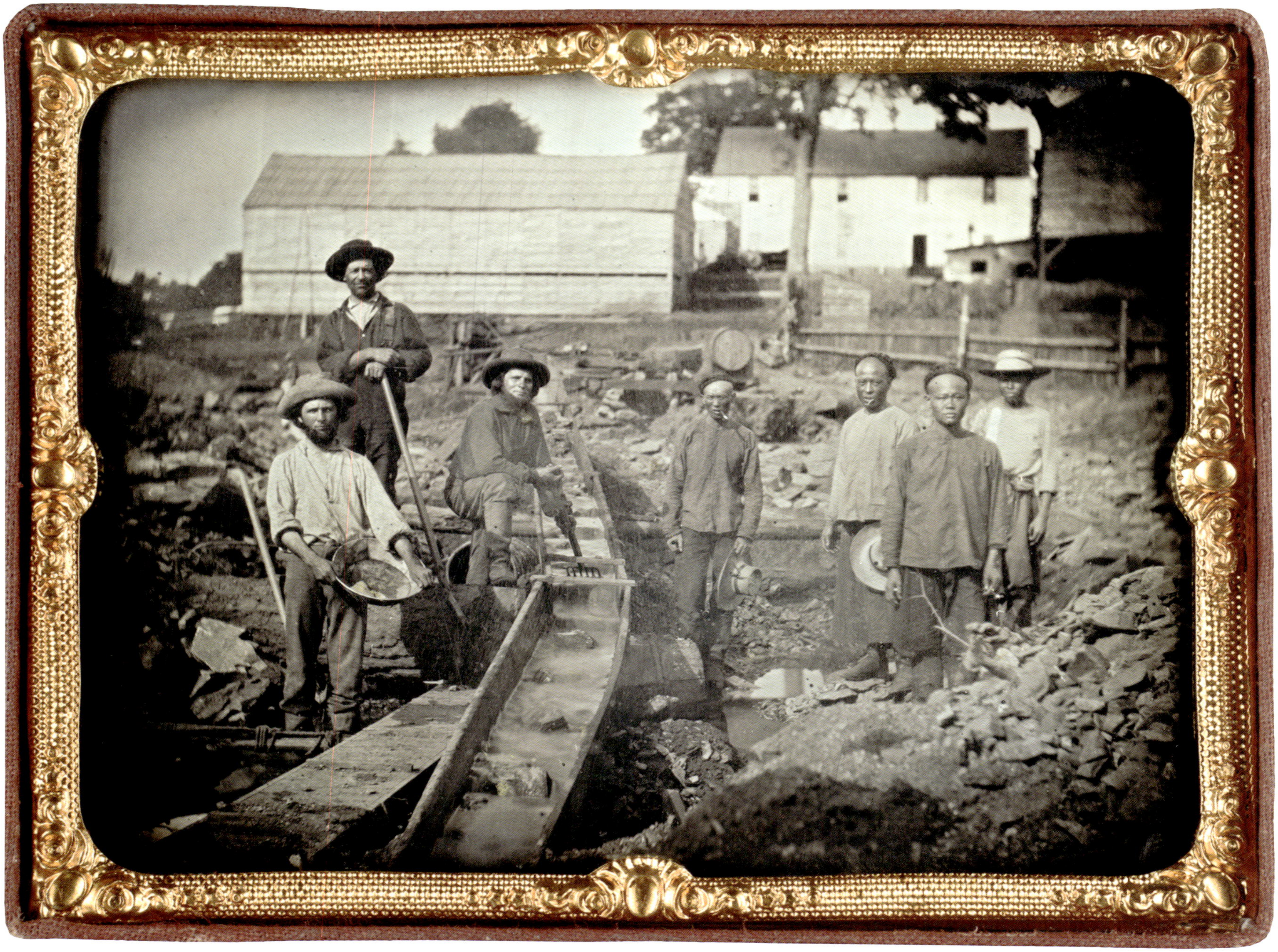

135 Joseph Starkweather, American (1822–ca. 1905). *Head of Auburn Ravine*, ca. 1852.
Quarter-plate daguerreotype. California History Room, California State Library, Sacramento.

CHAPTER 6 *Diversity in the Gold Fields*

During the years of the gold rush, California was a melting pot: native California residents (including Mexican, American Indian, and early pre-California settlers), Americans from other parts of the United States, and immigrants from abroad all shared in one goal—the pursuit of gold.[1] The nature of this cultural interaction varied with time. The initial immigration patterns were divided into three distinct periods: 1) 1848, the year of gold discovery; 2) 1849–51, the years of massive immigration; and 3) 1852 and thereafter, with the surge of Chinese immigration. During the first period, there were about 150,000 American Indians residing in California. The American Indians living in the gold region (around Coloma initially) were among the first to mine for gold in 1848, followed closely by native Californians who had lived under Mexican rule, and pre-gold rush European and American settlers [136]. People from countries in close geographic proximity to California with pre-established trade routes—including Hawaii, Chile, and Peru—arrived by ship, while Mexicans from Sonora journeyed north on foot. All were motivated to find gold, like this Chilean sailor [137], who reportedly jumped ship as soon as it reached San Francisco harbor.

In the second wave, Australians and New Zealanders arrived in early 1849, just before the onslaught of the forty-niners. Arriving by ship from the eastern United States, and overland from the South, Midwest, and North, Americans—over 90,000 strong—overwhelmed the territory. Europeans from Britain, Ireland, Scotland, France, and Germany gave a significant boost to the dominant white demographic in California. In the third period, the Chinese, a little late to the gold rush experience, arrived in large numbers. While some Chinese people had immigrated to California before 1850, most arrived in 1852 and later.

For Americans, there was a democracy to mining.[2] Indistinguishable in the field, wealth, education, and class took a back seat to hard work and luck. This did not apply to non-Americans, however. Subscribing to the idea of Manifest Destiny, American miners believed they were the rightful owners of the new land and its resources. In reality, all were trespassers—the territory had only recently come under US jurisdiction at the time of gold discovery and no legislation regarding gold extraction was passed until 1866. Regardless, resolutions were passed almost every year from 1849 onward to remove non-Americans and non-whites from the mines. Paradoxically, citizenship and associated rights were denied to American Indians because of their federally protected status. Rights were also denied to the Chinese purportedly because non-Christian belief prevented the swearing of a legal oath of allegiance. Additionally, large groups of non-white workers were perceived as threatening to the individual white miner; American Indians working on ranchos, the Chinese allegedly laboring for slave masters in China, Mexicans bonded under the peonage system, and black slave gang labor from the Southern United States were all unwelcome. The Foreign Miners' Tax (1850) required all Mexican and Chinese miners to pay monthly fees—a further legislative attempt to penalize non-white people.

Hinton Helper was a white farmer from North Carolina turned California miner. Unimpressed with California, he wrote his book *The Land of Gold: Reality Versus Fiction* (1855) to discourage immigration. Undoubtedly a man of racist tendencies, he proposed a solution to the "race problem":

> No inferior race of men can exist in these United States without becoming subordinate to the will of the Anglo-Americans, or foregoing [*sic*] many of the necessities and comforts of life. . . . It is so with the negroes in the South . . . it was so with the Indians in New England; and it will be so with the Chinese in California. The Indians, it is true, would not submit to be enslaved; but they had to suffer exile, hunger and death as a consequence of their intractability. Certain it is, that the greater the diversity of colors and qualities of men, the greater will be the strife and conflict of feeling.[3]

This racial bias, prevalent in nineteenth-century Californian society, generalized that people of color were in one inferior and subordinate category.

During the gold rush, large tribes of American Indians lived in all regions of California, tens of thousands of Chinese immigrated to the state, and a

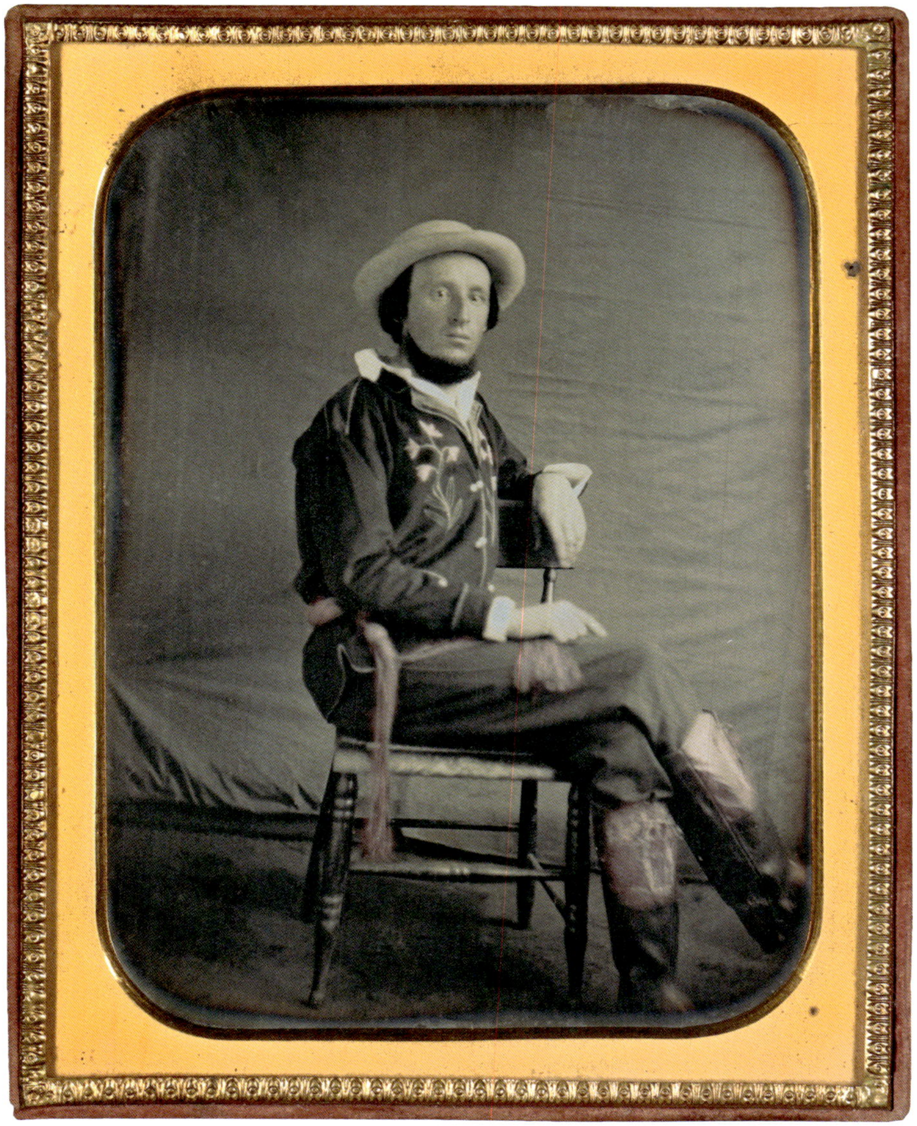

136 Unknown maker, American. *Portrait of man in embroidered shirt*, ca. 1850–54. Half-plate daguerreotype. The Art Institute of Chicago, The W. Bruce and Delaney H. Lundberg Collection, restricted gift of The Phillip Leonian and Edith Rosenbaum Leonian Charitable Trust.

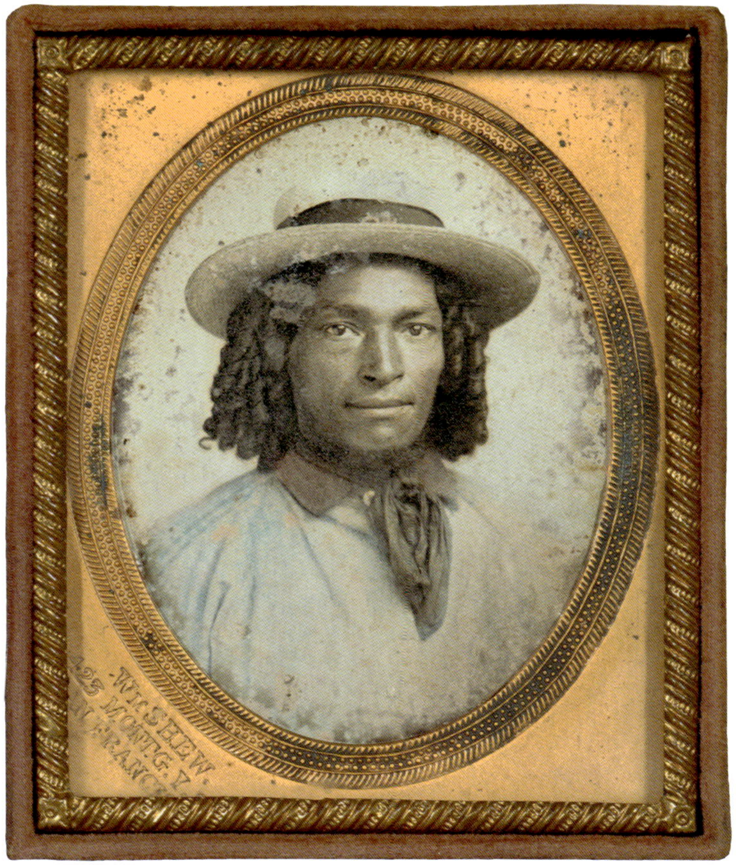

137 William Shew, American (1820–1903). *Portrait of Chilean sailor*, ca. 1850. Ninth-plate daguerreotype.

number of black people of African descent were working there. Nonetheless, the pictorial record of these groups is astonishingly thin. This chapter explores the following questions: Where did American Indian, Chinese, and black miners live and work? What mining technologies did they use? Did these groups achieve success at mining?

A word of caution: there are relatively few extant accounts written by individuals from these minority groups, making it difficult to determine their own perceptions of their experiences. What dominates the contemporary historical record is information from the white perspective—some sympathetic, most condemning, all a product of the thinking of the time.[4]

American Indian Miners

Hundreds of American Indians mined for gold during the California gold rush, but there are few daguerreotype records of their participation. Some factors accounting for this lack of visual representation include the absence of daguerreotypists in the gold fields during the earliest days of the rush, when American Indians mined most actively, as well as a rapidly declining American Indian population due to violence, disease, and forced deportation to distant reservations. In 1848, it is estimated that 150,000 American Indians lived in California; by 1860, there were around 30,000—an eighty percent decline in twelve years.[5]

For decades before the discovery of gold in California, unfree American Indian labor fueled the regional economy.[6] Large Mexican and American landowners—recipients of sizeable Spanish and Mexican grants—routinely exploited Indian labor in exchange for little more than subsistence. According to historian Michael Magliari, this racially based system of unfree labor was "primarily used to satisfy the state's high demand for domestic servants and agricultural laborers. . . . Forms included minor custodial wardship, indentured servitude or 'apprenticeship,' convict leasing, and debt peonage."[7] When gold was discovered in 1848 at Sutter's Mill, Indian laborers digging a new raceway made the find. Indian labor forces were subsequently directed away from the agricultural fields and toward the gold mining region.

Initially, many American Indians were engaged in gold mining. From 1848 to 1850, Indians working for rancho owners and in independent tribal groupings often panned side by side with miners of various nationalities. Colonel Richard B. Mason noted one of the earliest accounts of Indian gold mining activity in his official report in August 1848. Touring near the site where gold was first discovered, Mason witnessed "the Indians, and those who have nothing but pans or willow baskets, gradually wash out the earth, and separate the gravel by hand."[8] Moving down the American River to Weber's Creek, Mr. Weber himself reported to Mason, "two men had employed four white men and about 100 Indians" and mined $17,000 in gold. Additionally, John Sinclair employed "about fifty Indians on the north fork . . . engaged about five weeks . . . and up to that time his Indians had used simply closely-woven willow baskets." The simple technique had netted the wealthy ranchero over $16,000 in gold, after the deduction of expenses. Mason's recap of early mining activity included an estimate that "upwards of 4,000 men were working in the gold district, of whom more than one-half were Indians."[9]

Coexisting with fellow miners, American Indians not bonded to a rancho mined in independent groups either for themselves or as hired laborers for others. Gold or wages were then traded for needed supplies. In Mason's opinion, the barter was especially favorable to the American Indian workers who were exposed to "large quantities of goods . . . daily sent forward to the mines, as the Indians, heretofore so poor and degraded, have suddenly become consumers of the luxuries of life."[10] Contrary to Mason's first impression, however, most American Indians lived in appalling conditions on ranchos. On August 19, 1848, a correspondent for the *New York Herald* described "the Diggor [*sic*] tribe . . . are kept in a kind of slavery and bondage by the rancheros, and often flogged and punished. Their performing all the drudgery and heavy labor, leaves but little demand for laborers of white complexion."[11]

Independent American Indian miners were gaining a foothold by 1849. William Johnston, an early gold-seeking visitor to the northern region, noted that the area around Placerville in July 1849 was full of such miners:

> Each carried a neatly made willow basket, for washing gold, instead of the tin pan ordinarily used by miners. A few months prior to this, as we were told, thousands of these Indians were employed by the whites in gold gathering, and for the service rendered had been fed and blanketed, besides being supplied with gew-gaws of trifling value. Acquiring, however, a knowledge concerning gold dust, by seeing what could be purchased with it at the stores, they had of late been setting up business for themselves.[12]

Unfortunately, this push for economic self-sufficiency was short-lived. Newly arriving miners from the Oregon Territory objected to the use of Indian gang labor by the rancheros because it displaced the individual miner. Escalating racial tension led to a violent confrontation.[13] Miner William Case detailed the provocation:

> The Indians were the victims; but the old California system was the real cause. The attempt was made [by the rancheros] to work the mines upon a system of inequality—of proprietors and peons. The Oregonians, accustomed to a system of equality, finding themselves exposed to outlawry . . . struck as they could. . . . It was not mere personal vengeance, but the purpose to establish the system of free labor, and to root out the contract system, or rather the peon system.[14]

Fearful of further conflict, many of the Indians located in the vicinity of the American River fled south. E. Gould Buffum noted the exodus:

> A redskin is scarcely ever seen in the inhabited portion of the northern mining region. Their rancherias are deserted, the graves of their ancestors are left to be desecrated by the white man's footprint, and they have gone . . . the whole race is fast becoming extinct.[15]

Around this same time, traveler Theodore Johnson, informed of the mistreatment of Indians while visiting John Sutter, was outraged:

> Thus has been renewed in California the war of extermination against the aborigines, commenced in effect at the landing of Columbus, and continued to this day . . . and never has this policy proved so injurious to the interests of the whites as in California. The profitable trade for their gold dust is entirely at an end. Their labor once very useful, and, in fact, indispensable in a country where no other species of laborers were to be obtained at any price . . . has been utterly sacrificed by this extensive system of indiscriminate revenge.[16]

In the fall of 1849, the constitution of the territory of California included a seemingly favorable antislavery clause proclaiming, "Neither slavery, nor involuntary servitude, unless for the punishment of crimes, shall ever be tolerated." The following year, after California achieved statehood, the ironically named Act for the Government and Protection of Indians was included in the state's constitution. Unfortunately, rather than protecting Indians, this Act reinforced the Mexican debt peonage system and in effect sanctioned the slavery of American Indians. Visiting several ranchos (including John Sutter's) on the way to Mormon Diggings, John Letts was appalled by the deplorable conditions:

> The Indians on the ranchos in California, are considered as stock, and are sold with it as cattle, and the purchaser has the right to work them on the rancho, or take them into the mines. They are extremely squalid in appearance, and in the most abject servitude. I have never found the natives, anywhere, in a condition so degraded.[17]

Despite the racial persecution, some American Indian miners continued to assist new arrivals to the diggings. On Mariposa River in the southern mining region, Sam Ward was eager to join them but simply could not master the panning technique. He was astounded by

> the aptitude of the savages—men, women, and children—for this delicate mechanical operation surpassed any exhibition I witnessed of the skill of white miners; and was only equaled by the handiness of the Mexican adventurers. . . . Despairing to attain anything like this dexterity, I formed a league with two or three young shavers of the tribe, who gladly undertook, on shares, the beneficiation of the results of my delvings.[18]

White miners, it would seem, continued to benefit from an ongoing relationship with American Indians whether through gold trade, hired help, or direct control from the rancho system.

By 1852, California tribes were beginning to realize the consequence of close contact with the new residents living near them. An article in the *Alta California* newspaper reported on the alarming conditions in the south, in Mariposa County: "Much sickness of a fatal character have prevailed among these tribes during the past summer; nearly all the aged males and females have died, as well as very many of those of younger years." The reason for the deaths, the writer contended, was "attributed to the fact of their having had food in greater abundance, of a character to which they had before been unaccustomed."[19] In essence, instead of ascribing the fatalities to disease, the newspaper absurdly attributed the deaths to the excessive prosperity and success of the American Indian population. As the death toll continued to escalate, the cause became irrefutable:

> The small pox has prevailed to a great extent among the Indians the present season, and that it is computed by those best acquainted with the details of Indian life, that not less than four hundred of all sexes and ages of the Indians have been destroyed by this disease the past six months—that is one tenth of the whole number. The Indians are totally helpless when thus attacked . . . the most common sufferers are children, which are swept off in numbers.[20]

John Sutter, whose fort and farm were once replete with Indian laborers, felt the immensity of the tragedy. He reported to the *Sacramento Union* newspaper:

> As an example of the decimation of the Indian population of our country, we need but refer to the Hock Farm digger tribe, which consisted of over five hundred souls a few years since . . . of that entire number but *fifteen* are now living. The decrease has been far more rapid since the settlement of the State by Eastern emigrants.[21]

By 1854, there were few American Indians mining, especially in the north. Available claims were scarce and much of the Indian labor had shifted away from mining and toward the agriculture fields. Some Indians were able to scrounge up mining work by reworking the discarded claims of other miners:

> Sometimes a miner will permit them to take a pan of dirt from his claim from which they get some gold. They scrape up the dirt about the end of the sluice boxes which sometimes pays them very well. On the rivers they obtain gold by scraping out the crevices that have been abandoned by the whites.[22]

In addition to the small pox epidemic, the issue of "relocation" was also at odds with a thriving local Indian population in the mining region. Not surprisingly, "a great portion of the Indians are opposed to removal, and resist every overture made to them . . . preferring to roam at freedom, with a precarious subsistence" and refusing "the adoption of the manners and customs of the white man, whom they feel to be infinitely removed above them in native and cultivated superiority."[23] Many Californio rancheros were equally opposed to this solution, depending as they did on Indian labor for domestic and agricultural work. In the end, however, rancho owners reluctantly abided by the federal suggestion to capture the remaining Indians in the mining district and remove them to reservation land. As a result, by 1855, American Indian gold miners were almost non-existent.[24] While some historians have attributed this to the movement away from simple technologies to the more advanced drift, hydraulic, and quartz mining techniques, the reason is more basic: far fewer Indians were there. Small pox had drastically reduced the number of eligible working Indians, countless others were exterminated by white aggression, and the few that remained were deported to reservations or relocated to the agricultural fields.[25]

There is only one known California daguerreotype dedicated exclusively to an American Indian subject [138]. Unfortunately, the image is difficult to read. Seven Indians are gathered in a circle, but it is unclear what they are doing. This piece has variously been classified as Indians fishing or mining. The Indians are situated in rocky terrain in front of a river with a waterwheel; they hold long poles that may be shovels, and they are intently interested in something on the ground. The waterwheel is a sign of mining activity, but no characteristic mining baskets or pans are visible. Despite the ambiguity, this plate is important for documenting a photographically underrepresented facet of the mining region population. Photographic historian Richard Rudisill underscored the importance of this piece nearly fifty years ago, observing that the "blurring of the figures of the men" was vital in "conveying a developing activity with seeming spontaneity."[26]

In another image, two boys—presumably Indian—are saddling mules for a group of four white men, possibly heading into the Sierra Nevada foothills to mine [139]. Enslaved Indian juveniles were not uncommon; an

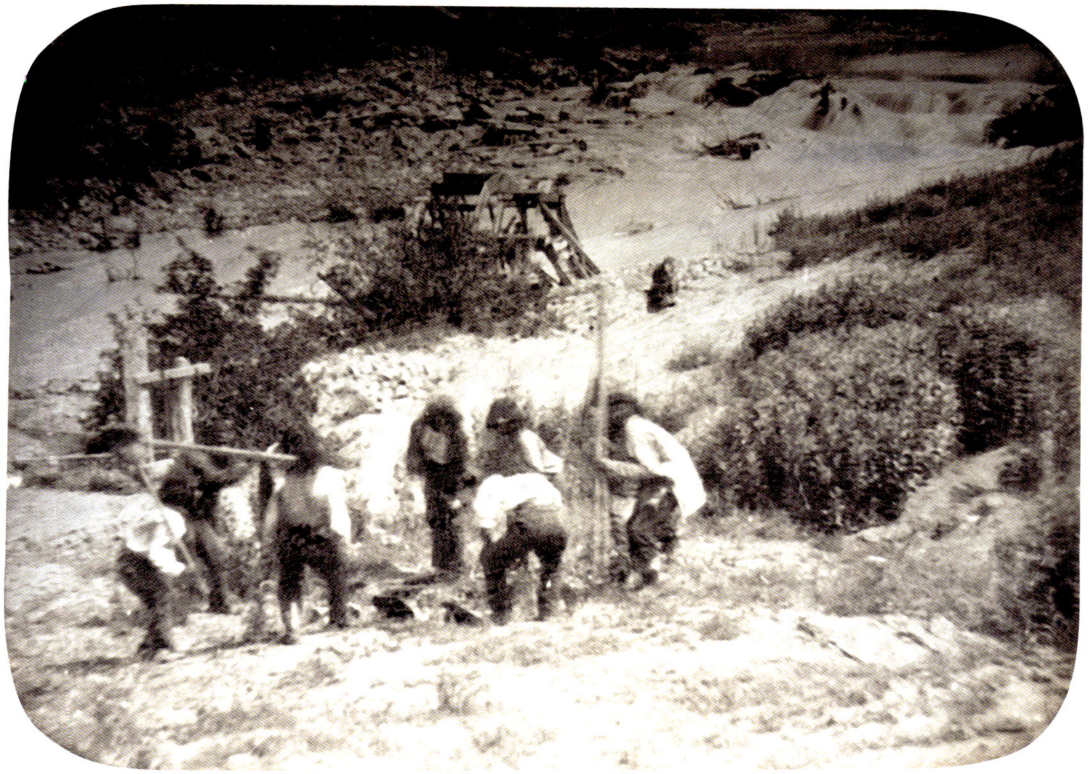

138 **Unknown maker**, American. *Indians fishing*, ca. 1850. Half-plate daguerreotype. Society of California Pioneers, San Francisco.

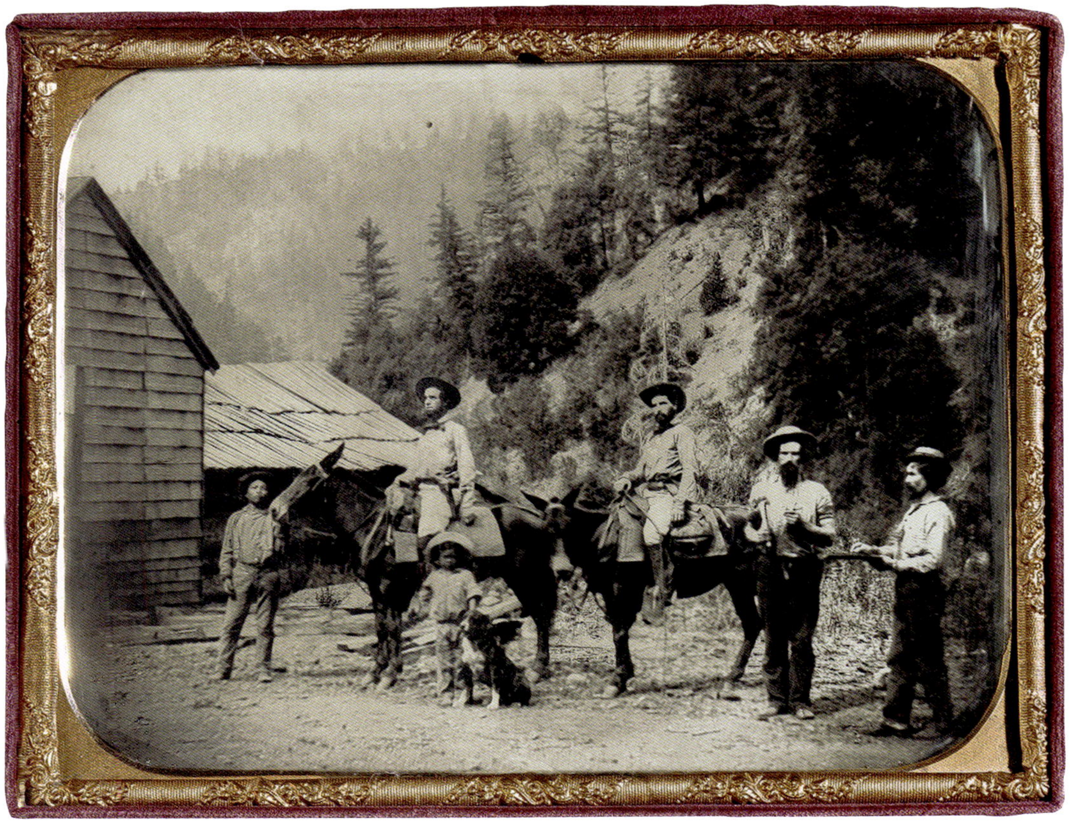

139 **Unknown maker**, American. *Two miners being outfitted for the high Sierra*, ca. 1855–60. Half-plate ambrotype. Oakland Museum of California, History Guild Purchase.

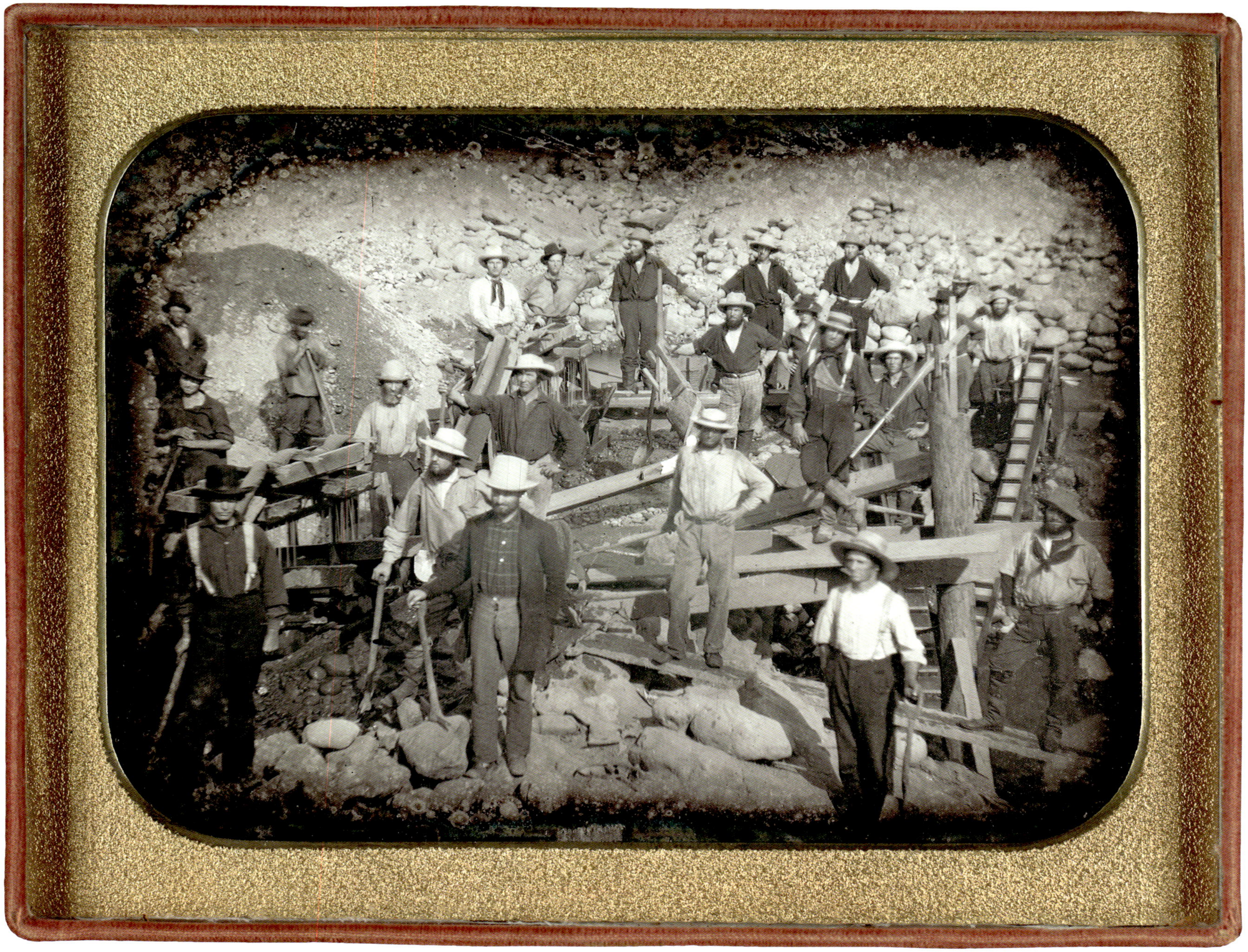

140 Unknown maker, American. *Portrait of twenty-three miners at sluice*, ca. 1852.
Half-plate daguerreotype. California History Room, California State Library, Sacramento.

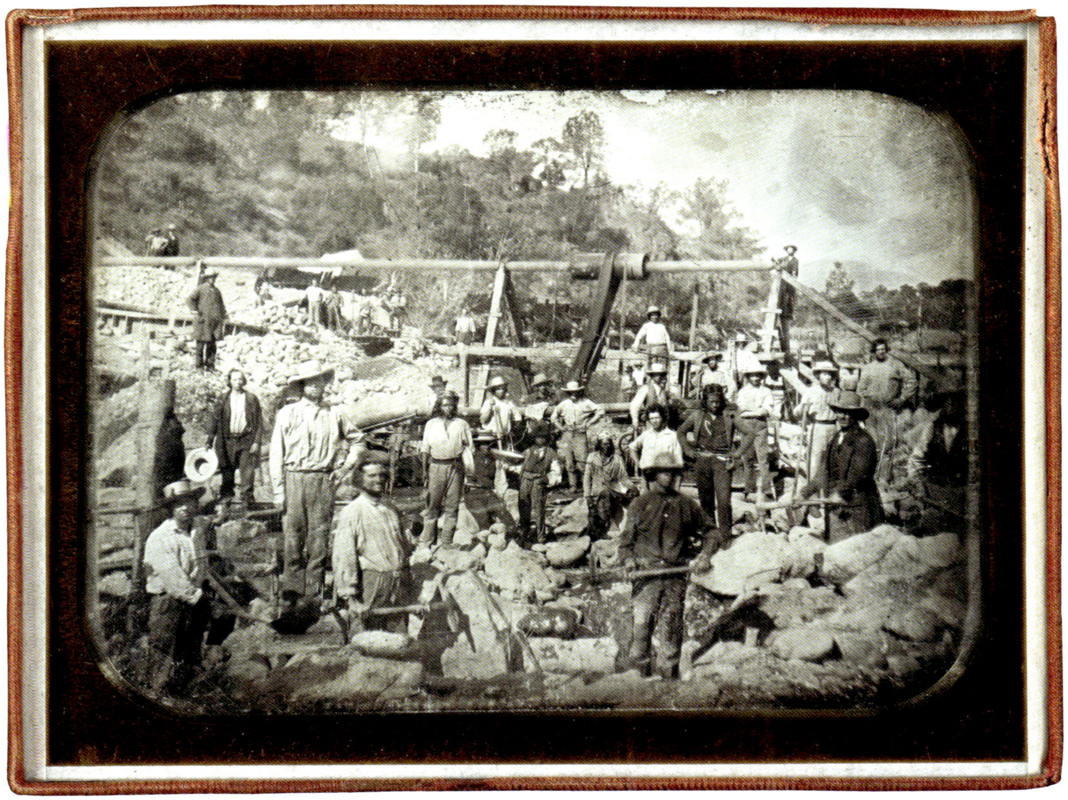

141 **Unknown maker**, American. *Miners at Taylorsville, California*, ca. 1851. Half-plate daguerreotype. Huntington Library, San Marino, California.

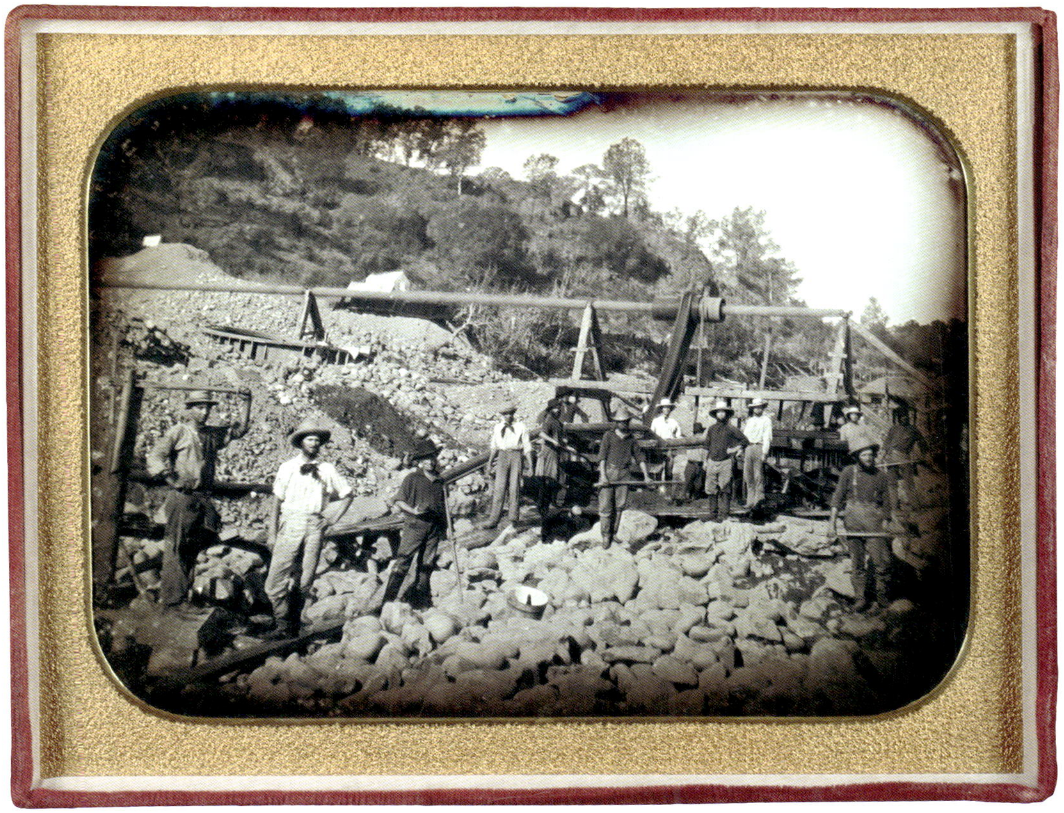

142 **Unknown maker**, American. *Riverbed mining scene with fifteen miners, including Elmer Bliss*, ca. 1852–58. Half-plate daguerreotype. Bancroft Library, University of California, Berkeley.

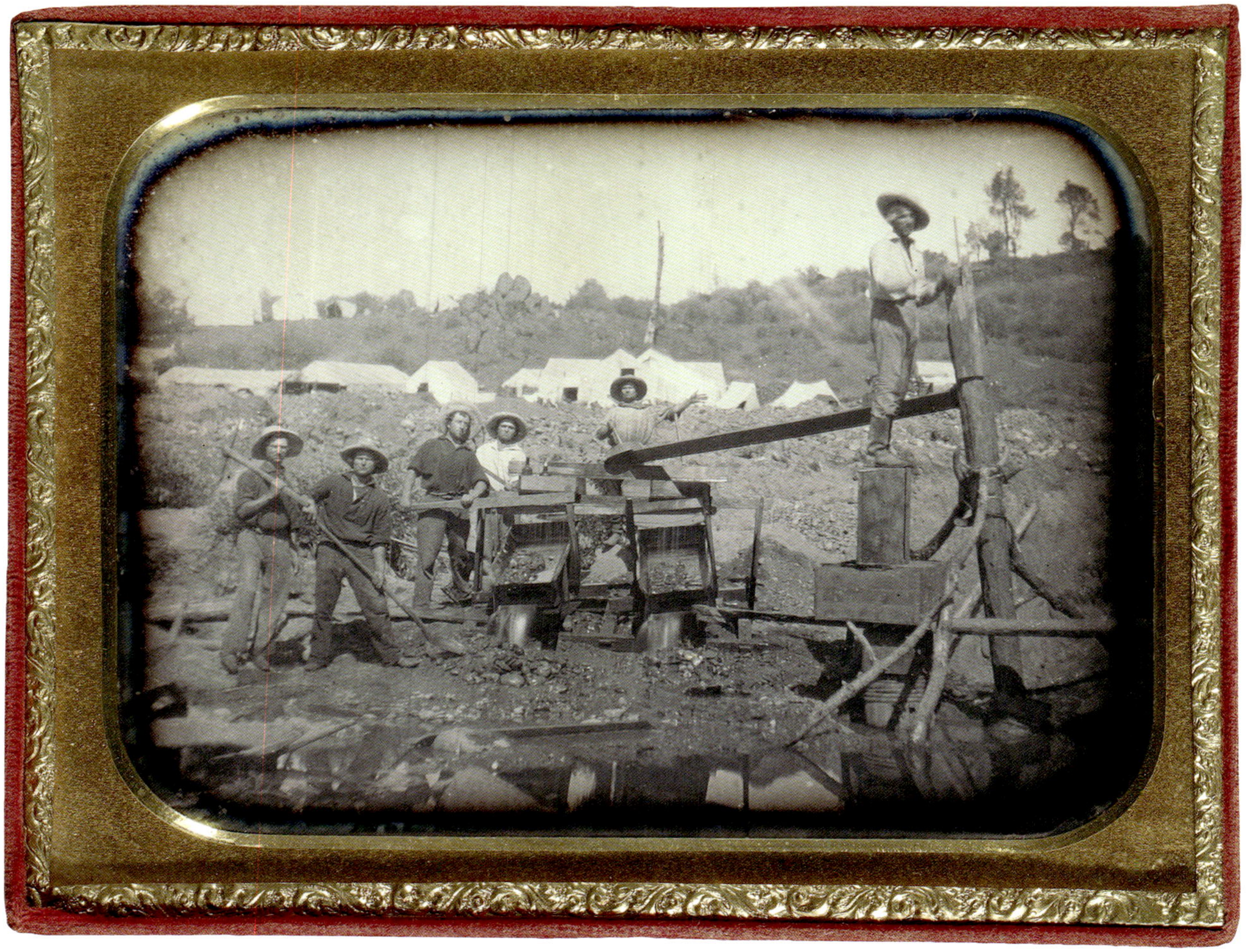

143 **Unknown maker**, American. *Placer mining scene*, ca. 1850–53. Half-plate daguerreotype. The J. Paul Getty Museum, Los Angeles, Open Content Program.

especially disturbing provision in the 1850 Act for the Government and Protection of Indians, Section 3, granted white employers custody of minor American Indian children who could be "retained" until the age of eighteen for males and fifteen for females.[27] Historian Michael Magliari maintains that Section 3 led to a "flourishing trade in Indian children kidnapped from their parents or seized as the spoils of war by California militiamen who campaigned throughout the state during the 1850s and 1860s."[28] In 1854, the *Alta California* reported that the abduction of Indian children "has become quite common. Nearly all the children belonging to some of the Indian tribes in the northern part of the State, have been stolen. They are taken to the southern part of the State and there sold."[29]

Other daguerreotype views that include American Indian miners are more obscure. Indian miners were sometimes included as a part of large labor forces, as with river diversion mining. In these larger group images, American Indians have been tentatively identified by the occasionally worn headband or the distinctively short-cropped hair [140], indicative of mourning.

In [141], miners are interrupted from their work of digging and breaking up rock in the riverbed of a diverted river. Standing with tools in hand or

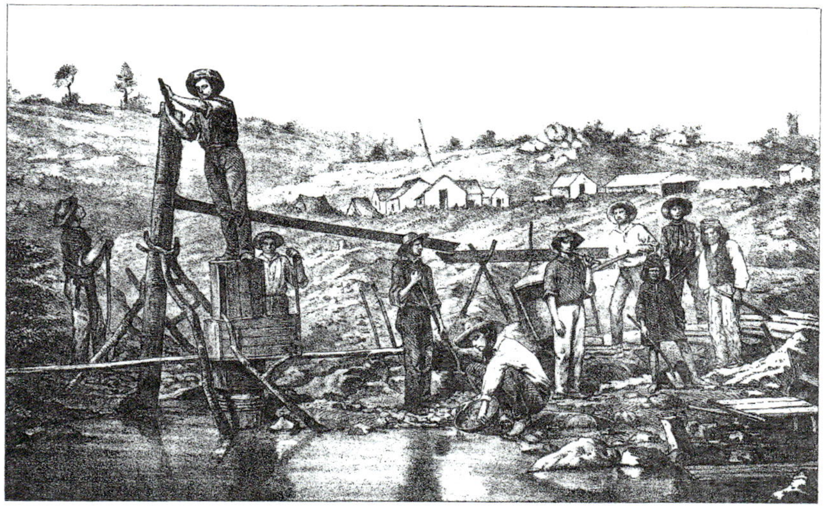

FIG. 22 *The Miners*, from Joseph Armstrong Baird, Jr., *California's Pictorial Letter Sheets, 1849–1869* (San Francisco: David Magee, 1967).

hands on hips, the men relax for the few moments necessary to capture the view. Of the miners in this image, several are possibly American Indians. Another daguerreotype from this same location [142] is taken from a slightly higher, more distant vantage point and is laterally reversed. Miners again are paused at their work. Several hold shovels or picks—tools necessary for breaking up large boulders and scooping the gravel lying beneath. One man in the bottom left with his hand on hip and a tie around his neck holds a prominent position within the composition; this may be the foreman or owner of the river company. Conspicuously absent from [142] are any of the Indian miners seen in [141]. It is possible they appear in a small grouping in the far distance; regardless, they have been relegated to a position of unimportance.

An interesting record of American Indian and white miners can be found in the daguerreotype-engraving pairing seen in [143, FIG. 22]. In the daguerreotype, six inventive miners have rigged a sort of sluice down which water could be poured. The water is directed into two rockers which could be operated at the same time—making quick work of gold washing. The man in the center props his outstretched arm on a shovel handle as if to claim the entire operation as his own. Another man balances precariously on a stack of wooden boxes. A variant of this scene was produced as a letter sheet titled *The Miners*, first published by Quirot & Co., and then by Britton & Rey.[30] The lithographic print is laterally reversed, an indication that it was based on an original view.[31] However, the double rocker contraption is missing—perhaps disassembled for end-of-the-day cleaning—and there are ten miners in the engraving rather than six. Notably, two of the four added miners are American Indians. One suspects that the Indian miners were indeed present, working as unfree labor for the white foreman.

American Indians are underrepresented in California daguerreotypes, in part due to timing. American Indian miners were most active in the early years of the gold rush, when few daguerreotypists were working in the field. In addition, white animosity resulted in their routine dismissal from mining operations and, thus, from daguerreotype images. White miners saw American Indian labor as disposable and replaceable, not valued as an essential part of the mining endeavor. Thus, the full measure of American Indian participation in the gold rush is missing from the historical visual record.

Miners of African Descent

Black people, or people of African descent, were present in the California mining region.[32] By the end of 1848, in addition to black persons of Mexican descent already residing in California, black men were arriving from Mexico, Chile, and Peru, and aboard American whaling ships from eastern US seaports. An important whaling port of the nineteenth century, New Bedford, Massachusetts, reacted early to news of the gold discovery, outfitting at least eleven vessels, each carrying 160 passengers, by February 1849.[33] This was

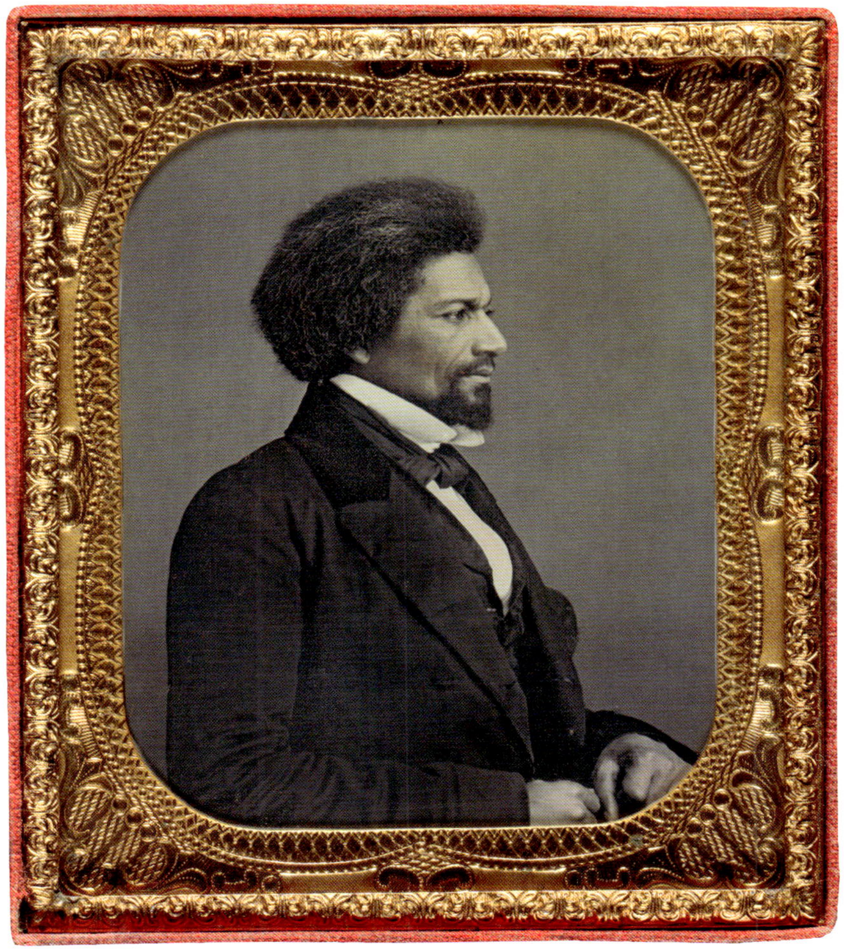

144 **Unknown maker**, American. *Profile portrait of Frederick Douglass*, ca. 1858. Sixth-plate daguerreotype.

significant to black men considering transit to California; New Bedford was a major hub of antislavery activity, referred to by Frederick Douglass [144] as the place where "the Anti-Slavery cause found me, and summoned me forth to defend the rights and . . . dignity of my oppressed and plundered people."[34] One antislavery captain of a ship from New Bedford proudly proclaimed his company as "having no narrow feelings of caste. The descendants of Africa and the sons of New England and Pennsylvania" were bound together seeking "one fortune and one fate."[35]

With the possibility of slavery in California undecided, miners from cities like New Bedford imbued the mining region with abolitionist sentiment. Corroborating the impact of northern immigration, Thomas Clingman of North Carolina made a "frank admission" on the floor of Congress:

> California . . . would have been settled by slave-owners . . . had there not been such a general agitation at the North upon this slavery question; but they had been prevented from moving there from this cause, and therefore California was populated mostly by Northern men.[36]

Nonetheless, calls to exclude black people from California and the threat of slavery were constant worries for white abolitionist and black miners alike.

The first governor of California, Peter Burnett, recommended "the total exclusion of free negroes," concerned that "if allowed to emigrate, they will form contracts in the Southern States . . . and thus be, to all intents and purposes, slaves."[37] Newspaper accounts boldly noted that the "citizens of the Southern States are taking things in their own hand so far as regards the establishment of slavery in California," and sending "several slave droves."[38] Newly formed mining companies in the southern states sanctioned "that each member shall take with him at least one, and not more than four slaves."[39]

As news of the gold rush spread, free black men in the northern United States took notice of early black successes. About one major find, a report in the *New York Tribune* boasted,

> California gold valued $600, [was] dug out at Stanislaus River by a *free* colored man, Reuben Ruby. . . . One queer shaped lump weighs 11 ounces . . . another four ounces, the rest are of various sizes, from the size of a chestnut down to a grain of wheat. All this he dug and paid his expenses, in less than four weeks.[40]

The real turning point for black immigration came in October 1849 when California declared its intention to become a free state. Antislavery newspapers, initially wary, became enthusiastic about the prospect. *The Liberator*, the country's leading abolitionist newspaper, reported on forty black men from New Bedford already in California and another thirty-seven who had organized a mutual aid society, earning between $100 and $300 a month.[41] Frederick Douglass confirmed that there were "industrious and enterprising [black] men, not fewer than forty now in California . . . as keenly alive to the attractions of gold as their white fellow-citizens." Appreciating gold mining as an equalizing activity for white and black men, Douglass stated, "I am glad of this proof of a common origin—a common identity."[42]

Men accustomed to hard manual labor had an advantage in the gold fields. In a letter reprinted in the antislavery newspaper the *North Star*, a Southerner confirmed, "the whole country . . . is filled with gold," but that "it is not to be obtained without great labor and loss of health." The writer maintained that to earn the average of ten to sixteen dollars a day in gold, a man must "work as hard as any negro on a cotton or sugar plantation . . . exposed to the burning sun" with "bad and unwholesome food and sleeping upon the ground at night unsheltered . . . disease is no stranger . . . and death is not of rare occurrence." This Southerner concluded, "There are but three classes of individuals that can ever work these mines, the Negro, Indian and Irish."[43]

But perhaps the most motivating rhetoric for black immigration to California came from Frederick Douglass himself. In the *North Star* in November 1849, Douglass wrote of California's potential for enterprising black men:

> I had the pleasure of perusing several letters from a number of old and intimate colored friends now in the gold region. These letters gave me a far more favorable impression as to the probable success of the gold hunter than any letters which I have seen floating about in the newspapers. It is quite evident . . . that the wealth of California is, as it ought to be, shared by colored as well as white men. Not one of the company of colored persons . . . expresses any regret at going to California, and all seem delighted with the prospect before them.[44]

The prospects in California appeared so favorable, in fact, that Douglass proposed, "the Colonization Society send some of its victims to California instead of sending them all to Liberia."[45]

By the end of 1849, "the proposed clause of the Constitution forbidding free negroes from immigrating into California, was finally rejected."[46] Black people of African descent were by then a solid presence in the mining region. Once in California, free black miners worked both in groups and alone. In one instance, Scotsman William Downie successfully mined on the Yuba River with a company of men unusually composed of "two white men . . . a white boy . . . seven colored men . . . a Kanaka [Hawaiian] and an Indian."[47] Writing about one of the black men, Downie noted in his journal "he came originally from Matthews County, Virginia, and I believe, was a runaway slave."[48] In October 1849, at Hawkins Bar on the Tuolumne River, a group of black miners working on one side of the river spotted a group of white miners working independently on the other side. Working together, the two companies pooled resources to construct a dam at an area just above where they were mining. However, a white miner from the southern United States who had observed the entire transaction objected to the presence of black miners on the claim. Backed by an armed posse, the Southerner took possession of the partially constructed dam and ejected both groups.[49]

Although slavery was outlawed in California, slaveholders still migrated westward with hundreds of slaves.[50] Historian Rudolph Lapp noted, however, that there were hundreds more free than enslaved black miners working in California.[51] Initially, slaveholders were reluctant to bring slaves to California. Some of this apprehension was eased after the passing of the 1850 Fugitive Slave Act, which gave slaveholders everywhere the right to apprehend and punish runaway slaves. A further refinement of the Act, passed in 1852 as the California Fugitive Slave Act, mandated slaves who had entered California prior to statehood (September 9, 1850) to remain slaves.

Even with these measures, slaveholders viewed California as a risky place to bring slaves. The territory was vast and largely unfamiliar, which could allow for easy flight, and many of the white miners were antislavery sympathizers from the East who would help an enslaved person attempting to escape. Many slaves ran away after their arrival in California and were never caught.[52] Historian Stacey Smith maintains that "enslaved African-Americans often recognized the disruptive, destabilizing potential of California. Using this instability to their advantage, they pressed against the authority of their masters and renegotiated the terms of their enslavement."[53] Some agreed to work for a specific amount of time in exchange for freedom; others looked beyond their immediate liberation and worked to free enslaved family members back home.[54] In addition to the work done for the slaveholders, in some instances, enslaved people were allowed "Sunday claims," in which they were permitted to stake their own mining claims and keep the gold they dug there on Sundays.

Some slaveholders, including many from the Midwest border states, traveled to California with only one slave After establishing a small claim, both men worked it together, side by side. J. D. Borthwick shared a "charming" anecdote about the geniality he observed between a slave and a slaveholder:

> There was a young Southerner in Hangtown at this time, who had brought one of his slaves with him to California. They worked and lived together, master and man sharing equally the labours and hardships of the mines. . . . The slave dreamed that they had been working the inside of a certain cabin . . . and had taken out a great pile of gold. . . . He succeeded at last in persuading his master to believe it also . . . wishing to become the owner of the cabin and finally succeeded in buying it. . . . He and his slave . . . set to work digging up the earthen floor . . . before they had worked all the ground they had taken out twenty thousand dollars.[55]

That the $20,000 would have been shared equally between the two men seems unlikely, however.

Slaveholders had long employed slave labor in mines throughout the southern United States. In Burke County, North Carolina—the heart of mining country from 1828 to 1833—gangs of four to thirty enslaved laborers were used to dig and wash gold. With an already "trained" workforce, Burke County slaveholders traveled to California with large contingents of slaves.[56] Southerners with these larger parties created slaveholding enclaves in California; families often supervised each other's slaves in an attempt to re-create plantation life in the new territory. This practice was short-lived: in the end, white miners protested the use of gangs of enslaved laborers not for reasons of immorality, but because it muscled out independent white workers. One *Alta California* newspaper editor relayed an encounter with "a Mississippi planter" who had arrived with five slaves. The planter was quickly advised by sympathetic Southerners already established in California "to remove his property beyond the passing gaze of travelers along the road."[57]

Despite slavery and racial discrimination, black miners achieved success in the mines and made some exceptional finds. An especially fruitful location was discovered in late 1849 or early 1850, on the American River in El Dorado County. A group of black miners working the deep sand bank of Spanish Ravine unearthed gold-laden gravel which "paid three hundred dollars and upwards, per day, to a company of five men." The area was named "Negro Hill" in celebration of the initial discovery.[58] This location continued to be productive, and in 1851, a second group of black miners made an additional discovery. So rich was the find that "nearly every man in town has a claim staked out, and for miles, they are taken up."[59] Eventually, the town of Big Negro Hill became home to a large black population.[60]

In 1852 in Tuolumne County, a traveling black miner "noticed a gleaming object poking its nose skyward. Not wishing to carry thirty-five pounds of gold . . . he buried the chunk." After three weeks' time, he returned to retrieve it: "Fortunately the nugget was not lost."[61] Farther south, in Mariposa County, a black miner named Duff and a German companion "found a block of gold bearing quartz, weighing one hundred and ninety-three pounds . . . one of the largest and most beautiful specimens . . . estimates of the value of this lump, ranging from $5,000 to $10,000."[62]

A few reports credited the perseverance of black miners. In 1851, a discovery made "within three hundred yards of Mokelumne Hill, by some negroes" was challenging to work efficiently due to an insufficient water supply. Undaunted, the miners resolved to "'back' their dirt some distance to wash it."[63] Other significant discoveries were made in Calaveras and Mariposa Counties, Indian Gulch, and Spanish Flat near Auburn.[64]

Many white miners refused to acknowledge that the success of black miners was the result of tenacity and ability. Instead, black miners were singled out as "lucky" and undeserving of success. J. D. Borthwick contended, "As miners they were proverbially lucky, but they were also inveterate gamblers, and did not long remain burdened with their unwonted riches."[65]

Daguerreotype views of miners of African descent working in the California gold fields are extremely rare. Although views exist of persons with darker skin, only two daguerreotypes have been identified as definitively depicting black subjects. Significantly, the same daguerreotypist, Joseph Starkweather, made both. Starkweather's visit to California in 1852 lasted only a few months, into 1853. From his few identified pieces, it appears he daguerreotyped primarily in Nevada and Placer Counties, at Nevada City, Auburn, the Auburn Ravine, and along Deer Creek. Starkweather did not have an established studio in California, nor are there advertisements for his daguerreian services; he may have been daguerreotyping strictly for his own interests. Originally from Roxbury, Massachusetts (near Boston), he operated a studio there from 1850 to 1852. Boasting a large free African-American population, Boston was at the center of the antislavery movement; it was where William Lloyd Garrison published *The Liberator*, beginning in 1831, and where Frederick Douglass lived for seven years. Many Bostonians belonged to the powerful New England Anti-Slavery Society. Although Starkweather's political leanings are not known and can only be surmised, it is revealing that he was the only daguerreotypist known to focus on black mining experiences in California.

When Starkweather arrived in California in February 1852, gold had just been discovered in Placer County at Gold Hill.[66] Nearby, east of Gold Hill, was the larger town of Auburn. At the Auburn Ravine, Starkweather daguerreotyped a black miner using a long tom [**145**]. His pan, lying just to the side, is filled with gold, evidence of his success. Suspended from his belt is a small pouch presumably filled with more gold. It is possible that he is the sole proprietor of this claim. If he is enslaved, he may be either working a "Sunday

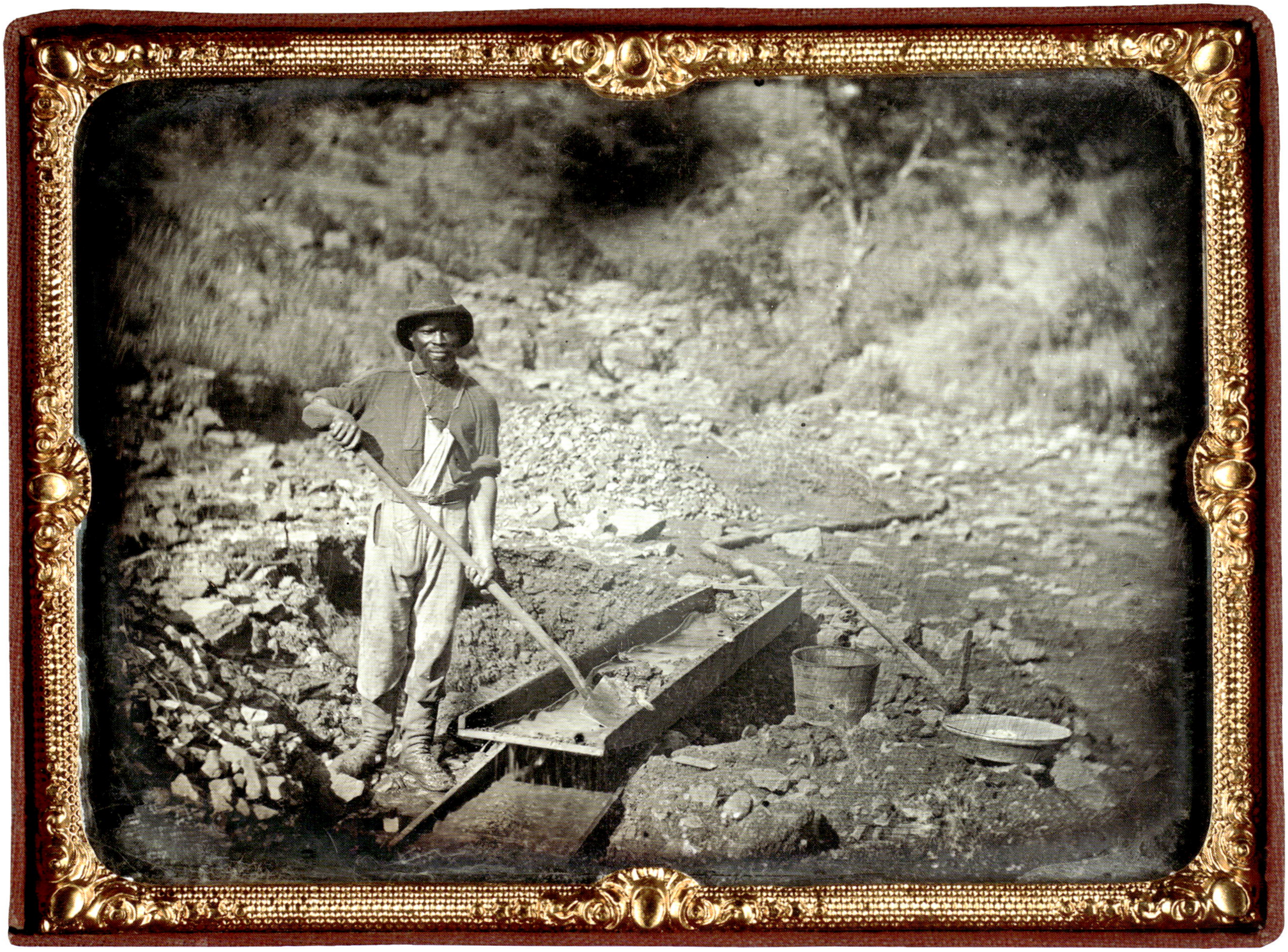

145 **Joseph Starkweather**, American (1822–ca. 1905). *Auburn Ravine*, 1852. Quarter-plate daguerreotype. California History Room, California State Library, Sacramento.

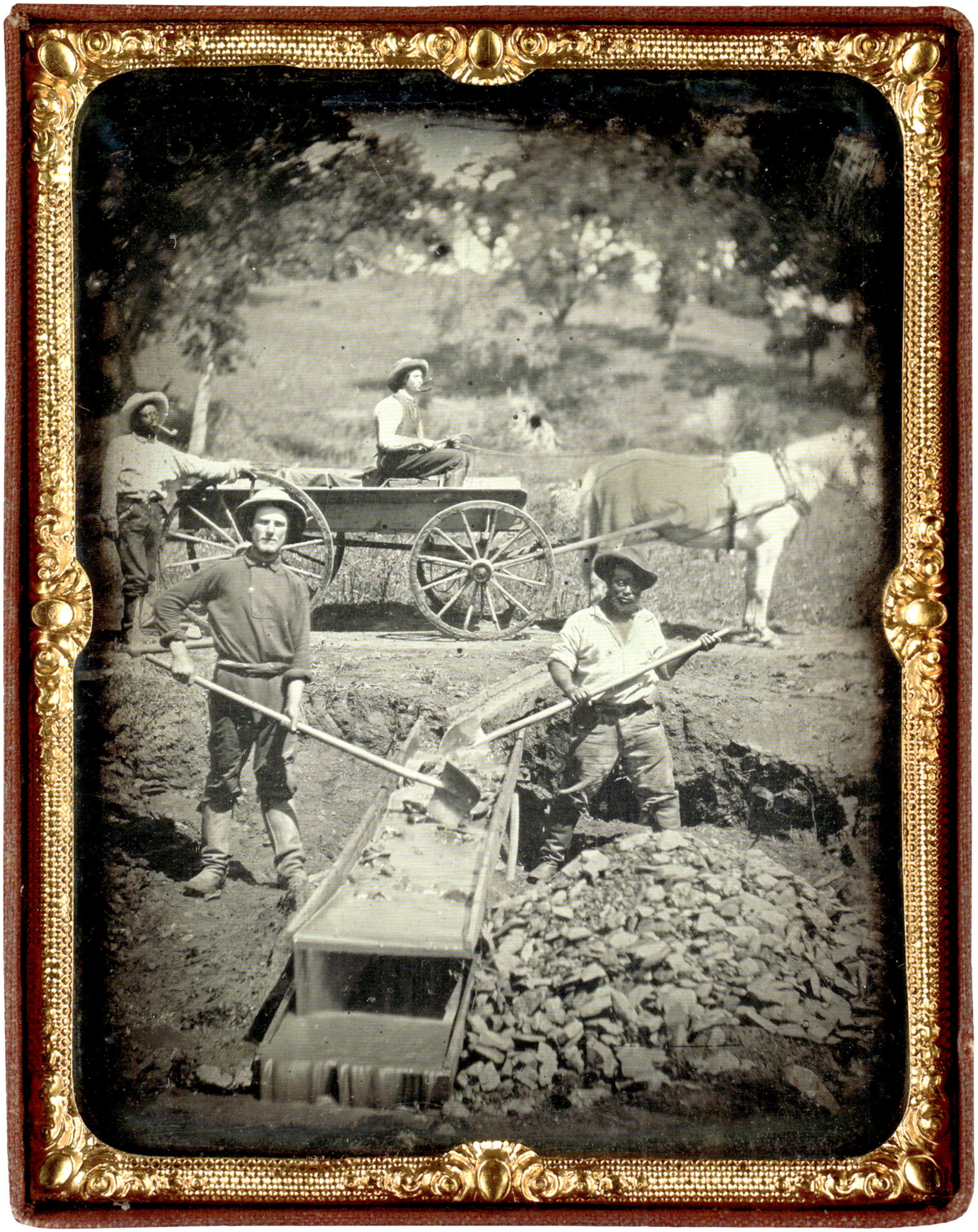

146 **Joseph Starkweather**, American (1822–ca. 1905). *Spanish Flat*, ca. 1852. Quarter-plate daguerreotype. California History Room, California State Library, Sacramento.

claim" or working unsupervised with all proceeds to be later relinquished to the slaveholder.

Adjacent to Auburn Ravine was an area known as Spanish Flat, where *Alta California* editors observed

> miners busily at work on their claims. . . . We should judge from all we saw that they were making good wages. Spanish Flat is well supplied with water . . . cut by the miners on the flat. . . . The gold in the vicinity of this place is solid and pure and of a very bright color. A negro dug from his claim . . . a piece weighing $97.[67]

It is impossible to know whether the man described was a free black man or a slave, although one suspects that the reference to "his claim" may imply a free man. Groups of Chinese men had settled in large numbers in the area around Auburn, and free black miners may have settled there as well. However, there was also a large contingent of white miners from the Georgia gold fields in Placer County.[68] These men were known to have used slave labor to work the gold mines in Georgia and undoubtedly would have brought slaves to work in California.

In Starkweather's daguerreotype of Spanish Flat **[146]**, one white man and one black man work on either side of a long tom. In the background, another black man smokes his pipe and leans against the back wheel of a horse-drawn cart, driven by a white man. There is no indication of a successful dig in this image; no gold is sighted in the long tom and no gold-filled pan is present. The side on which the white man stands shows no evidence of mining activity. On the black miner's side, however, stones that have been removed from the long tom are heaped in a pile at his feet. He is actively engaged in shoveling and washing rocks in the sluice. Without further information, it is difficult to determine whether this man is enslaved.

People of African descent, whether enslaved or free, faced discrimination in California. Even white abolitionists in support of black freedom did not necessarily believe in equality. Significant changes were afoot in the larger California cities, however. In San Francisco, the newspaper took note:

> What a change has California wrought in the organization and feelings of society. We were very much amused yesterday at seeing a gentleman of the colored persuasion, decked out in a full suit of broadcloth, and sporting a gold watch and chain, standing on the square having his boots blacked by a good looking white man.[69]

The gold fields, however, were another matter entirely. Frederick Douglass maintained that "the black man can dig gold as well as the white man" but for many white miners in California, this was irrelevant.[70] It was not a matter of whether black miners *could* mine, but whether they *should* be allowed to mine at all. Faced with this attitude, black miners—especially from the North—sought ways to avoid the harassment and prevailing racism. Although a few formed partnerships with white miners, most isolated themselves as much as possible. A regrettable result is a lack of photographic documentation; evidently, most black miners did not have daguerreotypes made of their claims. There are almost no known daguerreotypes of black miners working in the field, either alone or with white miners. It was truly remarkable, therefore, that Starkweather chose to document the culturally and racially diverse area around Auburn.

Chinese Miners

Canton, in the heart of the Guangdong Province (now Guangzhou), first received news of the California gold rush in October 1848. At first, few Chinese people made the journey across the Pacific, even though, at six weeks, it was much shorter than the trip from the American East Coast.[71] San Francisco was far from unknown to the Chinese—trade relations were first established with Canton in the eighteenth century, and by 1830, both cities benefitted from a flourishing trade in sea otter skins. Ships regularly traversed the route between the two, and by the time gold was discovered in California, Canton was the primary supplier of tea in San Francisco.

By the end of 1848, the Chinese population in California was less than one hundred. But the news from the California gold fields—combined with the population overcrowding, lack of economic opportunity, and outbreak of the Taiping Rebellion in China—enticed many Chinese to leave.[72] The Cantonese labor pool was both experienced and willing to travel for work opportunities. Many were already familiar with gold mining; as historian June Mei has noted, "Hired laborers could also be found by the thousands in the . . . gold and silver mines throughout the Guangdong countryside" and "metallurgical production in Guangdong was quite highly commercialized."[73] By the end of 1850, the Chinese population in California had increased to more than 4,000 **[147, 148]**.

At first, Chinese people were welcomed in California. In a letter dated December 2, 1850, Nevada City attorney Lorenzo Sawyer extolled the virtues of the new arrivals:

> There are many Chinese here, and they are the most interesting class of foreigners in the country. To all appearances they are the most sober, honest and industrious people. . . . Their deportment is grave and dignified. They seem never to meddle or interfere in any manner with the affairs of others. . . . Their treatment of others is always respectful . . . of all the people of these countries I have seen, I am most favorably impressed with the Chinese.[74]

The editors of the *Alta California* agreed: "We have a great deal of respect for the Chinese . . . and are pleased to find them of so quiet, peaceable, and industrious dispositions. We know of no class of citizens who conduct themselves more becomingly and are gratified to know that they meet with success."[75]

The Chinese rarely immigrated alone, preferring instead their clan tradition in which members of a family, village, or district banded together.[76] Once in California, they then lived and worked jointly in closely bonded

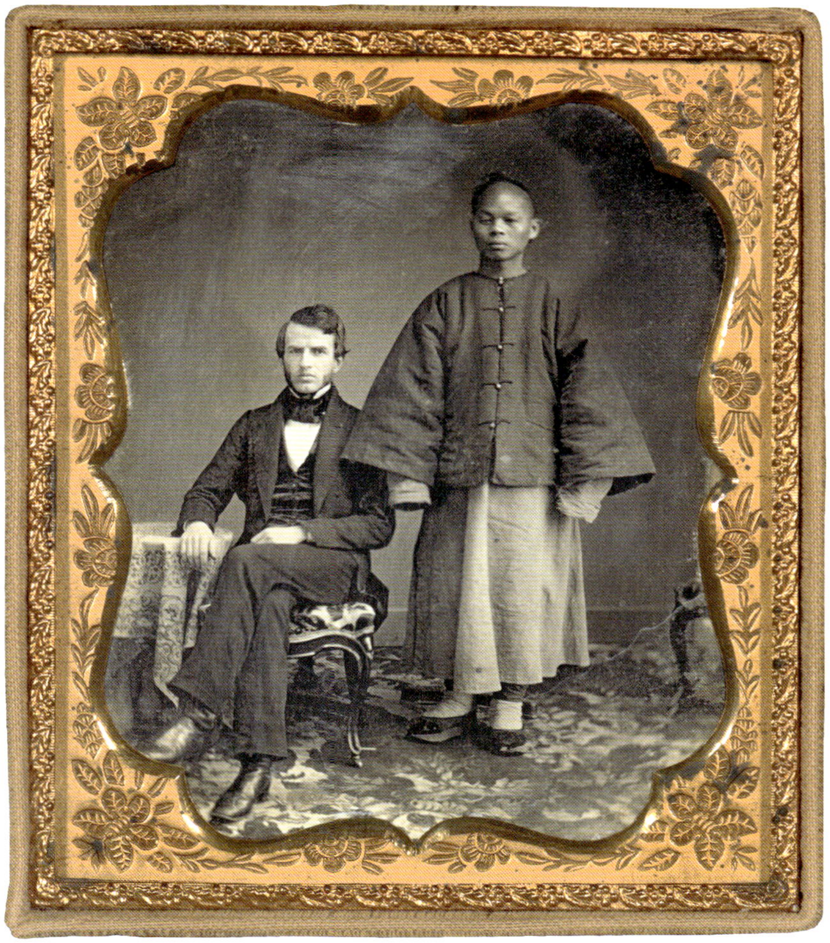

147 **Unknown maker**, American. *Portrait of a man and attendant*, ca. 1855. Sixth-plate daguerreotype.

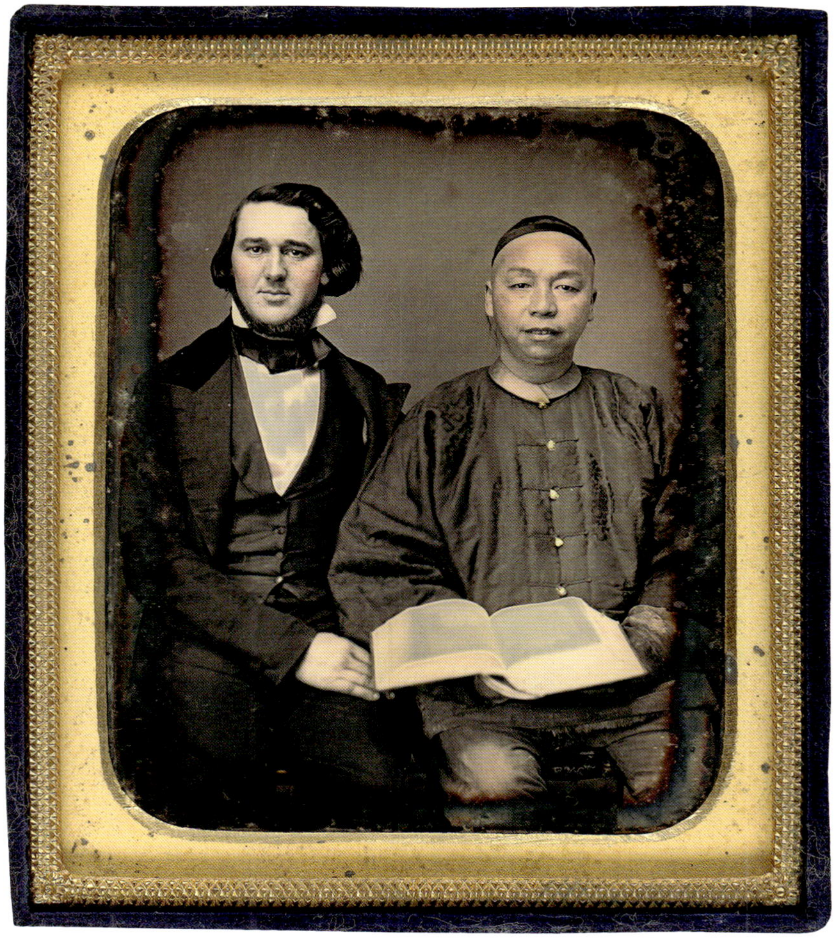

148 **Robert H. Vance**, American (1825–1876). *Portrait of two unidentified men*, ca. 1851. Sixth-plate daguerreotype. National Gallery of Canada, Ottawa.

communities. The ability to lead a cooperative lifestyle was seen as a benefit: "The Celestials [Chinese] are very useful, quiet, good citizens and are deserving the respect of all . . . they are all very happy and very clannish, the only real socialists in existence."[77]

Although some newspaper editors praised the Chinese and found their presence more palatable than many of the other immigrant groups, an undercurrent of anti-Chinese opinion was growing. Rumors circulated in the national newspapers of the "coolie" work system: Chinese laborers who mined for gold as slaves, usually for affluent and powerful masters back in China, but also for white men in California. An article in the *Baltimore Sun* asserted, "The number of Chinese arriving in California is enormous. They are brought in cargoes by English vessels, and sold as servants to the highest bidder, on the Cooley [*sic*] system, a shade less than absolute slavery."[78] According to June Mei, "the term 'coolie' here refers to those laborers who were taken abroad by force, deception, or both. Although very few of the Chinese emigrants in California were actual coolies, some of them had similar backgrounds."[79] For the coolie trade,

> abduction was necessary for the more undesirable destinations, but not for places like California and Hawaii. . . . Recruitment of unwilling coolies by deceit or abduction was naturally intended to supply labor to such places as Peru and Cuba, where the climate was severe, the working conditions harsh, and the pay minimal. . . . California, on the other hand, held out the lure of gold (real or imagined), and most of the Chinese bound for [California and Hawaii] seemed to have gone voluntarily. In the case of California, the desire to find a better job overseas was often further strengthened by the advertising of shipping firms, which stood to make large profits from the trans-Pacific traffic.[80]

Nineteenth-century missionary and Chinese historian S. Wells Williams vehemently rejected the idea of a coolie system at work in California. He maintained that Chinese immigrants "are not held at home as serfs by feudal barons or great landholders . . . nor compelled to work in mines, factories, or penitentiaries; they are in no particular danger of starving, from which and other evils they hope to escape by running away to America."[81] Despite no real proof that the system existed in gold rush California, belief in the possibility of the coolie system deepened the fear of a growing Chinese immigration among white Americans.

Like nearly all immigrant miners, most of the Chinese came to California with the intention of finding their fortune and returning home. Although the "come-and-go" mentality was endemic to the gold rush, many white Americans viewed the Chinese as a particularly unassimilable and economically aggressive group. Labeled "sojourners," they were accused of immigrating to the United States with the desire to make money through the depletion of national resources.[82] As a penalty, California instituted the California Foreign Miners' Tax of 1850, which required that a monthly fee be paid by miners who were not citizens. Aimed at both the Latin American and Chinese miners, the tax became a necessary cost of mining in California. Resigned to submit to this discriminatory legislation, as the *Sacramento Transcript* newspaper reported, "the Chinese were the first to answer the demand of the collector. They are said to have made no hesitation whatever from the first."[83] In later years, extortion of this tax from Chinese miners became a revenue source for some of the American Indians in the region.[84]

By 1852, more than 20,000 Chinese people had arrived. Although the Chinese may have missed the initial rush, they became the most dominant immigrant group in the gold region in the years 1852–54. Disturbed by the increasing number of Chinese people in California, most white miners were in favor of expelling all Chinese miners from the gold region. In an address to the California Senate, Governor John Bigler recommended that measures be adopted in order to "check this tide of Asiatic immigration and to prevent the exportation by them of the precious metal which they dig up from our soil."[85] Citing the differences of religion, skin color, and culture, he asserted that the Chinese could never become citizens of the United States.

Prevented from becoming citizens, the Chinese were prohibited from buying or selling property—including mining claims—and banned from mining in certain localities.[86] Nothing was said, however, about the sale of *abandoned* claims to non-citizens. By capitalizing on this loophole, the Chinese were able to purchase "exhausted" properties for reworking. Many times, success in these locations depended on the ability to import water into the area; fortunately, the Chinese were exceptional water managers. A successfully reworked claim came at a cost, however. If a white miner subsequently coveted that property, ownership would have to be relinquished since Chinese miners were "not permitted to work upon claims where other miners choose to work." For white miners, acceptance of these grossly unfair terms was nonnegotiable: "The Chinese have so far given way. And it is because they have given way that they have been permitted to stay at all."[87] Not surprisingly, the Chinese were allowed to be hired as laborers: "Anybody who is eligible to citizenship . . . can hire as many of these proscribed people as he chooses, and may work them in the mines at his pleasure."[88]

The Chinese suffered overt racial discrimination. The labor shortage plaguing the southern United States even had farmers there considering Chinese laborers as eventual and inevitable replacements for black slaves.[89] The Chinese were classified as forever subordinate to white male miners due to their perceived intellectual and physical inferiority—not unlike nineteenth-century women. To underscore this commonality, Chinese miners were feminized in the press and in contemporary accounts. J. D. Borthwick found the Chinese to be "on the whole . . . a harmless, inoffensive people" but determined that they "are certainly not calculated for gold-digging. They do not work with the same force or vigour [*sic*] as American or European miners, but handle their tools like so many women, as if they were afraid of hurting themselves."[90] Chinese dress and hairstyle were also considered feminine. Hinton Helper found the androgynous nature of Chinese clothing frustrating: "You would be puzzled to distinguish the women from the men, so inconsiderable are the differences in dress and figure. The only apparent difference is, that they are of smaller stature and have smoother features."[91] The braid or queue, a common hairstyle among Chinese men, was ridiculed for its lack of masculinity: A Chinese man "very seldom, however, wears [his hair] tucked up in his hat, but generally allows it to trail about his back and legs, as young girls sometimes do ribbons."[92] Although the two groups were usually compatible, American Indians also used a feminized term, "Chinaman squaw," as a common derogatory designation.[93]

There were a few areas where larger populations of Chinese miners did manage to thrive—in Placer County between the North and Middle Forks of the American River, and in El Dorado County between the Middle and South Forks. Initially overwhelmed by the number of Chinese people moving into the Gold Hill and Auburn region, white miners made sporadic efforts to get Chinese workers out. In 1852, for example, white residents resolved that "no foreigner can hold a claim in this district, unless he has declared his purpose to become a citizen. . . . This was done with a view to prevent the Chinese from settling here, and should any now make their appearance, they will doubtless receive a notice to leave."[94] However, by July, a writer noted that this "war on the Chinese has pretty much died away in this section, and I hope it will elsewhere." Finding the Chinese "the most peaceable and honest of our population," the writer was puzzled by the intolerance of others, concluding: "I think that there is room enough for all."[95] The relatively welcoming environment apparently attracted many Chinese to this area:

> There are undoubtedly a greater number of Chinamen at Auburn and in the immediate vicinity, than in any other mining precinct of the State. The streets . . . swarm with them; there hieroglyphics stare one in the face on almost every building, and these "children of the sun" are almost monopolizing the "small trade" of that flourishing town. Among the speculations entered into by this wonderful race, is one of a benevolent character, which, we trust, will be encouraged.[96]

Working in and around Auburn in 1852 and 1853, Joseph Starkweather took an astonishing daguerreotype of two groups—one of white miners, one of Chinese—working in Auburn Ravine [135]. The composition is meaningful and poignant: the Chinese miners stand separated from the white miners by two sluice boxes. They are united by work across a wide cultural divide; their only shared space is the sluice. Four Chinese miners stand, most holding their wide-brimmed straw hats in their hands. They all wear traditional tunics and sport the distinctive queue and shaved forehead, but none appears to be holding mining implements. The three white miners, on the other hand, are at a momentary rest. One man leans on the sluice with his rake positioned in the middle of the box, ready to remove larger rocks and debris; a second miner holds a shovel, while the third carries a gold pan, proudly displaying newly found gold. It is unclear whether the Chinese men are employed by the white miners, working for themselves, or simply included in the picture at Starkweather's request. Considering the year and location of this daguerreotype, one suspects that the Chinese miners are working an adjoining claim of their own.

The nearby town of Negro Hill also experienced a population boom; from 1852 to 1853, "Chinese began to flock in the camp," so that by the end of 1853, the town boasted 1,000–1,200 persons.[97] A correspondent for the *Sacramento Union* newspaper reported that Poverty Bar was "the nucleus too of an immense Chinese population. Throngs . . . daily reach these points, laden with . . . mining and camp equipage: whether they will eventually, if not shortly, take entire possession of the mineral lands of California, is a subject at this time hardly deemed worthy of consideration." Among the Chinese miners in this area, there were "many men who [had] at their command the requisite capital for the purchase of claims upon which to speculate or work."[98]

Auburn, the county seat of Placer County, discovered the economic advantage to encouraging Chinese settlement. Adaptive and welcoming, the town constructed "sixty buildings on the street . . . which were occupied exclusively by Chinese, and . . . had been built expressly to rent to that class of people. Unlike most of her sister towns, Auburn invites the Chinese instead of repulsing them, and she doubtless finds her interest promoted in so doing."[99] The increase in Chinese population was a boost to the local economy, including money "paid into [the town's] treasury annually . . . and working ground which was refused by the Americans." However, by 1855, white miners wanted everything: "The ground which was refused by miners in former days and given up as only fit for Chinamen, is now grasped at as excellent diggings."[100] With even this smallest scrap now contested, Chinese miners faced mounting pressure to vacate the mines.

Like the other non-white immigrants who traveled to California, the Chinese are woefully underrepresented in the pictorial narrative of this period. While Joseph Starkweather captured what has become perhaps the single most impressive daguerreotype of the Chinese during the California gold rush, there were at least a few other examples. A daguerreotype attributed to George Johnson features four white miners with one Chinese miner working side by side in a ravine.[101] The Chinese miner—the most prominent figure in the composition—stands closest to the camera at the end of the sluice, holding a gold pan under his arm. Other daguerreotypes of Chinese miners are more obscure. In this view by William Shew [**31, FIG. 4**], a Chinese worker (identified only by his conical-shaped hat) is pictured as one of a company of miners, probably engaged in drift mining. Positioned in the center of the composition, the overseer or owner, wearing a top hat and dark suit, stands with one leg proprietarily straddling the top of the ravine.

Despite the Chinese skill as large-scale diversion river miners, there are no known daguerreotypes of such a Chinese-owned claim. Given the scale of these operations, many were photographed from a distance, making it difficult to discern details of individuals in the scene. River mining equipment like paddlewheels and flumes were mostly standardized with no visual differences between Chinese and non-Chinese claims.

Although there were tens of thousands of Chinese immigrants living in California, very few were daguerreotyped. Most American miners were distrustful of Chinese miners from the moment they set foot in California. Highly distinctive in appearance and custom, they were an easy group to target. By 1855, the anti-Chinese movement reached a climax, as Chinese people were routinely harassed, swindled, ostracized, and denied basic human rights. There would have been few white people interested in owning daguerreotypes of Chinese miners and claims and, consequently, very few were made.

NOTES

INTRODUCTION

1 "California. San Francisco and Sacramento," *Illustrated London News*, October 19, 1850, 304. The phrase "prime cheerer of light" was used in the eighteenth-century poetry of John Milton and James Thomson.

2 William M. Ivins Jr., *Prints and Visual Communication* (Cambridge: Harvard University Press, 1953), 94.

3 Rodman W. Paul, *California Gold: The Beginning of Mining in the Far West* (Cambridge: Harvard University Press, , 1947), 16.

4 James K. Polk, "President's Message," *New York Tribune*, December 9, 1848.

5 This section is informed by: Sandra Phillips, *Crossing the Frontier: Photographs of the Developing West, 1849 to the Present* (San Francisco: San Francisco Museum of Modern Art, 1996).

6 John O'Sullivan, "Annexation," *Democratic Review*, July–August 1845. The term "Americans" refers here to white males from the existing American states and territories.

7 Phillips, *Crossing the Frontier*, 16.

8 Frederick Jackson Turner, *The Frontier in American History* (New York: Henry Holt and Co., 1930), 3.

9 Alan Trachtenberg, *Reading American Photographs: Images as History, Mathew Brady to Walker Evans* (New York: Hill and Wang, 1989), 8.

10 Trachtenberg, *Reading American Photographs*, 9.

11 William H. Goetzmann, *Exploration and Empire: The Explorer and the Scientist in the Winning of the American West* (New York: W. W. Norton & Company, 1966), 199.

12 Peter Bacon Hales, *Silver Cities: Photographing American Urbanization, 1839–1939* (Albuquerque: University of New Mexico Press, 2005), 2.

13 Hales, *Silver Cities*, 3.

14 Goetzmann, *Exploration and Empire*, 199.

15 Daguerreotype plate sizes were standardized in five basic formats: whole (6.5 × 8.5 inches), half (4.25 × 5.5 inches), quarter (3.25 × 4.25 inches), sixth (2.75 × 3.25 inches), and ninth (2 × 2.5 inches).

16 Few books have been written about California gold rush daguerreotypes. The last one of note, Drew Johnson and Marcia Eymann, eds., *Silver & Gold: Cased Images of the California Gold Rush* (Iowa City: University of Iowa Press, 1998) by the Oakland Museum of California, was published over twenty years ago and broadly covers the subject with essays by Johnson, John Wood, and Peter Palmquist. Johnson's essay reviews the practice of California daguerreian portraiture and Wood's positions the California daguerreotype in a larger social and national context. Prior to that, the museum published a small catalogue by Therese Heyman, *Mirror of California: Daguerreotypes* (Oakland: Oakland Museum of California, 1973). Several publications include sections about the California daguerreotype: Robert Taft, *Photography and the American Scene* (New York: Dover Publications, 1938); Beaumont Newhall, *The Daguerreotype in America* (New York: Duell, Sloan, & Pearce, 1961); Floyd and Marion Rinhart, *The American Daguerreotype* (Athens: University of Georgia Press, 1981); Keith F. Davis with contributions by Jane L. Aspinwall, *The Origins of American Photography, 1839–1885: From Daguerreotype to Dry-Plate* (Kansas City: Hall Family Foundation/The Nelson-Atkins Museum of Art, 2007); John Wood, *The Scenic Daguerreotype: Romanticism and Early Photography* (Iowa City: University of Iowa Press, 1995); and Richard Field, *American Daguerreotypes from the Matthew R. Isenburg Collection* (New Haven: Yale University Art Gallery, 1989). Although written nearly fifty years ago, Richard Rudisill's *Mirror Image: The Influence of the Daguerreotype on American Society* (Albuquerque: University of New Mexico Press, 1971) remains an essential reference on the medium's social history.

No study about California photography would be complete without acknowledging Peter Palmquist, who devoted himself to the history of nineteenth-century photography in California and the West. Following his accidental death in 2003, his archive of research notes and images was transferred to the Beinecke Library at Yale University, where it remains a major scholarly resource. Palmquist wrote many articles and essays focusing mainly on California photography. His most extensive works are the biographical dictionaries, done in collaboration with Thomas R. Kailbourn, *Pioneer Photographers of the Far West, 1840–1865* (2000) and *Pioneer Photographers from the Mississippi to the Continental Divide, 1839–1865* (2005). These meticulously researched volumes cover major makers as well as more obscure names. However, Palmquist's great historical contribution to the field focuses on biographical information, not art historical analysis. Other historians have also made significant contributions in biographical research in more recent years.

17 To build this personal database, this project utilized Microsoft Access, a program used to store and manage complex data points which can then be efficiently analyzed in myriad ways.

18 A noted historian of California history, Weinstein published essays on a variety of gold rush–related subjects in the 1960s and 1970s.

19 The San Francisco category includes urban views of businesses, busy city streets, and commercial districts as well as multi-plate panoramas of the city and waterfront. The Sacramento category includes urban views of businesses, busy city streets, and commercial districts. The Stockton category includes views by William Rulofson of the waterfront, channel, and associated buildings belonging to Captain Charles Weber.

20 Although mat style should never be exclusively relied on for a definitive maker identification, it is sometimes suggestive of maker.

CHAPTER 1

1 After a disappointing public response, Vance's 300 plates were transferred and displayed in the New York studio of daguerreotypist Jeremiah Gurney. They were then sold to the St. Louis daguerreotypist John H. Fitzgibbon, who exhibited them free of charge at his studio. Subsequent research by historian Gary W. Ewer traces the collection to Chicago, where they were part of the permanent exhibition of the private-venture "Chicago Museum." That museum subsequently changed hands and became "Colonel Wood's Museum," before it was destroyed in the Great Chicago Fire of 1871.

2 See Peter E. Palmquist and Thomas R. Kailbourn, *Pioneer Photographers of the Far West: A Biographical Dictionary, 1840–1865* (Stanford: Stanford University Press, 2000), 333–39; and Martha A. Sandweiss, *Print the Legend: Photography and the American West* (New Haven: Yale University Press, 2002).

3 The pantoscope was painted as if moving from east to west—Kansas to San Francisco. In actuality, the daguerreotypes were created from west to east—San Francisco to Kansas. This can be confusing because newspaper accounts of the trip are west to east while descriptions of the pantoscope are east to west.

4 J. Wesley Jones, "Jones' Pantoscope of California: A 'Lecture' by J. Wesley Jones, together with Pencil Sketches Depicting the Journey across the Plains to California," *California Historical Society Quarterly* 6, no. 2 (June 1927), 111. Jones's lecture was not published during the nineteenth century and remained more or less in its original form, including numerous typographical errors. To aid readability, I have corrected most typographical errors. The lecture was later reprinted in two parts: J. Wesley Jones, "Jones' Pantoscope of California: A 'Lecture' by J. Wesley Jones, together with Pencil Sketches Depicting the Journey across the Plains to

California," *California Historical Society Quarterly* 6, no. 2 (June 1927), 108–29; and J. Wesley Jones, "Jones' Pantoscope of California (Concluded)," *California Historical Society Quarterly* 6, no. 3 (September 1927), 238–53.

5 See P[eter] E. P[almquist], "Appendix: Miscellaneous Daguerreian Biographies and Chronologies—Shaw, Seth Louis," *Daguerreian Annual* (1990), 196–98. See also: Palmquist and Kailbourn, *Pioneer Photographers*, 489–90.

6 "Panorama of California and the Plains," *Alta California* (April 19, 1851), 2.

7 "Panorama of the Plains," *Sacramento Union* (May 6, 1851), 2.

8 "Panorama of the Plains, Salt Lake and California," *Sacramento Union* (May 8, 1851), 2.

9 "The Panorama of the Plains, Salt Lake, and California," *Marysville Herald* (May 31, 1851), 3.

10 On July 16, the *Alta California* reported on a mysterious wagon on the Plaza in San Francisco. By July 25, the mystery had been solved and it was identified as William Shew's "traveling daguerreotype establishment."

11 John Ross Dix, *Amusing and Thrilling Adventures of a California Artist while Daguerreotyping a Continent* (Boston: Published by the author, 1854), 38.

12 The lecture is broken into four sections, each illustrated with sketches copied directly from daguerreotypes now lost. There are twenty-three existing sketches, including fourteen California views. (Of the extant sketches, only two are drawn in a crude manner and thus probably not based directly on daguerreotype views.) The first section, the Nebraska plains, documents the journey from St. Joseph, Missouri, to Utah and is illustrated with seven extant sketches. The next section covers the deserts of Utah and the Sierra Nevada, moving from Utah to the eastern gold mining camp of Hangtown in California, and is illustrated with four extant sketches. It is the third and fourth sections, both devoted entirely to California, which will be the primary focus of this discussion. The third section moves through the heart of the gold region, from Weberville to Grass Valley, and is illustrated with five extant sketches (many others are missing). The fourth section continues west from the Yuba River, concluding at San Francisco, and is illustrated with seven extant sketches.

13 Dix, *Amusing and Thrilling Adventures*, 6. While gathering information for the short narrative, Phillips discovered that he had accumulated enough material for an entire book. He planned to illustrate the book with engravings of the daguerreotypes Jones had taken on the journey.

14 Dix, *Amusing and Thrilling Adventures*, 4.

15 Therefore, the opening images of the lecture and pantoscope—taken between Missouri and California—were made by Jones. This is confirmed by the fact that each of the first eleven sketches are signed "Daguerreotyped by J. Wesley Jones" (including two views made in California). Half of these sketches are also accompanied by the name of the artist who drew them. Although the twelve sketches in the final two sections devoted to California have no reference to any daguerreotypist, these images were most likely based on daguerreotypes made by William and Jacob Shew.

16 In the *Poetical Companion* section of Dix's narrative, sections three and four include descriptions of the journey through California, from the Sierra Nevada to the Missions of Santa Clara and Dolores. In Jones's unpublished lecture, as previously discussed, the end of section two and all of sections three and four are devoted to California.

17 Dix, *Amusing and Thrilling Adventures*, 73.

18 Jones, "Jones' Pantoscope of California," 128.

19 Jones, "Jones' Pantoscope of California," 138.

20 The views are made by the Shews, with the possible exception of later views taken in and around Stockton, Santa Clara, and San Francisco, which may have been taken by Seth Shaw.

21 There were three distinct properties owned by John Sutter and visited by many traveling through California: Sutter's Fort, located near Sacramento on the Sacramento River; Sutter's residence at Hock Farm, located south of Yuba City on the Feather River; and Sutter's Mill, where gold was first discovered, located on the American River near Coloma.

22 *A Nation's Benefactor: Gen'l John A. Sutter. Memorial of his Life and Public Services, and Appeal to Congress, To Citizens of California, and the People of the United States, by his Fellow Pioneers of California* (New York: Polydore Barnes, 1880), 7.

23 Dix, *Amusing and Thrilling Adventures*, 77.

24 Jones, "Jones' Pantoscope of California (Concluded)," 239.

25 Jones, "Jones' Pantoscope of California (Concluded)," 239.

26 Dix, *Amusing and Thrilling Adventures*, 78.

27 Jones, "Jones' Pantoscope of California (Concluded)," 240.

28 Although only one daguerreotype of an 1850s American Indian village is now known (taken by Solomon Carvalho and now in the collection of the Library of Congress), others were apparently taken.

29 For example, at Salmon Falls, Jones describes the essential work of American Indian women: after male tribe members caught salmon, the fish were passed to the women to dry upon the rocks. In Bartholomew's sketch of Salmon Falls, an American Indian male is pictured spear in hand next to the falls. However, despite Jones's careful description of the women in the narrative, there is no hint of their presence in this rendering.

30 Jones, "Jones' Pantoscope of California (Concluded)," 243.

31 Jones, "Jones' Pantoscope of California (Concluded)," 243.

32 Jones, "Jones' Pantoscope of California (Concluded)," 244–45

33 Jones, "Jones' Pantoscope of California (Concluded)," 245.

34 Jones, "Jones' Pantoscope of California (Concluded)," 247.

35 It is possible these views were taken by daguerreotypist Seth Shaw.

36 Jones, "Jones' Pantoscope of California (Concluded)," 250. The final illustration in the narrative is a crude sketch, *Sunday at Forbes' Diggings, Feather River*. This location is not mentioned in either Jones's or Dix's narratives. The sketch is signed with the initials "A. C." (probably Alonzo Chappell) and does not appear related to the pantoscope.

37 The reviews of "Daguerreotypes of California" are found on pages 34–43 of Dix, *Amusing and Thrilling Adventures*. Citations of specific excerpts in this section will be designated: *Placer Times and Transcript* on pages 34–35 [PT]; *Sacramento Union* on pages 35–36 [SU]; *St. Louis Republican* on pages 38–39 [STLR]; *Great Salt Lake Desert News* on page 39 [GSLDN]; and *Boston Journal* on pages 39–42 [BJ1].

38 The "Encomiums of the Press" are found on pages 44–50 of Dix, *Amusing and Thrilling Adventures*. Citations of specific excerpts in this section will be designated: *Boston Journal* on page 44 [BJ2]; *Boston Traveller* on page 45 [BT]; *Boston Herald* on page 45 [BH]; *The Congregationalist and Christian Times* on pages 45–46 [CCT]; *Boston Bee* on page 46 [BB]; *New York Tribune* on page 47 [NYT]; *New York Herald* on page 47 [NYH]; and *New York Mirror* on pages 47–48 [NYM].

39 I focus on the portions of reviews concerned with daguerreotypes, California daguerreotypes, or California subject matter.

40 SU.

41 Robert H. Vance, *Catalogue of Daguerreotype Panoramic Views in California* (New York: Baker, Godwin & Company, 1851), 3; and PT.

42 SU; BJ1.

43 PT.

44 There are several good biographies about von Humboldt including: Andrea Wulf, *The Invention of Nature: Alexander von Humboldt's New World* (New York: Vintage Books, 2015).

45 STLR.

46 CCT.

47 CCT.

48 CCT.

49 BJ2. During the California gold rush, the phrase "seeing the elephant" was used to describe the hardships encountered while experiencing the adventure of a lifetime.

50 Much information on Vance's biography was found in: Palmquist and Kailbourn, *Pioneer Photographers*, 559–66; Peter Palmquist, "Shadowcatching in El Dorado, 1849–1856," *Daguerreian Annual* (1990), 178–86; Abel Alexander, "Robert H. Vance: Pioneer of the Daguerreotype in Chile," *Daguerreian Annual* (1993), 11–30.

51 "Vance & Lerow Daguerreotype Rooms," *Christian Watchman* 27, no. 2 (January 9, 1846), 7. In an 1858 court case, Vance testified that he began work in the trade in 1845. Vance & Lerow advertising and business directory entry both begin in 1846. Thanks to Gary Ewer for this reference.

52 Alexander, "Robert H. Vance: Pioneer of the Daguerreotype in Chile," 11–30.

53 Views 109, 130, and 131 in Vance, *Catalogue of Daguerreotype Panoramic Views in California*, 8.

54 In Valparaiso, Vance worked with a partner, Mr. Mason, from 1849 to 1850. A July 1850 advertisement stated that "Vance and Mason, desiring to leave for California, offer for sale their establishment with very favorable terms and offer a month's instruction to the purchaser." "Miniaturas de daguerreotipo," *El Mercurio* (July 20, 1850) [translated from Spanish].

55 Views 105, 106, and 107 in Vance, *Catalogue of Daguerreotype Panoramic Views in California*, 8.

56 Views 103 and 104 in Vance, *Catalogue of Daguerreotype Panoramic Views in California*, 8. Vance also daguerreotyped a cathedral in Cuzco, Peru, possibly during his journey. Cuzco is not located on the coast, however, but in a mountainous region in central Peru.

57 See *San Francisco Public Balance*, December 9, 1850; *San Francisco Daily Pacific News*, January 21, 1851.

58 Frank Soulé, John H. Gihon, and James Nisbet, *The Annals of San Francisco* (New York: D. Appleton & Company, 1854), 305.

59 Palmquist, "Shadowcatching in El Dorado," 179.

60 In "Fine Arts," *Literary World* 9, no. 246 (October 18, 1851), 311. Thanks to Gary Ewer for providing sources of Vance exhibition reviews.

61 Mattakeesett, "Late From California," *Spirit of the Times: A Chronicle of the Turf, Agriculture, Field Sports, Literature and the Stage* 21, no. 10 (April 26, 1851), 114.

62 *Photographic and Fine Art Journal* 2, no. 3 (September 1851), 189.

63 Vance, *Catalogue of Daguerreotype Panoramic Views in California*, 3.

64 Vance, *Catalogue of Daguerreotype Panoramic Views in California*, 3.

65 Some titles clearly indicate at least two views (a before and after), or refer to "views," implying multiple plates beyond the single line item. The catalogue also includes seventeen panoramic views, each ranging from four to eight consecutive plates.

66 Fifty-two titles refer to the cities of San Francisco (39), Sacramento (10), and Stockton (3). Eight titles fall outside the gold region: Mission Dolores (5) and Benicia (3); nine titles refer to views taken outside the United States: Acapulco (2), Panama (3), Peru (1), and Valparaiso (3). The one remaining title has an unidentified location. Note that five titles refer to American Indian subject matter—these are assumed to have been taken in the gold region.

67 For the purpose of this publication, I have organized Vance's views by county in a reasonable geographic direction. I am not suggesting that Vance daguerreotyped all the views in each county chronologically nor am I proposing any specific timeline.

68 "New Diggings," *Sacramento Transcript* 1, no. 6 (April 12, 1850), 2.

69 Vance, *Catalogue of Daguerreotype Panoramic Views in California*, 7.

70 Vance, *Catalogue of Daguerreotype Panoramic Views in California*, 7.

71 Vance, *Catalogue of Daguerreotype Panoramic Views in California*, 7.

72 Vance, *Catalogue of Daguerreotype Panoramic Views in California*, 7. One could also make the counterargument that Sutter was, in fact, living on the land of the American Indians and not vice versa.

73 Vance, *Catalogue of Daguerreotype Panoramic Views in California*, 6.

74 Paolo Sioli, *Historical Souvenir of El Dorado County, California* (Oakland, CA: Paolo Sioli, 1883), 209.

75 Vance, *Catalogue of Daguerreotype Panoramic Views in California*, 6.

76 When founded in 1849, the town of Placerville was originally known as Hangtown. Vance uses both place names interchangeably in the catalogue. By 1850, a name change was being considered and in 1854, the name was officially changed to Placerville.

77 Vance, *Catalogue of Daguerreotype Panoramic Views in California*, 6.

78 The rich quartz vein discovered in September 1849 on the property of John Fremont in Mariposa branched north and was thought to underlie the entire area around Sonora. "Geological—Quartz Veins and Mining," *Alta California* 2, no. 368 (December 15, 1851).

79 "Geological—Quartz Veins and Mining."

80 Vance, *Catalogue of Daguerreotype Panoramic Views in California*, 7.

81 L. C. Branch, *History of Stanislaus County California* (San Francisco: Elliott & Moore, 1881), 93.

82 Madeline, "Correspondence of the Union," *Sacramento Union* 1, no. 70 (June 7, 1851).

83 Vance, *Catalogue of Daguerreotype Panoramic Views in California*, 3.

84 *Daguerreian Journal* 2, no. 10 (October 1, 1851), 308.

85 "Notices of New Books," *United States Magazine and Democratic Review* 29, no. 161 (November 1851), 480.

86 *Photographic Art-Journal* 5 (February 1853), 126.

87 "Gold Medal," *New York Evening Post* 52 (January 28, 1853), 2.

88 *Photographic Art-Journal* 5 (February 1853), 129.

89 For auction notice, see: *Photographic Art-Journal* 6, no. 1 (July 1853), 53. For notice of sale to Fitzgibbon, see: *Photographic Art-Journal* 6, no. 2 (August 1853), 129.

90 Vance had noted that he had invested $3,700 in this project. It is fair to assume that he lost money on this transaction.

91 The four issues are: "Notices of New Books," *United States Magazine and Democratic Review* 29, no. 161 (November 1851), 480; "Fine Arts," *Literary World* 9, no. 246 (October 18, 1851), 311; "Mr. Vance's California Views," *Photographic Art-Journal* 2, no. 4 (October 1851), 252–53; and "Dagurreotype [*sic*] Panoramic Views in California," *Daguerreian Journal* 2, no. 12 (November 1, 1851), 371. Subsequent citations of these specific articles in this section will be designated: *United States Magazine and Democratic Review* [USM], *Literary World* [LW], *Photographic Art-Journal* [PAJ], and *Daguerreian Journal* [DJ].

92 Citations taken from USM, LW, and DJ.

93 Michael Harvey, "Ruskin and Photography," *Oxford Art Journal* 7, no. 2 (1984), 28. For a thorough discussion of Ruskin's daguerreotypes, see: Ken and Jenny Jacobson, *Carrying Off the Palaces: John Ruskin's Lost Daguerreotypes* (London: Bernard Quaritch Ltd., 2015).

94 Ruskin quoted in Harvey, "Ruskin and Photography," 26.

95 LW.

96 LW; PAJ.

97 DJ.

98 PAJ.

99 Edmund Burke, *A Philosophical Enquiry into the Origin of Our Ideas of the Sublime and Beautiful* (London: R. and J. Dodsley, 1757).

100 H. W. Bellows, "The Moral Significance of the Crystal Palace: A Sermon, preached first to his own Congregation, and repeated in the Church of the Messiah, on Sunday Evening, October 30, 1853," *North American Review* 79, no. 164 (July 1854), 13. A graduate of Harvard Divinity School, Henry Whitney Bellows was a Unitarian minister and noted lecturer. During the Civil War, he created the United States Sanitary Commission as a means of raising money for the war effort. With friend Peter Cooper, Bellows also helped establish the Cooper Union, a free art and design school in New York City.

101 Bellows, "The Moral Significance of the Crystal Palace," 8.

102 Bellows, "The Moral Significance of the Crystal Palace," 25.

103 All citations in this paragraph from PAJ.

104 In 1840, John Banvard painted a large panorama of the entire Mississippi River valley measuring twelve feet high by half a mile long. By 1850, John Evers had created a moving panorama which included New York City, Brooklyn, and the Hudson River area. The panorama was reported to be six feet high and 3,000 feet long. Both panoramas were well received and were exhibited at venues in the eastern United States and abroad.

105 PAJ.

106 PAJ.

107 PAJ.

108 PAJ.

109 DJ.

110 M. A. Root, *The Camera and the Pencil or the heliographic art, its theory and practice in all its various branches* (Philadelphia: J. B. Lippincott & Co., 1864), 391. Samuel Morse was a painter and inventor of the telegraph. After meeting Louis-Jacques-Mandé Daguerre on a trip to Paris in 1839, Morse was also responsible for the early dissemination of daguerreotype information in the United States.

111 Root, *The Camera and the Pencil*, 391.

112 Edgar Allan Poe, "The Daguerreotype," *Alexander's Weekly Messenger* (January 15, 1840), 2.

113 PAJ.

114 LW.

CHAPTER 2

1 For background on this important subject, see, for example: Robert Phelps, "'All Hands Have Gone Downtown': Urban Places in Gold Rush California," in Kevin Starr and Richard J. Orsi, eds., *Rooted in Barbarous Soil: People, Culture, and Community in Gold Rush California*, special issue of *California History* 79, no. 2 (Summer 2000), 113–40.

2 For histories of Sacramento, see, for example: Mark A. Eifler, *Gold Rush Capitalists: Greed and Growth in Sacramento* (Albuquerque: University of New Mexico Press, 2002); and Thor Severson, *Sacramento: An Illustrated History: 1839 to 1874, From Sutter's Fort to Capital City* (Sacramento: California Historical Society, 1973).

3 http://www.sfgenealogy.org/sf/history/hgpop.htm

4 Gunther Barth, *Instant Cities: Urbanization and the Rise of San Francisco and Denver* (Albuquerque: University of New Mexico Press, 1988).

5 Charles A. Fracchia, *When the Water Came Up to Montgomery Street: San Francisco During the Gold Rush* (San Francisco: San Francisco Museum and Historical Society, 2009), 9–10.

6 For a superb overview of the city's formative history, see: Roger W. Lotchin, *San Francisco, 1846–1856: From Hamlet to City* (1974; reprint: Urbana: University of Illinois Press, 1997). For colorful descriptions of everyday life in these early years, see: Frank Soulé, *Annals of San Francisco* (1855; reprint: Loschberg, Germany: Jazzybee Verlag, n.d.); Malcolm E. Barker, ed., *San Francisco Memoirs, 1835–1851: Eyewitness accounts of the birth of a city* (San Francisco: Londonborn Publications, 1994); and Malcolm E. Barker, ed., *More San Francisco Memoirs, 1852–1899: The ripening years* (San Francisco: Londonborn Publications, 1996).

7 For a richly illustrated history of this period, see: Fracchia, *When the Water Came Up to Montgomery Street*.

8 Lotchin, *San Francisco, 1846–1856*, 175.

9 Lotchin, *San Francisco, 1846–1856*, 46.

10 Lotchin, *San Francisco, 1846–1856*, 57.

11 Peter E. Palmquist and Thomas R. Kailbourn, *Pioneer Photographers of the Far West: A Biographical Dictionary, 1840–1865* (Stanford: Stanford University Press, 2000), 153–54.

12 Palmquist and Kailbourn, *Pioneer Photographers*, 537.

13 Palmquist and Kailbourn, *Pioneer Photographers*, 489.

14 Palmquist and Kailbourn, *Pioneer Photographers*, 394.

15 Peter Palmquist, "The Daguerreotype in San Francisco," *History of Photography* 4, no. 3 (July 1980), 230, 234.

16 On the chronology of early photographic techniques in San Francisco, see: Peter E. Palmquist, "George Robinson Fardon: Photographer," in Rodger C. Birt, Marvin R. Nathan, Peter E. Palmquist, and Joan M. Schwartz, *San Francisco Album: Photographs of the Most Beautiful Views and Public Buildings: George Robinson Fardon* (San Francisco and New York: Fraenkel Gallery and Hans P. Kraus Jr., Inc., 1999), 13–16.

17 On this larger subject, see: "The Rise of Paper Photography," in Keith F. Davis with contributions by Jane L. Aspinwall, *The Origins of American Photography, 1839–1885: From Daguerreotype to Dry-Plate* (Kansas City: Hall Family Foundation/The Nelson-Atkins Museum of Art, 2007), 153–71; and David R. Hanlon, *Illuminating Shadows: The Calotype in Nineteenth-Century America* (Nevada City, CA: Carl Mautz, 2013).

18 On this enormously rich subject, see, for example: Davis, "The Face of a Nation," in *The Origins of American Photography, 1839–1885*, 83–151; and Richard H. Saunders, *American Faces: A Cultural History of Portraiture and Identity* (Hanover and London: University Press of New England, 2016).

19 For a recent biography of Love, see: William B. Secrest, *The Man from the Rio Grande: A Biography of Harry Love, Leader of the California Rangers who tracked down Joaquin Murrieta* (Spokane: Arthur H. Clark, 2005).

20 Peter Palmquist, "Shadowcatching in El Dorado, 1849–1856," *Daguerreian Annual* (1990), 176.

21 This is reproduced as plate 4, page 80, in Drew Johnson and Marcia Eymann, eds., *Silver & Gold: Cased Images of the California Gold Rush* (Iowa City: University of Iowa Press for the Oakland Museum of California, 1998).

22 The earliest advertisement for Coombs is in the *Alta California* 1, no. 178 (July 26, 1850), 3, as cited on Gary Ewer's website, http://www.daguerreotypearchive.org.

23 All three are reproduced in Peter Palmquist, "The Daguerreotype in San Francisco," *History of Photography* 4, no. 3 (July 1980), 224–25.

24 For a history of early panoramic photography in San Francisco, see: David Harris and Eric Sandweiss, *Eadweard Muybridge and the Photographic Panorama of San Francisco, 1850–1880* (Montreal: Canadian Centre for Architecture, 1993).

25 The following is based on Mike Robinson, "Sterling C. McIntyre's Panoramic Views of San Francisco," and "Conservation of the Panorama," in *Daguerreian Annual* (2013), 16–31, 32–37.

26 "Daguerreotype of San Francisco," *Alta California* 2, no. 40 (January 19, 1851), 2; as cited on Gary Ewer's website, http://www.daguerreotyparchive.org.

27 Mike Robinson argues convincingly that the first of these panoramas is now in the collection of the George Eastman Museum, Rochester, NY; a second five-plate panorama, made from a very similar location perhaps one or two months later, from the Matthew Isenburg collection, is now held by the National Gallery of Canada, Ottawa. Robinson, *Daguerreian Annual* (2013), 30.

28 Robinson, *Daguerreian Annual* (2013), 22–25.

29 "Panorama of San Francisco and the Gold Diggings," *Daguerreian Journal* 2, no. 4 (July 1, 1851), 115–16. Reproduced on Gary Ewer's website, http://www.daguerreotyparchive.org.

30 Palmquist and Kailbourn, *Pioneer Photographers*, 497.

31 Wendy Cunkle Calmenson, "'Likenesses Taken in the Most Approved Style': William Shew, Pioneer Daguerreotypist," *California Historical Quarterly* 56, no. 1 (Spring 1977), 12.

32 Reproduced in Palmquist, "The Daguerreotype in San Francisco," figure 16(a), 218–19.

33 "Johnson's Daguerrean Gallery," *Sacramento Transcript* 3, no. 9 (April 9, 1851), 2; as cited on Gary Ewer's website, http://www.daguerreotypearchive.org. Johnson's address did not change—he was still on the "North side of J Street, between Third and Fourth streets"—but he was now in the new Brick Block building.

34 "A Beautiful Present," *Daily Union* (Sacramento City) 1, no. 51 (May 16, 1851), 2; as cited on Gary Ewer's website, http://www.daguerreotypearchive.org.

35 The identification of the content of this view presents a challenge typical of research in this period. Two photographic skylights are visible in this scene: the prominent one at the upper left of the image, and a fragment of a lower one immediately behind the two daguerreotype signs. To our knowledge, Johnson never advertised any operation at 138 Montgomery Street. However, he is known to have worked at both 136 Montgomery ("second floor") and 142 Montgomery ("second floor"). The nearest structure shown here, the last address on this block, was 142 Montgomery. Given the height of the third building in from the corner—which seems too tall to have a studio on the second floor—we suspect that 136 Montgomery must have been the right hand door of the second structure from the corner—that is, that the two facades shown in their entirety had two entries each: 136–138, and 140–142. Thus, we think it is likely that Johnson may well have operated out of both of these gallery spaces, given the assumption that, over time, different entries from the street were used. Thus, while not maker-marked, we feel it is appropriate to attribute this view to him. It has all the attributes of Johnson's work and it records what appear to be both of his prime gallery spaces in San Francisco. Many of the city's best gallery spaces were clustered fairly closely together in the central business district and were used by a variety of photographers in succession. We know that James W. Johnston advertised at 136 Montgomery Street in 1852 and, for a short time in 1854, at 138 Montgomery—but the advertising sign recorded so prominently here is clearly not Johnston's.

36 Robert H. Vance, *Catalogue of Daguerreotype Panoramic Views in California* (New York: Baker, Godwin & Company, 1851); accessible on Gary Ewer's website, http://www.daguerreotyparchive.org. Peter Palmquist reordered this list by geography and probable chronology in Peter Palmquist, "The Sad but True Story of a Daguerreian Holy Grail," in Johnson and Eymann, eds., *Silver & Gold*, 43–73.

37 A full-plate view, looking along Sacramento Street toward the bay, dated ca. 1856, is held by the Bancroft Library. This is reproduced in Palmquist, "The Daguerreotype in San Francisco," 212.

38 According to Palmquist and Kailbourn, Vance was located at the corner of Sacramento and Commercial streets in January 1853, and the corner of Sacramento and Montgomery in September 1854. *Pioneer Photographers*, 561.

39 For example, see: Rodger C. Birt, "The San Francisco Album and its Historical Moment: Photography, Vigilantism, and Western Urbanization," in Birt et al., *San Francisco Album*, 98–125.

40 These plates, held by the Metropolitan Museum of Art and the Nelson-Atkins Museum of Art, were taken a few minutes apart from the same camera position. The most obvious differences between the two involve the position of the large flag or banner in the upper central area of the image and the position of the individual men on the sidewalk in the front of the building. For the making of the NAMA plate, the camera was rotated very slightly to the right, revealing more of the flag in the upper right background of the scene.

41 See Palmquist, "George Robinson Fardon: Photographer," in Birt et al., *San Francisco Album*, 11–32.

42 Birt, "The San Francisco Album and Its Historical Moment," in Birt et al., *San Francisco Album*, 99–125.

43 For an overview of this work, see: Peter Bacon Hales, *Silver Cities: Photographing American Urbanization, 1839–1939* (Albuquerque: University of New Mexico Press, 2005), 77–87.

44 The following is based on a variety of sources, including: Anthony Kirk, "'As jolly as a clam at high water': The Rise of Art in Gold Rush California," in *California History* 79, no. 2 (Summer 2002), 169–203; Janice T. Driesbach, Harvey L. Jones, and Katherine Church Holland, *Art of the Gold Rush* (Oakland: Oakland Museum of California/Crocker Art Museum/University of California Press, 1998); and Moreland L. Stevens, *Charles Christian Nahl: Artist of the Gold Rush, 1818–1878* (Sacramento: E. B. Crocker Art Gallery, 1976).

45 One of the original forty-niners, New York painter William S. Jewett, found that he could make two or three portrait paintings per week, for which he charged the enormous sum of $150 to $800 each. Kirk, "'As jolly as a clam at high water,'" 175.

46 Kirk, "'As jolly as a clam at high water,'" 185.

47 For classic works on this subject, see: John W. Reps, *Cities on Stone: Nineteenth Century Lithograph Images of the Urban West* (Fort Worth: Amon Carter Museum, 1976); and Harry T. Peters, *California on Stone* (Garden City, NY: Doubleday, Doran & Co., 1935).

48 For example, see: Douglas S. Watson, *California in the Fifties* (San Francisco: John Howell, 1936).

CHAPTER 3

1 There were many other daguerreotypists and ambrotypists working in California from 1850 to 1860 in addition to the men covered here. This text focuses on the known makers working outdoors in the gold region.

2 "Daguerrotype [*sic*]," *Pensacola Gazette* (June 14, 1845).

3 "Daguerreotype of San Francisco," *Alta California* 2, no. 40 (January 19, 1851).

4 "Daguerreotype of San Francisco," *Alta California* 2, no. 40 (January 19, 1851).

5 "The Panorama of San Francisco," *Alta California* (January 20, 1851).

6 "View of the Plaza," *Alta California* (January 28, 1851).

7 "A Handsome Picture," *Sacramento Transcript* 2, no. 98 (February 18, 1851).

8 "Panorama of San Francisco and the Gold Diggings," *Daguerreian Journal* 2, no. 4 (July 1, 1851), 115.

9 "Panorama of San Francisco and the Gold Diggings," *Daguerreian Journal* 2, no. 4 (July 1, 1851), 115–16.

10 "Panorama of San Francisco and the Gold Diggings," *Daguerreian Journal* 2, no. 4 (July 1, 1851), 116.

11 Relocating permanently to Nevada City in September 1851, McIntyre resumed his profession of dentistry. There is no evidence that he ever returned to daguerreotyping, although he did share an office space with daguerreotypist George Kilbourne in Nevada City in 1853 (probably rented shortly after George Dornin's departure to Grass Valley). McIntyre returned to the East in 1855. See: "New Daguerrean Gallery—S. C. McIntyre," *Nevada City Journal* (April 19, 1851); "Dentistry—S. C. McIntyre," *Nevada City Journal* (September 13, 1851); "Dentistry—Dr. S. C. McIntire [*sic*]," *Nevada City Journal* (January 6, 1854); "Departure," *Nevada City Journal* (November 30, 1855).

12 By the fall, Shew was spotted just outside of Monterey, where adventurer Bayard Taylor "lame and sore" accepted "the kind offer of Mr. Shew of Baltimore, who gave me a seat in his wagon." Monterey was located well outside the gold mining region, but it was an important city where the first California constitution was written in the fall of 1850. Bayard Taylor, *El Dorado, or, Adventures in the Path of the Empire*, vol. 1 (New York: George P. Putnam, 1850), 133.

13 Peter Palmquist has claimed Shew worked as a miner in Calaveras County in 1850 according to census records. Close inspection of the records, however, reveals the birthplace of that particular "Jacob Shew" to be Georgia and not New York State.

14 Biographical information on Jacob and William Shew is found in Wendy Cunkle Calmenson, "Likenesses Taken in the Most Approved Style: William Shew, Pioneer Daguerreotypist," *California Historical Quarterly* 56, no. 1 (Spring 1977), 2–19; and O. V. Lange, "William Shew: A Portrait Photographer for More Than Half a Century in San Francisco," *Daguerreian Annual* (1991), 15–26.

15 Jacob Shew worked alternatively for his brother, in partnership with Charles Hamilton, and at the studio of James Ford. In 1856, focusing primarily on studio portraiture, he moved to Sacramento where he operated a studio until 1860. He continued to work in photography until his suicide in 1879.

16 "The Big Wagon," *Alta California* 2, no. 223 (July 22, 1851).

17 "The Daguerreotype Caravan," *Alta California* 2, no. 229 (July 28, 1851).

18 "Improved Daguerreotypes," *Sacramento Union* 2, no. 230 (December 15, 1851).

19 This project's image database references four views—two half plates and one whole plate all maker-marked, and an additional attributed half plate.

20 "Placer County Correspondence," *Sacramento Union* 10, no. 1458 (November 27, 1855).

21 For Rulofson's biography, see: Robert Bartlett Haas, "William Herman Rulofson: Pioneer Daguerreotypist and Photographic Educator," *California Historical Society Quarterly* 34, no. 3 (September 1955), 289–300; and Peter E. Palmquist, "William Herman Rulofson: The P. T. Barnum of American Photography," *Daguerreian Annual* (1993), 137–54.

22 *Anthony's Photographic Bulletin* 5, no. 11 (November 1874), 358.

23 "Daguerreotype Miniatures," *Stockton Times and Tuolumne County Intelligencer* (July 27, 1850).

24 "Our Picture," *Philadelphia Photographer* 12, no. 133 (January 1875), 9.

25 Edna Bryan Buckbee, *The Saga of Old Tuolumne* (New York: The Press of the Pioneers, Inc., 1935), 195.

26 The Weber family daguerreotypes are all mounted in distinctive passe-partout mounts. Complete titles of the views are: *View of Weber home from the south*; *View of the Weber home from the west, seen across Fremont's channel from Banner Island* (2); *Distant view of Weber home from the northwest, with a longer perspective of the Stockton Channel*; *View west from the head of the Stockton Channel* (2); *View of the Sagamore in Stockton Channel, Weber's levee in background* (2); *View of the Stockton waterfront* (2); *View of Corinthian building across the Stockton Channel* (2).

27 According to historian Edna Bryan Buckbee, the Hendee brothers "established the first daguerreotype parlor in the town [of Sonora] in the fall of 1849." In Buckbee, *The Saga of Old Tuolumne*, 194.

28 "Daguerreian Artists' Registry," *Daguerreian Journal* (November 1850). Although Coombs daguerreotyped different areas of San Francisco (*Looking south on Montgomery Street*; *Ferry* Erastus Corning, *San Francisco Bay*; and *Montgomery and Clay streets, San Francisco*), he focused mostly on studio portraiture. He made no known views of the gold fields.

29 Harvey Hine, *An Illustrated History of the State of Oregon* (Chicago: The Lewis Publishing Company, 1893), 328. It is unclear whether the brothers continued to work together from January to May 1851.

30 Hine, *An Illustrated History of the State of Oregon*, 328. Edwin Hendee opened a daguerreotype studio in San Francisco in December 1851 and ran continuous advertisements until May 1852. See "Hendee's New Daguerrean Gallery," *Sacramento Union* (May 13, 1851) and (December 17, 1851).

31 "Removal," *Marysville Herald* 1, no. 91 (May 13, 1851).

32 There has been confusion between Alfred Edwards and D. H. Edwards, who may be the same person.

33 "Daguerreotyping in the Mines," *Sacramento Union* (October 20, 1851).

34 *Wilson's Photographic Magazine* 28, no. 407 (1891), 735.

35 "P. M & B. P. Batchelder Gallery," *Stockton Journal* (October 23, 1852). Unfortunately, there are no known maker-marked outdoor views by the Batchelder brothers.

36 The brothers continued to operate in this manner until May 1854 when Perez left California for the Australian gold rush. Benjamin continued the business, traveling north into Amador County where in May 1855 a miner visited his "sort of Daguerreotype saloon on wheels (Batchelder's)," to have his "likeness taken," which "all who saw it said it was a first rate likeness." Clearly pleased with the result, the same miner had his portrait taken again at "Batchelder's saloon" in Volcano a week later. In Alfred Doten, *The Journals of Alfred Doten, 1849–1903*, ed. Walter Van Tilburg Clark, vol. 1 (Reno: University of Nevada Press, 1973), 221, 224. In 1856, Benjamin left California to join his brother in Australia.

37 Although Isaac Baker wrote three journals while in California, he provided no information about his daguerreian experiences. Journal 1 covers August 1849–November 1850 and is titled *Journal of the Proceedings on board the Barque San Francisco, Thomas Remmonds Master, Of and from Beverly, for California, Commencing August 15, 1849*; Journal 2 covers May–October 1852 and is titled *Journal of some of the Sayings & Doings on board the Ship John Q. Adams From Boston for San Francisco*; Journal 3 covers Winter 1852–October 1853 and is untitled. These journals are in the collection of the Bancroft Library, University of California, Berkeley.

38 Although Baker was not a daguerreotypist during his first trip to California, journal entries include thoughts on ideal "views." After first sighting the city of Sacramento, Baker wrote: "By climbing a tree on the opposite side of the river . . . a fine view may be taken, otherwise, as the country around is so level, not much can be seen" (Isaac W. Baker, Journal 1, 94).

39 At least two other daguerreotypes taken in Vallecito: a half plate titled *Miners and cabin, near Vallecito* and a half plate attributed to Baker titled *Our California Home*. All Baker daguerreotypes are in the collection of the Oakland Museum of California with the exception of *Our California Home*, which is in the collection of Sutter's Fort State Historical Park, Sacramento. There are also two portrait daguerreotypes: a ninth-plate, *Portrait of an Indian boy*, and a sixth-plate, *Portrait of a Chinese man*. A sixth-plate occupational ambrotype, *Isaac Baker and friend playing poker*, may not be a California piece; the ambrotype became commercially popular in 1854, which postdates Baker's time in California.

40 "Proclamation!!" broadside printed by the *Sonoran Herald* (July 1853). In the collection of the Oakland Museum, 2009.35.2.1. This full-page advertisement/poem is illustrated with a wood engraving of Batchelder's traveling daguerreotype wagon.

41 Perez M. Batchelder manuscript letter to Isaac W. Baker, Sonora, California, September 2, 1853 in the collection of the late Frederick S. Baker and Mrs. Pine Lea (Baker's grandchildren), Berkeley, California, as cited in Richard Rudisill, *Mirror Image: The Influence of the Daguerreotype on American Society* (Albuquerque: University of New Mexico Press, 1971), 133.

42 En route to San Francisco, Vance stopped in Panama, where he set up a temporary studio. See "Secure the Shadow Ere the Substance Fades," *Panama Herald* (February 9, 1852), 2. According to the passenger list from the steamboat *Golden Gate* from Panama, Vance arrived back in San Francisco "with 2 boys." See: "Passengers," *Sacramento Union* 2, no. 293 (February 28, 1852).

43 *San Francisco Daily Herald* (January 26, 1852) as cited in Peter Palmquist and Thomas R. Kailbourn, *Pioneer Photographers of the Far West: A Biographical Dictionary, 1840–1865* (Stanford: Stanford University Press, 2000), 561.

44 Vance received several boxes of daguerreian supplies from Edward Anthony; see "Consignees," *Alta California* 3, no. 121 (May 1, 1852).

45 *Sacramento Union* 3, no. 383 (June 12, 1852).

46 "El Dorado," *Sacramento Union* 4, no. 550 (December 28, 1852).

47 Vance's mining views appear to have survived the Sacramento fires and flood. *The Photographic Art-Journal* reported "the numerous specimens of his skill" installed in his San Francisco studio included "mining scenes, panoramic views of cities, towns, etc., landscapes" in addition to portraiture. See: *Photographic Art-Journal* 5 (February 1853), 130.

48 "Daguerreotypes," *Alta California* 4, no. 21 (January 1, 1853).

49 "Letter-Sheet Engraving of the Flood," *Sacramento Union* 4, no. 574 (January 25, 1853).

50 "Letter-Sheet Engraving of the Flood," *Sacramento Union* 4, no. 574 (January 25, 1853).

51 *Photographic Art-Journal* 5 (March 1853), 190–91.

52 "Premium Daguerrean Gallery. R. H. Vance, Artist," *Alta California* 4, no. 22 (January 3, 1853).

53 "Premium Daguerrean Gallery. R. H. Vance, Artist," *Alta California* 4, no. 22 (January 3, 1853).

54 "Premium Daguerrean Gallery. R. H. Vance, Artist," *Alta California* 4, no. 22 (January 3, 1853).

55 *Hale & Emory's Marysville City Directory August 1853* (Marysville, CA: Marysville Herald, 1853). This branch was closed in August 1855.

56 Vance began receiving mail at the Sacramento Post Office by October 13, 1853. "List of Letters," *Sacramento Union* 6, no. 797 (October 13, 1853).

57 "Vance & Beals'," *Sacramento Union* 6, no. 853 (December 17, 1853). Beals was further identified as an "Operator, for the last 12 years of New York City."

58 An editor described the stereoscopic process as an "adaptation of two lenses, through which two likenesses taken at the same moment, at different angles, are viewed and blended into one picture." From "The Stereoscopic Daguerreotype," *Sacramento Union* 6, no. 830 (November 21, 1853).

59 "The Stereoscopic Daguerreotype," *Sacramento Union* 6, no. 830 (November 21, 1853). This technique appears to have been used exclusively for portraiture and city views. There are no known mining views taken using this method.

60 The Beals and Vance partnership did not end amicably; instead, their very public disagreement was documented in the newspaper. "Beware of Jealousy!" *Sacramento Union* 8, no. 1121 (October 26, 1854).

61 "Delinquent City Tax List," *Sacramento Union* 8, no. 1145 (November 23, 1853).

62 "Operator," *California Farmer and Journal of Useful Sciences* 4, no. 12 (September 21, 1855). A portrait of Horatio Finch in the collection of the Bancroft Library at Berkeley is an example of one of these oversized daguerreotypes.

63 An unattributed ambrotype was taken in Vacaville around this same time (see [94]). Located on the Wells Fargo & Company Express route, E. F. Gillespie's general store also served as the area post office. Ambrotypists McKown & Bishop worked in this area and supplied an ambrotype view of Vaca Valley for the March 1858 issue of *Hutchings' California Magazine*. George McKown may have opened a studio over Gillespie's store in 1857 which was soon after destroyed by fire.

64 "Abduction of Mr. Vance—Extraordinary Outrage," *Sacramento Union* 13, no. 2018 (September 14, 1857).

65 "The Vacaville Mystery," *Sacramento Union* 14, no. 2024 (September 21, 1857).

66 "The Riot at Sacramento City," *Illustrated California News* (September 1, 1850), 6. Also in "Sacramento Squatter's Riot—G. H. Johnson Captured the Scene," *Daguerreian Annual* (1990), 19–20.

67 George H. Johnson is listed on the passenger list of the *South Carolina*, which traveled from New York City and arrived in San Francisco on January 1, 1849, according to Palmquist and Kailbourn, *Pioneer Photographers*, 327.

68 "Daguerreotype Miniatures," *Placer Times* 1, no. 21 (September 29, 1849), 2.

69 Johnson's Sacramento studio locations include: on Front Street (September 1849); on J Street (May 1850); on J Street a few doors above Third, opposite Paul, White, & Co. (July 1850); on north side of J Street, between Third and Fourth (September 1850); No. 83 J Street, Brick Row, between Third and Fourth streets (April 1851); the brick block of Brown, Henry & Co. (April 1851); and with Selleck at Johnson's Pacific Pioneer Daguerrean Gallery at No. 79 J Street opposite the Crescent City and Missouri Hotels (September 1852).

Johnson's San Francisco studios include: with Shaw at Eureka Daguerrean Rooms at 197 Montgomery Street (January 1852); 136 Montgomery Street (March 1852); with Selleck at Pacific Pioneer Daguerreian Gallery at 142 Montgomery Street, corner of Clay Street, second floor, opposite Well's Building (November 1852); satellite location in Yerba Vista Cemetery (September 1853); with brother Bryan, Johnson Brothers at Pioneer Daguerrean Gallery 185 Clay Street two floors of the Freestone Building opposite the Court Block (November 1855); dissolved partnership (June 1857); 649 Clay Street, southeast corner of Clay and Kearny Streets (1861). He continued in San Francisco doing paper photography until at least 1873. See Palmquist, "George Johnson," *Pioneer Photographers*, 327–30.

70 "Johnson's Daguerrean Gallery," *Sacramento Transcript* (April 9, 1851).

71 "Daguerrean Gallery," *Placer Times*, May 10, 1850, 3.

72 "Daguerreian Artists' Registry," *Daguerreian Journal*, November 1850.

73 "Prices Reduced at G. H. Johnson's Daguerrean Gallery," *Sacramento Union* (April 1, 1851), 3.

74 Another daguerreotypist, James Pierpont, was making outdoor views at the same time as Johnson. He had a short-lived gallery (until May 1851) in San Francisco on Clay Street. He took a daguerreotype view of "the plaza and eastern side of San Francisco" and was "quite as clever with his portraits as with his landscape views." In "Daguerreotyping," *Alta California* 1, no. 68 (March 19, 1850).

75 "Johnson, George H.," *Bogardus' San Francisco, Sacramento City and Marysville Business Directory for July 1850* (San Francisco: William B. Cook & Co Bookseller, 1850).

76 "Daguerreotypes," *Sacramento Transcript* (July 11, 1850).

77 "Daguerreotypes," *Sacramento Transcript* (July 11, 1850).

78 "Daguerreotypes," *Sacramento Transcript* (January 8, 1851).

79 "Johnson's Daguerrean Gallery," *Illustrated California News* (September 15, 1850), 16.

80 "Sacramento Squatter's Riot—G. H. Johnson Captured the Scene," *Daguerreian Annual* (1990), 19–20.

81 "The Riot at Sacramento City," *Illustrated California News* (September 1, 1850), 5–6. Some scholars contend that Johnson was commissioned to provide this view. The accompanying article states, "We offer our thanks to Mr. Johnson . . . for his courtesy in volunteering to further the purpose of our visit to Sacramento City, by furnishing our engraver with views of the locality where the battle scene was enacted." The unbiased nature of the view also received praise; the engraving "would never have been rendered, had it not been in perfect consonance with [the editors'] unbiased judgment in the matter."

82 "Prices Reduced at G. H. Johnson's Daguerrean Gallery," *Sacramento Union* (April 1, 1851), 3.

83 "A Beautiful Present," *Sacramento Union* (May 16, 1851), 2.

84 "Daguerreotype View," *Sacramento Union* (May 20, 1851), 2.

85 Daguerreotypes and other photographic materials were shipped to Johnson in June. *San Francisco Picayune* (June 27, 1851).

86 Seth Shaw previously had a daguerreotype studio in Nashville, Tennessee, where he had practiced the art since 1840. In 1847, he had advertised his ability to make "copies from painting, engravings, or daguerreotypes." *Nashville Daily Union* (August 12, 1847).

87 Although Johnson may have been making regular trips to the gold fields prior to this time, there is no documented evidence.

88 "Eureka Daguerrean Rooms," *San Francisco Daily Evening Picayune* (March 3, 1852). This advertisement referred only to Johnson and not Shaw. Some historians maintain that the omittance of Shaw's name indicates that the partnership was dissolved by March.

89 Wallace W. Elliott, *History of Humboldt County, California* (San Francisco: Wallace W. Elliott & Co., 1881), 191.

90 "World's Fair Pictures at Johnson's Pacific Pioneer Daguerrean Gallery," *Sacramento Union* (September 22, 1852), 2.

91 *Photographic Art Journal* 5 (June 1853), 380.

92 Sources show that in September 1852, Silas Selleck worked with Johnson; by November 1852, with James Ford; by December 1852, with Johnson; by February 1854, with Henry Bradley; by June 1854, severed from Henry Bradley; by July 1854, operating alone; and by September 1854, with Henry Beals.

93 "Daguerreotype Landscapes," *Alta California* (September 23, 1853).

94 "Daguerreotype Landscapes," *Alta California* (September 23, 1853).

95 *Humphrey's Journal* 5 (October 1, 1853), 190. The full notation reads: "Johnson & Selleck of Sacramento, Cal., are doing a fine business in that part of the diggings." The incorrect reference to Sacramento instead of San Francisco may stem from the fact that the *Daguerreian Journal* (which later became *Humphrey's Journal*) listed Johnson at his Sacramento address in the *Daguerreian Artists' Registry* from November 1850 to September 1851 and for the October 1 publication, *Humphrey's Journal* had overlooked the city change.

96 A colorful character, Selleck was challenged to a duel in October 1854, which he survived. See "A Duel," *Sacramento Union* 8, no. 1124 (October 30, 1854). In August 1855, he was elected Assemblyman to the California legislature for Placer County. He returned to active duty as an operator at Henry Beals's studio in April 1856 and by June had opened his own studio in San Francisco. He dabbled in politics and continued to photograph until his death in 1885.

97 "Letter Sheet," *Sacramento Union* (August 28, 1852).

98 Engravings based on daguerreotype views were also used on bank notes. An Adams Express and Banking Office promissory note from December 1853 sports an illustration based on a daguerreotype view made in Nevada City, showing four miners using a long tom.

99 "Steamer Paper," *Sacramento Union* 4, no. 499 (October 28, 1852).

100 "Photographs from California," *Illustrated London News* (January 29, 1853), 69; and Pierre Charles Fournier de Saint-Amant, *Voyages en Californie et dans l'Orégon* (Paris: Librairie L. Maison, 1854), 600.

101 Based on aesthetic style, the use of Johnson daguerreotypes in publications, and brass mat style, this daguerreotype is most likely attributed George Johnson. In addition to *Notion Company's Works* and *North Fork, American River*, other engravings in this issue (also most likely based on daguerreotypes) include *Parks' Bar Company Works, California* and *Ross' Bar, California*.

102 Seven views are currently attributed to Johnson's visit to Grizzly Flats, though others may exist. Johnson did not maker-mark all the daguerreotypes in this series; some of the seven views here were discovered through a sorting of the database images.

103 Marcos Armstrong noted a change in lighting direction (as time passed) in several of the daguerreotypes: "Sunlight is directed from opposite directions in two of the views, while in another view, there are no pronounced shadows." In Marcos R. Armstrong, "The California Gold Rush: Approaches to Producing Daguerreotype Views, An Examination of Views in the Matthew R. Isenburg Collection at AMC Toronto," Master's thesis, Ryerson University, 2013, 43 n184.

104 Armstrong, "The California Gold Rush," 42.

105 The second image, a variant of *Mining on the American River, North Fork, near Sacramento*, is in the collection of Los Angeles County Natural History Museum.

106 For more information on the Gulicks, see: Jane L. Aspinwall, "More From the Gold Fields: The Gulick Brothers," *Daguerreian Annual* (2009/2010), 71–74.

107 A copy plate of this image, maker-marked by Johnson, is held by the California State Library in Sacramento. It has a significant flaw at the top edge of the plate. This work, and its companion held by the Nelson-Atkins Museum of Art, have oval-shaped brass mats.

108 Other trends noted in Johnson's gold field views include the predominant use of half plates (although quarter- and whole-plate daguerreotypes are known), no known ambrotypes, and the fairly consistent use (with a few exceptions) of a simple elliptical-cornered brass mat.

109 Robert A. Carden, "Photography in California," *Photographic and Fine Art Journal* 10, no. 4 (April 1857), 112–13.

110 "Daguerreotypes," *Sacramento Transcript* 2, no. 63 (January 8, 1851).

111 "Daguerreotype View," *Sacramento Union* 1, no. 54 (May 20, 1851); *Illustrated California News* 1, no. 1 (September 1, 1850).

112 "Passengers," *Sacramento Union* 2, no. 279 (February 12, 1852).

113 After returning to Massachusetts in 1853, Starkweather eventually returned to California to photograph from 1867 to 1904.

114 *Report of the Fifteenth Industrial Exhibition of the Mechanics' Institute of the City of San Francisco* (San Francisco: P. J. Thomas, 1880), 44.

115 Described as "Historical Views—Days of '49," the daguerreotypes were all dated 1852 and identified as: *Deer Creek*; *Sluice Mining*; *Nevada City*; *Surface Diggings—Auburn*; *Log Cabin—Nevada*; *Sluice Mining*; *Photographic Studio*; *Mining with Long Tom*; *Mining—Auburn Ravine*; and *Head of Auburn Ravine*. In *Report of the Fifteenth Industrial Exhibition*, 56–57. Eight of the ten daguerreotypes are owned by the California State Library. One piece was retitled *Spanish Flat* according to historians Gary E. Strong and Gary F. Kurutz, *Western Americana in the California State Library* (Sacramento: California State Library Foundation, 1985), 12.

116 *Report of the Fifteenth Industrial Exhibition*, 118.

117 There is a more extensive discussion of these daguerreotypes in Chapter 6.

118 It is not known if any additional daguerreotypes by Starkweather exist. His extant pieces suggest that he worked exclusively in the quarter-plate format. His works are further distinguished by their lack of brass mat; only the preserver frames the image package.

119 George D. Dornin, *Thirty Years Ago* (Berkeley: George Dornin, 1879), republished as: George D. Dornin, ed. Peter E. Palmquist, *Thirty Years Ago: Gold Rush Memories of a Daguerreotype Artist* (Nevada City, CA: Carl Mautz Publishing, 1995), 50. Before his death, Dornin recorded memories of his life during the California gold rush. Although the account is detailed, there is little specific information about his daguerreian practice.

120 A tantalizing mention of a daguerreotype view made in Grass Valley in 1852 by an unknown daguerreotypist was reported in the *Sacramento Union*: "We are indebted to Mr. Atkins, of the firm of Atkins & Stewart, of this city, for interesting mining information from Grass Valley, and for a striking Daguerreotype view of a railroad car, with the miners at their work. The railroad is near a mile in length and belongs to a claim of which Mr. Atkins is part owner. It is used to cary [*sic*] dirt to water, from what is called the Dry Slide. The paying dirt lies some sixty feet below the surface and is reached by sinking shafts and then drifting into the side of the hill to them. It pays finely when reached, and claims sell high." In "Grass Valley," *Sacramento Union* 3, no. 468 (September 22, 1852).

121 "Grass Valley Telegraph," *Sacramento Union* 7, no. 1020 (June 30, 1854). This half-plate daguerreotype was reported to be in the collection of the Nevada County Historical Society in Nevada City, although I was unable to locate the piece at that institution.

122 Dornin, *Thirty Years Ago*, 51.

123 Dornin, *Thirty Years Ago*, 52.

124 Dornin, *Thirty Years Ago*, 52.

125 Edwin F. Bean, *The History and Directory of Nevada County, California* (Nevada City: The Daily Gazette and Job Office, 1867), 341.

126 "Pacific Coast Amateur Photographic Association," *Anthony's Photographic Bulletin* 21, no. 19 (October 11, 1890), 601.

127 Known ambrotypes by Silver include *Dutch Flat*; *O. B. Silver's Ambrotype Gallery*; *Unidentified residence, Dutch Flat*; *Home in Dutch Flat*; *Dutch Flat, in summer*; and *Dutch Flat, in winter*. Historian Peter Palmquist has also attributed *Store fronts in Washington, Nevada County* and *Street with large crowd of miners, women, etc. in Sierraville* to Silver.

128 O. B. Silver advertisement, *Dutch Flat Enquirer* (May 28, 1863). The ad continued into 1865, as cited in Palmquist, *Pioneer Photographers*, 501–02.

129 *History of Placer County, California* (Oakland: Thompson & West, 1882), 380.

130 *History of Placer County, California* (Oakland: Thompson & West, 1882), 380.

CHAPTER 4

1 William Welling, *Photography in America: The Formative Years, 1839–1900, A Documentary History* (New York: Crowell, 1978), 69.

2 T. A. Barry and P. A. Patten, *Men and Memories of San Francisco in the Spring of '50* (San Francisco: Bancroft, 1873), 143–44.

3 "Daguerreotype Miniatures," *Placer Times* 1, no. 21 (September 29, 1849), 2.

4 J. S. Holliday, *The World Rushed In: The California Gold Rush Experience* (New York: Simon and Schuster, 1981), 59.

5 Drew Johnson and Marcia Eymann, eds. *Silver & Gold: Cased Images of the California Gold Rush* (Iowa City: University of Iowa Press for the Oakland Museum of California, 1998), 40.

6 "From the Mines," *Alta California* 1, no. 2 (May 31, 1849).

7 "Pen-Knife Sketches," *Marysville Herald* 1, no. 31 (November 18, 1850).

8 Joan Severa, *Dressed for the Photographer: Ordinary Americans and Fashion, 1840–1900* (Kent, OH: Kent State University Press, 1995), 121.

9 For more information, see Max Bell, *California Gold Rush Belt Buckles* (Auburn, CA: Max Bell, 2013).

10 William Gilpin, *Mission of the North American People: Geographical, Social, and Political* (Philadelphia: J. B. Lippincott & Co., 1873), 124.

11 "Sacramento Intelligence—Placerville," *Alta California* 1, no. 196 (August 15, 1850).

12 [Samuel Colville], *Colville's San Francisco Directory* (San Francisco: Monson, Valentine & Co., 1856), v–vi. The ideas outlined here are the language and thoughts of the dominant American culture of the time.

13 Robert Phelps, "'All Hands Have Gone Downtown': Urban Places in Gold Rush California," *California History* 79, no. 2 (Summer 2000), 120. Much information for the following discussion was taken from this comprehensive article.

14 In 1850, the recorded population of San Francisco was 34,776, Sacramento was 6,820, and Marysville was 4,500. Stockton was unrecorded. In Phelps, "Urban Places," 121.

15 Ralph Mann, *After the Gold Rush: Society in Grass Valley and Nevada City, California, 1849–1870* (Stanford: Stanford University Press, 1982), 19. Mann's study focused on Nevada City and Grass Valley from 1849 to 1870. Although both communities evolved over time, Grass Valley remained a predominantly male population centered around mining while Nevada City developed a diversified economy. By 1860, Nevada City was an established community with families and various social institutions. Mann's study was first published as: Ralph Mann, "The Decade after the Gold Rush: Social Structure in Grass Valley and Nevada City, California, 1850–1860," *Pacific Historical Review* 41, no. 4 (November 1972), 484–504.

16 Randall E. Rohe, "The Geography and Material Culture of the Western Mining Town," *Material Culture* 16, no. 3 (Fall 1984), 108.

17 Mann, *After the Gold Rush*, 20.

18 "Letter from the Mines—Mokelumne Hill," *Alta California* 4, no. 287 (November 5, 1853).

19 John E. Fletcher to Ruth Fletcher, June 20, 1850, John E. Fletcher Correspondence, mss. F6131849, Holt Atherton Collection, University of the Pacific, Stockton, California.

20 A. A. Sargent, "A Sketch of Nevada County," *Brown & Dallison's Nevada, Grass Valley, and Rough and Ready Directory* (San Francisco: The Town Talk Office, 1856), 26.

21 "Letter from the Dry Diggings," *Sacramento Transcript* 1, no. 115 (September 13, 1850).

22 Rohe, "Geography and Material Culture," 104.

23 "Latest from the Mines," *Alta California* 1, no. 13 (March 29, 1849); "From the Mines," *Placer Times* 2, no. 64 (May 27, 1850).

24 "Sacramento City," *Alta California* 1, 11 (March 15, 1849).

25 Charles E. Peterson, "Prefabs in the California Gold Rush, 1849," *Journal of the Society of Architectural Historians* 24, no. 4 (December 1965), 319.

26 In 1849, Peter Naylor, a metal roofer in New York City advertised "galvanized iron houses constructed by me for California. . . . The iron is gro[o]ved in such a manner that all parts of the house, roof and side slide together, and a house 20 × 15 can be put up in less than a day. They are far cheaper than wood, are fireproof, and much more comfortable than tents." Peter Naylor, "Portable Iron House," advertisement, *Emigrant's Guide* (February 12, 1849).

27 Harold Kirker, *California's Architectural Frontier: Style and Tradition in the Nineteenth Century* (Santa Barbara: Peregrine Smith, Inc., 1973), 43.

28 Rohe, "Geography and Material Culture," 107.

29 In his influential study of urban development, Kevin Lynch discusses the ways in which the conventional imaging of any city makes the foreign familiar. With a need "to recognize and pattern [their] surroundings," newly arriving town visitors relied on "environmental images" to navigate the unfamiliar terrain. Kevin Lynch, *The Image of the City* (Cambridge, MA: M.I.T. Press, 1960), 4.

30 *Daguerreian Journal* (May 1, 1852), 32.

31 S. D. Humphrey, *A System of Photography, containing an explicit detail of the whole process of daguerreotype* (Albany: C. Van Benthuysen, 1849), 69.

32 In this study's database, fewer than five daguerreotypes are not right reading.

33 Mann, *After the Gold Rush*, 15.

34 Daniel B. Woods, *Sixteen Months at the Gold Diggings* (New York: Harper & Brothers, 1851), 121.

35 Kirker, *California's Architectural Frontier*, 33.

36 Rohe, "Geography and Material Culture," 104.

37 E. Gould Buffum, *Six Months in the Gold Mines: From a Journal of Three Years' Residence in Upper and Lower California in 1847-8-9* (London: Richard Bentley, 1850), 70.

38 Mann, "The Decade after the Gold Rush," 484–504. This study should be taken with a grain of salt. Statistics were amassed using very early computer technology (IBM 360/67) so data was limited. Also, this study contains some blatantly racist and unfounded conclusions.

39 Kirker, *California's Architectural Frontier*, 34.

40 Kirker, *California's Architectural Frontier*, 34.

41 Buffum, *Six Months in the Gold Mines*, 182.

42 Sandy Gulch was located in Calaveras County near the Mokelumne River. Erwin G. Gudde, *California Gold Camps* (Berkeley: University of California Press, 1975), 306.

43 George Johnson was known to use this convention.

44 A Californio was a native or foreign-born resident of California before statehood.

45 According to the Bancroft Library object description, the faintest outline of a cabin may be visible behind the trees.

46 "An Evening Scene," *Hutchings' California Magazine* 2, no. 5 (November 1857), 203. Although no information is known about daguerreotypist H. M. Bacon, he apparently submitted several pieces for use as engravings to *Hutchings' California Magazine*. In June, a note to "H. M., Boston Flat" reported that "the view of the cabin is received, and with others, will appear by-and-by." "To Contributors and Correspondents," *Hutchings' California Magazine* 1, no. 12 (June 1857), 576.

47 Hubert Bancroft, *The Works of Hubert Howe Bancroft*, vol. 23, *The History of California, 1848–1859* (San Francisco: The History Company, 1888), 434.

48 Jesse D. Mason, *History of Amador County, California* (Oakland: Thompson & West, 1881), 303. "Mr. Hanford had charge of the stores, Mr. Downs generally remaining in the city purchasing and forwarding goods."

49 Many miners did mine year-round, varying activities according to the season. During periods of low water, miners dug and saved pay dirt to be washed when water was more abundant. Miners also traveled to areas known as the "dry diggings" where gold was gathered from the underlying rock crevices of ravines and gulches.

50 H. I. Long-Tom, "Communicated," *Sacramento Transcript* 2, no. 107 (February 28, 1851).

51 For example, the Oak Valley House on Pilot Hill in Yuba County was a first-class lodging establishment that hosted special events like weddings and an annual ball "attended by the most respectable citizens of our county." "El Dorado County Correspondence," *Sacramento Union* 10, 1435 (October 31, 1855). The first ball was held in November 1851 and continued every fall until 1860; see "Ball," *Sacramento Union* 6, 794 (October 10, 1853).

52 Myron Angel, *History of Placer County, California* (Oakland, CA: Thompson & West, 1882), 365.

53 Angel's *History of Placer County* contains excerpts from a journal kept by gold miner John Markle who arrived at Sacramento on September 2, 1849. Angel used the journal to precisely date the naming of the town of Auburn: "[The journal] records the time, nearly, when the name was given to the place, for thus he relates that on September 27th, he started from

Sacramento for the 'North Fork Dry Diggings,' the only name by which the locality was then known; and that in returning from Sacramento upon a subsequent trip, November 15th, he speaks of arriving at Auburn—circumstances which tend to prove that the nomenclature was applied between those dates." In Angel, *History of Placer County*, 80.

54 In 1852, Wells, Fargo & Co. was established as a joint stock venture in New York mainly to take advantage of business opportunities in California. Gold dust, bullion, mail, packages, and freight were moved between the East Coast and San Francisco, as well as to the various mining camps throughout the gold region. By the end of 1852, Wells Fargo was a firmly established leader in the field of express transport, and they began purchasing other express lines operating in California—including associated stage and banking businesses. These ancillary businesses enlarged the Wells Fargo business plan to include banking and exchange services as well as stagecoach transportation. For additional information about the Wells Fargo company in California, see "Wells, Fargo & Company's California Express," *New York Times* (May 20, 1852).

55 W. Turrentine Jackson, "A New Look at Wells Fargo, Stage-Coaches and the Pony Express," *California Historical Society Quarterly* 45, no. 4 (December 1966), 292.

56 Scholarship is plentiful on the subject of women in the California gold rush. Referenced works include: Nancy J. Taniguchi, "Weaving a Different World: Women and the California Gold Rush," *California History* 79, no. 2 (Summer 2000), 141–68; Susan Lee Johnson, "'Domestic' Life in the Diggings: The Southern Mines in the California Gold Rush," in Valerie Matsumoto and Blake Allmendinger, *Over the Edge: Remapping the American West* (Berkeley: University of California Press, 1999), 108–26; and Yolanda Venegas, "The Erotics of Racialization: Gender and Sexuality in the Making of California," *Frontiers: A Journal of Women Studies* 25, no. 3 (2004), 63–89.

57 Jean-Nicolas Perlot, *Gold Seeker: Adventures of a Belgian Argonaut During the Gold Rush Years*, trans. Helen Harding Bretnor, ed. Howard Lamar (New Haven: Yale University Press, 1985), 218.

58 "Digger Indians," *Sacramento Union* 8, no. 1177 (December 30, 1854). White individuals of the nineteenth-century regularly used the word "squaw" as a ubiquitous term for any Native American woman. The use of this word has been largely discontinued.

59 "Sacramento and Placer Intelligence," *Alta California* 1, no. 38 (February 12, 1850).

60 "Industrious Trio," *Alta California* 3, no. 15 (January 16, 1852).

61 "Marie Suize Arrested," *Alta California* 23, no. 7700 (April 22, 1871).

62 A daguerreotype image in the collection of the Huntington Library, San Marino, CA, reputedly of Mary McCloskey dressed as man was circulated for years by historians. The portrayed person was later identified as John Colton. L. Dow Stephens, in his account of the Jayhawkers in gold rush California, included the following information about the image: "This is a picture of John B. Colton . . . taken by an artist at Long Wharf, San Francisco, in 1850. The artist retained the negative of this picture and represented it to be a girl miner in boy's clothing, explaining that she had crossed the plains in 1849. Her parents both died on the trail but a woman in the train took charge of her and brought her safely through to the mines. Finding a rich placer mine she adopted boy's clothing and successfully worked her claim and soon made her pile. She started for the States, and while in San Francisco had this picture taken before changing to woman's attire. By telling this story the artist sold hundreds of copies of the photo at five dollars each to the miners. . . . Colton, the original of the picture upon returning from the mines, saw the crowd about the artist's shack and proceeded to investigate, and recognized the picture at once." In L. Dow Stephens, *Life Sketches of a Jayhawker* (San Jose, CA: L. Dow Stephens, 1916), 64. Despite the impossibility of the artist retaining the negative to make copies (daguerreotypes are one-of-a-kind images, without negatives), a letter from Stephens to Colton dated May 15, 1916 (MSS JA 944 in the Huntington Library archives) seeking permission to use the image and tell the true story, confirms Colton's identity. Thank you to Jennifer Watts, Huntington Library, for noting this.

63 Although a segment of the female population from all races engaged in prostitution, this form of employment did not define the extent of women's participation in the professional realm.

64 "An Enterprising Woman in California," *Hunt's Merchant's Magazine and Commercial Review* 26, no. 6 (June 1852), 777.

65 "An Enterprising Woman in California," 777.

66 Edith Sparks, *Capital Intentions: Female Proprietors in San Francisco, 1850–1920* (Chapel Hill: University of North Carolina Press, 2006), 222–23.

67 Walker D. Wyman, ed. "Running a Boarding House in the Mines," *California Historical Society Quarterly* 24, no. 4 (December 1945), 347.

68 Frank Marryat, *Mountains and Molehills* (London: Longman, Brown, Green, and Longmans, 1855), 32.

69 "Washerwoman's Bay," *Alta California* 2, no. 66 (February 14, 1851).

70 For an informative article about domesticity and the role of Chinese laborers in the California laundry industry, see: Joan S. Wang, "Race, Gender, and Laundry Work: The Roles of Chinese Laundrymen and American Women in the United States," *Journal of American Ethnic History* 24, no. 1 (Fall 2004), 58–99.

71 Marryat, *Mountains and Molehills*, 265.

72 James Hutchings, "The World in California," *Hutchings' California Magazine* 1, no. 9 (March 1857), 387.

73 Hutchings, "The World in California," 388.

74 See, for example, David V. DuFault, "The Chinese in the Mining Camps of California: 1848–1870," *Historical Society of Southern California Quarterly* 41, no. 2 (June 1959), 166. Current scholarship also includes Sylvia Sun Minnick, *Samfow: The San Joaquin Chinese Legacy* (Fresno: Heritage West Books, 1988) 239. See also: George Anthony Peffer, "From Under the Sojourner's Shadow: A Historiographical Study of Chinese Female Immigration to America, 1852–1882," *Journal of American Ethnic History* 11, no. 3 (Spring 1992), 41–67. Based on the assumption that all Chinese women were prostitutes, the Act to Prevent the Kidnapping and Importation of Mongolian, Chinese, and Japanese Females for Criminal or Demoralizing Purposes was passed in 1870 under the pretense of protection; in reality, it was a ban on Chinese female immigration.

75 Johnson, "'Domestic' Life in the Diggings, 110. See also: Mignon Duffy, "Doing the Dirty Work: Gender, Race, and Reproductive Labor in Historical Perspective," *Gender and Society* 21, no. 3 (June 2007), 313–36.

76 Excellent studies on gold rush architecture can be found in: Harold Kirker, "El Dorado Gothic: Gold Rush Architects and Architecture," *California Historical Society Quarterly* 38, no. 1 (March 1959), 31–46; Harold Kirker, *California's Architectural Frontier: Style and Tradition in the Nineteenth Century* (Santa Barbara: Peregrine Smith, 1973); and Harold Kirker, "California Architecture and Its Relation to Contemporary Trends in Europe and America," *California Historical Quarterly* 51, no. 4 (Winter 1972), 289–305.

77 Franklin Street, *California in 1850* (Cincinnati: R. E. Edwards and Co., 1851), 32.

78 "Farmer's Daguerreotypes," *California Farmer and Journal of Useful Sciences* 14, no. 12 (November 16, 1860).

79 "Farmer's Daguerreotypes," *California Farmer and Journal of Useful Sciences* 14, no. 12 (November 16, 1860).

80 Kirker, "El Dorado Gothic," 31.

81 Kirker, *California's Architectural Frontier*, 26.

82 Kirker, *California's Architectural Frontier*, 43.

83 Oscar Lewis, *Sea Routes to the Gold Fields: The Migration by Water to California in 1849–1852* (New York: Alfred A. Knopf, 1949), 43.

84 "The Diggings South-East," *Sacramento Transcript* 3, no. 14 (April 15, 1851).

85 For more about this daguerreotype, see Jane L. Aspinwall, "Found Treasure: The Bond & Molyneaux California Daguerreotype," *Daguerreian Annual* (2008), 70–75.

86 This business, designated by the "bakery" sign, may be visible on the left in [**100**].

87 This view was made after May 1851. The *California Gazette* headquartered in Benicia, and seen in this daguerreotype view, was founded in May 1851.

88 Gray arrived in Benicia in 1849 and served on the first board of directors of the Young Ladies' Seminary established in 1852. J. P. Munro Fraser, *History of Solano County* (San Francisco: Wood, Alley, & Co., 1879), 441.

89 "View of Georgetown," *Pictorial Union* (April 1854), 1. This daguerreotype view was used as the basis for an engraving in this issue.

90 Mark Johnson has attributed this daguerreotype (and others) to William Shattuck. See Mark S. Johnson, "Argonaut Moses Warren & the Quinebaug Gold Company," *Daguerreian Annual* (2012), 39–69.

91 "El Dorado County Correspondence," *Sacramento Union* 10, no. 1435 (October 31, 1855).

92 I am defining the bird's eye perspective as the view looking down at the city from a significant height, as if from a hot air balloon.

93 The patent on Barker's panoramic paintings expired in 1802. Twenty years later, Louis-Jacques-Mandé Daguerre began his work painting dioramas. He would later, along with Joseph Nicéphore Niépce, invent the first commercially viable form of photography, the daguerreotype, in 1839.

94 Alan Wallach, "Making a Picture of the View from Mount Holyoke," in David C. Miller, ed. *American Iconology: New Approaches to Nineteenth-Century Art and Literature* (New Haven: Yale University Press, 1993), 83.

95 Wallach, "Making a Picture of the View from Mount Holyoke," 83.

96 William Gilpin, *Observations on the River Wye, and Several Parts of South Wales, &c. relative chiefly to Picturesque Beauty: Made in the Year 1770*, 5th ed. (London: T. Cadell Junior and W. Davies, 1800), 128.

97 Louis L. Noble, *The Life and Works of Thomas Cole, N.A.* (New York: Sheldon, Blakeman and Company, 1856), 88.

98 Captain Basil Hall, *Forty Etchings from sketches made with the camera lucida in North America in 1827 and 1827* (London: Simpkin & Marshall, and Moon, Boys, & Graves, 1829), ii. The camera lucida is an optical device in which rays of light are refracted through a prism. Clamped to the side of a table, the camera lucida superimposes the object (or landscape) being viewed onto a sheet of paper upon which the artist is drawing. Similarly, the camera obscura is a small box with a lens through which a view is transmitted (upside down and reversed) onto ground glass where it can be traced on translucent paper by an artist. Both the camera lucida and the camera obscura are considered precursors to the photographic camera.

99 Peter Galassi has argued that the oil sketch was the transitionary mode between painting and photography. Galassi noted that the landscape sketch was used by artists "as exploratory rather than didactic" and presented a new "pictorial syntax of immediate perceptions . . . also the syntax of photography." Peter Galassi, *Before Photography: Painting and the Invention of Photography* (New York: The Museum of Modern Art, 1981), 25.

100 The staff of the Bancroft Library have reattributed the geographic location of this daguerreotype to Mormon Bar, in Mariposa County. A lithograph titled *View of Goodyears Creek, Sierra Co. Cala. With Monte-Cristo in the distance* was done by Britton & Rey around this same time. Although the exact location of this daguerreotype has yet to be determined, it does not picture the town of Marysville.

101 At least seven examples are known.

102 Robert H. Vance, *Catalogue of Daguerreotype Panoramic Views in California* (New York: Baker, Godwin & Company, 1851), 7.

103 Kenneth N. Owens, ed. *Riches for All: the California Gold Rush and the World* (Lincoln: University of Nebraska Press, 2002).

104 "Yerba Buena Cemetery," *Alta California* 1, no. 70 (March 21, 1850).

105 "Mortality," *Sacramento Transcript* 1, no. 93 (August 19, 1850).

106 "Mayor's Message," *Alta California* 1, no. 139 (June 10, 1850).

107 "Mayor's Message," *Alta California* 1, no. 139 (June 10, 1850).

108 "Removal of the Dead," *Alta California* 1, no. 76 (March 28, 1850).

109 Rohe, "Geography and Material Culture," 111.

110 Mann, *After the Gold Rush*, 31.

111 "Placer County Correspondence," *Sacramento Union* 5, no. 698 (June 18, 1853).

CHAPTER 5

1 This study focuses only on the mining technologies used from 1848 to 1865.

2 James Hutchings, "Mining for Gold in California," *Hutchings' California Magazine* 2, no. 1 (July 1857), 1–14; "River Mining," *Hutchings' California Magazine* 2, no. 3 (September 1857), 97–100; and "Quartz Mining in California," *Hutchings' California Magazine* 2, no. 4 (October 1857), 145–54. Later guidebooks like *A Trip to the Mining Regions in the Spring of 1859* by Eduard Vischer also made use of these same descriptions and illustrations.

3 James Hutchings, *The Miners' Own Book, Containing Correct Illustrations and Descriptions of the Various Modes of California Mining* (San Francisco: Hutchings & Rosenfield, 1858), 6.

4 E. Gould Buffum, *Six Months in the Gold Mines: From a Journal of Three Years' Residence in Upper and Lower California in 1847-8-9* (London: Richard Bentley, 1850), 72–73.

5 Hutchings, "Mining for Gold in California," 4.

6 Hutchings, "Mining for Gold in California," 4.

7 Historian Otis Young contends that all forms of mining technology, from the pan to the sluice, were brought to California by miners from the American South. Otis E. Young Jr., "The Southern Gold Rush: Contributions to California and the West," *Southern California Quarterly* 62, no. 2 (Summer 1980), 127–41.

8 Vincente Peréz Rosales, Diary entry from March 16, 1849, in Edwin Beilharz and Carlos López, ed. and trans., *We Were 49ers! Chilean Accounts of the California Gold Rush* (Pasadena: Ward Ritchie Press, 1976), 52.

9 Miners regularly referred to the north and south sections of the mining region. See Maps, pgs. 160–161.

10 William Redmond Ryan, *Personal Adventures in Upper and Lower California*, vol. 2 (London: William Shoberl, 1852), 13–14.

11 Fayette Robinson, *California and Its Gold Regions* (New York: Stringer & Townsend, 1849), 23.

12 Rosales, in Beilharz and López, ed. and trans., *We Were 49ers!*, 50.

13 Letter from R. B. Mason to R. Jones, August 17, 1848, H.R. Ex. Docs., 30 Congress, 2 session, Doc. I, 60.

14 Hutchings, "Mining for Gold in California," 4–5.

15 S. W., "From the Mines, Jamestown, May 13, 1849,' *Alta California* 22, no. 31 (May 31, 1849), 2.

16 *Alta California* 22, no. 31 (May 31, 1849), 2.

17 "Latest From the Mines, Mokelumne Diggings, May 29, 1849," *Alta California* 25 (June 21, 1849), 2.

18 Buffum, *Six Months in the Gold Mines*, 132.

19 Another form of rocker, variously called the Quicksilver Machine, Burke Rocker, Virginia Rocker, or the Grizzly Bumper, was developed during this time but soon fell out of favor because of construction expense and the difficulty of transporting the heavy machine to the mining region. Randall Rohe, "Origins & Diffusion of Traditional Placer Mining in the West," *Material Culture* 18, no. 3 (Fall 1986), 132.

20 Louise Clapp, "California, In 1852—Letter Fifteenth. Residence in the Mines. From Our Log Cabin, Indian Bar," *Pioneer of California Monthly Magazine* 3, no. 5 (May 1855), 309.

21 Roscoe, "Letter from Sonora, April 23, 1854," *Alta California* 5, no. 119 (April 30, 1854), 2.

22 Hutchings, "Mining for Gold in California," 5.

23 In his study on tool acculturation of the Chinese in California, Robert Spier maintains that motor habit patterns of a cultural group are fairly rigid and that the Chinese working in California would have continued to use their own tools and working methods where applicable after arriving in the United States. The prolonged usage of the rocker by the Chinese in California, therefore, may be due to the prior experience of a similar tool in China. See Robert F. G. Spier, "Tool Acculturation among 19th-Century California Chinese," *Ethnohistory* 5, no. 2 (Spring 1958), 97–117.

24 Rodman Wilson Paul, *Mining Frontier of the Far West, 1848–1880* (New York: Holt, Rinehart, and Winston, 1963), 28–29; and Otis E. Young Jr., *Western Mining: An Informal Account of Precious-Metals Prospecting, Placering, Lode Mining, and Milling on the American Frontier from Spanish Times to 1893* (Norman: University of Oklahoma Press, 1970), 111.

25 *San Francisco Evening Bulletin* (January 4, 1858).

26 Hutchings, "River Mining," 98.

27 A variant of this view was published as an engraving in "Scenes in California," *Gleason's Drawing Room Companion* 6, no. 12 (March 25, 1854), 184.

28 Rohe, "Origins & Diffusion of Traditional Placer Mining," 141.

29 In later years, in areas where the volume of water in a river was too great for fluming, wing dams continued to be used.

30 J. D. Borthwick, *Three Years in California* (Edinburgh and London: William Blackwood and Sons, 1857), 262.

31 Borthwick, *Three Years in California*, 263.

32 "Mining Works at Coloma," *Alta California* 1, no. 223 (September 11, 1850), 2.

33 "Mining Works at Coloma," *Alta California* 1, no. 223 (September 11, 1850), 2.

34 "Placer Intelligence," *Alta California* (October 1, 1849), 2.

35 "Placer Intelligence—Successful Gold Digging," *Alta California* 35 (August 30, 1849).

36 "Placer Intelligence—The Mines," *Alta California* 35 (August 30, 1849).

37 For more information on river mining in the southern region, see: "San Joaquin and Placer Intelligence," *Alta California* 1, no. 125 (May 24, 1850), 2; George Henry, "Labor upon the Tuolumne," *Alta California* 1, no. 184 (August 2, 1850), 2; "San Joaquin Intelligence," *Alta California* 1, no. 192 (August 11, 1850), 2.

38 "Editorial Correspondence," *Alta California* 1, no. 175 (July 23, 1850), 2. See also "Mining Works at Coloma," *Alta California* 1, no. 223 (September 11, 1850), 2.

39 "Goodyear's Bar," *Marysville Daily Herald* 16 (August 25, 1853), 2.

40 In river mining, the word "flume" refers to a large canal used to carry diverted water. For water companies, a flume refers to a sluice-like wooden structure used to carry water from mountain streams to claims.

41 MAC, "Downieville Correspondence," *Marysville Herald* 68 (March 20, 1851), 2.

42 Longobardus, "Placer County Correspondence," *Sacramento Union* 5, no. 698 (June 18, 1853), 2.

43 The following section is indebted to: Randall E. Rohe, "After the Gold Rush: Chinese Mining in the Far West, 1850–1890," *Montana: The Magazine of Western History* 32, no. 4 (Autumn 1982), 2–19; Randall Rohe, "Chinese River Mining in the West," *Montana: The Magazine of Western History* 46, no. 3 (Autumn 1996), 14–29; and Liping Zhu, "No Need to Rush: The Chinese, Placer Mining, and the Western Environment," *Montana: The Magazine of Western History* 49, no. 3 (Autumn 1999), 42–57.

44 Borthwick, *Three Years in California*, 265.

45 For another example of Chinese construction of a wing dam, see: "Letter from Placer County," *Sacramento Union* 16, no. 2349 (October 7, 1858), 2.

46 Borthwick, *Three Years in California*, 265–66.

47 Borthwick, *Three Years in California*, 265–66.

48 U., "Special Correspondence," *Sacramento Union* 11, no. 1696 (September 2, 1856), 2.

49 The newspapers made free use of the many racial slurs aimed at the Chinese miners: "Chinaman," "Celestial," and "China John" are but a small sample.

50 "Mining on the Stanislaus," *Alta California* 10, no. 280 (October 12, 1858), 2.

51 "Mining Items," *Alta California* 10, no. 277 (October 9, 1858), 2.

52 American miners found the "Middle [Fork of the] American river mining [was] mostly left to the Chinamen." Poco Man, "Placer County Correspondence," *Sacramento Union* 12, no. 1772 (November 29, 1856), 2.

53 Poco Man, "Placer County Correspondence," *Sacramento Union* 12, no. 1772 (November 29, 1856), 2.

54 "Tamaroo Bar," *Sacramento Union* 13, 1988 (August 10, 1857), 2. Another example of Chinese and American flume construction: "Letter from Placer County," *Sacramento Union* 16, no. 2349 (October 7, 1858), 2.

55 Howard R. Lamar, *Gold Seeker: Adventures of a Belgian Argonaut during the Gold Rush, Jean-Nicolas Perlot* (New Haven: Yale University Press 1985), 138, 140–41.

56 "Latest from the Placer," *Alta California* 1, no. 183 (August 1, 1850), 2.

57 Robert L. Kelley, "Forgotten Giant: The Hydraulic Gold Mining Industry in California," *Pacific Historical Review* 23, no. 4 (November 1954), 343–356.

58 Hutchings, "Mining for Gold in California," 5–6.

59 S. Shufelt, "March 3, 1850, Placerville, Eldorado Co. California," in *A Letter From a Gold Miner, Placerville, California, October 1850, with an introduction by Robert Glass Cleland* (Los Angeles: Anderson & Ritchie with the Friends of the Huntington Library, 1944), 11.

60 Another daguerreotype (in the collection of the Bancroft Library), inscribed "J. Y. Hutchins & Co. June 5, 1852" was probably made by the same daguerreotypist just two days prior.

61 "From the Diggings," *Placer Times*, 2, no. 60 (May 17, 1850), 2.

62 J. C., "Near Sonora, Jan. 17, 1851," *Alta California* 2, no. 60 (February 8, 1851), 2. The long tom was used in El Dorado by September 1851. "Mining Intelligence," *Alta California* 2, no. 284 (September 22, 1851), 2.

63 "Mining Intelligence—North and South," *Alta California* 3, no. 65 (March 6, 1852), 2. As of November 1851, "very few have ever used long toms." "Mountain Intelligence," *Alta California* 2, no. 341 (November 18, 1851), 2.

64 J. C., "Near Sonora, Jan. 17, 1851," *Alta California* 2, no. 60 (February 8, 1851), 2.

65 Clapp, "California, In 1852—Letter Fifteenth," 309.

66 Hutchings, "Mining for Gold in California," 6.

67 "Sluice Washing," *Marysville Daily Herald* 84 (April 26, 1851), 2.

68 "San Joaquin intelligence: Sluicing," *Alta California* 2, no. 375 (December 22, 1851), 2.

69 "Sluice Washing," *Marysville Daily Herald* 84 (April 26, 1851), 2.

70 Hutchings, "River Mining," 98.

71 "Latest from the Placer," *Alta California* 1, no. 183 (August 1, 1850).

72 Herbert O. Lang, *A History of Tuolumne County California* (San Francisco: B. F. Alley, 1882), 100.

73 "Statistics of the Tuolumne Water Companies," *Alta California* 3, no. 215 (August 4, 1852).

74 Hutchings, "Mining for Gold in California," 11–12.

75 Hutchings, "Mining for Gold in California," 11–12.

76 Information in this section was informed by two excellent articles about water rights/law: Douglas R. Littlefield, "Water Rights During the California Gold Rush: Conflicts over Economic Points of View," *Western Historical Quarterly* 14, no. 4 (October 1983), 415–34; and Donald J. Pisani, "The Origins of Western Water Law: Case Studies from Two California Mining Districts," *California History* 70, no. 3 (Fall 1991), 242–57.

77 Pisani, "Origins of Western Water Law," 244.

78 "Coyota Mining in the Gold Region," *Sacramento Transcript* 1, no. 146 (October 19, 1850), 2.

79 Historians have attributed the shallow-mining technologies like drift mining to the arrival of immigrants from Cornwall, England, and Cornish-trained Americans from the southern states.

80 "New Mining Operation," *Alta California* (July 20, 1850), 2.

81 Hutchings, "Mining for Gold in California," 9.

82 W. W. Jenkins, "History of the Development of Placer Mining in California" *Annual Publication of the Historical Society of Southern California* 7, no. 1 (1906), 69–77.

83 "Latest from the Placer," *Alta California* 1, no. 183 (August 1, 1850), 2.

84 Lorenzo Sawyer, *Way Sketches* (New York: Edward Eberstadt, 1926), 120. Lorenzo Sawyer traveled to California from Ohio in 1850. Written for the *Ohio Observer*, Sawyer's travel accounts were published in western newspapers and served as guides for others traveling west. He later served as judge on the California Supreme Court, handing down an 1884 decision that effectively ended hydraulic mining in northern California.

85 Clapp, "California, In 1852—Letter Fifteenth," 308-9.

86 Kelley, "Forgotten Giant," 343–56.

87 Hutchings, "Mining for Gold in California," 9–11.

88 "Tunnel Mining," *Sacramento Daily Union* 8, no. 1118 (October 23, 1854), 2.

89 "Tunnel Mining," *Sacramento Daily Union* 8, no. 1118 (October 23, 1854), 2.

90 "Sacramento News: The Old Jersey Flat" *Alta California* 3, no. 189 (July 9, 1852), 2; "Letter from the Mountains," *Alta California* 4, no. 112 (April 23, 1853), 2.

91 "Sierra Nevada Correspondence: Description of Mining Claims," *Sacramento Daily Union* 17, 2602 (July 30, 1859), 2.

92 In most instances, articles and diaries using the term "sluice" refer only to the board sluice. Ground sluicing is usually specifically identified as such.

93 John Ross Browne, *Report of J. Ross Browne on the Mineral Resources of the States and Territories West of the Rocky Mountains* (Washington, DC: Government Printing Office, 1868), 117–18.

94 Hutchings, "Mining for Gold in California," 8.

95 Randall E. Rohe, "Hydraulicking in the American West: The Development and Diffusion of a Mining Technique," *Montana: The Magazine of Western History* 35, no. 2 (Spring 1985), 19.

96 For a detailed account, see H. P. Davis, *Gold Rush Days in Nevada City* (Nevada City, CA: Berliner & McGinnis, 1948).

97 Hutchings, "Mining for Gold in California," 12–13.

98 Hydraulic mines were founded in the Yuba and American River watersheds in the northern mining region: in Yankee Jim (1852); La Porte, Iowa Hill, Camptonville, Gold Hill, Georgetown, North Bloomfield, and Michigan Bluff (1853); Bidwell, Smartsville, and You Bet (1854–55). Later mines included: Dutch Flat (1857), Cherokee (1858), and Gold Run and Weaverville (1862). Hydraulic mining was much more prevalent in the north than in the south from 1852 to 1854 due to a lack of deep gravel deposits, absence of water, and a relatively flat terrain. Although there were a few notable exceptions in the south along the Consumnes and Mokelumne River watersheds in the towns of Volcano (1855) and Columbia (1858), "there has not been one large hydraulic claim such as abound north of El Dorado." Mining peaked in 1856–57, then declined before a renewal of activity in 1864. Quote from John Ross Browne, *Resources of the Pacific Slope: A Statistical and Descriptive Summary . . .* (San Francisco: H. H. Bancroft, 1869), 13. See also: Rohe, "Hydraulicking in the American West," 21; and Kelley, "Forgotten Giant," 346.

99 Jeffrey LaLande's archaeological survey noted that Chinese hydraulic mining sites did not look any different from the American sites. Although Chinese miners retained certain cultural standards (dress, food, medicine, religion), they rapidly adopted the foreign technology of hydraulic mining. See Jeffrey M. LaLande, "Sojourners in Search of Gold: Hydraulic Mining Techniques of the Chinese on the Oregon Frontier," *Journal of the Society for Industrial Archeology* 11, no. 1 (1985), 29–52.

100 As quoted in Rohe, "Hydraulicking in the American West," 27.

101 "Letter from the Mountains," *Alta California* 4, no. 157 (June 7, 1853), 2.

102 The tailings are the materials left over from the process of washing gold and include rocks, dirt, and mercury-tainted water.

103 Mercury was found in minute particles floating on surface water as far as twenty miles downstream from hydraulic mines. See Charles Alpers, Michael Hunerlach, Jason May, and Roger Hothem, *Mercury Contamination from Historical Gold Mining in California, Fact Sheet 2005-3014* (Washington, DC: Department of the Interior: US Geological Survey, 2005).

104 Gold production in California reached a high point of $62.5 to $69.5 million in 1853–54 when most gold was placer gold. In Herbert Sawin, "One Hundred Years of California Placer Mining," *Scientific Monthly* 69, no. 1 (July 1949), 56–62.

105 A concise overview of quartz mining can be found in: Maureen A. Jung, "Documenting Nineteenth-Century Quartz Mining in Northern California," *American Archivist* 53, no. 3 (Summer 1990), 406–18.

106 Hutchings, "Quartz Mining in California," 146–48.

107 Ronald Limbaugh points out that popular literature today often confuses the initial quartz discovery in the south with the more productive foothill deposits in the north. See Ronald H. Limbaugh, "Making Old Tools Work Better: A Pragmatic Adaptation and Innovation in Gold-Rush Technology," *California History* 77, no. 4 (Winter 1998/1999), 36.

108 *Placer Times* 2, no. 65 (May 29, 1850).

109 "Startling Discovery," *Sacramento Transcript* 1, no. 38 (June 14, 1850).

110 "Local Matters," *Alta California* 1, no. 147 (June 19, 1850).

111 "Gold Quartz Mining," *Scientific American* 11, no. 33 (April 26, 1856), 262.

112 Thomas Allsop, *California and Its Gold Mines, Being a Series of Recent Communications from the Mining Districts, Upon the Present Condition and Future Prospects of Quartz Mining . . .* (London: Goombridge & Sons, 1853), 85.

113 "The Grass Valley Quartz Veins," *Sacramento Transcript* 2, no. 101 (February 21, 1851).

114 Hutchings, "Quartz Mining in California," 146.

115 In nineteenth-century mining literature, the term is commonly spelled "arrasta." Another variant is "rasta."

116 In an archaeological study of mining sites, arrastras were found to range from eight to twenty feet in diameter. They were powered by water or steam by 1859. It was most usual for camps to have only a single arrastra. Because they were easily built, arrastras were semipermanent structures found in all mining districts irrespective of terrain. See Roger E. Kelly and Marsha C. S. Kelly, "Arrastras: Unique Western Historic Milling Sites," *Historical Archaeology* 17, no. 1 (1983), 85–95.

117 Browne, *Resources of the Pacific Slope*, 8.

118 In a rock-lined circular pit, a center post, turned by a mule, was attached to a large stone wheel. A stream of water was kept continually running to which mercury was added to bond with the gold.

119 "Quartz Mines," *Alta California* 4, no. 316 (December 5, 1853).

120 Hutchings, "Quartz Mining in California," 151.

121 Guido Kustel, *Nevada and California Processes of Silver and Gold Extraction for General Use and Especially for the Mining Public of California and Nevada* (San Francisco: Frank D. Carlton, 1868), 66–71.

122 Per John Ross Browne, the California Stamp Mill was developed after the discovery of the Comstock Lode in Nevada. Scientific machinery designed for Nevada was subsequently used in California. Browne, *Resources of the Pacific Slope*, 8.

123 Duane A. Smith, "The Stamp Mill," *Montana: The Magazine of Western History* 58, no. 1 (Spring 2008), 63–65.

124 Mark Twain, *Roughing It* (New York: Harper & Brothers Publishers, 1872), 245–46. For this book, Twain drew from his personal experience working in a stamp mill.

125 Eduard Vischer, "A Trip to the Mining Regions in the Sprint of 1859," translated by Ruth Frey Axe, *California Historical Society Quarterly* 11, no. 3 (September 1932), 227.

126 Buffum, *Six Months in the Gold Mines*, 141–42.

127 Limbaugh, "Making Old Tools Work Better," 46.

128 Lacking additional information, images of miners working a sluice located in a rocky landscape could be interpreted as mining any of the following: the bed of a turned river (river diversion), the bottom of a ravine between hills (drifting, ground sluicing, or quartz mining), or the floor of a deep chasm (caused by hydraulic mining).

129 "Sierra County Correspondence," *Sacramento Union* 17, no. 2602 (July 30, 1859).

130 Rossiter W. Raymond, *Statistics of Mines and Mining in the States and Territories West of the Rocky Mountains* (Washington, DC: Government Printing Office, 1870), 728.

131 Browne, *Resources of the Pacific Slope*, 9–10.

132 Raymond, *Statistics of Mines and Mining*, 727.

CHAPTER 6

1 This section is informed by Sucheng Chan, "A People of Exceptional Character: Ethnic Diversity, Nativism, and Racism in the California Gold Rush," *California History* 79, no. 2 (Summer 2000), 44–85.

2 The term "Americans" refers here to white males from the existing American states and territories.

3 Hinton R. Helper, *The Land of Gold: Reality Versus Fiction* (Baltimore: Henry Taylor, 1855), 96. Helper was a critic of slavery, arguing that it retarded the economic and cultural growth of the South. His book provides insight on predominant views of white male Americans at the time.

4 Throughout this book, original language regarding many non-white groups has been retained in the citations. Recognizing the offensive nature of many of the names used, this book strives for historical accuracy but does not condone or embrace any such bias.

5 Albert H. Hurtado, *Indian Survival on the California Frontier* (New Haven: Yale University Press, 1988), I.

6 Mexican California relied on California's large Indian population to solve labor shortages. Over time, Indian workers became the sole source of agricultural labor on the vast ranchos. Due to notions of American Indian racial inferiority, unemployed Indians deemed "vagrants" were automatically assigned to labor duty. Dishonest employers falsely claimed that Indians owed labor for "wages advanced," thus forcing them into debt peonage. Kidnappers raided Indian villages, violently abducting victims for forced servitude. See: Benjamin Madley, "'Unholy Traffic in Human Blood and Souls' Systems of California Indian Servitude Under U.S. Rule," *Pacific Historical Review* 83, no. 4 (November 2014), 626–67.

7 Michael Magliari, "Free Soil, Unfree Labor," *Pacific Historical Review* 73, no. 3 (August 2004), 349–50.

8 All citations in this paragraph are from: R. B. Mason to R. Jones, August 17, 1848, *H. R. Ex. Documents*, 30th Congress, 2nd Session, Document 1, 60.

9 Other early mining operations dependent on Indian labor included, in the north: James Bidwell on the Feather River (1848), and John Marsh in the gold fields above Marysville (1848); and in the south: Charles Weber of the Stockton Mining Company on the Stanislaus River (1848), John Murphy in Calaveras County on the Stanislaus River (1848), and James Savage on the Tuolumne River near Jamestown and in the Big Oak Flat mining district (1848). In James J. Rawls, "Gold Diggers: Indian Miners in the California Gold Rush," *California Historical Society Quarterly* 55, no. 1 (Spring 1976), 32–37.

10 R. B. Mason to R. Jones, August 17, 1848, *H. R. Ex. Documents*, 30th Congress, 2nd Session, Document 1, 60.

11 "Diggor Indian," *New York Herald* (August 19, 1848), 1.

12 William G. Johnston, *Experiences of a Forty-Niner, A Member of the Wagon Train First to Enter California in the Year 1849* (Pittsburgh: 1892), 240.

13 The confrontation began when white miners entered a Maidu village on the American River and raped several Indian women. After Indians retaliated, the conflict ended with the execution of Indian prisoners at Coloma.

14 H. S. Lyman, "Reminiscences of Wm. M. Case," *Quarterly of the Oregon Historical Society* 1, no. 3 (September 1900), 288.

15 E. Gould Buffum, *Six Months in the Gold Mines: From a Journal of Three Years' Residence in Upper and Lower California in 1847-48-49* (London: Richard Bentley, 1850), 134. American Indians are variously referred to as "redskins," "diggers," "savages," and other racially biased and derogatory terms used by white people in the nineteenth century.

16 Theodore T. Johnson, *California and Oregon; or, Sights in the Gold Region and Scenes by the Way* (Philadelphia: J. B. Lippincott & Co., 1865), 140.

17 John M. Letts, *California Illustrated: Including a Description of the Panama and Nicaragua Route By a Returned Californian* (New York: William Holdredge Publisher, 1852), 63.

18 Carvel Collins, ed., *Sam Ward in the Gold Rush* (Stanford: Stanford University Press, 1949), 162.

19 "Mariposa County-Valuable Statistics," *Alta California* 3, no. 313 (November 12, 1852).

20 "From the Interior—Nevada," *Sacramento Union* 5, no. 680 (May 28, 1853).

21 "Fatality Among Indians," *Sacramento Union* 7, no. 1046 (August 1, 1854).

22 "Digger Indians," *Sacramento Union* 8, no. 1177 (December 30, 1854).

23 "Digger Indians," *Sacramento Union* 8, no. 1177 (December 30, 1854).

24 Rawls, "Gold Diggers," 28–45.

25 It should be noted that a significant number of American Indians continued the unfree system of labor in the agricultural fields through the 1870s. See Madley, "'Unholy Traffic in Human Blood and Souls,'" 657–67.

26 Richard Rudisill, *Mirror Image: The Influence of the Daguerreotype on American Society* (Albuquerque: University of New Mexico Press, 1971), 159.

27 This system of child enslavement continued until the repeal of section 3 in April 1863. Later, the Anti-Peonage Act of 1867 ended the entire system.

28 Magliari, "Free Soil, Unfree Labor," 353.

29 "Abducting Indian Children," *Alta California* 5, no. 273 (October 2, 1854).

30 In his landmark book, *California's Pictorial Letter Sheets*, Joseph Baird confirmed that some letter-sheet illustrations "were adapted from contemporary ambrotypes and daguerreotypes," and that "the artistic character . . . patently indicates that they have been transcribed directly from such sources, even though the source is not acknowledged." Using the letter sheet of *The Miners* as an example, Baird noted that the "faces of the men are veritable portraits" and that "such individual attention to facial detail" suggested a daguerreotype was "almost certainly" used as the model. Joseph Armstrong Baird Jr., *California's Pictorial Letter Sheets, 1849–1869* (San Francisco: David Magee, 1967), 18.

31 According to contemporary daguerreotypist Robert Shlaer, "the fact that daguerreotypes are usually laterally reversed from left to right was well understood by the artists and engravers of the period. When presented with one they would normally correct it laterally while preparing an illustration from it for printing." Robert Shlaer, *Sights Once Seen: Daguerreotyping Fremont's Last Expedition through the Rockies* (Santa Fe: Museum of New Mexico Press, 2000), 48.

32 In the nineteenth century, the term "negro" was used interchangeably to refer to people of African descent in Latin America and Jamaica, as well as Americans—free men and women from the northern states or enslaved men and women from the southern states.

33 "New Bedford," *The Liberator* (February 9, 1849), 18.

34 Frederick Douglass, "Letter from the Editor," *North Star* (November 30, 1849).

35 *New Bedford Mercury* (March 30, 1849), as cited in the landmark study by Rudolph M. Lapp, *Blacks in Gold Rush California* (New Haven: Yale University Press, 1977), 17.

36 "What the 'Fanatics' Have Done," *The Liberator* 20, no. 7 (February 15, 1849).

37 "Late From California," *The Liberator* (February 15, 1849).

38 "Slaves on Their Way," *The Liberator* 20, no. 17 (April 27, 1849), reprinted from the *Wetumpka (AL) Guard* newspaper; "Slaves for California," *The Liberator* 20, no. 17 (April 27, 1849), reprinted from the *Washington Era* newspaper.

39 "Southern Proposition," *The Liberator* 20, no. 17 (April 27, 1849).

40 "California Gold," *New York Tribune* 9, no. 111 (August 17, 1849). News of this discovery was not mentioned in the California newspapers.

41 *The Liberator* (December 21, 1849; February 15, 1850) as cited in Lapp, *Blacks in Gold Rush California*, 13.

42 F[rederick] D[ouglass], "Letter from the Editor," *North Star* (November 30, 1849).

43 "Southerner's View of Gold Digging," *North Star* 2, no. 49 (November 30, 1849).

44 F[rederick] D[ouglass], "Letter from the Editor," *North Star* (November 30, 1849).

45 The American Colonization Society was established in 1816 for the purpose of removing free black people from the United States. A controversial organization, the Society was supported by many southern slaveholders who saw free black people as a threat. Black people held in bondage were not permitted to immigrate to Liberia. Many abolitionists opposed the Society and saw it as a racist strategy aimed at protecting slavery. See Frankie Hutton, "American Colonization Society's Early Effort to Emigrate Free Blacks to Liberia, 1816–36," *Journal of Negro History* 68, no. 4 (Autumn 1983), 376–89.

46 "Free Negroes Admitted," *North Star* (December 21, 1849).

47 William Downie, *Hunting for Gold: Reminiscences of Personal Research in the Early Days of the Pacific Coast From Alaska to Panama* (San Francisco: The California Publishing Company, 1893), 34–35.

48 Downie, *Hunting for Gold*, 51.

49 William W. Miller, diary, October 6 and 28, 1849, Beinecke Library, Yale University, as cited in Lapp, *Blacks in Gold Rush California*, 56–57.

50 See Stacey L. Smith, "Remaking Slavery in a Free State: Masters and Slaves in Gold Rush California," *Pacific Historical Review* 80, no. 1 (February 2011), 28–63.

51 Historian Rudolph Lapp maintained that "most [black people] came from Northern states and from those Upper South states that had immense free [black] populations. States like South Carolina, Georgia, Alabama, and Mississippi contributed only a very small part of the [black people] who participated in the Gold Rush; thus there is the probability that many of the [black people] who arrived in California were free men." Lapp also states that "in the early days of the Gold Rush, the overwhelming majority of the [black] population was involved in mining" and black people from the southern states were a majority in the southern gold mining region in California. See Rudolph M. Lapp, "The Negro in Gold Rush California," *Journal of Negro History* 49, no. 2 (April 1964), 81–98.

52 Hoping to escape the racism prevalent in the California mines, many black men later immigrated to British Columbia in the Fraser River gold rush of the late 1850s. See: Malcolm Edwards, "The War of Complexional Distinction: Blacks in Gold Rush California & British Columbia," *California Historical Quarterly* 56, no. 1 (Spring 1977), 34–45.

53 Smith, "Remaking Slavery in a Free State," 30.

54 Chan, "A People of Exceptional Character," 68.

55 J. D. Borthwick, *Three Years in California* (Edinburgh: William Blackwood and Sons, 1857), 163.

56 "Slaves for California," *Alta California* 3, no. 55 (February 25, 1852). Not all slaves worked as miners, however. It was often more lucrative to hire out a slave to other white employers in the city than it was to have him work in the gold fields.

57 "What does it mean?" *Alta California* 1, no. 108 (May 4, 1850).

58 Paolo Sioli, *Historical Souvenir of El Dorado County, California* (Oakland, CA: Paolo Sioli, 1883), 201. In more loathsome terms, the claim was advertised in the *Alta California*: "About four miles below Mormon Island, on the American River, there have been new diggings discovered which prove to yield exceedingly well. They are called 'Nigger Diggings,' from the fact that some colored gentlemen first discovered them.' "San Joaquin Intelligence," *Alta California* 2, no. 354 (December 1, 1851).

59 "San Joaquin Intelligence," *Alta California* 2, no. 354 (December 1, 1851).

60 Sioli, *Historical Souvenir*, 201. Black mining populations were also found at Lancha Plana, Poverty Bar, and Murphys Camp; see "Colored Men in the Mines," and "Indians at Murphy's," *Alta California* 10, no. 45 (February 15, 1858).

61 Edna Bryan Buckbee, *The Saga of Old Tuolumne* (New York: The Press of the Pioneers, Inc., 1935), 329.

62 "The Big Lump," *Alta California* 5, no. 50 (February 20, 1854).

63 "From the Interior," *Sacramento Union* 2, no. 228 (December 1, 1851).

64 "Old Jenkins," *Sacramento Union* 2, no. 222 (November 22, 1851); "Indian Gulch," *Alta California* 4, no. 204 (August 4, 1853); "Auburn and Vicinity," *Alta California* 4, no. 18 (January 18, 1853); and "Summary of News in the Southern Mines," *Alta California* 4, no. 204 (August 4, 1853).

65 Borthwick, *Three Years in California*, 164.

66 J. B. Starkweather arrived from Panama on the steamship *Oregon*. "Passengers," *Sacramento Union* 2, no. 279 (February 12, 1852).

67 "Auburn and Vicinity," *Alta California* 4, no. 18 (January 18, 1853).

68 C. L., "Placer County Correspondence," *Sacramento Union* 3, no. 346 (April 30, 1852).

69 "Black and White," *Alta California* 2, no. 53 (February 1, 1851).

70 F[rederick] D[ouglass], "Letter from the Editor," *North Star* (November 30, 1849).

71 This section is indebted to the scholarship of Yong Chen, "The Internal Origins of Chinese Emigration to California Reconsidered," *Western Historical Quarterly* 28, no. 4 (Winter 1997), 520–46; and June Mei, "Socioeconomic Origins of Emigration: Guangdong to California, 1850–1882," *Modern China* 5, no. 4 (October 1979), 463–501.

72 Doris Marion Wright, "The Making of Cosmopolitan California: An Analysis of Immigration, 1848–1870," *California Historical Society Quarterly* 19, no. 4 (December 1940), 329–30.

73 Mei, "Socioeconomic Origins," 469. See also Chen, "The Internal Origins," 545 n89.

74 Lorenzo Sawyer, *Way Sketches Containing Incidents of Travel Across the Plains from St. Joseph to California* (New York: Edward Eberstadt, 1926), 125.

75 "Celestial," *Alta California* 1, no. 114 (May 11, 1850).

76 Chinese immigrants belonged to one of the Six Companies headquartered in San Francisco. In an attempt to retain the traditional Chinese social structure, each of the Six represented a geographical region of the Guangdong Province. In exchange for financial and legal assistance, each member paid dues and pledged allegiance to their respective company. In David V. DuFault, "The Chinese in the Mining Camps of California: 1848–1870," *Historical Society of Southern California Quarterly* 41, no. 2 (June 1959) 155–70.

77 "Our Population," *Alta California* 1, no 59 (March 8, 1850). The Chinese were referred to interchangeably as "China John," "Chinaman," and "Celestial." Hinton Helper suggested the origin of the term "Celestial": "So exalted in opinion have they of themselves that they think they are the most central, civilized and enlightened people on earth, and that they are the especial favorites of heaven—hence they are sometimes called 'Celestials.'" Helper, *The Land of Gold*, 90.

78 Reprinted from the *Baltimore Sun* as "Chinese Slaves in California," *Placer Times* 1, no. 42 (March 2, 1850).

79 Mei, "Socioeconomic Origins," 478.

80 Mei, "Socioeconomic Origins," 484–85.

81 S. Wells Williams, *Chinese Immigration, A Paper Read before the Social Science Association at Saratoga, September 10, 1879* (New York: Charles Scribner's Sons, 1879), 45.

82 Yuen-fong Woon, "The Voluntary Sojourner among the Overseas Chinese: Myth or Reality?" *Pacific Affairs* 56, no. 4 (Winter 1983–1984), 673–90.

83 "The Foreign Taxes," *Sacramento Transcript* 1, no. 30 (June 5, 1850).

84 "From Stockton," *Sacramento Union* 5, no. 687 (June 6, 1853). For a thorough discussion on the interactions of American Indians and Chinese in California, see Daniel Liestman, "Horizontal Inter-Ethic Relations: Chinese and American Indians in the Nineteenth-Century American West," *Western Historical Quarterly* 30, no. 3 (Autumn 1999), 327–49.

85 "Governor's Special Message," *Sacramento Union* 3, no. 341 (April 24, 1852). For the Chinese American response to Governor Bigler's message, see Noman Asing, "To His Excellency Gov. Bigler," *Alta California* 3, no. 125 (May 5, 1852). In his letter to Governor Bigler, Asing points out the hypocrisy of excluding immigrants from the US, stating, "immigration made *you what you are*." He also stressed that the Chinese were not a "degraded race," and emphasized the hundreds of years of arts and culture enjoyed in China while the US was but a wilderness.

86 Sue Fawn Chung, *In Pursuit of Gold: Chinese American Miners and Merchants in the American West* (Urbana: University of Illinois Press, 2011), 41–45.

87 "The Chinese," *Alta California* 6, no. 51 (February 21, 1855).

88 "The Chinese," *Alta California* 6, no. 51 (February 21, 1855).

89 Dan Caldwell, "The Negroization of the Chinese Stereotype in California," *Southern California Quarterly* 53, no. 2 (June 1971), 123–31.

90 Borthwick, *Three Years in California*, 143–44.

91 Helper, *The Land of Gold*, 89.

92 Helper, *The Land of Gold*, 87.

93 J. Ross Browne, *Adventures in the Apache Country: A Tour Through Arizona and Sonora, with Notes on the Silver Region of Nevada* (New York: Harper & Brothers, 1868), 388.

94 C. L., "Gold Hill Diggings—Rules and Regulations of the Miners," *Sacramento Union* 3, no. 346 (April 30, 1852).

95 Longobardus, "Fluming Companies—Immigration—The Chinamen—Secret Diggings," *Sacramento Union* 3, no. 420 (July 27, 1852).

96 "Chinese Hospital," *Sacramento Union* 4, no. 484 (October 11, 1852).

97 "Negro Hill," in Sioli, *Historical Souvenir*, 201.

98 Copperhead, "History of Poverty Bar," *Sacramento Union* 8, no. 1115 (October 19, 1854).

99 "Auburn," *Sacramento Union* 9, no. 1360 (August 4, 1855).

100 Quill Driver, "El Dorado County Correspondence," *Sacramento Union* 10, no. 1450 (November 17, 1855).

101 Attributed to George H. Johnson, *Chinese Miner at the Sluice*, ca. 1850–55. Quarter plate. In the *Stephen R. Anaya Collection of Gold Rush Daguerreotypes and Other Photographs* sale, "Photographs," Sotheby's New York, April 6, 2000, lot 35.

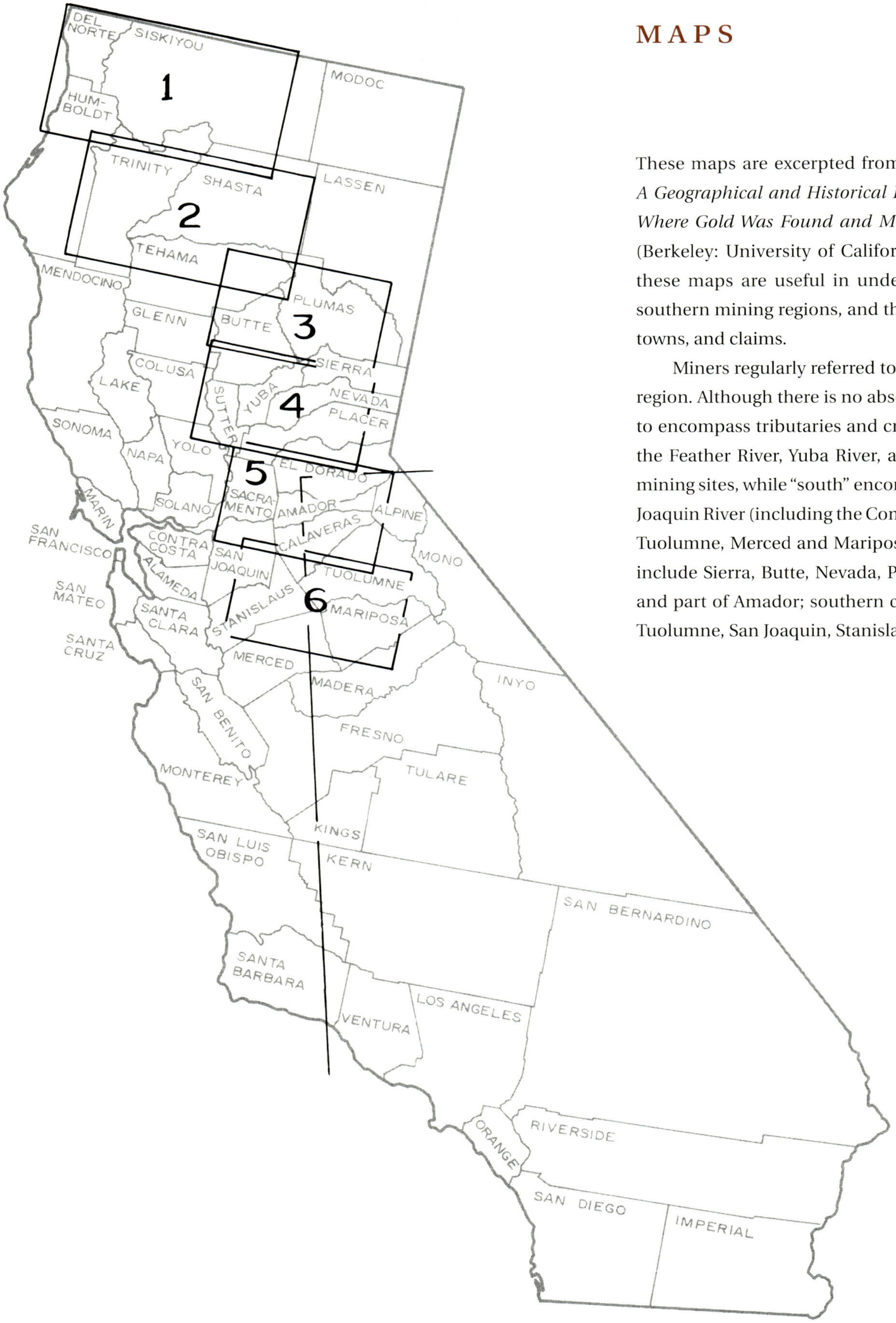

MAPS

These maps are excerpted from Erwin G. Gudde, *California Gold Camps: A Geographical and Historical Dictionary of Camps, Towns, and Localities Where Gold Was Found and Mined; Wayside Stations and Trading Center* (Berkeley: University of California Press, 1974). While not finely detailed, these maps are useful in understanding the scope of the northern and southern mining regions, and the general location of various counties, gold towns, and claims.

Miners regularly referred to the north and south sections of the mining region. Although there is no absolute rule, "north" was generally considered to encompass tributaries and creeks from the Sacramento River (including the Feather River, Yuba River, and American River) and the Sierra Nevada mining sites, while "south" encompassed tributaries and creeks from the San Joaquin River (including the Consumnes, Mokelumne, Calaveras, Stanislaus, Tuolumne, Merced and Mariposa Rivers). For this book, northern counties include Sierra, Butte, Nevada, Placer, Yuba, Sutter, El Dorado, Sacramento, and part of Amador; southern counties include part of Amador, Calaveras, Tuolumne, San Joaquin, Stanislaus, and Mariposa.

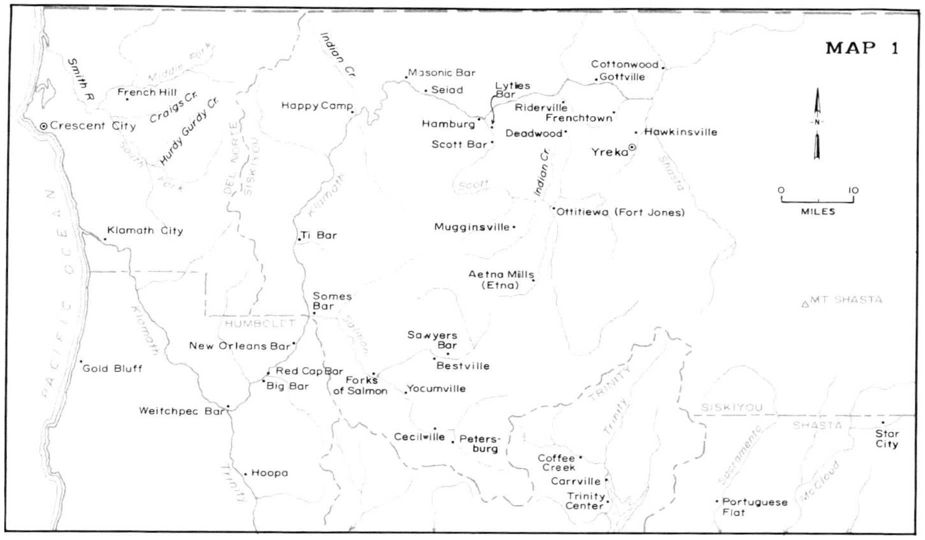
MAP 1
MILES
0
10
Smith R.
French Hill
Crescent City
Craigs Cr.
Hurdy Gurdy Cr.
Happy Camp
Indian Cr.
Masonic Bar
Seiad
Lytles Bar
Riderville
Frenchtown
Cottonwood
Gottville
Hamburg
Deadwood
Scott Bar
Hawkinsville
Yreka
Indian Cr.
Ottitiewa (Fort Jones)
Klamath City
Ti Bar
Mugginsville
Aetna Mills (Etna)
Somes Bar
MT SHASTA
HUMBOLDT
New Orleans Bar
Sawyers Bar
Bestville
Gold Bluff
Red Cap Bar
Big Bar
Forks of Salmon
Yocumville
Weitchpec Bar
Cecilville
Peters-burg
SISKIYOU
SHASTA
Star City
Coffee Creek
Carrville
Trinity Center
Hoopa
Portuguese Flat
PACIFIC OCEAN
DEL NORTE
SISKIYOU
TRINITY
Sacramento
McCloud

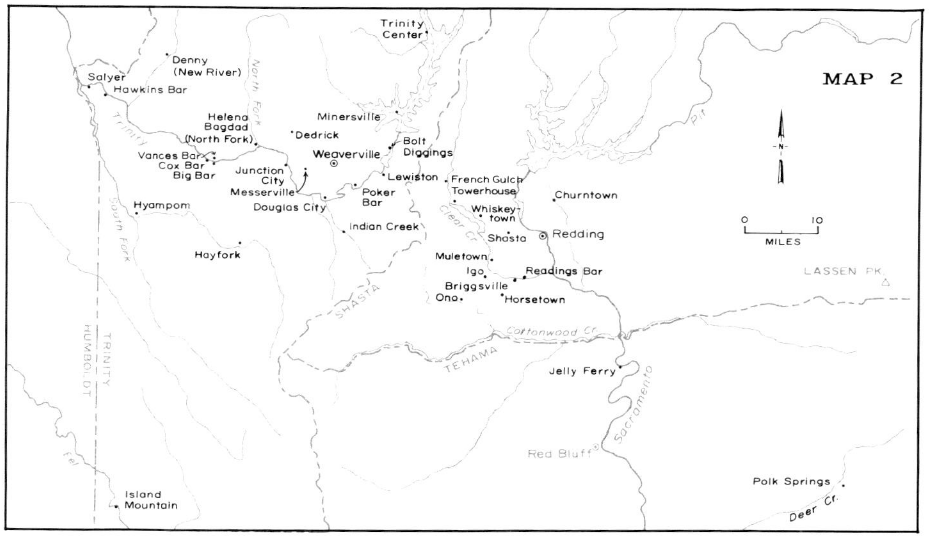
MAP 2
MILES
0
10
Trinity Center
Denny (New River)
Salyer
Hawkins Bar
Minersville
Helena
Bagdad
(North Fork)
Dedrick
Bolt Diggings
Vances Bar
Cox Bar
Big Bar
Weaverville
Junction City
Lewiston
French Gulch
Towerhouse
Messerville
Poker Bar
Churntown
Douglas City
Hyampom
Whiskey-town
Indian Creek
Shasta
Redding
Hayfork
Muletown
Igo
Readings Bar
LASSEN PK.
Briggsville
Ono
Horsetown
HUMBOLDT
TRINITY
SHASTA
TEHAMA
Cottonwood Cr.
Jelly Ferry
Red Bluff
Sacramento
Island Mountain
Polk Springs
Deer Cr.
South Fork

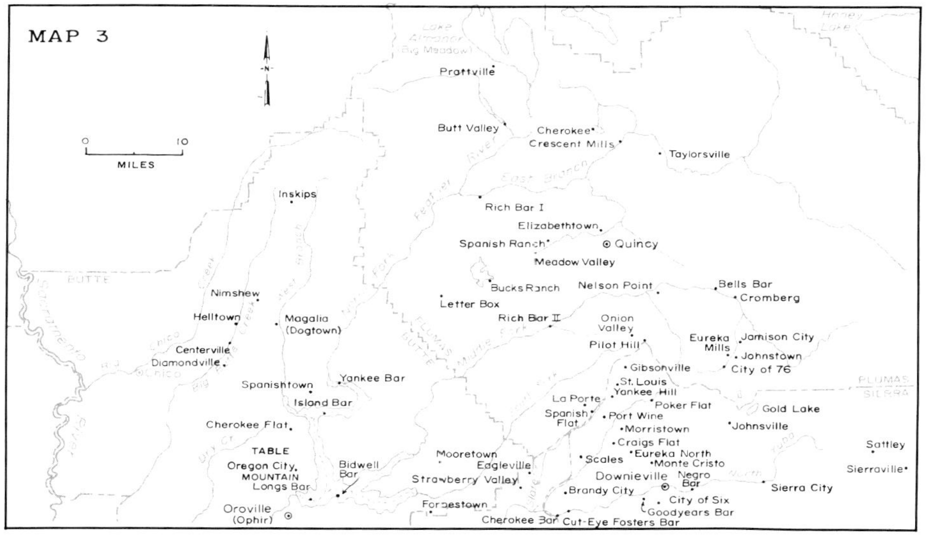
MAP 3
MILES
0
10
Prattville
Butt Valley
Cherokee
Crescent Mills
Taylorsville
Inskips
Rich Bar I
Elizabethtown
Spanish Ranch
Quincy
Meadow Valley
BUTTE
Nimshew
Bucks Ranch
Nelson Point
Bells Bar
Cromberg
Helltown
Magalia (Dogtown)
Letter Box
Rich Bar II
Onion Valley
Centerville
Diamondville
Pilot Hill
Eureka Mills
Jamison City
Johnstown
City of 76
Gibsonville
Spanishtown
Yankee Bar
St. Louis
Yankee Hill
PLUMAS
SIERRA
Island Bar
La Porte
Poker Flat
Gold Lake
Spanish Flat
Port Wine
Cherokee Flat
Morristown
Johnsville
Craigs Flat
TABLE
Mooretown
Eureka North
Sattley
Oregon City
MOUNTAIN
Longs Bar
Bidwell Bar
Eagleville
Scales
Monte Cristo
Sierraville
Strawberry Valley
Downieville
Negro Bar
Brandy City
Sierra City
Oroville (Ophir)
Forbestown
City of Six
Goodyears Bar
Cherokee Bar
Cut-Eye Fosters Bar

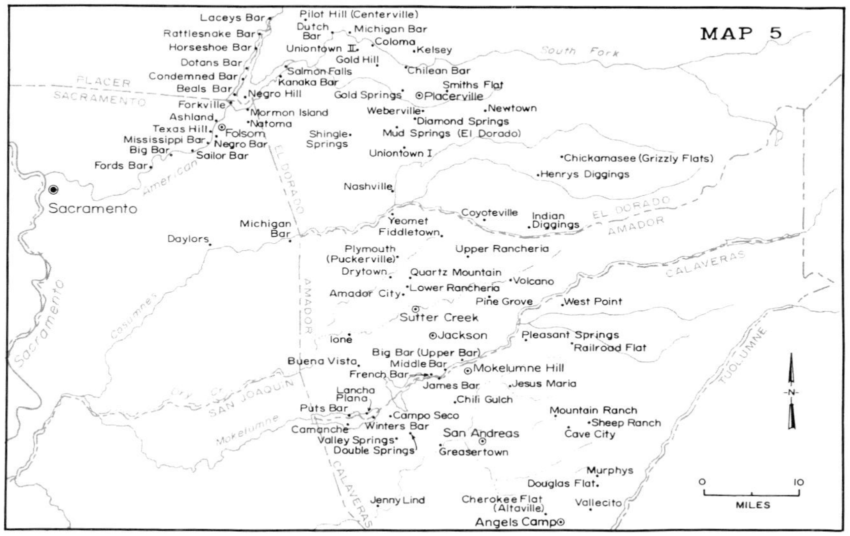
MAP 5
MILES
0
10
Laceys Bar
Pilot Hill (Centerville)
Rattlesnake Bar
Dutch Bar
Michigan Bar
Horseshoe Bar
Coloma
Uniontown II
Kelsey
Dotans Bar
Gold Hill
Salmon Falls
Chilean Bar
South Fork
Condemned Bar
Kanaka Bar
Smiths Flat
PLACER
SACRAMENTO
Beals Bar
Negro Hill
Gold Springs
Placerville
Forkville
Mormon Island
Newtown
Ashland
Natoma
Weberville
Diamond Springs
Texas Hill
Folsom
Shingle Springs
Mud Springs (El Dorado)
Mississippi Bar
Negro Bar
Big Bar
Sailor Bar
Uniontown I
Chickamasee (Grizzly Flats)
Fords Bar
Henrys Diggings
Nashville
Sacramento
Yeomet
Coyoteville
Indian Diggings
Michigan Bar
Fiddletown
EL DORADO
AMADOR
Daylors
Plymouth (Puckerville)
Upper Rancheria
Drytown
Quartz Mountain
Volcano
Amador City
Lower Rancheria
Pine Grove
CALAVERAS
West Point
Sutter Creek
Ione
Jackson
Pleasant Springs
Railroad Flat
Buena Vista
Big Bar (Upper Bar)
Middle Bar
Mokelumne Hill
French Bar
TUOLUMNE
James Bar
Jesus Maria
Lancha Plana
Chili Gulch
Puts Bar
Mountain Ranch
Campo Seco
Sheep Ranch
Camanche
Winters Bar
San Andreas
Cave City
Valley Springs
Double Springs
Greasertown
SAN JOAQUIN
Mokelumne
Murphys
Douglas Flat
Jenny Lind
Cherokee Flat (Altaville)
Vallecito
Angels Camp
CALAVERAS

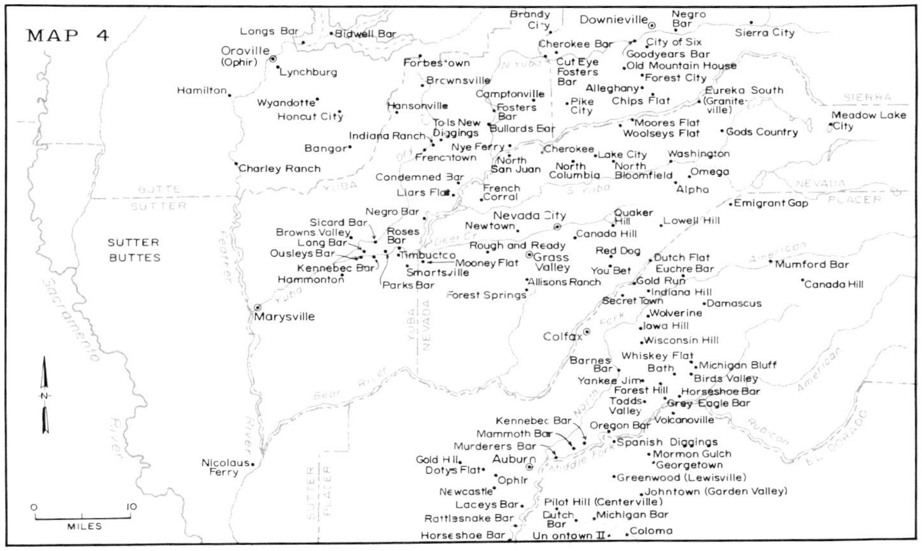
MAP 4
MILES
0
10
Brandy City
Downieville
Negro Bar
Sierra City
Longs Bar
Bidwell Bar
Cherokee Bar
City of Six
Goodyears Bar
Oroville (Ophir)
Forbestown
Cut Eye Fosters Bar
Old Mountain House
Lynchburg
Forest City
Brownsville
Hamilton
Camptonville
Alleghany
Eureka South
Wyandotte
Hansonville
Fosters Bar
Pike City
Chips Flat
(Granite-ville)
SIERRA
Meadow Lake City
Honcut City
Tols New Diggings
Bullards Bar
Indiana Ranch
Moores Flat
Woolseys Flat
Gods Country
Bangor
Nye Ferry
Cherokee
Frenchtown
Lake City
Washington
Charley Ranch
North San Juan
North Columbia
North Bloomfield
Omega
Condemned Bar
BUTTE
SUTTER
YUBA
French Corral
Alpha
NEVADA
PLACER
Llars Flat
Emigrant Gap
Negro Bar
Nevada City
Quaker Hill
Sicard Bar
Newtown
Lowell Hill
Browns Valley
Roses Bar
Canada Hill
SUTTER BUTTES
Long Bar
Ousleys Bar
Timbuctoo
Rough and Ready
Red Dog
Kennebec Bar
Mooney Flat
Grass Valley
Dutch Flat
Mumford Bar
Hammonton
Smartsville
You Bet
Euchre Bar
Parks Bar
Allisons Ranch
Gold Run
Canada Hill
Forest Springs
Indiana Hill
Secret Town
Damascus
Marysville
Wolverine
Iowa Hill
Colfax
Wisconsin Hill
Whiskey Flat
Barnes Bar
Bath
Michigan Bluff
Yankee Jims
Birds Valley
Forest Hill
Horseshoe Bar
Todds Valley
Grey Eagle Bar
Kennebec Bar
Volcanoville
Oregon Bar
Mammoth Bar
Spanish Diggings
Murderers Bar
Mormon Gulch
Gold Hill
Auburn
Georgetown
Nicolaus Ferry
Dotys Flat
Greenwood (Lewisville)
Ophir
Newcastle
Johntown (Garden Valley)
Laceys Bar
Pilot Hill (Centerville)
Rattlesnake Bar
Dutch Bar
Michigan Bar
Horseshoe Bar
Uniontown II
Coloma
Sacramento
Feather
Bear
American
Rubicon
EL DORADO
SUTTER
PLACER

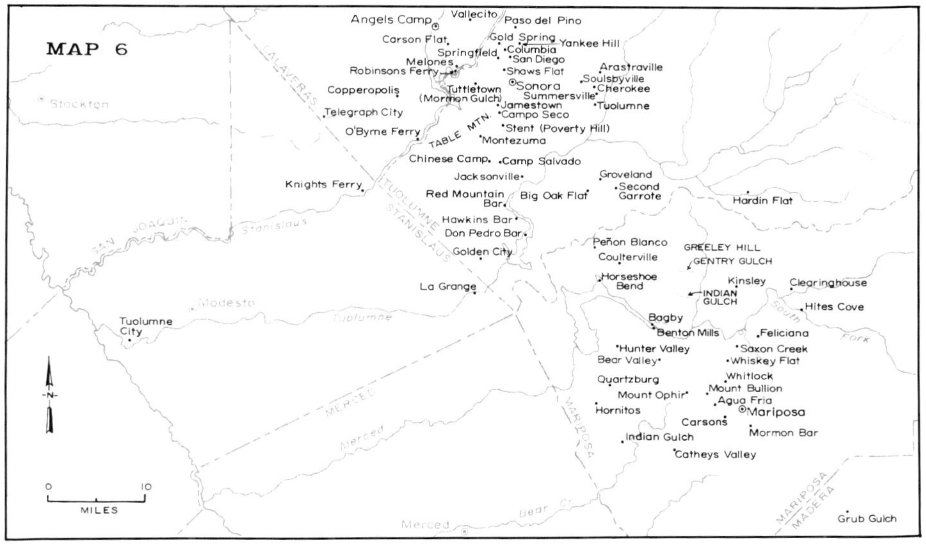
MAP 6
MILES
0
10
Angels Camp
Vallecito
Paso del Pino
Carson Flat
Gold Spring
Yankee Hill
Springfield
Columbia
San Diego
Melones
Robinsons Ferry
Shows Flat
Arastraville
Soulsbyville
Copperopolis
Tuttletown
Sonora
Cherokee
(Mormon Gulch)
Summersville
Tuolumne
Stockton
Telegraph City
Jamestown
Campo Seco
O'Byrne Ferry
TABLE MTN.
Stent (Poverty Hill)
Montezuma
Chinese Camp
Camp Salvado
Jacksonville
Groveland
Knights Ferry
Second Garrote
Red Mountain Bar
Big Oak Flat
Hardin Flat
Hawkins Bar
Don Pedro Bar
Peñon Blanco
Golden City
GREELEY HILL
Coulterville
GENTRY GULCH
Horseshoe Bend
Kinsley
Clearinghouse
La Grange
INDIAN GULCH
Hites Cove
Modesto
Tuolumne City
Bagby
Benton Mills
Feliciana
Hunter Valley
Saxon Creek
Bear Valley
Whiskey Flat
Quartzburg
Whitlock
Mount Bullion
Mount Ophir
Agua Fria
Hornitos
Mariposa
Carsons
Indian Gulch
Mormon Bar
Catheys Valley
MERCED
Merced
Grub Gulch
MARIPOSA
MADERA
SAN JOAQUIN
STANISLAUS
TUOLUMNE
CALAVERAS
Stanislaus
Tuolumne
Bear Cr.

SELECTED BIBLIOGRAPHY

Alexander, Abel. "Robert H. Vance: Pioneer of the Daguerreotype in Chile." *Daguerreian Annual* (1993): 11–30.

Armstrong, Marcos R. "The California Gold Rush: Approaches to Producing Daguerreotype Views, An Examination of Views in the Matthew R. Isenburg Collection at AMC Toronto." Master's thesis, Ryerson University, 2013.

Aspinwall, Jane L. "Found Treasure: The Bond & Mollyneaux California Daguerreotype." *Daguerreian Annual* (2008): 70–75.

———. "Like a Bird Before a Snake: Nineteenth-century Portraiture and Its Relationship to the American Daguerreotype." Master's thesis, University of Missouri-Kansas City, 2001.

———. "More From the Gold Fields: The Gulick Brothers." *Daguerreian Annual* (2009/2010): 71–74.

Baird Jr., Joseph Armstrong. *California's Pictorial Letter Sheets, 1849–1869.* San Francisco: David Magee, 1967.

Baker, Isaac W. "Journal of the Proceedings on Board the Barque San Francisco, Thomas Remmonds Master, Of and from Beverly, for California Commencing August 15, 1849." Unpublished diary, Bancroft Library, University of California Berkeley, 1849–1852.

Bancroft, Hubert. *The Works of Hubert Howe Bancroft*, vol. 23, *The History of California, 1848–1859.* San Francisco: The History Company, 1886.

Barth, Gunther. *Instant Cities: Urbanization and the Rise of San Francisco and Denver.* Albuquerque: University of New Mexico Press, 1988.

Bean, Edwin F. *The History and Directory of Nevada County, California.* Nevada City: The Daily Gazette and Job Office, 1867.

Birt, Rodger C., Marvin R. Nathan, Peter E. Palmquist, and Joan M. Schwartz. *San Francisco Album: Photographs of the Most Beautiful Views and Public Buildings: George Robinson Fardon.* San Francisco and New York: Fraenkel Gallery and Hans P. Kraus Jr., Inc., 1999.

Borthwick, J. D. *Three Years in California.* Edinburgh: William Blackwood and Sons, 1857.

Browne, John Ross. *Report of J. Ross Browne on the Mineral Resources of the States and Territories West of the Rocky Mountains.* Washington, DC: Government Printing Office, 1868.

Buckbee, Edna Bryan. *The Saga of Old Tuolumne.* New York: The Press of the Pioneers, Inc., 1935.

Buffum, E. Gould. *Six Months in the Gold Mines: From a Journal of Three Years' Residence in Upper and Lower California in 1847-8-9.* London: Richard Bentley, 1850.

Calmenson, Wendy Cunkle. "Likenesses Taken in the Most Approved Style: William Shew, Pioneer Daguerreotypist." *California Historical Quarterly* 56, no. 1 (Spring 1977): 2–19.

Chan, Sucheng. "Chinese Livelihood in Rural California: The Impact of Economic Change, 1860–1880." *Pacific Historical Review* 53, no. 3 (August 1984): 273–307.

———. "A People of Exceptional Character: Ethnic Diversity, Nativism, and Racism in the California Gold Rush." In Kevin Starr and Richard J. Orsi, eds., *Rooted in Barbarous Soil: People, Culture, and Community in Gold Rush California*, special issue of *California History* 79, no. 2 (Summer 2000): 44–85.

Chandler, Robert. "Integrity amid Tumult: Wells, Fargo & Co.'s Gold Rush Banking." *California History* 70 (Fall 1991): 258–77.

Chen, Yong. "The Internal Origins of Chinese Emigration to California Reconsidered." *Western Historical Quarterly* 28, no. 4 (Winter 1997): 520–546.

Chung, Sue Fawn. *In Pursuit of Gold: Chinese American Miners and Merchants in the American West.* Urbana: University of Illinois Press, 2011.

Clapp, Louise. "California, In 1852—Letter Fifteenth. Residence in the Mines. From our Log Cabin, Indian Bar, April 10, 1852," *Pioneer of California Monthly Magazine* 3, no. 5 (May 1855), 309.

Colton, Walter. *Three Years in California.* New York: A. S. Barnes & Co., 1850.

Davis, Keith F., with contributions by Jane L. Aspinwall. *The Origins of American Photography, 1839–1885: From Daguerreotype to Dry-Plate.* Kansas City: Hall Family Foundation/The Nelson-Atkins Museum of Art, 2007.

Dix, John Ross [George Spencer Phillips]. *Amusing and Thrilling Adventures of a California Artist while Daguerreotyping a Continent.* Boston: Published by the author, 1854.

Dornin, George D. *Thirty Years Ago.* Berkeley: George Dornin, 1879. Republished as George D. Dornin, *Thirty Years Ago: Gold Rush Memories of a Daguerreotype Artist.* Edited by Peter E. Palmquist. Nevada City, CA: Carl Mautz Publishing, 1995.

Downie, William. *Hunting for Gold: Reminiscences of Personal Research in the Early Days of the Pacific Coast From Alaska to Panama.* San Francisco: The California Publishing Company, 1893.

Driesbach, Janice T., Harvey L. Jones, and Katherine Church Holland. *Art of the Gold Rush.* Oakland: Oakland Museum of California/Crocker Art Museum/University of California Press, 1998.

DuFault, David V. "The Chinese in the Mining Camps of California: 1848–1870." *Historical Society of Southern California Quarterly* 41, no. 2 (June 1959): 155–170.

Edwards, Malcolm. "The War of Complexional Distinction: Blacks in Gold Rush California & British Columbia." *California Historical Quarterly* 56, no. 1(Spring 1977): 34–45.

Eifler, Mark A. *Gold Rush Capitalists: Greed and Growth in Sacramento.* Albuquerque: University of New Mexico Press, 2002.

Field, Richard, et al. *American Daguerreotypes from the Matthew R. Isenburg Collection.* New Haven: Yale University Art Gallery, 1989.

Fracchia, Charles A. *When the Water Came Up to Montgomery Street: San Francisco During the Gold Rush*. San Francisco: San Francisco Museum and Historical Society, 2009.

Fraser, J. P. Munro. *History of Solano County*. San Francisco: Wood, Alley & Co., 1879.

Fremont, John. *Memoirs of My Life by John Charles Fremont*. New York: Belford, Clarke, & Company, 1887.

Gudde, Erwin G. *California Gold Camps: A Geographical and Historical Dictionary of Camps, Towns, and Localities Where Gold was Found and Mined, Wayside Stations and Trading Centers*. Berkeley: University of California Press, 1975.

Haas, Robert Bartlett. "William Herman Rulofson: Pioneer Daguerreotypist and Photographic Educator." *California Historical Society* 34, no. 3(September 1955): 288–300.

Hales, Peter Bacon. *Silver Cities: Photographing American Urbanization, 1839–1939*. Albuquerque: University of New Mexico Press, 2005.

Harris, David, and Eric Sandweiss. *Eadweard Muybridge and the Photographic Panorama of San Francisco, 1850–1880*. Montreal: Canadian Centre for Architecture, 1993.

Heizer, Robert F., ed. *They Were Only Diggers: A Collection of Articles from California Newspapers, 1851–1866, on Indian and White Relations*. Ramona, CA: Ballena Press, 1974.

Helper, Hinton. *The Land of Gold*. Baltimore: Henry Taylor, 1855.

Heyman, Therese. *Mirror of California: Daguerreotypes*. Oakland, CA: Oakland Museum, 1973.

Holliday, J. S. *The World Rushed In: The California Gold Rush Experience*. New York: Simon and Schuster, 1981.

Hurtado, Albert H. *Indian Survival on the California Frontier*. New Haven: Yale University Press, 1988.

Hutchings, James. "Mining for Gold in California." *Hutchings' California Magazine* 2, no. 1 (July 1857): 1–14.

———. "River Mining." *Hutchings' California Magazine* 2, no. 3 (September 1857): 97–100.

———. "Quartz Mining in California." *Hutchings' California Magazine* 2, no. 4 (October 1857): 145–54.

Illustrated History of Plumas, Lassen & Sierra Counties. San Francisco: Fariss & Smith, 1882.

Jacobs, Margaret. "Western History: What's Gender Got to Do With It?" *Western Historical Quarterly* 42 (Autumn 2011): 297–304.

Jenkins, W. W. "History of the Development of Placer Mining in California." *Annual Publication of the Historical Society of Southern California* 7, no. 1 (1906): 69–77.

Johnson, Drew, ed. *Capturing Light: Masterpieces of California Photography, 1850 to the Present*. Oakland: Oakland Museum, 2001.

———. "Silver & Gold: A Preview of Cased Images from Northern California Collections." *Daguerreian Annual* (1995): 75–114.

———, and Marcia Eymann, eds. *Silver & Gold: Cased Images of the California Gold Rush*. Iowa City: University of Iowa Press for the Oakland Museum of California, 1998.

Johnson, Mark S. "Argonaut Moses Warren & The Quinebaug Gold Company from the Isenburg Collection at AMC Toronto." *Daguerreian Annual* (2012): 39–69.

Johnson, Susan Lee. "'Domestic' Life in the Diggings: The Southern Mines in the California Gold Rush." In Valerie Matsumoto and Blake Allmendinger, *Over the Edge: Remapping the American West*. Berkeley: University of California Press, 1999.

———. "A Memory Sweet to Soldiers: The Significance of Gender in the History of the American West." *Western Historical Quarterly* 24 (November 1993): 495–517.

———. "My Own Private Life: Toward a History of Desire in Gold Rush California." In Kevin Starr and Richard J. Orsi, eds., *Rooted in Barbarous Soil: People, Culture, and Community in Gold Rush California*, special issue of *California History* 79, no. 2 (Summer 2000): 316–346.

———. *Roaring Camp: The Social World of the California Gold Rush*. New York: W. W. Norton, 2000.

Johnston, William G. *Experiences of a Forty-Niner, A Member of the Wagon Train First to Enter California in the Year 1849*. Pittsburgh, 1892.

Jones, J. Wesley. "Jones' Pantoscope of California: A Lecture by J. Wesley Jones, together with Pencil Sketches Depicting the Journey Across the Plains of California." Reprinted in *California Historical Society Quarterly* 6, no. 2 (June 1927): 109–129.

———. "Jones' Pantoscope of California (Concluded)." Reprinted in *California Historical Society Quarterly* 6, no. 3 (September 1927): 238–53.

Jung, Maureen A. "Documenting Nineteenth-Century Quartz Mining in Northern California." *American Archivist* 53, no. 3 (Summer 1990): 406–18.

Kelley, Robert L. "Forgotten Giant: The Hydraulic Gold Mining Industry in California." *Pacific Historical Review* 23, no. 4 (November 1954): 343–56.

Kirk, Anthony. "As Jolly as a Clam at High Water: The Rise of Art in Gold Rush California." In Kevin Starr and Richard J. Orsi, eds., *Rooted in Barbarous Soil: People, Culture, and Community in Gold Rush California*, special issue of *California History* 79, no. 2 (Summer 2000): 169–203.

Kirker, Harold. "California Architecture and Its Relation to Contemporary Trends in Europe and America." *California Historical Quarterly* 51, 4 (Winter 1972): 289–305.

———. *California's Architectural Frontier: Style and Tradition in the Nineteenth Century*. Santa Barbara: Peregrine Smith, Inc., 1973.

———. "El Dorado Gothic: Gold Rush Architects and Architecture." *California Historical Society Quarterly* 38, no. 1 (March 1959): 31–46.

Kowalewski, Michael. "Imagining The California Gold Rush: The Visual and Verbal Legacy." *California History* 71 (Spring 1992): 60–73.

Kurutz, Gary. "Culture on the Golden Shore." In Kevin Starr and Richard J. Orsi, eds., *Rooted in Barbarous Soil: People, Culture, and Community in Gold Rush California*, special issue of *California History* 79, no. 2 (Summer 2000): 280–315.

———. *The Triumph of Helios: Photographic Treasures of the California State Library*. Sacramento: California State Library Foundation, 2006.

LaLande, Jeffrey M. "Sojourners in Search of Gold: Hydraulic Mining Techniques of the Chinese on the Oregon Frontier." *Journal of the Society for Industrial Archeology* 11, no. 1 (1985): 29–52.

Lang, Herbert O. *A History of Tuolumne County California*. San Francisco: B. F. Alley, 1882.

Lange, O. V. "William Shew: A Portrait Photographer for More Than Half a Century in San Francisco." *Daguerreian Annual* (1991): 15–26.

Lapp, Rudolph M. *Blacks in Gold Rush California*. New Haven: Yale University Press, 1977.

———. "The Negro in Gold Rush California." *Journal of Negro History* 49, no. 2 (April 1964): 81–98.

Lewis, David. "Argonauts and the Overland Trail Experience: Method and Theory." *Western Historical Quarterly* 16 (July 1985): 285–305.

Lewis, Oscar. *Sea Routes to the Gold Fields: The Migration by Water to California in 1849–1852*. New York: Alfred A. Knopf, 1949.

Liestman, Daniel. "Horizontal Inter-Ethnic Relations: Chinese and American Indians in the Nineteenth-Century American West." *Western Historical Quarterly* 30, no. 3 (Autumn 1999): 327–349.

Limbaugh, Ronald. "Making Tools Work Better: Pragmatic Adaptation and Innovation in Gold-Rush Technology." *California History* 77, no. 4 (Winter 1998/1999): 24–51.

———. "The Chinese of Knight's Ferry, 1850–1920." *California History* 72, no. 2 (Summer 1993): 106–127.

Littlefield, Douglas. "Water Rights During the California Gold Rush: Conflicts over Economic Points of View." *Western Historical Quarterly* 14, no. 2 (October 1983): 415–34.

Lönnberg, Allan. "The Digger Indian Stereotype in California." *Journal of California and Great Basin Anthropology* 3, no. 2 (Winter 1981): 215–23.

Lotchin, Roger W. *San Francisco, 1846–1856: From Hamlet to City*. Urbana: University of Illinois Press, 1977.

Madley, Benjamin. "'Unholy Traffic in Human Blood and Souls' Systems of California Indian Servitude Under U.S. Rule." *Pacific Historical Review* 83, no. 4 (November 2014): 626–67.

Magliari, Michael. "Free Soil, Unfree Labor: Cave Johnson Couts and the Binding of Indian Workers in California, 1850–1867." *Pacific Historical Review* 73 (August 2004): 349–90.

Mann, Ralph. *After the Gold Rush: Society in Grass Valley and Nevada City, California, 1849–1870.* Stanford: Stanford University Press, 1982.

Mansfield, George C. *History of Butte County California.* Los Angeles: Historic Record Company, 1918.

Marryat, Frank. *Mountains and Molehills.* London: Longman, Brown, Green, and Longmans, 1855.

Mason, Jesse D. *History of Amador County California.* Oakland, CA: Thompson & West, 1881.

Mei, June. "Socioeconomic Origins of Emigration: Guangdong to California, 1850–1882." *Modern China* 5, no. 4 (October 1979): 463–501.

Naef, Weston J. and James N. Wood. *Era of Exploration: The Rise of Landscape Photography in the American West, 1860–1885.* Buffalo: Albright-Knox Art Gallery, 1975.

Newhall, Beaumont. *The Daguerreotype in America.* New York: Duell, Sloan, & Pearce, 1961.

Palmquist, Peter. "The Daguerreotype in San Francisco." *History of Photography* 4, no. 3 (July 1980): 207–38.

———. "Frederick Coombs: Eccentric Daguerreian in California." *The American West* 19 (July/August 1982): 60–61.

———. "Mirror of our Conscience: Photographic Images of California Indians Produced Before 1860." *Journal of California Anthropology* 5 (Winter 1978): 162–78.

———. "Robert H. Vance, The Maine and Boston Years, 1825–c. 1850." *Daguerreian Annual* (1991): 199–216.

———. "Shadowcatching in El Dorado, 1849–1856." *Daguerreian Annual* (1990): 167–86.

———. and Thomas R. Kailbourn. *Pioneer Photographers of the Far West: A Biographical Dictionary, 1840–1865.* Stanford: Stanford University Press, 2000.

Paul, Rodman W. *California Gold: The Beginning of Mining in the Far West.* Cambridge: Harvard University Press, 1947.

———. *The California Gold Discovery: Sources, Documents, Accounts, and Memoirs Relating to the Discovery of Gold at Sutter's Mill.* Georgetown, CA: Talisman Press, 1966.

———. *Mining Frontiers of the Far West, 1848–1880.* New York: Holt, Rinehart and Winston, 1963.

Peffer, George Anthony. "From Under the Sojourner's Shadow: A Historiographical Study of Chinese Female Immigration to America, 1852–1882." *Journal of American Ethnic History* 11, no. 3 (Spring 1992): 41–67.

Perlot, Jean-Nicolas. *Gold Seeker: Adventures of a Belgian Argonaut during the Gold Rush Years.* Reprint edited by Howard R. Lamar. Translated by Helen Harding Bretnor. New Haven: Yale University Press, 1985.

Peters, Harry T. *California on Stone.* Garden City, NY: Doubleday, Doran & Co., 1935.

Phelps, Robert. "All Hands Have Gone Downtown: Urban Places in Gold Rush California." In Kevin Starr and Richard J. Orsi, eds., *Rooted in Barbarous Soil: People, Culture, and Community in Gold Rush California*, special issue of *California History* 79, no. 2 (Summer 2000): 113–40.

Phillips, Sandra. *Crossing the Frontier: Photographs of the Developing West, 1849 to the Present.* San Francisco: San Francisco Museum of Modern Art, 1996.

Pisani, Donald J. "The Origins of Western Water Law: Case Studies from Two California Mining Districts." *California History* 70, no. 3 (Fall 1991): 242–57.

Rawls, James J. "Gold Diggers: Indian Miners in the California Gold Rush." *California Historical Quarterly* 55, no. 1 (Spring 1976): 28–45.

Raymond, Rossiter W. *Statistics of Mines and Mining in the States and Territories West of the Rocky Mountains.* Washington, DC: Government Printing Office, 1870.

Riley, Glenda. "Feminizing the History of the Gold Rush." *Western Historical Quarterly* 30 (Winter 1999): 445–48.

Rinhart, Floyd and Marion. *American Daguerreian Art.* New York: C.N. Potter, 1967.

———. *The American Daguerreotype.* Athens: University of Georgia Press, 1981.

Robinson, Fayette. *California and Its Gold Regions.* New York: Stringer & Townsend, 1849.

Robinson, Mike. "Sterling C. McIntyre's Panoramic Views of San Francisco," and "Conservation of the Panorama," *Daguerreian Annual* (2013): 16–31, 32–37.

Rohe, Randall E. "After the Gold Rush: Chinese Mining in the Far West, 1850–1890." *Montana: The Magazine of Western History* 32, no. 4 (Autumn 1982): 2–19.

———. "Chinese River Mining in the West." *Montana: The Magazine of Western History* 46, no. 3 (Autumn 1996): 14–29.

———. "The Geography and Material Culture of the Western Mining Town." *Material Culture* 16, no. 3 (Fall 1984): 99–120.

———. "Hydraulicking in the American West: The Development and Diffusion of a Mining Technique." *Montana: The Magazine of Western History* 35, no. 2 (Spring 1985): 18–35.

———. "Origins & Diffusion of Traditional Placer Mining in the West." *Material Culture* 18, no. 3 (Fall 1986): 127–66.

Rohrbough, Malcolm. "The California Gold Rush as a National Experience." *California History* 77 (Spring 1998): 16–29.

———. *Days of Gold: The California Gold Rush and the American Nation.* Berkeley: University of California Press, 1997.

———. "No Boy's Play: Migration and Settlement in Early Gold Rush California." In Kevin Starr and Richard J. Orsi, eds., *Rooted in Barbarous Soil: People, Culture, and Community in Gold Rush California*, special issue of *California History* 79, no. 2 (Summer 2000): 25–43.

Rosales, Vincente Peréz. Journal account in Edwin Beilharz and Carlos López, ed. and trans., *We Were 49ers! Chilean Accounts of the California Gold Rush.* Pasadena: Ward Ritchie Press, 1976.

Royce, Josiah. *California, from the Conquest in 1846 to the Second Vigilance Committee in San Francisco.* Boston: Houghton Mifflin, 1886.

Rudisill, Richard. *Mirror Image: The Influence of the Daguerreotype on American Society.* Albuquerque: University of New Mexico Press, 1971.

Ryan, William Redmond. *Personal Adventures in Upper and Lower California.* London: William Shoberl, 1852.

Sandos, James. "Because He Is a Liar and a Thief: Conquering the Residents of 'Old' California, 1850–1880." In Kevin Starr and Richard J. Orsi, eds., *Rooted in Barbarous Soil: People, Culture, and Community in Gold Rush California*, special issue of *California History* 79, no. 2 (Summer 2000): 86–112.

Sandweiss, Martha. *Print the Legend: Photography and the American West.* New Haven: Yale University Press, 2002.

Sargent, A. A. "A Sketch of Nevada County." *Brown & Dallison's Nevada, Grass Valley, and Rough and Ready Directory.* San Francisco: The Town Talk Office, 1856.

Sawyer, Lorenzo. *Way Sketches Containing Incidents of Travel Across the Plains from St. Joseph to California.* New York: Edward Eberstadt, 1926.

Shew, William. "Photography." *California Monthly Magazine.* 2 (July 1854): 34–40.

Shlaer, Robert. *Sights Once Seen: Daguerreotyping Fremont's Last Expedition through the Rockies.* Santa Fe: Museum of New Mexico Press, 2000.

Sioli, Paolo. *Historical Souvenir of El Dorado County, California.* Oakland, CA: Paolo Sioli, 1883.

Smith, Stacey L. "Remaking Slavery in a Free State: Masters and Slaves in Gold Rush California." *Pacific Historical Review* 80, no. 1 (February 2011): 28–63.

Sparks, Edith. *Capital Intentions: Female Proprietors in San Francisco, 1850–1920.* Chapel Hill: University of North Carolina Press, 2006.

Spier, Robert F. G. "Tool Acculturation among 19th-Century California Chinese." *Ethnohistory* 5, no. 2 (Spring 1958): 97–117.

Starr, Kevin. "Rooted in Barbarous Soil: An Introduction to Gold Rush Society and Culture." In Kevin Starr and Richard J. Orsi, eds., *Rooted in Barbarous Soil: People, Culture, and Community in Gold Rush California*, special issue of *California History* 79, no. 2 (Summer 2000): 1–24.

Stevens, Moreland L. *Charles Christian Nahl: Artist of the Gold Rush, 1818–1878*. Sacramento: E. B. Crocker Art Gallery, 1976.

Street, Franklin. *California in 1850*. Cincinnati: R. E. Edwards and Co., 1851.

Taft, Robert. *Photography and the American Scene*. New York: Macmillan, 1938; repr. New York: Dover Publications, 1964.

Taniguchi, Nancy J. "Weaving a Different World: Women and the California Gold Rush." In Kevin Starr and Richard J. Orsi, eds., *Rooted in Barbarous Soil: People, Culture, and Community in Gold Rush California*, special issue of *California History* 79, no. 2 (Summer 2000): 141–68.

Taylor, Bayard. *El Dorado, or, Adventures in the Path of the Empire*, vol. 1. New York: George P. Putnam, 1850.

Trachtenberg, Alan. *Reading American Photographs: Images as History, Mathew Brady to Walker Evans*. New York: Hill and Wang, 1989.

Van Nostrand, Jeanne. *California Pictorial: A History in Contemporary Pictures, 1786 to 1859*. Berkeley: University of California Press, 1948.

———. *The First Hundred Years of Painting in California 1775–1875*. San Francisco: John Howell Books, 1980.

Vance, Robert H. *Catalogue of Daguerreotype Panoramic Views in California*. New York: Baker, Godwin & Company, 1851.

Venegas, Yolanda. "The Erotics of Racialization: Gender and Sexuality in the Making of California." *Frontiers: A Journal of Women Studies* 25, no. 3 (2004): 63–89.

Villegas, Hernan Rodriguez. *Historia de la Fotografia: Fotografos en Chile Durante el Siglo XIX*. Chile: Centro Nacional del patrimonio fotografio, 2001.

Vischer, Eduard. "A Trip to the Mining Regions in the Spring of 1859." Translated by Ruth Frey Axe. *California Historical Society Quarterly* 11, no. 3 (September 1932): 224–46.

———. "A Trip to the Mining Regions in the Spring of 1859." Translated by Ruth Frey Axe. *California Historical Society Quarterly* 11, no. 4 (December 1932): 321–38.

Watson, Douglas S. *California in the Fifties*. San Francisco: John Howell, 1936.

Wells, Harry L. *History of Nevada County, California*. Oakland: Thompson & West, 1880.

Williams, Mary Floyd. *History of the San Francisco Committee of Vigilance of 1851*. Berkeley: University of California Press, 1921.

Wood, John. *America and the Daguerreotype*. Iowa City: University of Iowa Press, 1991.

———. *The Daguerreotype*. Iowa City: University of Iowa Press, 1989.

———. *The Scenic Daguerreotype: Romanticism and Early Photography*. Iowa City: University of Iowa Press, 1995.

Woods, Daniel B. *Sixteen Months at the Gold Diggings*. New York: Harper & Brothers, Publishers, 1851.

Woon, Yuen-fong. "The Voluntary Sojourner among the Overseas Chinese: Myth or Reality?" *Pacific Affairs* 56, no. 4 (Winter 1983–1984): 673–690.

Wright, Doris Marion. "The Making of Cosmopolitan California: An Analysis of Immigration, 1848–1870." *California Historical Society Quarterly* 19, no. 4 (December 1940): 329–30.

Young, Jr., Otis E. "The Southern Gold Rush: Contributions to California and the West." *Southern California Quarterly* 62, no. 2 (Summer 1980): 127–41.

Zhu, Liping. "No Need to Rush: The Chinese, Placer Mining, and the Western Environment." *Montana: The Magazine of Western History* 49 (Autumn 1999): 42–57.

ACKNOWLEDGMENTS

This volume is the result of the assistance and contributions of many skilled and generous people. I am tremendously thankful to those directors, curatorial colleagues, and museum professionals who have supported this project. Many thanks to the institutions which generously agreed to lend rare and important works to the exhibition and to the individuals who assisted in those loans. These include: the Bancroft Library, University of California, Berkeley (James Eason, principal archivist, pictorial; Jack von Euw, curator, pictorial collections); National Gallery of Canada, Ottawa (Ann Thomas, acting director of the Canadian Photography Institute and senior curator of photographs); and Art Institute of Chicago (Elizabeth Siegel, curator of photography). I am equally grateful to the institutions which will host this exhibition after its debut in Kansas City: Peabody Essex Museum, Salem, Massachusetts (Sarah Kennel, former curator of photography); and Yale University Art Gallery, New Haven, Connecticut (Judy Ditner, associate curator of photography and digital media).

Research assistance has been generously provided by: the California State Library, Sacramento (Kathleen Correira, supervising librarian, California History Section), and Sariah Groff (museum curator); The J. Paul Getty Museum, Los Angeles (Mazie Harris, assistant curator of photography); California Historical Society, San Francisco; Society of California Pioneers, The Presidio, San Francisco; Oakland Museum of California, Oakland; Huntington Library, San Marino, California (Stephanie Arias, librarian); Beinecke Library, Yale University, New Haven, Connecticut (George Miles, curator, Western Americana collection); Amon Carter Museum of Art, Fort Worth, Texas (John Rohrbach, senior curator of photographs); Library of Congress, Washington, DC; and the private collections of Bruce Lundberg, Michael Peterson, Doug Scougale, Len Walle, and Greg French. Special thanks to my program advisors at the University of Missouri-Kansas City: Dr. Burton Dunbar, Dr. Linna Place, Dr. Frances Connelly, and Dr. Larson Powell.

This book is the result of a superbly talented production team: Thomas Palmer, Newport, RI, image separations; Malcolm Grear Designers, Providence, RI, design; and Meridian Printing, East Greenwich, RI, printing. Special thanks go to Thomas Palmer; Pat Appleton of Malcolm Grear Designers; and Daniel Frank at Meridian for their care and attention. Thanks, too, to Molly Tarbell for manuscript and copy editing. We are grateful to Yale University Press, and particularly Patricia J. Fidler, publisher, art and architecture, for their partnership in distributing this book.

At The Nelson-Atkins Museum of Art, this book would not have been possible without the support, guidance, and encouragement of senior curator Keith F. Davis. He took on the enormous task of converting a lengthy dissertation into a cohesive book; reading, editing, and making suggestions to numerous revisions and drafts. I have been greatly assisted by Kaitlyn Bunch, our exhibitions and publications coordinator—our one-woman-publications-department. Every book project we do involves all the members of our photography department; special thanks for assistance and advice provided by April M. Watson, curator, and Natalie Boten, senior coordinator. Thanks also to Tara Brungardt, collections manager and Saori Lewis, associate conservator of photographs. Many other museum personnel helped in the course of this project and in the preparation of the accompanying exhibition. These include museum director Julián Zugazagoitia, for his foreword to this volume and his ongoing support and guidance, and Karen Christiansen, chief operating officer. Deep thanks also go to the members of the other museum departments that contributed to this project, including collections management, presentation, curatorial, education, marketing and communications, and the Spencer Art Reference Library for their invaluable efforts towards this catalogue and the accompanying exhibition.

As always, the generosity of the Hall Family Foundation is deeply appreciated. For their ongoing support of our photography program as well as this book, we offer sincere thanks to the Foundation, its Board of Directors, and, in particular, William A. Hall, president, and Donald J. Hall, chairman.

Finally, for their patience, understanding, and inspiration, I thank my family and dedicate this book to my children: Luke, Caleb, Gabriel, and Eve Aspinwall.

J. L. A.

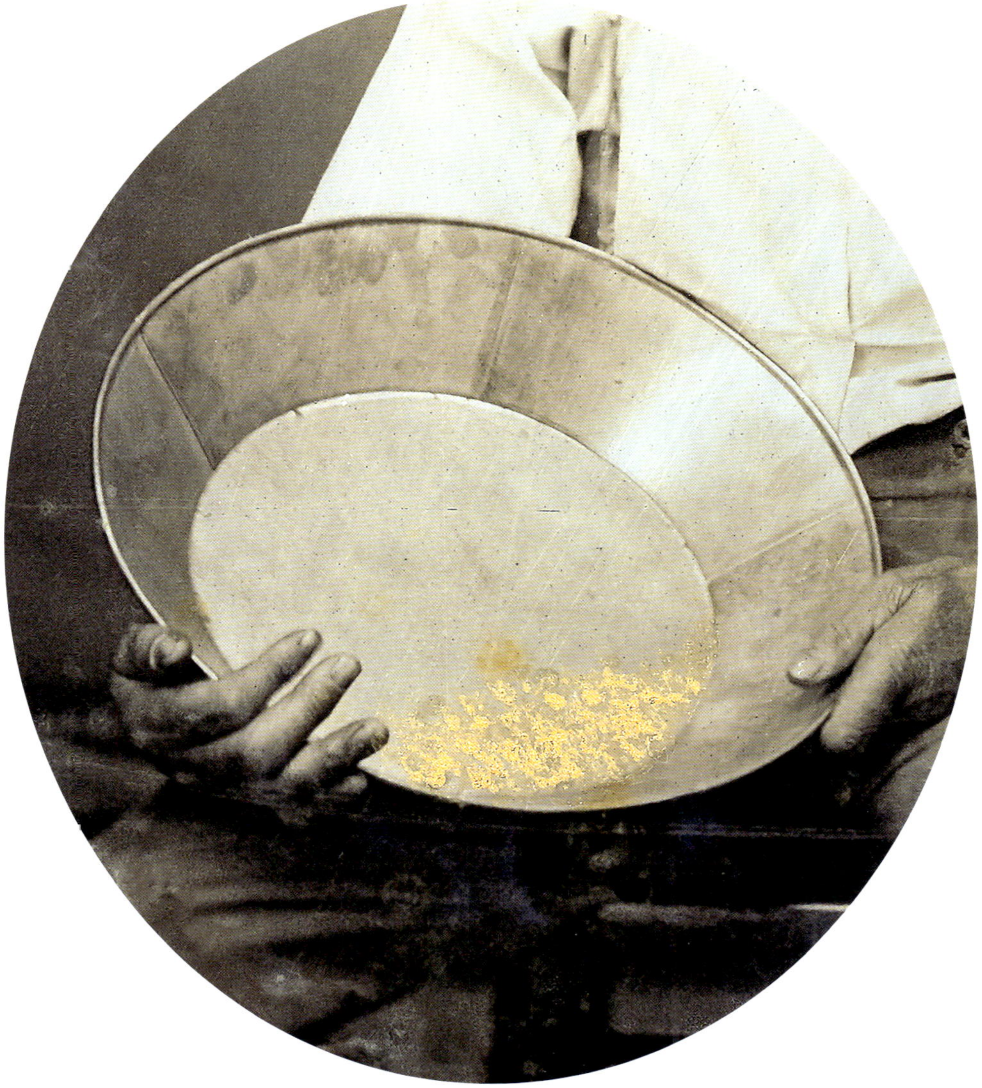

This book was designed
and set in type by
Malcolm Grear Designers
Providence, Rhode Island.

The typeface is Utopia.
Printed on Sterling Premium Matte
with Brillianta bookcloth and
Mohawk Superfine endpapers.

All reproductions are 240-line screen
four-color with varnish.
Separations by Thomas Palmer,
Newport, Rhode Island.

3,300 hardcover copies
were printed at Meridian Printing
East Greenwich, Rhode Island
and bound by Superior Bindery
Braintree, Massachusetts.
August 2019

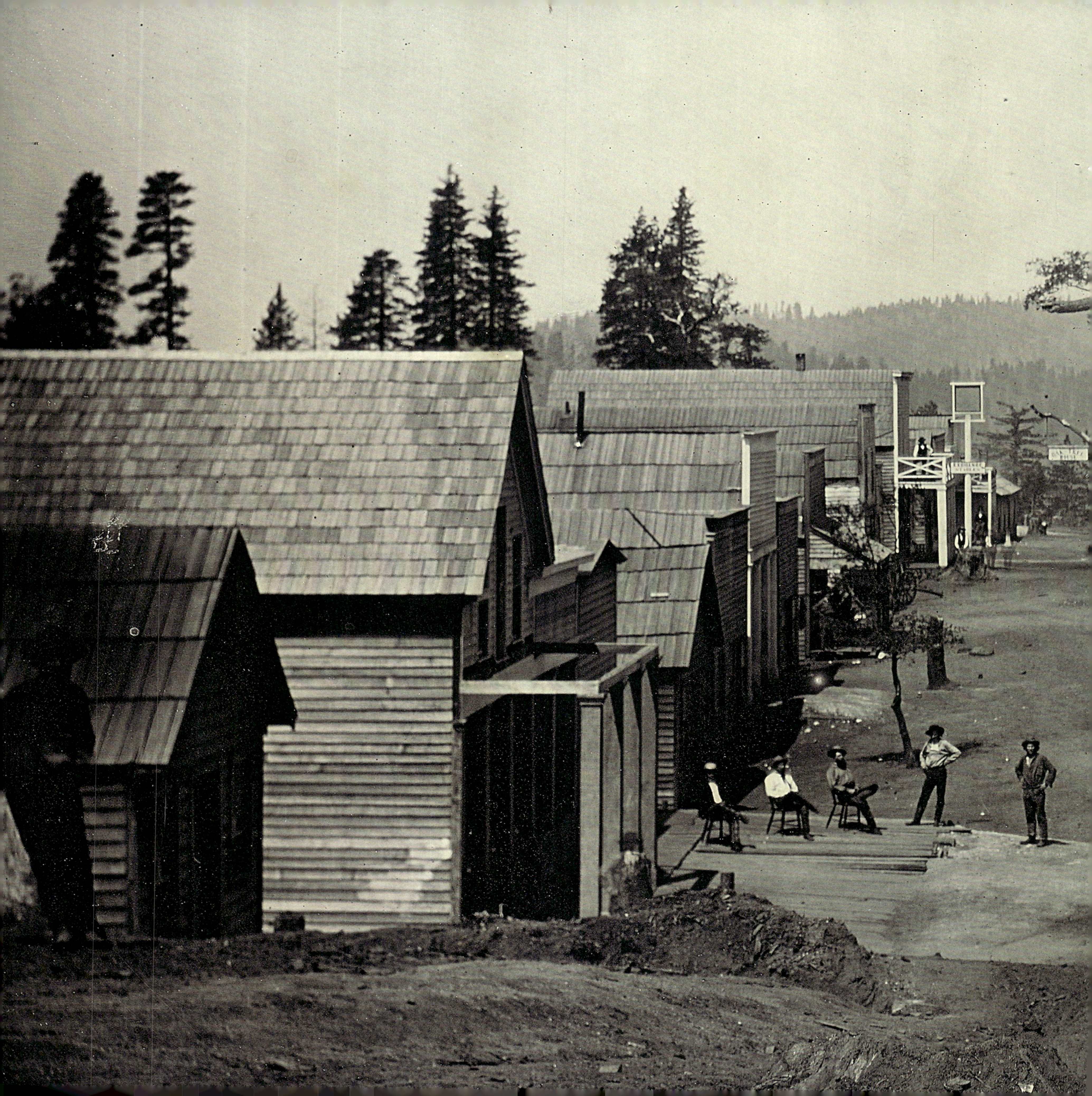